Biblical Hebrew for All

Volume 5
Lifting the Veil

מִזְמוֹר לְדָוִד
יְהוָה רֹעִי לֹא אֶחְסָר׃

Psalm 23:1

The London Press

Copyright © 2022 Tian Hattingh

Disclaimer: The views, meanings and values presented in this work are the author's and thus not necessarily those of the publisher. The author therefore assumes and accepts full responsibility and legal liability for the contents of this work.

The moral right of the author has been asserted.

Apart from any fair dealing for the purposes of research or private study, or criticism or review, as permitted under the Copyright, Designs and Patents Act 1988, this publication may only be reproduced, stored or transmitted, in any form or by any means, with the prior permission in writing of the publishers, or in the case of reprographic reproduction in accordance with the terms of licenses issued by the Copyright Licensing Agency. Enquiries concerning reproduction outside those terms should be sent to the publishers.

This work may contain copyrighted material the use of which has not always been specifically authorized by the copyright owner. Such material is made available for educational purposes, to advance understanding of human rights, democracy, scientific, moral, ethical, and social justice issues, etc. It is believed that this constitutes a "fair use" of any such copyrighted material as provided for in Title 17 U.S.C. section 107 of the US Copyright Law.

ISBN 978-1-907313-50-9

British Library Cataloguing in Publication Data.
A catalogue record for this book is available from the British Library.

Design, Typeset, and Cover by Scribe Inc., Philadelphia, Pennsylvania, United States

Published by The London Press, London, England, UK.

Dedicated to

my son

Charel Hattingh

and

daughter-in-law

Michieu Ché Hattingh (neé Lourens)

Contents

Foreword ix
Preface x
Abbreviations xiv
Series Overview xvi
Acknowledgments xviii

CONCISE CONTENTS

XVI	Translations		XVII	Names of God	
80	Ruth	2	84	Introduction	236
81	Jonah	22	85	EL	237
82	Selected Passages	26	86	YHWH	264
83	Birds in the Tanakh	216	87	Other Names	272

DETAILED CONTENTS

XVI TRANSLATIONS

80 RUTH

1. Introduction 2
2. Ruth 1 4
3. Ruth 2 7
4. Ruth 3 10
5. Ruth 4 16

81 JONAH

1. Introduction 22
2. Jonah 1 22

82 SELECTED PASSAGES

1. Introduction 26
2. Tiqquney Sopherim 27
3. Ittur Sopherim 32
4. Hapax legomena 33
5. Genesis 34
6. Exodus 58
7. Leviticus 76
8. Numbers 81

9	Deuteronomy	83
10	Joshua	91
11	Judges	93
12	Ruth	95
13	1 Samuel	96
14	2 Samuel	99
15	1 Kings	103
16	2 Kings	104
17	1 Chronicles	106
18	2 Chronicles	108
19	Ezra	109
20	Nehemiah	110
21	Esther	112
22	Job	113
23	Psalms	120
24	Proverbs	150
25	Ecclesiastes	153
26	Song of Solomon	156
27	Isaiah	161
28	Jeremiah	175
29	Lamentations	179
30	Ezekiel	181
31	Daniel	185
32	Hosea	188
33	Joel	192
34	Amos	194
35	Obadiah	196
36	Jonah	197
37	Micah	198
38	Nahum	201
39	Habakkuk	204
40	Zephaniah	207
41	Haggai	208
42	Zechariah	209
43	Malachi	212

83 BIRDS IN THE TANAKH

1	Introduction	216
2	Flightless Birds	216
	1 Ostrich	216
3	Diurnal Birds of Prey	217
	1 Introduction	217
	2 Eagles	218
	3 Vultures	219

	4	Kites	220
	5	Falcons	220
4	Fowl-like Birds		221
	1	Introduction	221
	2	Partridges	221
	3	Quail	222
	4	Red Junglefowl	223
	5	Indian Peafowl	224
5	Nocturnal Raptors		224
	1	Introduction	224
	2	Barn-owl	224
	3	Typical Owls	225
6	Pigeons and Doves		227
	1	Introduction	227
	2	Doves	227
7	Perching Birds / Songbirds		228
	1	Introduction	228
	2	Swallows	228
	3	Ravens	228
	4	Sparrows	229
8	Unclean Birds		230
	1	Introduction	230
9	Bird Species in the Hebrew Bible		230

XVII NAMES OF GOD

84 INTRODUCTION

85 EL

1 El 237
2 Variations of El 241
  1 Elohim 241
    1 Introduction 241
    2 Derivation and Meaning 241
    3 Plural absolute 242
    4 Plural construct 243
    5 Inseparable Prepositions 245
    6 Declensional Suffixes 247
    7 Waw 247
  2 Elah 248
    1 Introduction 248
    2 Elah(a) combinations 249
    3 Inseparable Prepositions 249
    4 Declensional Suffixes 249
    5 Waw 250

		6 Aramaic	250
		7 'illaya	250
		8 Elah(a), illaya	251
	3	Eloah	251
		1 Introduction	251
		2 Derivation and Meaning	251
		3 Name Literal Meaning Examples	252
		4 Inseparable Prepositions	252
		5 Declensional Suffixes, Waw	253
	4	Elyon	253
		1 Introduction	253
	5	Elah(a)	253
		1 Introduction	253
3	El Constructions		254
	1	El Shaddai	254
		1 Introduction	254
		2 Derivation and Meaning	254
	2	El Gibbor	255
		1 Introduction	255
		2 Derivation and Meaning	255
		3 Messiah	255
		4 Scriptural Requirements	256
	3	El Eljon	257
		1 Introduction	257
		2 Derivation and Meaning	257
	4	El Olam	258
		1 Introduction	258
		2 Derivation and Meaning	258
	5	El Roiy	259
		1 Introduction	259
		2 Derivation and Meaning	259
	6	El Qanna'	260
		1 Introduction	260
	7	El hay	260
		1 Introduction	260
	8	Other Names	261
4	Proper Names Containing El		262

86 YHWH

1	YHWH	264
	1 Introduction	264
	2 YHWH Spelling	264
	3 Derivation and Meaning	264
2	Combinations with Elohim	265

3 Other Combinations with YHWH 266
1. Yahweh-yireh 266
2. Yahweh-mkaddeish 267
3. Yahweh-nissi 267
4. Yahweh-osenu 267
5. Yahweh-ro'iy 268
6. Yahweh-roph'eka 268
7. Yahweh-tseva'ot 268
8. Yahweh-shalom 269
9. Yahweh-shamma 269
10. Yahweh-tsidqenu 269
11. Yahweh-bore 269
12. Yahweh-qedoshchem 270
13. Yahweh-elyon 270

4 Proper names containing YAH(WEH) 270

87 OTHER NAMES

1. Adon 272
2. Adonay 274
3. Yah 276
4. Attiq yomin 277
5. Ehyeh Asher Ehyeh 278
6. Melek Gadol 278
7. Pachad Jitschad 278
8. Abir Ja'aqoph 279
9. Abir Jisrael 279
10. Even Jisrael 279
11. Ro'eh 279
12. Ro'eh Jisrael 279
13. Qadosh 280
14. Qadosh Jisrael 280
15. Qadosh Ja'aqoph 280
16. Moshia' 280
17. Go'el 281
18. Neitsach Jistael 281

INDEX — 282

REFERENCES — 290

Publications 290
Audio book 290
Websites 291
Bible Versions Online 291

BIOGRAPHY — 292

Foreword

When, in the early centuries, the Church spread rapidly across North Africa, historians of the biblical text tell us that its teaching and debate were hampered by a profusion of Latin translations of varying quality. The solution was to produce a new translation on the basis of the Hebrew text. Apparently one man was thought most capable of doing this work, namely Jerome, translator of the Vulgate.

That at such a critical hour the scholarship of the Church in the area of Hebrew was sufficiently depleted as to depend so heavily on the work of a single scholar must surely give cause for reflection to anyone who loves the Scriptures and understands the inestimable value of the Masoretic text. I therefore warmly encourage the work of Tian Hattingh in making available to non-academics the basics of biblical Hebrew. His presentation is sound and will provide a firm basis for any who wish to build thereon, either as they study the Masoretic text for themselves, or as they proceed along more formal channels of study.

There can be little doubt that the careful spreading of a knowledge of Classical Hebrew will greatly enrich the Church and strengthen its evangelistic outreach. May God bless this endeavor and its author.

Prof. J. C. Lübbe
Johannesburg
September 2017

Preface

1. INTRODUCTION

Religion, politics, and sports are arguably examples of inexact sciences. Therefore it is common to find that anyone and/or everyone has formed an opinion regarding controversial issues existing in these disciplines. Sadly, this situation occurs irrespective of how informed or how ignorant, on how misinformed and ill-informed these individuals are.

In the case of religion, opinions are often formed by how people read and interpret those Holy Scriptures that are available to them in a language that they are familiar with. Christianity is based on the faith that believers acquire by either hearing the Christian Gospel and/or by reading the Christian Bible. This Bible contains a so-called Old Testament (the Hebrew Bible), originally written in Hebrew, and a so-called New Testament, originally written in Koine Greek.

The work of the Great Assembly (c. 430–320 BCE) resulted in the acceptance of the Jewish Canon, written in Hebrew consonants (Chapter 65.6 in Volume 4 of this series). For the next 13 centuries, this Jewish Canon underwent a complex developmental process that eventually culminated into, what is know today as, the Masoretic Text (MT). The Canon was almost immediately translated into the Greek Septuagint (c. 250–100 BCE). The Targumim (paraphrases, explanations, and expansions of the Canon), were written in Hebrew (c. 50 BCE-100 CE). A few centuries later, Eusebius Hieronymus (Jerome), used the Septuagint to translate the Canon into the Latin Vulgate (c. 390–405 CE). Another few centuries later (c. 600 CE), the work of the Masoretes started and lasted for three centuries (c. 900 CE) and ended the developmental era. Since then the Masoretic Text has been translated into a myriad of languages and versions.

Except for those few who are able to read the Hebrew Bible and the Christian New Testament in the original languages, everyone else has to make do with reading the available translations that they understand. These translations are inevitably flawed for a number of obvious reasons. First of all, inherent to any translation process, it is often impossible to exactly convey the meaning of the original (source) text into the target (receptor) language. Second, translators are imbedded in a specific cultural, social and ideological environment, which may or may not influence their views on the meaning of the source text. In addition, these translators often have to rely on dictionaries that were compiled by individuals that also were from a specific set of cultural, social and ideological circumstances, and also interpreted their sources in a particular way.

All of the above have played a significant role in the profound changes that took place in the Christian Church over the past two thousand years. For example:

a) **The Reformation**

"The Reformation (more fully the Protestant Reformation or the European Reformation) was a movement within Western Christianity in the 16th-century Europe that posed a religious and political challenge to the Roman Catholic Church—and papal authority in particular. Although the Reformation is usually considered to have started with the publication of the Ninety-five Theses by Martin Luther in 1517, there was no schism between the Catholic Church and the nascent Luther until the 1521 Edict of Worms. The edict condemned Luther and officially banned citizens of the Holy Roman Empire from defending or propagating his ideas."[1]

Rom 1:17 is considered to be the verse that inspired Luther to change his views. It is a quotation of Hb 2:4 in the Hebrew Bible, and is quoted in Gal 3:11 and Heb 10:38 as well. Luther knew biblical Hebrew, and his Luther Bible is a German language Bible translation from Hebrew and Koine Greek and not the Latin Vulgate. His knowledge of the original languages arguably assisted in his understanding of the texts.

b) **Denominations** are defined as "recognized autonomous branches of the Christian Church." Christianity comprises of about 2.42 billion people found all over the globe. These are divided into seven families of Christian denominations:

1. Catholic Church—1.285 billion.
2. Protestantism—920 million.
3. Eastern Orthodox Church—270 million.
4. Oriental Orthodoxy—80 million.
5. Non-trinitarian Restorationism—35 million.
6. Independent Catholicism—18 million.
7. Minor branches—3 million.[2]

However, there are no less than 33,790 individual denominations:

1. Independents (about 22000).
2. Protestants (about 9000).
3. Marginals (about 1600).
4. Orthodox (780).
5. Roman Catholics (242).
6. Anglicans (168).[3]

Creationism is the religious belief that the universe and living organisms originated from specific acts of divine creation. According to this definition, one could still believe in the scientific evidence on how the universe and living creatures developed. One could even subscribe to the theory of evolution, with the added assumption that during the evolutionary stages of species, a divine act set humans apart from other living creatures and resulted in the unique features displayed by this species.

Young Earth Creationism however, resulted from people interpreting Genesis Chapters 1–11 as being a literal account of how the universe and living creatures came to be. They believe that the Earth is 6,000 to 10,000 years old. This conflicts with the age of approximately 4.54 billion years measured using independently cross-validated geochronological methods including radiometric dating.

---

1 Wikipedia contributors. *"Reformation."* Wikipedia, The Free Encyclopedia, 5 July, 2019. Web: 9 July, 2019. Slightly edited.
2 Wikipedia contributors. *"List of Christian denominations by number of members."* Wikipedia, The Free Encyclopedia, 2 July, 2019. Web: 8 July, 2019. Slightly edited.
3 Barret, et al. (2012), Vol. 1, p. 16–18.

2. OBJECTIVES

How does everything that was said and done in Volumes 1–4 of this series come to fruition? The objective of this volume is not to present definitive translations as a product of basic grammatical knowledge and textual criticism skills, but rather to present the relevant facts and then leave the final conclusions up to the student. The following chapters are presented:

XVI TRANSLATIONS

a) Illustrations of how footnotes are taken into consideration when one is attempting to derive at a possible dynamic equivalent. This objective is achieved by looking at actual footnotes found in the books of Ruth and Jonah in *BHS*. (Chapters 80, 81)

   The book of Jonah contains one of the best known, and highly controversial, narratives in the Hebrew Bible. In addition, the book is an excellent example of how the author's originally intended message can be understood much more clearly when the original Hebrew text is carefully analyzed.

b) A selection of 424 texts taken from 179 chapters, where the reader is able to understand the texts more clearly by consulting the MT. These passages do not always involve footnotes. Actually, 24 of these texts are not problematic at all. (Chapter 82)

   The majority of these passages are well known and beloved within both the Jewish and Christian communities. In addition, a number of lesser known passages were included to illustrate the premise made by Bialik in section 3 below.

c) A concise description of all 343 references to birds and avian terms found in the Hebrew Bible. (Chapter 83)

XVII NAMES OF GOD

a) To clarify all the names, titles, and descriptions of God in the Hebrew Bible, we have grouped and listed 188 instances were the MT mentions God. (Chapters 84—87)

3. FIVE VOLUMES

"Translating Hebrew into another language is like kissing your bride through her veil." This quote, most often attributed to Hayim Nahman Bialik (1873–1934), one of the greatest Hebrew poets of the 20th century, has been the genesis for including Volume 5 into this series. The statement by Bialik is in answer to the often asked question as to what difference does it make to read the original Hebrew Bible as apposed to reading any number of translations.

All four previous volumes are utilized and combined into this volume in order to provide the student with a selection of some of the relatively simple but nevertheless vivid examples from the Hebrew Bible. The main objective of presenting these examples is to show that a basic understanding of the grammatical principles involved, together with the ability to apply the principles involved in sound textual criticism will bring the student to the following realization: That most modern translations have in many instances been unable to fully deal with texts that are open to different interpretations in two ways:

a) Correctly reproducing a literal translation of the original source text.

b) Showing the full extent of what meaning is to be found in the original source text and transferring this meaning into the target language by means of a dynamic equivalent.

4. SERIES PEDAGOGY

The guiding pedagogical principle in this series could be described as: "taking learners on a step-by-step progression from the most basic concepts in the language to the more complex phenomena, while staying closely in touch with the Hebrew Bible text."

This principle has diligently been pursued in the previous three volumes. Particularly in Chapter 79 of this volume, the stated principle becomes real.

Abbreviations

BOOKS OF THE HEBREW BIBLE

Genesis	Gen
Exodus	Ex
Leviticus	Lv
Numbers	Nm
Deuteronomy	Dt
Joshua	Js
Judges	Jgs
Ruth	Ru
1 Samuel	1 Sm
2 Samuel	2 Sm
1 Kings	1 Kgs
2 Kings	2 Kgs
1 Chronicles	1 Chr
2 Chronicles	2 Chr
Ezra	Ezr
Nehemiah	Neh
Esther	Est
Job	Jb
Psalms	Ps
Proverbs	Prv

Ecclesiastes	Eccl
Song of Solomon	Sg
Isaiah	Is
Jeremiah	Jer
Lamentations	Lam
Ezekiel	Ez
Daniel	Dn
Hosea	Hos
Joel	Jl
Amos	Am
Obadiah	Ob
Jonah	Jon
Micah	Mi
Nahum	Na
Habakkuk	Hb
Zephaniah	Zep
Haggai	Hg
Zechariah	Zec
Malachi	Mal

NEW TESTAMENT BOOKS

1 Corinthians	1 Cor
1 Timothy	1 Tim
Galatians	Gal
Hebrews	Heb

Mark	Mrk
Matthew	Mt
Romans	Rom

GENERAL

first person	1	literal	litr.
second person	2	masculine	m.
third person	3	masculine plural	mp.
absolute	abs.	masculine singular	ms.
adjective	adj.	New Testament	NT
adverb	adv.	participle	part.
Chapter	Chpt.	perfect	perf.
construct	cstr.	plural	pl.
direct definite object marker	DDOM	preposition	prep.
		proper noun	pn.
English	Eng.	particle	prtl.
feminine	f.	singular	sg.
feminine plural	fp.	Saint	St.
feminine singular	fs.	suffix	suff.
idiomatic	idm.	under the word	s.v.
imperfect	impf.	BDB	Brown-Driver-Briggs Hebrew and English Lexicon
infinitive	inf.		
interjection	intj.		

BIBLES

AB	Amplified Bible		KJB	King James Bible
ABP	Apostolic Bible Polyglot		LSV	Literal Standard version
ASV	American Standard Version		MSG	The Message
BHS	Biblia Hebraica Stuttgartensia		NASB	New American Standard Bible
BSV	Berean Standard Version		NHEB	New Heart English Bible
CEV	Contemporary English Version		NKJV	New King James Version
CSB	Christian Standard Bible		NIV	New International Version
DRB	Douay-Rheims Bible		NLT	New Living Translation
ERV	English Revised Version		WBT	Webster's Bible Translation
ESV	English Standard version		WEB	World English Bible
GNT	Good News Translation		YLT	Young's Literal Translation
ISV	International Standard Version			

Series Overview

VOLUME 1
Beginner

I. General

1–21	General Grammar
22	Verbs in General

II. Strong Verbs

23	Qal
24	Niph'al
25	Pi'el
26	Pu'al
27	Hiph'il
28	Hoph'al
29	Hithpa'el

III. Appendixes
IV. Paradigm Charts

VOLUME 2
Elementary

V. Weak Verbs

30	I א
31	I ע
32	I ח
33	I ה
34	II א
35	II ע
36	II ח / II ר
37	II ה
38	III א
39	III ע
40	III ח
41	III ה

VI. Irregular Verbs

42	I י
43	I ו
44	I נ
45	Biconsonantal
46	Geminate

VII. Appendixes
VIII. Paradigm Charts

Series Overview

VOLUME 3
Intermediate

IX. Doubly Weak Verbs

Introduction

47	I א	III ה
48	I ע	III ה
49	I ה	III ה
50	I ח	III ה
51	I י	IIG
52	I י	IIIG
53	I י	III ה
54	I נ	IIG
55	I נ	IIIG
56	I נ	III ה
57	IG	Gem
58	IIG	III ה
59	Unique Verbs	

X. General

60	Stative Verbs
61	Verbs with Suffixes
62	Hebrew Sentences
63	Minor Paradigms
64	General

XI. Appendixes
XII. Paradigm Charts

VOLUME 4
Textual Criticism

XIII. Manuscripts

65	Introduction
66	The Septuagint
67	The Targums
68	The Qumran Scrolls
69	The Vulgate
70	The Masoretic Texts
71	Other translations

XIV. Textual Criticism

72	Causes of Textual Corruption
73	Textual Criticism Methods
74	*BHK, BHS, BHQ*
75	Apparatus of *BHS*
76	General Abbreviations
77	Version Abbreviations
78	Masora Abbreviations

XV. Application

79	Examples from *BHS*

VOLUME 5
Lifting the Veil

XVI. Translations

80	Ruth
81	Jonah
82	Selected Passages
83	Birds in the Tanakh

XVII. Names of God

84	Introduction
85	El
86	YHWH
87	Other Names

Acknowledgments

Yahweh, the God of Abraham, Isaac and Jacob. He who is continuously revealing himself to us through Scripture and Nature.

All my former and present students in South Africa and China. Their enthusiasm and efforts have always been, and continues to be, a source of inspiration to me. Your feedback has been invaluable in helping me make this publication "student friendly."

The management and staff at Scribe Inc.: David Rech (CEO), Jason Hughes (book developer and manager), Jen Boeree and Megan Grande (editors), Tim Durning (designer), Jeffrey DeBlasio (typesetter) and Steve Ushioda (sales director).

The management and staff at The London Press.

XVI
TRANSLATIONS

80 Ruth

80.1 INTRODUCTION

1. In this chapter, the focus is only on the footnotes and other apparatus as found around the *Biblia Hebraica Stuttgartensia (BHS)* main text of the Book of Ruth in the Hebrew Bible.

2. For this analysis of the 57 footnotes found in the *BHS* version of the Hebrew Bible Book of Ruth, the information found in Chapter 8 of the following publication was heavily relied on: Brotzman, Ellis R.; Tully, Eric J., (2016). *Old Testament Textual Criticism: A Practical Introduction*. Grand Rapids, Michigan: Baker Academic.

3. At the beginning of their discussion of a footnote, Brotzman and Tully present the reader with the Masoretic Text (MT) as found in *BHS*, as well as what they call the "retroversions" of the sources mentioned in the footnote and/or other apparatus. These retroversions (verb: retrieve) are also known as "back-translations" or the *vorlage* of the MT. These retroversions are duplicated here with the permission of the authors. The following credit line applies, "Excerpt from *Old Testament Textual Criticism* by Ellis Brotzman and Eric Tully, copyright © 1994, 2016. Used by permission of Baker Academic, a division of Baker Publishing Group."

4. The discussion of a footnote starts by quoting the footnote. This is done according to the system followed in Volume 4 of this series (Item 7 below). This is followed by the MT text(s) in Hebrew (on the right), and a literal English translation (on the left). Then the retoversions are listed. The sources from where these retroversions originate, are indicated by their commonly known sigla. Lastly, numbered explanatory notes are added.

5. **vorlage** A German word (pronounced as foːɐ̯ˌlaːɡə), that in this context refers to the assumed or conjectured Hebrew-Aramaic original source-text for a translation that is before a scholar, translator, or scribe.

6. In the case of the Septuagint for example, one seeks to determine whether the Hebrew text (the *vorlage*) from which the Greek translation was made may have differed from the original MT. This determination is usually made based on a conjectured "back-translation" or "retroversion" from the Septuagint Greek back into Hebrew. (Conjecture: an opinion or conclusion formed on the basis of incomplete information.) As can be seen in Chapter 8 of the Brotzman and Tully publication, this strategy can be followed for any of the non-Masoretic sources mentioned in the *BHS* footnotes.

7. The modus operandi that was employed in compiling the list of footnotes in Vol. 4 is used in this volume as well. For the sake of convenience to the reader, those rules are repeated here:

    7.1 First the translation of the footnote is given in quotation marks (inverted commas). With some of the footnotes, this is then followed by a number of notes. These notes are usually references to any applicable section(s), and are not meant to be explanatory.

    7.2 When translating the footnotes, English words in parenthesis are sometimes added, indicating words added by the author of this publication. This is done in an attempt for the footnote to logically make more sense but is not an attempt to translate the footnotes into idiomatic English.

7.3 To accurately reproduce the footnotes into English, the word order of the footnotes was not changed, even in those cases where such a change would make the English translation more logical.

7.4 To describe items commonly found in the footnotes, a number of common sense abbreviations were created by the author and are used in this chapter only.

1	**Akk**	The word(s) in the footnote are transliterated from Akkadian (Js 13:3[a]).
2	**Arb**	The word(s) in the footnote are transliterated from Arabic (Js 17:7[b]).
3	**Arm**	The word(s) in the footnote are transliterated from Aramaic (Neh 3:15[d]).
4	**Cop**	The word(s) in the footnote are transliterated from Coptic (Jgs 5:14[d]).
5	**Eth**	The word(s) in the footnote are transliterated from Ethiopic (1 Sm 19:20[b]).
6	**Egy**	The word(s) in the footnote are transliterated from Egyptian (Is 2:16[a]).
7	**Grk**	Greek texts in a footnote are not translated and only indicated as such by this abbreviation (Gen 1:1[a]).
8	**Heb**	Hebrew words included in a footnote, either in square script or in transliterated form, are indicated as such by this abbreviation (Gen 1:1[a]).
9	**Lat**	Latin texts in a footnote are not translated and only indicated as such by this abbreviation. This should not be confused by the Fraktur symbol that indicates Old Latin Versions (Gen 31:46[a]).
10	**LXX**	The Septuagint in Greek (Gen 1:20[a]).
11	**MT**	Masoretic Texts in Hebrew (Gen 1:1[a]).
12	**SP**	Samaritan Pentateuch in SP alphabet (Gen 1:11[b]).
13	**SyP**	Syriac Peshitta (Ex 20:3[a-a]).
14	**Syr**	The word(s) in the footnote are transliterated from the Syriac language (Gen 1:11b).
15	**Syriac**	The Syriac language (Gen 1:11[b]).
16	**Uga**	The word(s) in the footnote are transliterated from Ugaritic (Jb 31:29[a]).
17	**Vulg**	The Latin Vulgate (Ru 2:18[a]).

7.5 **"Manuscripts"** is the abbreviation for "Medieval Hebrew Manuscript(s)" (Gen 1:11[b]). **"Editions"** (Gen 2:18[a]) and **"Versions"** (Gen 14:6[a]), are collective terms indicating a wide range of these types of documents.

7.6 Symbols in an Arial font are shown as they are (Chapter 77.3).

7.7 The directions given in Chapter 75.2 were implemented in reproducing the footnotes.

7.8 Manuscripts, Versions, Scrolls, Editions and so on, are identified but not described in detail. The exact details can be found in Chapters 77.1–3 of Vol. 4.

7.9 In the following sections of this chapter, the order of the books of the Hebrew Bible were changed to follow that of the Christian Old Testament as found in the King James Bible.

80.2 RUTH 1

1ᵃ⁻ᵃ	"The original LXX Grk = Heb; SyP it omits Heb."	
MT	in the days of the judging of the judges	בִּימֵי שְׁפֹט הַשֹּׁפְטִים
LXX*	when the judges judged	בִּשְׁפֹט הַשֹּׁפְטִים
SyP	in the days of the judges	בִּימֵי הַשֹּׁפְטִים

1. The MT is unusual in having an infinitive in the midst of a construct chain.

2. First, this footnote gives us the Greek text εν τω κρίνειν in the original Septuagint. The back-translation or retroversion into Hebrew is shown above. From this we can see that the Septuagint does not have "In the days of," but changed the infinitive into a temporal infinitive construct that is translated as "when judging."

3. As mentioned in this footnote, the Syriac Peshitta does not have the infinitive.

4. The MT likely represents the original (slightly cumbersome) text, with the translators of the Greek Septuagint and Syriac Peshitta attempting to clarify the syntax in their translations. They both present a way to simplify the text, each with their own solution but without changing the meaning. Therefore it is likely that they consulted the same reading as the MT in their Hebrew vorlage.

1ᵇ	"LXX (Syriac Peshitta) it omits Heb."	
MT	he and his wife and his **two** sons	הוּא וְאִשְׁתּוֹ וּשְׁנֵי בָנָיו׃
LXX	he and his wife and his sons	הוּא וְאִשְׁתּוֹ וּבָנָיו׃
SyP	he and his wife and his sons	הוּא וְאִשְׁתּוֹ וּבָנָיו׃

1. There is no clear reason why the Greek Septuagint and the Syriac Peshitta would not have the numeral. One possible explanation is that is was done to simplify the syntax.

2. This footnote does not mention any additional information, but it is noteworthy that other Versions and Manuscripts are in accordance with the MT.

8ᵃ	"LXX Vulgate as Qere Heb."	
MTᴷ	YHWH will do with you	יַעֲשֶׂה יְהוָה עִמָּכֶם
MTQ	May YHWH do with you	יַעַשׂ יְהוָה עִמָּכֶם
LXX	May YHWH do with you	יַעַשׂ יְהוָה עִמָּכֶם
Vulg	May YHWH do with you	יַעַשׂ יְהוָה עִמָּכֶם

1. This is a typical example of a Ketiv-Qere reading (Chapters 70.4.2.d.1.ii, and 78.1.2).

2. This footnote states that both the Greek Septuagint and the Latin Vulgate have the Qere form. The Ketiv is a qal impf. 3ms meaning, "he will do." The Qere suggest the qal jussive form that means, "may he do." It is well known that the impf. can also be used to express a wish or desire.

14ª	"LXX additional text Grk, perhaps read Heb."	
MT	and Orpah kissed her mother-in-law	וַתִּשַּׁק עָרְפָּה לַחֲמוֹתָהּ
LXX	and Orpah kissed her mother-in-law	וַתִּשַּׁק עָרְפָּה לַחֲמוֹתָהּ
	and returned to her people.	וַתָּשָׁב אֶל־עַמָּהּ

1. The variant found in the Greek Septuagint can easily be inferred by the reader in verse 15, just as it was inferred by the Greek translator. Therefore the variant does not have a significant effect on its interpretation.

19ª	"Read with multiple (20–60) Manuscripts Heb."	
MT^L	(L) So the two of them (**mp**) came	וַתֵּלַכְנָה שְׁתֵּיהֶם
Mss	So the two of them (**fp**) came	וַתֵּלַכְנָה שְׁתֵּיהֶן

1. It would seem obvious from the context that the suffix should be feminine, but the following points reminds us that we should be cautious not to erase the author's original intention in using this suffix:

   a) It is well known that in biblical Hebrew a m. pl. suffix can refer to feminine antecedents. In fact, m. pl. forms are used elsewhere in this book to refer to women for example in 1:8, 9, 11, 13.

   b) It might be that the author intentionally used less typical language for a specific purpose, like making his text more colorful.

19^{b-b}	"It lacks material the original LXX."	
MT	and when they came to Bethlehem	וַיְהִי כְּבֹאָנָה בֵּית לֶחֶם

1. The entire phrase marked by this footnote does not appear in the Greek Septuagint.

2. It could be argued that this is a case of a kind of dittography in the MT, or of homoioteleuton in the Septuagint. The MT admittedly contains some redundancy, and it could be that the Greek translator omitted the phrase which in his view was redundant.

3. However, the author could have included the phrase simply to emphasize that Ruth was actually from Moab (1:6) and now on her way to Bethlehem.

19ᶜ	"LXX Grk (LXX Grk) = Heb."	
MT	And the whole city was stirred up over **them**.	וַתֵּהֹם כָּל־הָעִיר עֲלֵיהֶן
LXX	And the whole city was stirred up over **her**.	וַתֵּהֹם כָּל־הָעִיר עָלֶיהָ

1. This footnote mentions three variants of the Greek Septuagint. As shown here, in Hebrew all three these variants have the same retroversion and similar meanings.

2. The MT has a plural pronominal suffix (them). This agrees with previous references to the two women in the verse. The Septuagint variants have a singular pronoun which fits into the context of the question "Is this Naomi?" at the end of the verse.

20ᵃ	"Read with multiple (20-60) Manuscripts Heb."	
MT	bitter, bitterness	מָרָא
Mss	bitter, bitterness	מרה

1. From the adjective מַר meaning, "bitter" (and the verb מָרַר meaning, "to be bitter"), we have two forms with different spellings but equal in meaning.

2. The form used in more than twenty medieval Manuscripts is the more usual one.

21ᵃ⁻ᵃ	"LXX (Syriac Peshitta Vulgate) Grk."	
MT	and YHWH has testified against me	וַיהוָה עָנָה בִי
LXX	and YHWH has humbled me	וַיהוָה עִנָּה בִי

1. Refer to Chapter 75.2.8 in Vol. 4 of this series for an explanation of when a version is mentioned in parentheses in a *BHS* footnote. In this case the Syriac Peshitta and the Latin Vulgate are in agreement with the Greek Septuagint text.

2. We should keep in mind that a translation like the Septuagint was made from an *abjad* (a consonantal Hebrew text with no vowels), which, like in this case, would not show the binyan of the verb. It could be a qal, a pi'el, or a pu'al binyan.

3. The Masoretes read the consonants as a qal 3ms of the verb עָנָה meaning, "to answer, testify, respond," but the translators of the Latin Vulgate read it to be the pi'el 3ms of this verb which in the pi'el binyan means, "to humble, afflict."

4. The objects of the verb "to answer" are usually preceded by the inseparable preposition *beit*, but the objects of the pi'el verb "to humble" do not use the preposition.

5. Therefore the MT vocalization should be preferred.

80.3 RUTH 2

1ᵃ	"Multiple (20-60) Manuscripts as Qere Heb; Ketiv Heb."	
MTᴸ	And Naomi had a relative (noun) (Qere)	וּלְנָעֳמִי מֻידָע
MTᴷ	And Naomi had a relative (pu'al part. active m. sg.) (Ketiv)	וּלְנָעֳמִי מְיֻדָּע
MTᵠ	And Naomi had a relative (noun) (Qere)	וּלְנָעֳמִי מוֹדָע
Mss	And Naomi had a relative (noun) (Qere)	וּלְנָעֳמִי מוֹדָע

1 Both the Qere and the Ketiv mean, "acquaintance or relative."

2 The Qere form is closely related to the noun used in the book at 3:2.

6ᵃ⁻ᵃ	"Lacks material Syriac Peshitta."	
MT		וַיַּעַן הַנַּעַר הַנִּצָּב עַל־הַקּוֹצְרִים וַיֹּאמַר
MT	And the young man who was in charge of the harvesters (answered) and said:	
SyP	And the young man (answered) and said:	וַיַּעַן הַנַּעַר וַיֹּאמַר

1 In the previous verse the man's full title is given. The translator of the Syriac Peshitta probably decided to omit the full title here to avoid repetition.

2 The Greek Septuagint is in accordance with the MT.

7ᵃ	"LXX Grk = Heb."	
MT	from (then) the morning until now	מֵאָז הַבֹּקֶר וְעַד־עַתָּה
LXX	from the morning until (the) evening	מֵאָז הַבֹּקֶר וְעַד־עָרֶב

1 Brotzman and Tully says: "This is probably the most difficult verse in the book of Ruth. Many commentators have attempted to emend the MT from this point to the end of the verse in order to make sense of it."[1]

2 This footnote and the next one are linked to each other and should be considered together.

---

1 All these names obviously refer to the same individual.

7ᵇ⁻ᵇ	"LXX Grk = Heb."	
MT	this is her sitting (in) the house (?)	זֶה שִׁבְתָּהּ הַבַּיִת
LXX	she has not rested in the field	לֹא שָׁבְתָה בַשָּׂדֶה
SyP	from the morning until the (time of) rest	מִן הַבֹּקֶר וְעַד־שִׁבְתָהּ

1. The Greek Septuagint has three completely different words.
2. *BHS* does not mention the Syriac Peshitta, but it would have been very helpful. The Syriac Peshitta actually combines both the footnotes.
3. It is clear that the MT is the most difficult with the Septuagint and Syriac Peshitta more clear and simple but in different ways. Therefore the MT should be regarded as the original.
4. "This verse is a good example of the limitations of the *BHS* apparatus. If we work only with the data that they provide, we do not have the full story."²

16ᵃ	"Verse 16 lacks information Syriac Peshitta."

1. Refer to Chapter 75.2.4 in Vol. 4 of this series.
2. The note states that this entire verse was omitted in the Syriac Peshitta.
3. The verse does appear in the Greek Septuagint, but with some differences from the MT.

18ᵃ	"A few (3–10) Manuscripts Syriac Peshitta Vulgate Heb."	
MT	And she saw	וַתֵּרֶא
Mss	And she showed	וַתַּרְא
SyP	And she showed	וַתַּרְא
Vulg	And she showed	וַתַּרְא

1. In the MT the verb is vocalized as the qal binyan of the verb "to see." Naomi is the subject of the verb, and the object is indicated by the definite direct object marker.
2. In a few Manuscripts, the Syriac Peshitta, and the Latin Vulgate the verb is vocalized as the hiph'il binyan of the verb "to see." Now Naomi is the first object of the verb (which is not marked by an object marker), and the relative clause ("what she had gleaned") the second object.
3. However, the verb occurs 63 times in the hiph'il, and in 60 of those instances the first object (the person being shown something) occurs as either an object suffix that is attached directly to the verb, or it is marked with the object marker.

---

2 In 1 Chr 2:11 we find another spelling namely *salma'*.

19ᵃ⁻ᵃ	"LXX Grk compare Syriac Peshitta."	
MT	with whom she had worked	אֵת אֲשֶׁר־עָשְׂתָה עִמּוֹ
LXX	where she worked	אַיֵּה עָשָׂתָה

1. In the Versions, Ruth first answers Naomi's question directly, and then goes on to identify Boaz as the man at that location.

2. However, in the MT the author is slowly building suspense when Ruth does not answer the question directly but rather shifts the focus to Ruth's interaction with Boaz.

20ᵃ	"One Manuscript Syriac Peshitta Heb."	
MT	Blessed is he **by** Yahweh	בָּרוּךְ הוּא לַיהוָה
LXX	Blessed is (he) Yahweh	בָּרוּךְ הוּא יְהוָה

1. One medieval Manuscript and the Syriac Peshitta does not have the inseparable preposition lamed before Yahweh.

2. Not mentioned in this footnote is that the Old Latin agrees with the mentioned variants, and that the Greek Septuagint agrees with the MT.

3. This phrase has an effect on how we see the next part of the verse. In the MT the personal preposition הוּא refers to Boaz, and either Boaz or Yahweh did not abandon his kindness. In the variants, the ambiguity is cleared up, and it is Yahweh who has not abandoned his loving-kindness.

4. As is often the case, we would prefer the variants as they make more sense to us or, like here, clears up an ambiguity, but this is not sufficient justification for us to reject the MT.

21ᵃ	"LXX (Syriac Peshitta) additional information Grk = Heb; lacks material LXX Syriac Peshitta Vulgate."	
MT	And Ruth the Moabitess said	וַתֹּאמֶר רוּת הַמּוֹאֲבִיָּה
LXX	And Ruth said to her mother-in-law	וַתֹּאמֶר רוּת לַחֲמוֹתָהּ

1. This footnote does not mention it, but actually the Targum and a scroll from Qumran namely 2QRuthᵃ, do support the MT.

2. The Septuagint, the Syriac Peshitta, and the Vulgate omit the word "the Moabitess."

3. "In biblical studies, 'inclusio' is a literary device based on a concentric principle, also known as 'bracketing' or an 'envelope structure,' which consists of creating a frame by placing similar material at the beginning and end of a section."³ This can be seen clearly in Ru 2:2 and here in Ru 2:21.

4. In the MT the author uses the phrase "And Ruth the Moabitess said" as an inclusio, and the use of this literary device by the author makes the MT preferable.

---

3. Scholars agree that it would be quite acceptable to say that these are three variants of the same name, and that the MT could be accepted.

23ᵃ⁻ᵃ	"A few (3–10) Manuscripts Vulgate Heb."	
MT	And she lived with her mother-in-law	וַתֵּשֶׁב אֶת־חֲמוֹתָהּ׃
Mss	And she returned to her mother-in-law	וַתָּשָׁב אֶל חֲמוֹתָהּ׃
Vulg	And she returned to her mother-in-law	וַתָּשָׁב אֶל חֲמוֹתָהּ׃

1. The MT vocalizes the verb as the qal preterite (Chapter 23.6.4.3 in Vol. 1) 3fs of the verb יָשַׁב meaning, "to sit, remain, dwell, live." A few medieval Manuscripts and the Latin Vulgate vocalize the verb as the qal impf. of the bi-consonantal stem שׁוּב meaning, "to return" (Chapter 45.2a in Vol. 2)

2. Neither of the above verbs are transitive. Therefore, in the MT, the word that looks like a definite direct object marker, is in fact an independent preposition meaning, "with" (Chapter 17.7.9 in Vol. 1).

80.4 RUTH 3

3ᵃ	"A few (3–10) Manuscripts as Qere Heb; Ketiv multitude (20–60) Manuscripts Heb."	
Mss	and you will put on your garments	וְשַׂמְתְּ שִׂמְלֹתַיִךְ
MTᵠ	and you will put on your garments	וְשַׂמְתְּ שִׂמְלֹתַיִךְ
Mss	and you will put on your garment(s)	וְשַׂמְתְּ שִׂמְלֹתֵךְ
MTᴷ	and you will put on your garment(s)	וְשַׂמְתְּ שִׂמְלֹתֵךְ

1. In MTᴸ (*BHS*) there is an attempt to show both the above variants, but the yod is omitted.
2. The Qere clearly is the plural form meaning, "your garments."
3. The Ketiv, however, could be singular, plural, or collective, and it is thought that the Qere "is a later clarification, intended to remove the ambiguity."[4]

3ᵇ	"Qere multitude (20–60) Manuscripts Heb; Ketiv Heb."	
MTᴷ	And **I / you** shall go down (to) the threshing floor	וְיָרַדְתִּי הַגֹּרֶן
Mss	And **you** shall go down (to) the threshing floor	וְיָרַדְתְּ הַגֹּרֶן
MTᵠ	And **you** shall go down (to) the threshing floor	וְיָרַדְתְּ הַגֹּרֶן

1. The Qere has the normal qal perf. 2fs of the verb meaning, "to come / go down." More than 20 medieval Manuscripts agree with the Qere.

---

[4] Brotzman, Tully (2016), p. 151.

2   The Ketiv can be either a qal perf. 1cs of the same verb, or an archaic form of the qal perf. 2fs, that does not make sense in the context.

4[a]	"Compare 3[b]."	
MT[K]	And I / you shall lie down	וְשָׁכַבְתִּי
Mss	And you shall lie down	וְשָׁכַבְתְּ
MT[Q]	And you shall lie down	וְשָׁכַבְתְּ

1   The explanation in the previous footnote is applicable here as well.

5[a]	"Multitude (20-60) Manuscripts as Qere Heb, the original LXX as Ketiv."	
MT[L]	everything that you say	כֹּל אֲשֶׁר־תֹּאמְרִי
Mss	everything that you say **to me**	כֹּל אֲשֶׁר־תֹּאמְרִי אֵלַי
MT[Q]	everything that you say **to me**	כֹּל אֲשֶׁר־תֹּאמְרִי אֵלַי
LXX*	everything that you say	כֹּל אֲשֶׁר־תֹּאמְרִי
MT[K]	everything that you say	כֹּל אֲשֶׁר־תֹּאמְרִי

1   This footnote does not mention it, but actually the Syriac Peshitta and Targum also agree with the Qere, and the Latin Vulgate also agrees with the Ketiv.

2   This footnote provides us with an example of how the Masorah Magna operates. Above the vowels without consonants there is a small circle that indicates that there is a note in the Masorah Parva in the left margin of *BHS*. The note in the margin begins with the assumed consonants of the Qere. It then states: "One of ten occurrences (of a word) that is read but not written." The superscript numeral 5 then directs us to the Masorah Magna that is located between the main text and the footnotes. Note number 5 in the Book of Ruth Chapter 3 reads, "Mm 2745," which means that we should have a look at entry number 2745 in the separate book Gérard E. Weil. *Massorah Gedolah: Juxta Codicem Leningradensem B 19 a* (1971). Rome. Pontificium Inst. Biblicum [u.a.], to find the locations of those ten occurrences.

6[a]	"A few (3-10) Manuscripts Syriac Peshitta Vulgate Heb."	
MT	And she did exactly as all that she commanded	וַתַּעַשׂ כְּכֹל אֲשֶׁר־צִוַּתָּה
Mss	And she did all that she commanded	וַתַּעַשׂ כֹּל אֲשֶׁר־צִוַּתָּה

1   The Syriac Peshitta and Latin Vulgate agree with the (3–10) medieval Manuscripts.

2   Waltke and O'Connor call this a *kaph veritatis* (*veritatis* means, "truth"), and state that "the agreement of the things compared is complete," and translate it with "in every way" like in Hos 5:12 and Neh 7:2.[5] Brotzman and Tully translate this kaph with, "exactly as."[6]

---

5   Brotzman, Tully (2016), p. 154.
6   Main source: Wikipedia contributors. "*Inclusio.*" Wikipedia, The Free Encyclopedia, 20 November, 2017. Web: 5 August, 2019.

3   There are two possibilities here. a) the MT contains a dittography (a scribe wrote two kaphs instead of one), or b) the variants contain a haplography (a scribe copied one kaph instead of two).

7ª	"Lacks material in the original LXX."	
MT	Boaz ate **and drank** and his heart was glad	וַיֹּאכַל בֹּעַז וַיֵּשְׁתְּ וַיִּיטַב לִבּוֹ
LXX*	Boaz ate and his heart was glad	וַיֹּאכַל בֹּעַז וַיִּיטַב לִבּוֹ

1   This footnote does not mention it, but in fact the Syriac Peshitta, the Targum, the Old Latin, the Latin Vulgate and 2QRuthª all agree with the MT in this instance.

2   It might be that the Greek Septuagint wants to avoid any possibility of impropriety between Ruth and Boaz, but the author actually might want to raise concerns, and then surprise the reader when they do act properly.

9ª	"LXX (Syriac Peshitta Vulgate) additional information Grk = Heb."	
MT	And he said: "Who are you?"	וַיֹּאמֶר מִי־אָתְּ
LXX^L	And he said **to her**: "Who are you?"	וַיֹּאמֶר לָהּ מִי־אָתְּ

1   The Syriac Peshitta and the Vulgate agree with the Lucianic revision of the Septuagint.

2   **polygenesis**: the hypothetical origination of language (or, as here, a phrase) from a number of independent sources in different places at different times.

3   This is probably a case of polygenesis. The prepositional phrase "to her" was independently added by all three variants because in the Book of Ruth, the preposition "le" often identifies the one who is addressed after the verb "to say."

9^b	"So Leningradensis, multitude (20-60) Manuscripts Editions Heb."	
MT^L	And he said: "Who are you?"	וַיֹּאמֶר מִי־אָתְּ
Mss	And he said: "Who are you?"	וַיֹּאמֶר מִי־אָתְּ

1   Here the Leningrad Codex has an obvious error in omitting the shewa in the feminine singular pronoun. It was corrected and standardized in the later medieval Manuscripts and Editions.

9^c	"Ketiv (Western) many (20-60) Manuscripts Heb, Ketiv (Eastern) Qere LXX Syriac Peshitta Heb."	
MT^L	Spread you garments	וּפָרַשְׂתָּ כְנָפֶךָ
MT^K-Oc	Spread you garments	וּפָרַשְׂתָּ כְנָפֶיךָ
MT^K-Or	Spread you garment	וּפָרַשְׂתָּ כְנָפְךָ

1   Actually, the Hebrew word כָּנָף means, "wing," or "extremity."

2   The Leningrad Codex has the dual even in the absence of the yod.

3. In addition, there are also two Ketiv readings:

   a) The Western / Tiberian / Palestinian form, indicated by superscript ᴼᶜᶜ, an abbreviation of "Occident(al)" meaning, "West(ern)." This reading, which is also found in many (20–60) later Manuscripts, includes the yod, to make the dual spelling complete.

   b) The Eastern / Babylonian form, indicated by superscript ᴼʳ as an abbreviation of "Orient(al)" meaning, "East(ern)." Together with the Greek Septuagint, the Syriac Peshitta, and the Qere, this form represents the singular.

4. We should keep in mind that the Greek Septuagint and Syriac Peshitta were translated from the unvocalized Hebrew text, and because there was no yod, they naturally translated the word as singular.

11ᵃ	"A few (3–10) Manuscripts LXX Syriac Peshitta Targum Vulgate adds information Heb."	
MT	All that you say, I will do for you.	כֹּל אֲשֶׁר־תֹּאמְרִי אֶעֱשֶׂה־לָּךְ
Mss	All that you say **to me**, I will do for you.	כֹּל אֲשֶׁר־תֹּאמְרִי אֵלַי אֶעֱשֶׂה־לָּךְ

1. A few (3–10) medieval Manuscripts, the fifth column in Origen's Greek Hexapla, the Syriac Peshitta, the Targum, and the Latin Vulgate all add the preposition "to her."

2. There is no explanation as to why the preposition was lost in the MT.

12ᵃ	"Multitude (20–60) Manuscripts as Qere."	
MTᴷ	that if I am a redeemer	כִּי אִם גֹּאֵל אָנֹכִי
MTᴷ	that surely I am a redeemer	כִּי אִם גֹּאֵל אָנֹכִי
MTᴷ	but I am (not) a redeemer	כִּי אִם גֹּאֵל אָנֹכִי
MTQ	that I am a redeemer	כִּי גֹּאֵל אָנֹכִי

1. The meaning of the Qere is fairly straightforward and it appears in more than 20 other medieval Manuscripts. When the two consonants (aleph mem) are absent, the second *kiy* likely introduces the proposition that Boaz, in the previous phrase, says is true.

2. If the Ketiv is correct, and the two consonants remain and are pointed (given vowels) with a chireq (to become '*im*), then there are three possible translations.

3. This footnote does not mention the fact that in the Greek Septuagint, the Syriac Peshitta, and the Latin Vulgate, both the second *kiy* and the two consonants (aleph mem) are omitted.

4. We can therefore conclude that a dittography occurred in the MT, and that the Masoretes recognized this and did not vocalize the aleph and mem.

14ᵃ	"Multitude (20–60) Manuscripts as Qere Heb."	
MTᴷ	the place of his feet	מַרְגְּלֹתָו
MTꟴ	the place of his feet	מַרְגְּלֹתָיו

1. Twenty or more medieval Manuscripts agree with the Qere.

2. The 3ms suffix should have the yod, but this suffix is often written without the yod in accordance with the actual pronunciation namely "-aw," and thus the word is plural.

14ᵇ	"Ketiv Heb, multitude (20–60) Manuscripts as Qere Heb."	
MTᴸ	and she rose before	וַתָּקָם בְּטֶרֶום
MTᴷ	and she rose before	וַתָּקָם בְּטְרוֹם
MTꟴ	and she rose before	וַתָּקָם בְּטֶרֶם

1. For the word "before," the Leningrad codex text of *BHS* has the consonants of the Ketiv but the vowels of the Qere. This is unusual as it results in a strange spelling.

2. Many (20–60) medieval Manuscripts agree with the Qere, which is the usual spelling.

14ᶜ	"LXX (Vulgate) additional information Grk; Syriac Peshitta Syr = Heb."	
MT	And he said	וַיֹּאמֶר
LXX	And Boaz said	וַיֹּאמֶר בֹּעַז
SyP	And she said to him	וַתֹּאמֶר לוֹ

1. The LXX and Vulgate are making the subject more explicit by adding the name Boaz.

2. The Syriac Peshitta has a completely different reading, which is not mentioned fully in this footnote.

3. Footnotes *c*, *d*, and *e* have to be considered together. Refer to note 4 at footnote *e*.

14ᵈ	"Syriac Peshitta Syr = Heb."	
MT	that she came	כִּי־בָאָה
SyP	that I came	כִּי־בָאתִי

1. The Syriac Peshitta has a different overall understanding of this part of the verse.

2. This footnote equates the Syriac verb "to go down" with the Hebrew verb "to enter." This is not completely correct as Syriac has at least two other verbs (see 2:18) that are more closely equivalent to the Hebrew.

14ᵉ	"Additional information Syriac Peshitta, the LXX Grk = Heb."	
MT	that **the** woman has come (to) the threshing floor	כִּי־בָאָה הָאִשָּׁה הַגֹּרֶן
LXX	that **a** woman has come (to) the threshing floor	כִּי־בָאָה אִשָּׁה הַגֹּרֶן
SyP	that I came to you (at) the threshing floor	כִּי־בָאתִי אֵלֶיךָ הַגֹּרֶן

1. In the MT there might be a dittography of the hei, resulting in "the woman."

2. Conversely in the Greek Septuagint the hey could have been omitted due to a haplography.

3. The MT makes more sense as the concern of Boaz was directed at Ruth specifically.

4. Footnotes *c*, *d*, and *e* have to be considered as a unit. The MT and the Syriac Peshitta see the last sentence as follows:

MT: "And he said, 'Do not let it be known that the woman came (to) the threshing floor'."

Peshitta: "And she said (note *c*) to him, 'Do not let anyone know that I came down (note *d*) to you (note *e*) at the threshing floor'."

The MT has it that Boaz is speaking to himself and considering what has to be done to protect Ruth's (and his own) reputation. Because the previous two verbs in the verse are in the third person feminine ("she lay down" and "she got up"), the Syriac Peshitta was influenced by this and sees Ruth speaking to Boaz here (note *c*). The translator then was forced to make subsequent changes (notes *d* and *e*). The MT was not influenced and is the original and better reading.

15ᵃ	"The original LXX additional information Grk, the LXX additional information Grk."	
MT	And he said	וַיֹּאמֶר
LXX*	And he said to her,	וַיֹּאמֶר לָהּ
LXXᴸ	And he said to Ruth,	וַיֹּאמֶר אֶל־רוּת

1. The changes in both versions of the Greek Septuagint reflect the tendency of the Septuagint to make what has been implied more explicit.

2. The original Septuagint follows 1:10, 2:2, 2:14, 3:1 in using the inseparable preposition *lei*, whereas Lucian's recension (revised edition) follows 2:8 and 2:22 in using the independent preposition *'el* before Ruth.

15ᵇ	"Multiple (20–60) Manuscripts Syriac Peshitta Vulgate Heb."	
MT	And **he** entered the city	וַיָּבֹא הָעִיר׃
Mss	And **she** entered the city	וַתָּבֹא הָעִיר׃

1. The Syriac Peshitta and Vulgate agree with the many (20–60) medieval Manuscripts.
2. The MT makes more sense as it is in accordance with the agreement between Boaz and Ruth to return to the city separately.

17ᵃ	"The original LXX additional information Grk, compare (verse) 15ᵃ."	
MT	And she said,	וַתֹּאמֶר
LXX*	And she said to her,	וַתֹּאמֶר לָהּ

1. This footnote refers us to the first footnote in 3:15.
2. Although the context makes it quite obvious, once again the Greek Septuagint has made the implicit addressee of Ruth's statement more explicit. It now seems that this is becoming an identified characteristic of the Septuagint version of the Book of Ruth.
3. It is becoming more clear if and when the changes to the original Hebrew text were made by the translator of the Septuagint.

17ᵇ	"LXX (Syriac Peshitta) Targum as Qere Heb."	
MTᴷ	For he said, "Do not go . . ."	כִּי אָמַר אַל־תָּבוֹאִי
MTQ	For he said **to me,** "Do not go . . ."	כִּי אָמַר אֵלַי אַל־תָּבוֹאִי

1. Refer to footnote 3:5ᵃ.

80.5 RUTH 4

2ᵃ	"LXX (Vulgate) additional information Grk."	
MT	And **he** took ten men	וַיִּקַּח עֲשָׂרָה אֲנָשִׁים
LXX	And **Boaz** took ten men	וַיִּקַּח בֹּעַז עֲשָׂרָה אֲנָשִׁים

1. This footnote states that the Latin Vulgate agrees with the Greek Septuagint.
2. The apparatus in *BHS* does not mention it, but the Septuagint has also added the name Boaz in the previous verse (And Boaz said to him, "Turn aside").
4. In both verses the subject of the verb could be Boaz or the "redeemer." The Greek Septuagint therefore deemed it necessary to provide more explicit subjects. The MT is in fact coherent and the reader does not need to be helped.

3ᵃ⁻ᵃ	"LXX Grk."	
MT	Naomi has sold	מָכְרָה נָעֳמִי
LXX	which was given to Naomi	אֲשֶׁר נְתוּנָה לְנָעֳמִי

1. This footnote does not mention that other versions of the Greek Septuagint, as well as the Syriac Peshitta and Latin Vulgate, support the MT reading.

2. "However, this substitution in the Septuagint makes the sentence ungrammatical and impossible as it now has no main clause, only a string of relative clauses: 'The portion of the field, which belonged to our brother Elimelech, which was given to Naomi who returned from the territory of Moab'."⁷

4ᵃ	"Multiple (20-60) Manuscripts Versions Heb."	
MT	But if **he** will not redeem, tell me	וְאִם־לֹא יִגְאַל הַגִּידָה לִּי
Mss	But if **you** will not redeem, tell me	וְאִם־לֹא תִגְאַל הַגִּידָה לִּי

1. The medieval Manuscripts and all or most of the Versions, including the Greek Septuagint and the Syriac Peshitta, have the verb in the second person. The Targum Ruth has a completely different text construction.

2. The MT has the verb "redeem" in the third person, and as there is no plausible explanation as to how this came about, it is difficult to dismiss the MT.

3. However, because of the unified consensus in the Versions, in this case we have to accept as more likely that the second person is the more original reading.

4ᵇ	"Ketiv Heb; multitude (20-60) Manuscripts as Qere Heb."	
MTᴷ	that I may know	וְאֵדַע
MTǪ	that I may know	וְאֵדְעָה

1. In the Ketiv we find a qal impf. of the verb, but in the Qere we find the qal coh. of the same verb.
2. Both these forms indicate the purpose of the preceding clause, "Tell me so that I may know."

5ᵃ	"Vulgate Lat, read Heb."	
MT	**and from** Ruth the Moabitess	וּמֵאֵת רוּת הַמּוֹאֲבִיָּה
Vulg	**also** Ruth the Moabitess	גַּם אֶת־רוּת הַמּוֹאֲבִיָּה

1. In the MT we find the preposition min (Chapter 17.5.3.3 in Vol. 1) before a form that is either an object marker (Chapter 16.9 in Vol. 1), or the independent preposition "with" (Chapters 16.4.2.1 and 17.2 in Vol. 1).

---

7 Brotzman, Tully (2016), p. 160.

2. The Vulgate changed the form to two words in which case we could explain the MT as a scribal error (the gimmel became a waw) and a difference in the division of the words.

3. However, we first have to consider the next footnote before coming to a conclusion.

5ᵇ		"A few (3-10) Manuscripts as Qere Heb; Ketiv Heb; perhaps read Heb compare Versions."
MTᴸ	the wife of the deceased I acquire	אֵשֶׁת־הַמֵּת קָנִיתִי
MTᴷ	the wife of the deceased I acquire	אֵשֶׁת־הַמֵּת קָנִיתִי
MTᵠ	the wife of the deceased you acquire	אֵשֶׁת־הַמֵּת קָנִיתָה
Vrs	acquire the wife of the deceased	אֵשֶׁת־הַמֵּת קְנֵה

1. This footnote states that some medieval Manuscripts as well as some Versions (like the Greek Septuagint, the Targum Ruth, and the Syriac Peshitta) support the second person Qere in seeing Ruth as the object of the following, and the second appearance, of the verb "to buy."

2. The MT is too difficult to explain. The Vulgate form in footnote 5ᵃ coupled with the Ketiv in footnote 5ᵇ gives us the following reasonable reading: "On the day you buy the field from the hand of Naomi, I also buy Ruth the Moabitess, the wife of the deceased."

3. This seems a reasonable reading, especially in view of 4:10 where we learn that Boaz did in fact do what he is proposing here.

7ᵃ		"LXX additional information Grk compare Syriac Peshitta Targum Vulgate = Heb."
MT	Now this formerly	וְזֹאת לְפָנִים
LXX	Now this was the judgment formerly	וְזֶה הַמִּשְׁפָּט לְפָנִים

1. The Greek Septuagint adds a word that is usually translated with "justice" or "penalty," and a similar form is found in the SyP. But this does not make sense in this context.

2. The Targum and Latin Vulgate also include this word, but there it has the meaning of, "the custom" which makes sense.

3. The feminine gender of the demonstrative pronoun is changed to the masculine in the Versions, and therefore we can accept the MT as the original.

7ᵇ		"LXX Targum put before conjunction."
MT	a man would draw off his sandal	שָׁלַף אִישׁ נַעֲלוֹ
LXX	**and** a man would draw off his sandal	וְשָׁלַף אִישׁ נַעֲלוֹ

1. This footnote states that both the Greek Septuagint and the Targum add a waw before the verb. Refer to Chapter 23.6.3 in Vol. 1 for a discussion of the waw before a perf. verb.

2. Adding the waw would be a more standard syntax, but there is no reason not to accept the MT.

Ruth

8ᵃ	"LXX additional information Grk = Heb."	
MT	And he drew off his sandal	וַיִּשְׁלֹף נַעֲלוֹ׃
LXX	And he drew off his sandal and gave it to him.	וַיִּשְׁלֹף נַעֲלוֹ וַיִּתֶּן לוֹ׃

1. The words in the MT are quite terse (sparing in the use of words), and the Greek Septuagint again is attempting to make the implicit MT more explicit.

2. The apparatus in *BHS* does not mention it, but the Septuagint has actually added more words just before this phrase for the same reason as above.

10ᵃ⁻ᵃ	"Read Heb compare LXX."	
MT	from his brothers and from the gate of his place	מֵעִם אֶחָיו וּמִשַּׁעַר מְקֹמוֹ
LXX	from his brothers from his people	מֵעִם אֶחָיו מֵעַמּוֹ

1. "Metonymy is a figure of speech in which a thing or concept is referred to by the name of something closely associated with that thing or concept."⁸ For example, "The Kremlin" for "the primary complex of the Government of Russia or the USSR."

2. In the MT, "the gate" actually refers to the elders who are convened at the town gate.

3. The apparatus in *BHS* does not mention the following:

   a) The Syriac Peshitta is similar to the Greek Septuagint.

   b) The Latin Vulgate has, "his family and his brothers and his people."

4. However, the MT is likely the original with the versions attempting to interpret the MT.

11ᵃ⁻ᵃ	"LXX Grk, perhaps read Heb."	
MT	and the elders (said) "Witnesses"	וְהַזְּקֵנִים עֵדִים
LXX	"Witnesses." and the elders (said)	עֵדִים וַיֹּאמְרוּ הַזְּקֵנִים

1. In this case it seems unlikely that a different Hebrew text existed here, and more likely that the Greek Septuagint made an intentional change to achieve a better interpretation.

14ᵃ	"LXX Grk = Heb."	
MT	And may **his** name be called in Israel.	וְיִקָּרֵא שְׁמוֹ בְּיִשְׂרָאֵל׃
LXX	And may he call **your** name in Israel.	וְיִקְרָא שִׁמְךָ בְּיִשְׂרָאֵל׃

1. In the MT the pronominal suffix is 3ms (his), but in the Greek Septuagint it is 2ms ("your").

2. In verses 13–15 the focus is on Ruth's child. Therefore the MT makes more sense in the wider context. The Septuagint makes more sense in the immediate context.

---

8 Waltke and O'Connor (1990), p. 203.

15ª	"Thus Leningradensis, multitude (20–60) Manuscripts Editions Heb."	
MT^L	your daughter-in-law who loves you	כַּלָּתֵךְ אֲשֶׁר־אֲהֵבָתֶךְ
Mss	your daughter-in-law who loves you	כַּלָּתֵךְ אֲשֶׁר־אֲהֵבָתֶךְ

1. This is an example of the idiosyncrasies (a distinctive / peculiar feature or characteristic) that are sometimes found in the Leningrad Codex.

2. The difference in spelling has no influence on the meaning.

16ª⁻ª	"Additional information Syriac Peshitta."	
MT	and laid him on her lap	וַתְּשִׁתֵהוּ בְחֵיקָהּ
SyP	—	—

1. The next word after these two words is, "and she became." This word has the same two initial consonants and vowels medieval Manuscripts. It therefore seems very likely that this is an example of the copying error called homoioarcton (Chapter 72.2.1e in Vol. 4).

18ª	"Verse 18 following compare 1 Chr 2:5, 9–15."

1. Here the superscript ª is at the beginning (right side) of the first word of the verse. This usually means that the footnote applies to the whole verse (Chapters 75.2.3,4 in Vol. 4). In this case it actually pertains to Ru 4:18–20.

19ª	"LXX Grk; LXX Grk; read Heb compare Mt 1:3, 4."	
MT	Ram, and Ram	אֶת־רָם וְרָם
LXX^{A,B}	Aran, and Aran	אֶת־אֲרָן וְאֲרָן
LXX^{rel}	Aram, and Aram	אֶת־אֲרָם וְאֲרָם

1. Variable spellings of names is rather common in the MT, and therefore of no consequence here.

20ª	"LXX Grk; LXX Grk."	
MT	Salmah	אֶת־שַׂלְמָה׃
LXX^B	Salman	אֶת־שַׂלְמָן
LXX^{rel}	Salmon	אֶת־שַׂלְמוֹן׃

1. In Jgs 14:2 the footnote 2^d has the Latin "rel," which is an abbreviation of "reliqua" meaning, "remaining." LXX^{rel} would then mean, "The remaining versions of the LXX."

2. This note is related to the next one, and will be included in the discussion below.

21ᵃ	"A few (3–10) Manuscripts Heb; LXX Grk, LXX = MT."	
MTᴸ	And Salmon	וְשַׂלְמוֹן׃
Mss	And Salmah	וְשַׂלְמָה׃
LXXᴮ	And Salman	וְשַׂלְמָן׃
LXXʳᵉˡ	And Salmon	וְשַׂלְמוֹן׃

1. All these names obviously refer to the same individual.

2. In 1 Chr 2:11 we find another spelling namely *salma'*.

3. Scholars agree that it would be quite acceptable to say that these are three variants of the same name, and that the MT could be accepted.

81 Jonah

81.1 INTRODUCTION

1. In this chapter, we will focus on identifying the grammar involved in every word found in Chapter 1 of the Book of Jonah in the Hebrew Bible

2. The numbers appearing beneath the Hebrew text are references to the sections contained in Volumes 1–3 in this series that are relevant to this word.

81.2 JONAH 1

Verse								
1:1	וַיְהִי	דְּבַר־	יְהוָה	אֶל־	יוֹנָה	בֶּן־	אֲמִתַּי	לֵאמֹר:
	23.6.6	10.11.B	20.1	17.3.1	pn	10.11.A	pn	23.13.5
1:2a	קוּם	לֵךְ	אֶל־נִינְוֵה	הָעִיר	הַגְּדוֹלָה	וּקְרָא	עָלֶיהָ	
	45.2a	43.1	pn	12.2.5.1	12.2.3	13.3.1	17.7.12.2	
					15.2.2	38.1		
1:2b	כִּי־	עָלְתָה	רָעָתָם	לְפָנָי:				
	17.2	48.1	10.11.B.5.1	10.11.B.6				
1:3a	וַיָּקָם	יוֹנָה	לִבְרֹחַ	תַּרְשִׁישָׁה	מִלִּפְנֵי	יְהוָה	וַיֵּרֶד	יָפוֹ
	23.6	pn	17.4.6	pn	17.5.3	20.1	23.6	pn
	45.2a		40.1	19.1	10.11.B.6	43.1		
1:3b	יִמְצָא	אֳנִיָּה	בָּאָה	תַרְשִׁישׁ	וַיִּתֵּן	שְׂכָרָהּ	וַיֵּרֶד	בָּהּ
	38.1	10.11.B.5.1	45.2b	pn	23.6	10.11.B.2.1a	23.6	17.7.7
					44.2c	10.8.2	43.1	
1:3c	לָבוֹא	עִמָּהֶם	תַּרְשִׁישָׁה	מִלִּפְנֵי	יְהוָה:			
	17.4.4	17.7.9	pn	17.5.3	20.1			
	45.2b		19.1	10.11.B.6				

1:4a	וַיהוָה	הֵטִיל	רוּחַ־	גְּדוֹלָה	אֶל־	הַיָּם	וַיְהִי	סַעַר	גָּדוֹל	בַּיָּם
	23.6	45.6	15.1.3	17.2	12.2.3	23.6.6		15.1	17.7.7	
	20.1	10.11.A.3.3		10.11.A.2.1		10.11.B.1.4				

1:4b	וְהָאֳנִיָּה	חִשְּׁבָה	לְהִשָּׁבֵר:
	19.1	32.3.1	17.4.4 24.6

1:5a	וַיִּירְאוּ	הַמַּלָּחִים	וַיִּזְעֲקוּ	אִישׁ	אֶל־	אֱלֹהָיו
	42.2	12.2.3	35.1.1	10.11.A.3.1	17.3.1	20.1 18.8

1:5b	וַיָּטִלוּ	אֶת־הַכֵּלִים	אֲשֶׁר	בָּאֳנִיָּה	אֶל־הַיָּם	לְהָקֵל	מֵעֲלֵיהֶם
	45.6	10.11.B.4.1	16.6	17.4.8	10.11.A.2.1	46.6	17.5.3.3 17.7.12.2

1:5c	וְיוֹנָה	יָרַד	אֶל־יַרְכְּתֵי	הַסְּפִינָה	וַיִּשְׁכַּב	וַיֵּרָדַם:
	13.2.1	43.1a	10.11.B.7	10.11.B.5.1	23.4	(30.2.1)

1:6a	וַיִּקְרַב	אֵלָיו	רַב	הַחֹבֵל	וַיֹּאמֶר	לוֹ	מַה־לְּךָ	נִרְדָּם
	23.6.4	17.7.12.1	10.11.A	10.11.B.2.4	23.6.9	17.7.6	16.7.4	24.7

1:6b	קוּם	קְרָא	אֶל־	אֱלֹהֶיךָ	אוּלַי	יִתְעַשֵּׁת	הָאֱלֹהִים	לָנוּ	וְלֹא	נֹאבֵד:
	45.2a	38.1	17.2	10.11.B.6	adv	31.7	12.2.5.1	17.7.6	13.1	30.1.4.1

1:7a	וַיֹּאמְרוּ	אִישׁ	אֶל־	רֵעֵהוּ	לְכוּ	וְנַפִּילָה	גוֹרָלוֹת
	30.1.4.1	10.11.A.3.1	17.3.1	10.11.A.2.2	43.1.3a	44.6	10.11.B.2.4

1:7b	וְנֵדְעָה	בְּשֶׁלְּמִי	הָרָעָה	הַזֹּאת	לָנוּ	וַיַּפִּלוּ	גוֹרָלוֹת
	43.1	16.7 17.4	10.11.B.5.1	15.4.3	17.7.6	44.6	10.11.B.2.4

1:7c	וַיִּפֹּל	הַגּוֹרָל	עַל־	יוֹנָה:
	44.2b	12.2.3	17.2	pn

1:8a	וַיֹּאמְרוּ	אֵלָיו	הַגִּידָה־	נָּא	לָנוּ	בַּאֲשֶׁר	לְמִי־	הָרָעָה	הַזֹּאת	לָנוּ
	30.1.4.1	17.7.12	prtl 44.6	21.2.1	17.7.6	21.8	16.7	10.11.B.5.1	15.4.3	17.7.6

1:8b	מַה־	מְלַאכְתְּךָ	וּמֵאַיִן	תָּבוֹא	מָה	אַרְצֶךָ
	16.7.4	10.8	16.7	45.2b	16.7.4	10.11.B.1.1

אָֽתָּה׃	עַם	מִזֶּ֥ה	וְאֵֽי־		1:8c
16.4.1	10.11.A.1.1	17.5.3	16.7.7		
אֱלֹהֵ֣י הַשָּׁמַ֗יִם	וְאֶת־יְהוָ֞ה	אָנֹ֑כִי	עִבְרִ֣י	אֲלֵיהֶ֖ם	וַיֹּ֥אמֶר	1:9a
81.2.1.4c.2	86.2	16.4.1	pn	17.7.12.1	23.6.9	
הַיַּבָּשָֽׁה	וְאֶת־	הַיָּ֖ם	אֶת־	עָשָׂ֥ה	אֲשֶׁר־	יָרֵ֔א	אֲנִ֣י	1:9b
10.11.B.5.1	16.9.5	10.11.A.2.1	16.9.5	48.1	16.6	adj	16.4.1	
אֵלָ֔יו	וַיֹּאמְר֣וּ	גְדוֹלָ֔ה	יִרְאָ֣ה	הָֽאֲנָשִׁים֙	וַיִּֽירְא֤וּ	1:10a
17.7.12.1	30.1	15.2.1	10.11.B.5.1	10.6	42.2	
הָאֲנָשִׁ֔ים	יָדְע֣וּ	כִּֽי־	עָשִׂ֑יתָ	זֹּ֣את	מַה־	1:10b
10.6	12.2.5.1	52.1	prtl	48.1	15.4.3	16.7	
לָהֶֽם׃	הִגִּ֥יד	כִּֽי־	בֹרֵ֔חַ	ה֣וּא	יְהוָה֙	מִלִּפְנֵ֤י	כִּֽי־	1:10c
17.7.6	44.6	62.6	40.1	16.4.1	86.1	17.5.3.1	prtl	
לָּ֔ךְ	נַּֽעֲשֶׂ֣ה	מַה־	אֵלָיו֙	וַיֹּאמְר֤וּ	1:11a
17.7.6	48.1.1	16.7	17.7.12.1	30.1	
וְסֹעֵֽר׃	הוֹלֵ֥ךְ	הַיָּ֖ם	כִּ֥י	מֵֽעָלֵ֑ינוּ	הַיָּ֖ם	וְיִשְׁתֹּ֥ק	1:11b
34.1	33.1	10.11.A	62.6	17.5.3.3	10.11.A	23.4, 13.2	
מֵעֲלֵיכֶ֑ם	הַיָּ֖ם	וְיִשְׁתֹּ֥ק	אֶל־הַיָּ֔ם	וַהֲטִילֻ֣נִי	שָׂא֙וּנִי֙	אֲלֵיהֶ֗ם	וַיֹּ֣אמֶר	1:12a
17.7.12.2		23.4	44.6.1	44.2.1a	17.7.12.1	23.6.9	
עֲלֵיכֶֽם׃	הַזֶּ֖ה	הַגָּד֛וֹל	הַסַּ֧עַר	בְּשֶׁלִּ֗י	כִּ֣י	אָ֔נִי	יוֹדֵ֣עַ	כִּ֚י	1:12b
17.7.12.2	15.4.3	15.3.1	12.2.3	16.7	17.4	16.4.1	42.2	prtl	
יָכֹ֑לוּ	וְלֹ֣א	הַיַּבָּשָׁ֖ה	אֶל־	לְהָשִׁ֥יב	הָאֲנָשִׁ֛ים	וַיַּחְתְּר֣וּ	1:13a
42.2		12.2.3		45.6.1	12.2.5.1	23.6.5	
עֲלֵיהֶֽם׃	וְסֹעֵ֖ר	הוֹלֵ֥ךְ	הַיָּ֛ם	כִּ֣י	1:13b
17.7.12.2	35.1	33.1	10.11.A.2.1	17.5.3.3	

Jonah

1:14a	וַיִּקְרְא֞וּ	אֶל־	יְהוָה֙	וַיֹּאמְר֗וּ	אָנָּ֤ה	יְהוָה֙	אַל־	נָ֣א	נֹאבְדָ֗ה
	38.1	17.7.12	20.1	30.1	intj	20.1	23.4.3	21.2	23.8, 30.1

1:14b	בְּנֶ֙פֶשׁ֙	הָאִ֣ישׁ	הַזֶּ֔ה	וְאַל־תִּתֵּ֥ן	עָלֵ֖ינוּ	דָּ֣ם	נָקִ֑יא
	10.11.B.1.1	12.2.5.1	15.4.3	44.2.1c			adj

1:14c	כִּֽי־	אַתָּ֣ה	יְהוָ֔ה	כַּאֲשֶׁ֥ר	חָפַ֖צְתָּ	עָשִֽׂיתָ׃
	prtl	16.4.1		16.6	32.1	48.1.2

1:15	וַיִּשְׂאוּ֙	אֶת־יוֹנָ֔ה	וַיְטִלֻ֖הוּ	אֶל־הַיָּ֑ם	וַיַּעֲמֹ֥ד	הַיָּ֖ם	מִזַּעְפּֽוֹ׃
	44.2a		45.6.1 + suff		31.1		10.11.B.1.5

1:16a	וַיִּֽירְא֧וּ	הָאֲנָשִׁ֛ים	יִרְאָ֥ה	גְדוֹלָ֖ה	אֶת־יְהוָ֑ה
	42.2	10.6.1	10.11.B.5.1	15.2.1	

1:16b	וַיִּֽזְבְּחוּ־	זֶ֙בַח֙	לַֽיהוָ֔ה	וַֽיִּדְּר֖וּ	נְדָרִֽים׃
	40.1	10.11.B.1.2		44.2b	10.11.B.1.1

82 Selected Passages

82.1 INTRODUCTION

1. The main objective of this volume is to indicate how a basic knowledge of biblical Hebrew together with a basic process of textual criticism are able to enhance our understanding of the original MT text. To achieve this objective we will look at a number of selected passages from which the above assumption will become evident. It should be noted that the objective here is not to reach and/or present a final translation, but rather to present all the available evidence and then leave it to the reader to decide on a dynamic equivalent in a target language chosen by the reader.

2. As a logical consequence of the stance taken above, no theological, ethical, or moral arguments are to be found in any of the following chapters. Many of the passages dealt with in this volume are highly controversial. They have, in many cases over centuries, been the subject of debate and speculation expressed by Jewish and Christian clergy and academics in a vast number of publications and statements of believe.

   A current example which illustrates the above point clearly are the "clobber verses," so-called because of the often hurtful and damaging effect they have on the gay and lesbian communities against which they are lobbed. In the Hebrew Bible these verses are Gen 1:28, Gen 19:5, Lv 18:22, and in the Christian New Testament they are Rom 1:26–27, 1 Cor 6:9, 1 Tim 1:10. For example, in Lv 18:22 the word usually translated as "abomination" is used 117 times in the Hebrew Bible, and applied to a variety of situations. There are those who argue that this variety should caution us against simplistic interpretations of these texts.

3. In translation, the target language, also called the receptor language, is the language being translated to. In the following chapters, the target language is modern English. It is the antonym (a word opposite in meaning to another) of the source language, which is the language being translated from (Biblical Hebrew as found in the MT). While the form and style of the source language often cannot be reproduced in the target language, the meaning and content can. Refer to item 3, "Nida and Taber" in the Preface to Volume 4 of this series.

4. In dealing with passages from the Hebrew Bible in this volume, the following modus operandi was followed:

4.1 Firstly, the MT in question is reproduced exactly as found in the Codex Leningradensis.

4.2 This is followed by an absolute literal translation of the above MT text.

4.3 Then a number of the most popular English translations are listed. The KJB, NASB, and ESV are listed as examples of more literal (form equivalent) translations. The NLT and NIV represent more dynamic equivalent attempts at translating. Often other translations are included to illustrate a point mentioned in the notes.

   Biblehub.com is an extensive Bible portal featuring topical Greek and Hebrew study tools, concordances, commentaries, dictionaries, sermons and devotionals. The translations mentioned above are part of a list of 27 English Bibles found in the parallel Bible section of Biblehub.com.

4.4 Any footnote(s) found in *BHS* applicable to the phrase or sentence are reproduced in the same manner as was done in Chapter 79 in Volume 4 of this series. The content of these footnote(s) are explained by adding additional notes.

4.5 A number of Hebrew forms in the particular text might be parsed and, if needed, explained. Often, the reading of these forms have a bearing on the outcome of the preferred translation.

4.6 Lastly, further notes are made. These could include notes on different opinions and commentaries, and in a limited number of cases, criticisms leveled at one or more current Bible editions and their translations. Where deemed necessary, short essays dealing with relevant background information are presented.

5 The books are dealt with in the order as found in the Old Testament of the Christian King James Bible. The numbering of verses are according to those found in *BHS*. The literal translations in English are written from right to left in accordance with the Hebrew text in *BHS*. Although aligned to the right to appear under the literal translation, the English translations are written in the normal English format from left to right.

6 Readers are hereby reminded to keep Chapter 80.1.4 on how footnotes are translated in mind throughout the rest of this volume. In Chapter 82.2 we will look at the *tiqquney sopherim*; in Chapter 82.3 we list the five *ittur sopherim*; in Chapter 82.4 we deal with the *hapax legomenon*; and in Chapter 82.5 we will deal with 400 selected passages taken from each and every book of the Hebrew Bible.

7 For the sake of easier reading, in this chapter longer verses in *BHS* are arbitrarily divided into shorter lines and numbered in alphabetical order. However, it should be noted that there is no correlation between the numbers assigned to the lines and the alphabetical numbering of the footnotes as found in the complete verses of *BHS*.

82.2 TIQQUNEY SOPHERIM

1 *Tiqqun sopherim* (pl.: *tiqquney sopherim*) is a term from rabbinic literature meaning, "correction of scribes" or "scribal correction" and refers to a change of wording in the Hebrew Bible (Tanakh) in order to preserve the honor of God or for a similar reason. Most modern scholars believe that the text was corrected by later scribes, perhaps those of the Great Assembly that edited the biblical corpus. The rabbis mentioned *tiqquney sopherim* in several places in their writings, with a total of 18 *tiqquney sopherim* in all.[1]

2 According to ancient Jewish tradition the Great Assembly, also known as the Great Synagogue, or Synod, was an assembly of 120 scribes, sages, and prophets, in the period from the end of the biblical prophets and the beginning of the Second Temple period (537 BCE) to the early Hellenistic period (323–31 BC).

3 Some modern scholars question whether the Great Assembly ever existed as an institution as such and can rather be taken to mean that ideas, rules, and prayers (seen to be pre-Rabbinic but post-biblical), that were often fathered upon them.

4 Among the developments in Judaism that are attributed to the Great Assembly are the fixing of the Jewish biblical canon, including for the first time the Books of Ezekiel, Daniel, and Esther, and the Twelve Minor Prophets. In addition they introduced the celebration of the Feast of

---

[1] Brotzman, Tully (2016), p. 162.

Purim, the institution of the prayer known as the "Shemoneh 'Esreh," as well as other synagogue prayers, rituals, and benedictions.[2]

5   These changes were made by means of so-called "emendations" (the process of making a revision or correction to a text). However, in many cases it is debated whether the substitutions are true tiqquney sopherim (i.e., emendations by copyists), or whether they were euphemisms supplied by the original writers.

6   Here we will look at the 18 tiqquney sopherim. They are not clearly marked as such in the footnotes of BHS. In the first ten cases the changes were all made to avoid references to God. This was achieved by changing the pronominal suffix attached to the word in question. Refer to Chapter 75.3.4—A.b.4.ii, in Vol. 4.

McCarthy (1981), is of the opinion that all of these are cases of unauthentic emendations by a copyist.

6.1	**GENESIS 18**
22[a-a]	"Tiqqun sopherim, reading originally Heb."
	In this phrase the word order was changed by the sopherim from, "Yahweh was still before Abraham" to, "Abraham was still standing before Yahweh." Now it means that the standing *shekhinah* (the glory of the divine presence) is waiting for Abraham. To "stand before" someone usually means to minister to an authority who is sitting.
6.2	**NUMBERS 11**
15[c]	"Tiqqun sopherim probably Heb."
	To avoid a disrespectful expression toward God, the original 2ms suffix in "your distress / wretchedness" was changed to the 1cs, "my distress / wretchedness."
6.3	**NUMBERS 12**
12[c]	"Tiqqun sopherim probably Heb and Heb; the LXX (Vulgate) Grk."
	To avoid an expression of disrespect regarding the origins of Moses, the original pronominal suffixes of two words in the verse were changed. "Our mother's womb" and "our flesh" was changed to read "its mother's womb" and "its flesh."
6.4	**1 SAMUEL 3**
13[a]	"Tiqqun sopherim Heb compare LXX Old Latin; Heb compare Ginsburg."
	So that the reader of the Scriptures would not have to speak aloud of cursing God, "his sons were cursing God" was changed to "his sons were cursing themselves."
6.5	**2 SAMUEL 16**
12[a]	"Several (11–20) Manuscripts as Qere compare Targum; a few (3–10) Manuscriptscited Heb compare LXX SyP Vulgate."
	The footnote in *BHS* does not indicate that this is a *tiqqun sopherim*. To avoid an anthropomorphism, "Yahweh will look with His eye" was changed to "Yahweh will look on my eye."
	anthropomorphism: the attribution / ascription of human characteristics, behavior, emotions, feelings or passions to a non-human being, generally to a deity, but sometimes to an animal or a thing.

---

2   Brotzman, Tully (2016), p. 173.

6.6		**2 SAMUEL 20**
1		There is no footnote in *BHS* to point out a possible *tiqqun sopherim*. To avoid reading aloud a call to apostasy, "to his gods" was changed to "to his tents."
		apostasy: the abandonment or renunciation of a religious or political belief.
6.7		**1 KINGS 12**
16[d]		The word involved has been marked in the text of *BHS* but there is no footnote in the apparatus. To avoid reading aloud a call to apostasy, "to your gods" was changed to "to your tents."
		apostasy: the abandonment or renunciation of a religious or political belief.
6.8		**2 CHRONICLES 10**
16		There is no footnote in *BHS* to point out a possible tiqqun sopherim.
		To avoid reading aloud a call to apostasy, "to your gods" was changed to "to your tents."
		apostasy: the abandonment or renunciation of a religious or political belief.
6.9		**JOB 7**
20[a]		"Tiqqun sopherim the LXX Grk."
		Because of the unseemliness of speaking of becoming a burden to God, the original 2ms suffix in the second last word of the verse meaning, "upon you" was changed by the scribes to the 1cs meaning, "upon me" (Chapter 10.9 in Vol. 1).
6.10		**JOB 32**
3[a]		"Tiqqun sopherim, probably Heb."
		To avoid reading an expression of blasphemy, the words "yet they had condemned God" was changed to read "yet they had condemned Job."
6.11		**PSALM 106**
20[a]		"Tiqqun sopherim probably Heb or Heb."
		To soften the force of an expression of disrespect toward God, the original pronominal suffix of the word was changed from the 1cs or 3ms "my glory" or "his glory" was changed to the 3mp and then read "their glory."
6.12		**JEREMIAH 2**
11[a]		"Tiqqun sopherim probably Heb."
		To soften the force of an expression of disrespect toward God, the original 1cs suffix in "my glory" was changed to the 3mp to read, "their glory."
6.13		**LAMENTATIONS 3**
20[b]		"Tiqqun sopherim Heb."
		To avoid a strong anthropomorphism, the original 2ms suffix in "your soul" was changed to the 1cs, "my soul."
6.14		**EZEKIEL 8**
17[d]		"Tiqqun sopherim Heb or Heb."
		To avoid expressing the blasphemous idea of putting a branch to Yahweh's nose., the original 1cs suffix in "my nose" or "my noses" was changed to 3mp, "their noses."

6.15	**HOSEA 4**
7ᵃ	"Tiqqun sopherim Heb."
	To soften the force of an expression of disrespect toward God, the original 1cs suffix in "my glory" was changed to the 3mp to read, "their glory."
7ᵇ	"Targums, Syriac Peshitta third (person) plural, probably Heb (tiqqun sopherim)."
	The original was the hiph'il perf. 3mp which means, "they changed," but was changed to the hiph'il impf. 1cs then meaning, "I will change" (Chapter 45.6 in Vol. 2).
6.16	**HABAKKUK 1**
12ᵇ⁻ᵇ	"Read with tiqqun sopherim Heb."
	To avoid the unseemly concept of God's death, the original qal impf. 2ms which means, "you will die," was changed to the qal impf. 1cp then meaning, "we will die" (Chapter 45.2a in Vol. 2).
6.17	**ZECHARIAH 2**
12ᵉ	"Tiqqun sopherim instead of Heb compare the LXX, Tertullianus, Vulgate."
	To avoid it referring to God, the original 1cs pronominal suffix in the form "my eye" was changed to the 3ms, "his eye" so as to refer to the divine eye euphemistically.
6.18	**MALACHI 1**
13ᵇ	"Read Heb (tiqqun sopherim)."
	In order to avoid an expression of offense toward Yahweh the original 1cs suffix on the object marker meaning, "me," was changed to the 3ms "it" (Chapter 10.9 in Vol. 1).
	Some lists include Mal 1:12 instead of or in addition to Mal 1:13, claiming that "you profane me" was changed to "you profane it."

7   Although the above list is widely accepted, there is no consensus yet as to the exact list. In a number of other places in the Hebrew Bible it is suggested by ancient rabbinic sources, or by modern scholars, that certain words could have been substituted for theological and other reasons. However, in some other cases it is debatable whether these substitutions are true *tiqquney sopherim* (emendations by copyists), or whether they were simply euphemisms supplied by the original writers. Some of these cases include the following, with an evaluation from McCarthy (1981), p. 197–243. Refer to Chapter 75.3.4—A.b.4.ii, in Vol. 4.

   euphemism: A mild or indirect word or expression substituted for one considered to be too harsh or blunt when referring to something unpleasant or embarrassing

7.1	**NUMBERS 16**
14ᵃ⁻ᵃ	"LXX Grk = Heb."
	Also, the substitution of "these men" for "our." McCarthy: original euphemism (or not a substitution at all).
7.2	**JUDGES 18**
30ᵃ	"Leningrad multiple (20–60) Manuscripts nun raised, multiple Manuscripts Editions not raised; read with a few (3–10) Manuscripts LXX constructed form Vulgate Heb compare Syrohexaplaris."
	The substitution of "Manasseh" for "Moses." McCarthy: emendation

7.3	**1 SAMUEL 2**
17ᵃ	"This material lacking in one Manuscript Qumran LXX."
	Addition of "the men." McCarthy: probable emendation.
7.4	**1 SAMUEL 14**
47ᵃ	"A few (3–10) Manuscripts Cairo Geniza Heb."
	Also, changing "he prospered" or "he was victorious" to "he acted wickedly" or "he put them to the worse." McCarthy: emendation.
7.5	**1 SAMUEL 20**
16ᵃ⁻ᵃ	"LXX Grk compare Ru 4:10, but also 22:8."
	Also, insertion of "the enemies of" before a name. McCarthy: emendation.
7.6	**1 SAMUEL 25**
22ᵃ⁻ᵃ	"LXX Grk (LXX Grk), SyP Syr."
	Also, insertion of "the enemies of" before a name. McCarthy: emendation.
7.7	**1 SAMUEL 29**
4ᵃ⁻ᵃ	"Lacking this material in LXX SyP Vulgate."
	Also, the substitution of "these men" for "our." McCarthy: an original euphemism (or nota substitution at all).
7.8	**2 SAMUEL 5**
8ᵃ	"LXX Grk compare Old Latin."
	Also, changing "who hate David's soul" to "who are hated by David's soul." McCarthy: emendation.
7.9	**2 SAMUEL 12**
9ᵃ	"Lacking this in LXX Theodotion's Greek Version."
	Also, changing "Yahweh" to "the word of Yahweh." McCarthy: emendation.
14ᵇ	"Qumran Heb compare 1 Sm 25:22."
	Also, insertion of "the enemies of" before a name. McCarthy: emendation.
7.10	**1 KINGS 9**
8ᵃ	"Read Heb compare Old Latin SyP Targum."
	Also, changing "this house will become lofty" to "this house will become a ruin." McCarthy: an emendation.
7.11	**1 KINGS 10**
8ᵃ	"Probably read Heb compare LXX SyP."
	Also, changing "your wives" to "your men." McCarthy: an emendation.
7.12	**1 KINGS 19**
3ᵃ	"Read with a few (3–10) Manuscripts LXX SyP Vulgate Heb."
	Changing "he was afraid" to "he saw." McCarthy: emendation, but some feel this is not a true emendation, since it is only a difference in vocalization.

7.13	**1 KINGS 21**
10a	"Original LXX SyP Vulgate 3(rd person) singular; LXX (SyP Vulgate) additional Grk."
	Also, the substitution of "bless" for "curse." McCarthy: an original euphemism.
13c-c	"Original LXX Grk compare (verse) 10."
	Also, the substitution of "bless" for "curse." McCarthy: an original euphemism.
7.14	**2 CHRONICLES 7**
21a	"LXX has additional material Grk, Targum has additional material Heb compare 1 Kgs 9:8 Old Latin SyP Arabic Versions, insert Heb (haplography)."
	Refer to "haplography" in the "Terminology" section in the front of this volume.
	Also, changing "this house will become lofty" to "this house will become a ruin." McCarthy: an original euphemism.
7.15	**2 CHRONICLES 9**
7a	"Thus compare 1 Kgs 10:8, LXX Old Latin Grk."
	Refer to "sic" in the "Terminology" section in the front of this volume.
	Also, changing "your wives" to "your men." McCarthy: an original euphemism.
7.16	**JOB 1**
5a	"Correction or euphemism instead of Heb or similar."
	The substitution of "bless" for "curse." McCarthy: an original euphemism.
11a	"Compare 5a."
	The substitution of "bless" for "curse." McCarthy: an original euphemism.
7.17	**JOB 2**
5b	"Compare 1:5a."
	The substitution of "bless" for "curse." McCarthy: an original euphemism.
9a	"Compare 1:5a."
	The substitution of "bless" for "curse." McCarthy: an original euphemism.
7.18	**ISAIAH 19**
18a	"Qumran several (11–20) Manuscripts Symmachus's Greek Version Targum Vulgate Arabic Versions Heb; LXX Grk = Heb LXX Grk."
	Changing "The City of the Sun" to "the City of Destruction." McCarthy: emendation.

82.3 ITTUR SOPHERIM

1   *Ittur sopherim* is a term from rabbinic literature meaning, "omission of scribes" and refers to the five instances where a conjunctive waw is expected but had been omitted as superfluous (unnecessary). Refer to Chapter 70.4.2.c.8 and Chapter 75.3.4—A.b.4.ii, in Vol 4.

1.1	**GENESIS 18**
5[a]	"A few (3–10) Manuscripts SP LXX SyP Targum Jonathan Heb."
1.2	**GENESIS 24**
55[c]	"Some / several (11–20) Manuscripts SP Versions Heb."
1.3	**NUMBERS 31**
2[b]	"Several (11–20) Manuscripts SP LXX SyP Targum Jonathan Vulgate Heb."
1.4	**PSALM 36**
7[a]	"Cairo Geniza multiple (20–60) Manuscripts LXX Heb, several (11–20) Manuscripts Heb."
1.5	**PSALM 68**
26	The *ittur sopherim* is not mentioned in the apparatus of *BHS*, but the relevant word ("afterward") does appear in the text.

82.4 HAPAX LEGOMENA

1   *Hapax legomena* (sg. *hapax legomenon*) is the term used to describe words that occur only once within a context, either in the written record of an entire language, in the works of an author, or in a single text like the Hebrew Bible.

2   There are about 1,500 *hapax legomena* in the Hebrew Bible; but only 400 are strictly *hapax legomena* that are either absolutely new coinages of roots, or can not be derived in their formation or in their specific meaning from other occurring stems. The remaining 1,100, while appearing once only as a form, can easily be connected with other existing words; as for instance, Job 17:9, Zec 12:5, Am 9:11, Is 49:19, Ez 24:26, Job 34:25, and Ps 69:3. These ones would obviously refer to verbs etc., which are of frequent occurrence in the Bible.[3]

3   The following *hapax legomena* will be dealt with in upcoming sections of Chapter 82.

Hebrew	Reference	English
עֲצֵי־גֹפֶר	Gen 6:14	wood of gopher
סִבֹּלֶת	Jdg 12:6a	ear of wheat
וְכַגְּבִנָּה	Job 10:10	and like cheese
וּזְכוֹכִית	Job 28:17	and glass
וַיְהִי	Ps 95:10	fought
גָּלְמִי	Ps 139:16	embryo
הֵילֵל	Is 14:21a	to shine
וַיְהִי	Is 34:14	night ghost

---

3   Wikipedia contributors. *"Metonymy."* Wikipedia, The Free Encyclopedia, 14 August 2019. Web: 1 September, 2019.

82.5 GENESIS

1. GENESIS 1

BHS	בְּרֵאשִׁ֖ית* בָּרָ֣א אֱלֹהִ֑ים אֵ֥ת הַשָּׁמַ֖יִם וְאֵ֥ת הָאָֽרֶץ׃	1
Ltrl	the earth—and DDOM—the heavens—DDOM—God—he created—in a beginning	
KJB	In the beginning God created the heaven and the earth.	
NASB	In the beginning God created the heavens and the earth.	
ESV	In the beginning God created the heavens and the earth.	
NLT	In the beginning God created the heavens and the earth.	
NIV	In the beginning God created the heavens and the earth.	

1ª "Originally Grk or Grk (Grk), Samaritan Heb."

1. The two Greek forms in this footnote show no deviation from the MT, but the Samaritan form is "in the beginning," as opposed to the "in **a** beginning" of the MT and the Greek Septuagint.

2. בְּרֵאשִׁית — Preposition + noun, f. sg. abs. There is no definite article in the MT.

3. Some scholars argue that the shewa indicates that the word is in a construct chain and could imply "In the beginning of the story."

4. Remembering that the original documents consisted of consonants only, we could question the vowels that the Masoretes added to the second word in the verse. They took the three consonants to be a qal perfect verb 3ms בָּרָא then meaning, "he created." It has been suggested that the consonants could also be given different vowels and so change it into a qal infinitive form בְּרֹא meaning, "to create." This would then open the possibility to translate the phrase as, "beginning to create . . ." This would make even more sense if we kept in mind that the punctuation mark (a soph pasuq) does not necessarily mean a full stop or period.

5. אֵת — DDOM = Definite Direct Object Marker (Chapter 16.9, Vol. 1).

6. Before the first word in this chapter, we find the Hebrew letter samek in the margin. This indicates the beginning of the first of the so-called *parashot*, and is named *"Parashah Bereishit."* Gen 1:1–6:8 is the first parashah in the Hebrew Bible.

7. "The term parashah (plural: *parashot*) formally means a section of a biblical book in the Masoretic Text (MT) of the Tanakh (Hebrew Bible). The division of the text into *parashot* for the biblical books is independent of chapter and verse numbers, which are not part of the Masoretic tradition. *Parashot* are not numbered, but some have special names. In some manuscripts and in many printed editions, an 'open portion' (*petuhah*) is abbreviated with the Hebrew letter *pei*, and a 'closed portion' (*setumah*) with the Hebrew letter *samek*. The parashot also are used to indicate a portion of the Torah that is chanted or read each week in the synagogue on the Sabbath."[4]

---

4 Main source: Wikipedia contributors. *"Tiqqun soferim."* Wikipedia, The Free Encyclopedia, 16 October, 2018. Web: 21 December, 2018. Slightly edited.

BHS	וְהָאָרֶץ הָיְתָה תֹהוּ וָבֹהוּ וְחֹשֶׁךְ עַל־פְּנֵי תְהוֹם	2a
Ltrl	—upon—and darkness—and emptiness—formlessness—she was—and the earth the sea / abyss—face of	
KJB	And the earth was without form, and void; and darkness was upon the face of the deep.	
NASB	The earth was formless and void, and darkness was over the surface of the deep,	
ESV	The earth was without form and void, and darkness was over the face of the deep	
NLT	The earth was formless and empty, and darkness covered the deep waters.	
NIV	Now the earth was formless and empty, darkness was over the surface of the deep,	

1. הָיְתָה Qal perf 3fs of the doubly weak verb הָיָה meaning, "to be, to become, to come to pass." In total it appears 3,576 times in the Hebrew Bible (Vol.1, Chapter 49.1). The preterite form is the most common and occurs 781 times, like in Gen 1:5b below.

2. תֹהוּ Noun, m. sg. abs. meaning, "formlessness, confusion, unreality, emptiness."

BHS	וְרוּחַ אֱלֹהִים מְרַחֶפֶת עַל־פְּנֵי הַמָּיִם׃	2b
Ltrl	the water—the face of—intensely hovering—God—and the Spirit of	
KJB	And the Spirit of God moved upon the face of the waters.	
NASB	and the Spirit of God was moving over the surface of the waters.	
ESV	And the Spirit of God was hovering over the face of the waters.	
NLT	And the Spirit of God was hovering over the surface of the waters.	
NIV	and the Spirit of God was hovering over the waters.	

1. The third word in this line is the pi'el part. active m. sg. of the doubly weak verb רָחַף that in the qal binyan means, "to hover." The pi'el binyan is the intensive form of a verb, so the literal "intensely hover over" is often translated as "brood over." Refer to Dt 32:11 for a rather famous metaphor where an eagle will "intensely hover" over his eaglet.

2. The masculine noun פָּנֶה meaning, "face" appears 2,128 times in the Hebrew Bible and, except for 97 cases, only in the plural, and then mostly in the construct form. For example, the construct with the inseparable preposition *le* occurs 989 times, and with the preposition מִן it occurs 369 times.

3. Here it takes on the meaning of "surface," but elsewhere it has a wide variety of meanings and applications like for example, "the presence of" or "the front of."

3	וַיֹּאמֶר אֱלֹהִים יְהִי אוֹר וַיְהִי־אוֹר:	BHS
	light—and it was—light—it will be—God—and he said	Ltrl
	And God said, "Let there be light," and there was light.	KJB
	And God said, "Let there be light," and there was light.	NASB
	And God said, "Let there be light," and there was light.	ESV
	And God said, "Let there be light," and there was light.	NLT
	And God said, "Let there be light," and there was light.	NIV

1. יְהִי Qal imperfect jussive of the verb הָיָה "to be, to become." Refer to Chapter 23.9 in Vol. 1 for a discussion on the translation of the jussive.

2. וַיְהִי Waw conversive + qal imperfect of the verb הָיָה "to be, to become." Refer to Chapter 49.1 in Vol. 3.

4a	וַיַּרְא אֱלֹהִים אֶת־הָאוֹר כִּי־טוֹב	BHS
	good—that—the light—DDOM—God—and he saw	Ltrl
	And God saw the light, that it was good:	KJB
	God saw that the light was good,	NASB
	God saw that the light was good,	ESV
	God saw that the light was good,	NLT
	God saw that the light was good,	NIV

1. The first word in this verse is the apocopated form of the qal impf. 3ms יִרְאֶה that appears here with a waw conversive (Chapter 23.6 in Vol. 1).

2. The transitive verb "to apocopate" means, "to omit the final sound(s) or syllable of a word." This is often done in English, like in "gym" as the apocopated form of "gymnasium."

3. In total, this verb occurs 1,310 times in the Hebrew Bible, and the apocopated form with the waw conversive occurs 131 times like in Gen 1:10, 12, 18, 21, 25, 31.

4b	וַיַּבְדֵּל אֱלֹהִים בֵּין הָאוֹר וּבֵין הַחֹשֶׁךְ:	BHS
	the darkness—and between—the light—between—God—and he divided	Ltrl
	and God divided the light from the darkness.	KJB
	and God separated the light from the darkness.	NASB
	And God separated the light from the darkness.	ESV
	Then he separated the light from the darkness.	NLT
	and he separated the light from the darkness.	NIV

1. The first word in this line is the hiph'il impf. 3ms of the verb בָּדַל "to separate, divide," which means that the action was caused by the subject (God). The verb is preceded by a waw conversive which changes the impf. into the past tense.

Selected Passages

BHS	וַיִּקְרָ֨א אֱלֹהִ֤ים ׀ לָאוֹר֙ י֔וֹם וְלַחֹ֖שֶׁךְ קָ֣רָא לָ֑יְלָה	5a
Ltrl	night—he called—and the darkness—day—to the light—God—and he called	
KJB	And God called the light Day, and the darkness he called Night.	
NASB	God called the light day, and the darkness He called night.	
ESV	God called the light Day, and the darkness he called Night.	
NLT	God called the light "day" and the darkness "night."	
NIV	God called the light "day," and the darkness he called "night."	

BHS	וַֽיְהִי־עֶ֥רֶב וַֽיְהִי־בֹ֖קֶר י֥וֹם אֶחָֽד׃ פ	5b
Ltrl	one—day—morning—and it was—evening—and it was	
KJB	And the evening and the morning were the first day.	
NASB	And there was evening, and there was morning, one day.	
ESV	And there was evening, and there was morning, the first day.	
NLT	And evening passed and morning came, marking the first day.	
NIV	And there was evening, and there was morning—the first day.	

1. At the end of this verse and before the beginning of the next verse, we find the Hebrew letter *pei* in a wide space. This is the first *parashah petuhah* in the Hebrew Bible text. Refer to Gen 1:1 above.

2. Other than a few English synonyms that could be used to convey the same meaning, these five verses do not present any major challenge to the translator.

BHS	תַּֽדְשֵׁ֤א הָאָ֙רֶץ֙ דֶּ֔שֶׁאᵃ עֵ֚שֶׂב מַזְרִ֣יעַ זֶ֔רַע	11b
Ltrl	the earth—she will cause to shoot forth seed—the ones that yield—herbage—fresh shoots—	
KJB	Let the earth bring forth grass, the herb yielding seed,	
NASB	"Let the earth sprout vegetation, plants yielding seed,	
ESV	"Let the earth sprout vegetation, plants yielding seed,	
NLT	"Let the land sprout with vegetation—every sort of seed-bearing plant,	
NIV	"Let the land produce vegetation: seed-bearing plants	

11ᵃ⁻ᵃ "LXX Vulgate compare Heb with Heb."

1. From the parsings below it will be seen that the suggestion in this footnote is useful.

2. תַּֽדְשֵׁא Hiph'il impf. 3fs of the verb דָּשָׁא which in the qal means, "to sprout, shoot forth, grow green." In the hiph'il the earth is causing the action.

3. דֶּשֶׁא Noun, m. sg. abs. meaning, "fresh shoots." This is believed to be a generic term for mere greenness, maybe plants without visible seeds or stalks.

4   עֵשֶׂב Noun, m. sg. abs. meaning, "herb, herbage." Paying attention to this footnote is useful here. The noun should be understood as "herbage." These higher developed plants would serve as food for the grazers. This not a "herb" as in modern English meaning, "a plant with leaves, seeds, or flowers used for flavoring food, medicine, or perfume."

5   מַזְרִיעַ Hiph'il part. m. pl. active of the verb זָרַע which in the qal means, "to sow, to scatter seed," and in the hiph'il then means, "produce seed."

6   The information above applies equally to verse 12, where the same wording is repeated almost verbatim.

BHS	וְהָיוּ לְאֹתֹת וּלְמוֹעֲדִים	14c
Ltrl	and for appointed festivals—for sings—and they will be	
KJB	and let them be for signs, and for seasons,	
NASB	and they shall serve as signs and for seasons,	
ESV	And let them be for signs and for seasons,	
NLT	Let them be signs to mark the seasons,	
NIV	and let them serve as signs to mark sacred times,	

1   וּלְמוֹעֲדִים Waw consecutive + prep. + noun, m. pl. abs. The noun מוֹעֵד means, "appointed time, place, meeting."

2   "It is most probable that in Gen 1:14, the reference is to the sacred seasons as fixed by the moon's appearance, although many Lexicons and Commentaries refer these to the *seasons* of the year."[5]

3   According to the former view expressed above, the word does not refer to the annual seasons, but means, "appointed gatherings," used both, to identify the time of commanded gatherings (i.e. the Holy Days), and also to identify the place of these gatherings (i.e. the tabernacle of the congregation).

BHS	וַיִּבְרָא אֱלֹהִים אֶת־הַתַּנִּינִם	21a
Ltrl	the sea-monsters—DDOM—God—and he created	
KJB	And God created great whales,	
NASB	God created the great sea monsters	
ESV	So God created the great sea creatures	
NLT	So God created great sea creatures	
NIV	So God created the great creatures of the sea	

1   הַתַּנִּינִם Definite article + noun, m. sg. meaning, "serpent, dragon, sea-monster."

2   In Hebrew and Phoenician belief, this noun refers to sea monsters or dragons that were associated with chaos and creation myths, and not merely large aquatic animals.

---

5   Main source: Wikipedia contributors. *"Great Assembly."* Wikipedia, The Free Encyclopedia, 17 October, 2018. Web: 10 January, 2019. Slightly edited.

3   A number of translations use "sea-monsters" in places like Is 27:1, Jb 7:12, and Ps 74:13. It is said that they are reluctant however to mention mythological creatures in a text that is interpreted very literally when forming the "creationist" ideology.

BHS	בְּצַלְמֵנוּ כִּדְמוּתֵנוּa	26a
Ltrl	as our likeness—in our image	
KJB	in our image, after our likeness:	
NASB	in Our image, according to Our likeness;	
ESV	in our image, after our likeness.	
NLT	in our image, to be like us.	
NIV	in our image, in our likeness,	

26a "Samaritan Pentateuch Heb compare LXX Vulgate."

1   The inclusion or not of a waw does not alter the meaning of the term.

2   בְּצַלְמֵנוּ Prep. + noun, m. sg. cstr. + suffix 1cp meaning, "in our image."

3   כִּדְמוּתֵנוּ Prep. + noun, f. sg. cstr. + suffix 1cp meaning, "as our likeness, similitude (the quality or state of being similar to something)."

4   Modern expositors (people who explain complicated ideas or theories) generally find no distinction whatsoever between these two words. For example:

    a)   Luther renders them as, "Let us make a man with an image that is like us."

    b)   Calvin denies that any difference exists between the two words.

5   An alternative view is of the opinion that the words indicate the unique qualities of the genus *Homo* as apposed to others in the animal kingdom. This view contends that God was saying "let us make man conceptually like us, but with the same capacities of spirituality of his being, as an intelligent and free agent; with moral integrity." In other words, "a man that looks like us, and has a soul."

2. GENESIS 2

BHS	וַיְכַל . . . וַיִּשְׁבֹּת	2b
Ltrl	and he stopped . . . and he completed	
KJB	he ended . . . and he rested	
AB	he completed . . . and He rested (ceased)	
NLT	he had finished . . . so he rested	
NIV	he had finished . . . and he rested	
YLT	he completeth . . . and ceaseth	

1   וַיְכַל Waw conversive + pi'el impf 3ms of the verb כָּלָה meaning, "to be complete, at an end, finished, accomplished, spent."

2   וַיִּשְׁבֹּת Waw conversive + qal impf. 3ms of the verb שָׁבַת meaning, "to cease,"

3   There is a footnote at the Hebrew word for "seventh" that informs us that the Greek Septuagint the Samaritan Pentateuch, and the Syriac Peshitta has "sixth" instead of "seventh." This probably was in order to avoid even the appearance of God having put the finishing touches to creation on the Sabbath.

4   וַיָּנַח Waw consecutive + qal impf. 3ms of the verb נוּחַ meaning, "to rest." This verb is not used in the creation narratives. The first time this verb appears is in referring to Noah's ark in Gen 8:4. It is then also used in Ex 20:11b where it is used to describe God's "rest" on the seventh day.

BHS	אֲשֶׁר־בָּרָא אֱלֹהִים לַעֲשׂוֹת׃ פ	3c
Ltrl	to make—God—he created—that	
KJB	which God created and made.	
NASB	which God had created and made.	
YLT	which God had prepared for making.	

1   לַעֲשׂוֹת Prep. + qal inf. cstr. of the verb עָשָׂה meaning, "to do, to make." There are several ways in which this word has been interpreted:

   a)   As an emphatic infintive, intensifying the action of the first, and conveying the idea of a perfect creation.

   b)   As an epexegetic (explanatory) infintive, as in the similar phrases, "spoke, saying" (literally, spoke to speak) (Ex 6:10), and "labored to do" (Eccl 2:11).

   c)   In a relic (surviving from an earlier time) sense, as expressive of the purpose for which the heavens and the earth were at first created. In other words, that by the six days' work they might be fashioned into a cosmos.

BHS	וְעֵץ הַדַּעַת טוֹב וָרָע׃	9c
Ltrl	and evil—good—the discernment between—and the tree of	
KJB	and the tree of knowledge of good and evil.	
NASB	and the tree of the knowledge of good and evil.	
ESV	and the tree of the knowledge of good and evil.	
NLT	and the tree of the knowledge of good and evil.	
NIV	and the tree of the knowledge of good and evil.	
GNT	and the tree that gives knowledge of what is good and what is bad.	

1   הַדַּעַת Definite article + noun, f. sg. abs. meaning, "knowledge, perception, discernment." The GNT is a modern translation that attempts to indicate that not only knowledge itself, but also the nuance of moral discernment is meant by the word.

BHS	וַיִּצֶר יְהוָה אֱלֹהִים	19a
Ltrl	God—Yahweh—and he formed	
KJB	And . . . . the LORD God formed	
NASB	And . . . . the LORD God formed	
ESV	Now . . . . the LORD God had formed	
NLT	So the LORD God formed	
NIV	Now the LORD God had formed	

1. וַיִּצֶר Waw conversive + qal impf. 3ms of the verb יָצַר meaning, "to form, to fashion" as a potter or creator would. This verb occurs 63 times in the Hebrew Bible.

2. This form of the verb is extremely common and should be translated as, "And he formed."

3. The NIV and ESV have changed the transalation for it to indicate that the animals were created after the creation of man in 2:7. This would then prevent this verse from contradicting the order of creation in Gen 1:20–25.

4. There is no reason for us to attempt to harmonize the two creation narratives. We should rather recognize that they present different theological perspectives of what God did when he created the world.

5.

Order of creation	
Genesis 1	**Genesis 2**
light	man created from the dust
heavens	the garden
earth, seas	trees and vegetation
vegetation, trees	Animals
sun, moon, and stars	Birds
sea monsters, fish, birds	woman created from man
animals	
man and woman (created together)	

3. GENESIS 3

BHS	וַיִּשְׁמְעוּ אֶת־קוֹל יְהוָה אֱלֹהִים מִתְהַלֵּךְ בַּגָּן	8a
Ltrl	in the garden—moving around—God—YHWH—the voice of—DDOM—and they heard	
KJB	And they heard the voice of the LORD God walking in the garden	
NASB	Now they heard the sound of the LORD God walking in the garden	
ESV	And they heard the sound of the LORD God walking in the garden	
NLT	the man and his wife heard the LORD God walking about in the garden	
AB	And they heard the sound of the LORD God walking in the garden	

1. מִתְהַלֵּךְ Hithpa'el part. m. sg. of the root הלך which in the qal means, "to walk, go, come." However, in the hithpa'el it means, "to walk, wander, walk about, move to and fro."

2. קוֹל Noun, m. sg. cstr. meaning, "voice of" but also, "sound of."

3. Many modern English translations (NLT) have it wrong in two ways:

    a) The antecedent of the verb is "the voice of" or "the sound of" and not God.

    b) The meaning of the verb is much more nuanced than mere "walking." This banyan has a reflexive and/or repetitive meaning, which in this case would be "walking to and fro." It usually means, "walking" (with legs and feet), but here also means, "moving (without body parts)." On the repetitive nature of this verb form Kushner (2015) says, "You can hear the voice of God from all directions in the garden. God asks Adam where he is, and so the voice is going in different directions repeatedly. It's the voice, not the feet that are taking a walk."[6]

	הוּא יְשׁוּפְךָ רֹאשׁ	15c
Ltrl	head—he shall bruise you—he	
KJB	it shall bruise thy head,	
NASB	He shall bruise you on the head,	
ESV	he shall bruise your head,	
NLT	He will strike your head,	
NIV	he will crush your head,	

1. יְשׁוּפְךָ Qal impf. 3ms + suffix 2ms of the verb שׁוּף meaning, "to bruise." The verb occurs only here and in Jb 9:17 and Ps 139:11.

2. הוּא Personal pronoun 3ms meaning, "he."

3. Because of the context being God speaking to the snake about the woman and her descendants, many have argued that the above pronoun was an error by the copyist and that it should be הִיא (3fs "her") in accordance with the Latin Vulgate. However, the antecedent in the previous phrase is the "seed" which is masculine.

---

6 The Apostolic Bible Polyglot (ABP), originally published in 2003 is a Bible translation by Charles Vander Pool. The ABP is an English translation with a Greek interlinear gloss and is keyed to a concordance.

4   The Greek Septuagint chose αυτός ("he"). This choice is noteworthy since the Greek, as apposed to Hebrew, has a choice of m., f., and neuter, and the Greek word for "seed" σπέρμα is a neuter. Yet, the Septuagint chose the masculine.

5   <u>Mariology</u>: the part of Christian theology dealing with the Virgin Mary.

   <u>The Militia Immaculatae</u>: "Army of the Immaculate One," is a worldwide Catholic evangelization movement founded by St. Maximilian Kolbe in 1917.

6   Mariologists strongly prefer the f. pronoun, as evidenced by the Militia Immaculata. They see Mary as the second Eve, and being the one who crushes the serpent's head.

BHS	וּלְאָדָ֞םa אָמַ֗ר כִּֽי־שָׁמַעְתָּ֮ לְק֣וֹל אִשְׁתֶּךָ֒	17
Ltrl	your wife—to voice of—you listened—because—he said—and to Adam	
KJB	And unto Adam he said, "Because thou hast hearkened unto the voice of thy wife,"	
NASB	Then to Adam He said, "Because you have heeded the voice of your wife,	
ESV	And to Adam he said, "Because you have listened to the voice of your wife	
NLT	And to the man he said, "Since you listened to your wife	
NIV	To Adam he said, "Because you listened to your wife,"	

17ᵃ "Read Heb."

1   This footnote suggests that the word should be pointed (given vowels) as וְלָאָדָם which would then mean, "and to the man."

2   אָדָם This is a masculine noun meaning, "man" or "mankind."

3   אָדֹם This is an adj. meaning, "red," referring to the ruddy color of human skin.

4   אֲדָמָה This is a feminine noun meaning, "ground" or "earth."

5   According to Gen 2:19, Adam was created from the earth by God, and his name would be closely associated with the above mentioned terms.

4. GENESIS 4

BHS	קָנִ֥יתִי אִ֖ישׁ אֶת־יְהוָֽה׃	1c
Ltrl	Yahweh—DDOM—a man—I have gotten	
KJB	I have gotten a man from the LORD.	
YLT	'I have gotten a man by Jehovah;'	
NASB	"I have gotten a manchild with the help of the LORD."	
ESV	"I have gotten a man with the help of the LORD."	
NLT	"With the LORD'S help, I have produced a man!"	
NIV	"With the help of the LORD I have brought forth a man."	

1ᵃ⁻ᵃ "LXX Grk."

1   The Greek in the Septuagint does indeed read διά τοῦ θεοῦ meaning, "through God."

2   קָנִיתִי Qal perf. 1cs of the verb קָנָה meaning, "to get, acquire, gain, etc."

3   The word קַיִן could mean, "spear" (2 Sm 21:16); the name of a tribe (Jgs 4:11); and the proper name "Cain." It is not certain that the name is derived from the above verb. It could be derived from קִינָה which means, "elegy (a poem of serious reflection, typically a lament for the dead), dirge (a lament for the dead)."

4   The KJB and YLT are correct in translating the MT literally. Other modern English translations have inserted "with the help of" which does not appear in the MT.

BHS	וְהֶבֶל הֵבִיא גַם־הוּא מִבְּכֹרוֹת צֹאנוֹ וּמֵחֶלְבֵהֶן ᵃ	4a
Ltrl	—of his flock—from the female firstlings—he—also—he brought—and Abel and from their fat parts	
KJB	And Abel, he also brought of the firstlings of his flock and of the fat thereof.	
NASB	Abel, on his part also brought of the firstlings of his flock and of their fat portions.	
ESV	and Abel also brought of the firstborn of his flock and of their fat portions.	
NLT	Abel also brought a gift—the best portions of the firstborn lambs from his flock.	
NIV	And Abel also brought an offering—fat portions from some of the firstborn of his flock.	
YLT	and Abel, he hath brought, he also, from the female firstlings of his flock, even from their fat ones;	

4ᵃ "Cairo Geniza SP Heb; perhaps read Heb—compare (footnote) 1:21ᵃ."

1   This footnote shows alternative forms of the pl. suffix. However, the suffixes in the MT make perfect sense.

2   הֵבִיא Hiph'il perf. 3ms of the verb בוֹא which in the qal binyan means, "to come (in), go (in)," and in the hiph'il binyan means, "to cause to come (in)" or in other words, "bring (in)."

3   מִבְּכֹרוֹת Preposition + the f. pl. form of the noun בְּכוֹר meaning, "first-born."

4   וּמֵחֶלְבֵהֶן Waw consecutive + preposition + the f. pl. form of the noun חֵלֶב (which in the plural means, "fat parts" or "fat pieces") + pronominal suffix 2 f. pl. meaning, "their" (female plural).

5   Both the nouns indicate that females are involved. Of the main English translations, it is only the YLT that clearly indicates the gender of the mentioned firstborn.

6   In contrast to male first-born, which are common in the Hebrew Bible (Gen 35:23 for example), female firstborn are only mentioned here and in Dt 12:6, 17 and Dt 14:23.

BHS	כִּי אִישׁ הָרַגְתִּי לְפִצְעִי וְיֶלֶד לְחַבֻּרָתִי:	23c
Ltrl	for my blow—and a youngster—for my wound—I have killed—a man—because	
KJB	for I have slain a man to my wounding, and a young man to my hurt.	
NASB	For I have killed a man for wounding me; And a boy for striking me;	
ESV	I have killed a man for wounding me, a young man for striking me.	
NLT	I have killed a man who attacked me, a young man who wounded me.	
NIV	I have killed a man for wounding me, a young man for injuring me.	

1. לְפִצְעִי Preposition + noun, m. sg. + suffix 1 cs. The noun פֶּצַע means, "wound" or "bruise," and this form could the be translated as, "for wounding me."

2. לְחַבֻּרָתִי Preposition + noun, f. sg. + suffix 1 cs. The noun חַבּוּרָה means, "stripe" or "blow," and this form could the be translated as, "for striking me."

3. It has been suggested that both the above forms are actually infinitive construct forms of the corresponding verbs.

5. GENESIS 6

BHS	לֹא־יָדוֹן רוּחִי בָאָדָם לְעֹלָם	3a
Ltrl	forever—with man—my spirit—he will judge—not	
KJB	My spirit shall not always strive with man,	
NASB	"My Spirit will not remain with man forever,	
ESV	"My Spirit shall not abide in man forever,	
NLT	"My Spirit will not put up with humans for such a long time,	
NIV	"My Spirit will not contend with humans forever,	

1. יָדוֹן Qal impf. 3ms of the verb דִּין meaning, "to judge."

2. The wrong translation of this verb comes to us via the Greek Septuagint and the Latin Vulgate. The LXX Greek translation for the verb is καταμείνῃ meaning, "to abide, remain." The Latin Vulgate followed the Greek Septuagint and rendered this verb as *permanebit*, which also means, "to abide, to remain." The influence of the Greek Septuagint and the Vulgate can be seen in such translations as NASB and ESV.

3. "Translating from the Latin Vulgate, John Wycliffe rendered this as "shall not dwell in man." It was William Tyndale who first introduced the word "strive" into his translation of Genesis for the Matthew's Bible in 1537. This verb "strive" was then retained by the Geneva Bible in 1560 and the later Bishops Bible, both of which formed the foundation for the 1611 KJV. From there the verb "strive" was accepted by many subsequent translators."[7]

---

7 Hattingh, Tian (2012), p. 96.

BHS	הַנְּפִלִים הָיוּ בָאָרֶץ	4a
Ltrl	in the earth—they were—the fallen ones	
KJB	There were giants on the earth	
YLT	The fallen ones were in the earth	
ESV	The Nephilim were on the earth	
NIV	The Nephilim were on the earth	

1. הַנְּפִלִים BDB lists this as a noun, m. pl. abs. meaning, "giants." They mention that this meaning is also found in Nm 13:33. The KJB follows this directive.

2. However, many modern English translations translate it as a proper noun, "Nephilim."

3. YLT sees the consonants of the original abjad with the vowels of the qal part. m. pl. נֹפְלִים as found in Jos 8:25 as well.

4. רְפָאִים Proper noun, referring to an old race of giants. This term appears 25 times in the Hebrew Bible, and is often used to describe giants (Dt 3:11, Jos 12:4).

BHS	וַיִּנָּחֶם יְהוָה	6a
Ltrl	YHWH—and he was sorry	
KJB	And it repented the LORD	
NASB	So the LORD was sorry	
ESV	And the LORD regretted	
NLT	So the LORD was sorry	
NIV	The LORD regretted	

1. וַיִּנָּחֶם Waw conversive + niph'al impf 3ms of the root נחם meaning, "to be sorry, console oneself."

2. In biblical terms, "to repent" comprises of sorrow and regret, followed by a turning back toward God. In the Hebrew Bible it is customary to use the verb שׁוּב to express the concept of "repentance" (1 Kgs 8:47, 2 Chr 6:37, Is 6:10, Jer 4:1, Ez 14:6).

BHS	עֲצֵי־גֹפֶר	14a
Ltrl	wood of gopher	
KJB	gopher wood;	
NASB	gopher wood;	
ESV	gopher wood.	
NLT	cypress wood	
NIV	cypress wood	

1 עֲצֵי־ Noun, m. pl. cstr. meaning, "trees of" or "wood of."

2 גֹפֶר Noun, m. sg. This is an example of a *hapax legomenon* (a word that is found only once in a body of work like the Hebrew Bible). It has no connection to any other verb root, making it impossible to ascertain with certainty what the original author meant.

3 Because of its single appearance, its literal meaning of this word is lost. "Gopher" is simply a transliteration of the Hebrew word.

4 Some are of the opinion that the word should be compared to כֹפֶר meaning, "pitch" and the resulting literal "pitch wood" to mean a resinous wood like that of a cypress tree.

6. GENESIS 8

BHS	וַיְשַׁלַּח אֶת־הָעֹרֵב^a	7
Ltrl	the raven—DDOM—and he sent	
KJB	And he sent forth a raven,	
NASB	and he sent out a raven,	
ESV	and sent forth a raven.	
NLT	and released a raven.	
NIV	and sent out a raven,	

7ª "LXX adds Grk compare (verse) 8."

1 This footnote states that the Greek Septuagint adds του ιδείν ει κεκόπακε το ύδωρ "to see if abated the water." (Take note that in the Septuagint this phrase in the MT and the phrase added by the Septuagint are included in the end of verse 6).

BHS	וַיְשַׁלַּח^a אֶת־הַיּוֹנָה	8a
Ltrl	the dove—DDOM—and he sent	
KJB	Also he sent forth a dove from him,	
NASB	Then he sent out a dove from him,	
ESV	Then he sent forth a dove from him,	
NLT	He also released a dove	
NIV	Then he sent out a dove	

8ª "Put before Heb."

1 This footnote suggests that we put (insert) before the beginning of the MT verse, the Hebrew phrase וַיִּיָּחֶל נֹחַ שִׁבְעַת יָמִים which means, "and he waited Noah seven days." Apparently, this is in response to the use of the word עוֹד which means, "another" and implies that a similar action occurred previously.

2 The Greek Septuagint uses the word ετέρας ("another") in verse ten, but as in the MT, it does not have the proposed phrase in verse 8. Neither the Aleppo Codex, nor the SP has the proposed phrase in verse 8.

3   "It is extremely dangerous to draw conclusions from Gen 1–11, but in the case of the 'Great Flood' we have many confirmations from extra-biblical sources. The so-called 'flood myths' in many cultures suggest that something happened, capturing the imagination of ancient man. In the recent past there have been attempts to scientifically motivate the possibility of an earth-covering flood. I, for one, am not convinced, yet. However, I firmly believe that some natural phenomena did occur, but where, when and on what scale, I am not prepared to speculate. That somebody, because of divine intervention, believed it necessary to take evasive action, I am prepared to accept, even if this included humans taking care of other living creatures. The only indication to the extent of this incident becomes clear if we keep in mind that the concept had been transferred orally for many generations until eventually being recorded. The author of Genesis, for example, deemed it necessary to describe the unfolding of this particular drama in the first part of his book that he was writing. His objective was to describe the results when an individual acts in obedience to a divine command against all odds. To what extent the whole story had been the product of an overly productive imagination is of no consequence here. The fundamental premise involved is: when something had been told or written, somebody had to possess sufficient intellectual resources to produce such a narrative. These intellectual resources originate from observations of either natural or manipulated phenomena, which today are known as field observations and laboratory research. The following example is a case in point: Somebody, let us also call him Noah, reportedly took fourteen specimens (seven pairs, and not one pair, as is commonly envisaged) of each living species into a watertight vessel. Common sense should prevail here and make us realize that containing all of the species of the world in a single vessel is a matter of impossibility. In addition, today the symbolic value of the number seven is widely accepted by laymen and scholars of many religious persuasions. They regard the number seven as signifying 'completeness,' or 'perfect wholeness.' Notwithstanding this, it has to be admitted that here the author's intentions can be seen as being twofold:

a) To describe the first attempt by a human being to not only consider the survival of himself and his kind but to, at the same time, prevent the eminent extinction of all or a number of species in the face of detrimental circumstances.

b) But even more important: to utilize the above incident to convey the message that obedience to a divine command, is in the best interest of man and beast. At that time, and in those circumstances it meant engaging in completely irrational behavior. In other words, acting in faith was the right thing to do.

The incident provides us with the first ever mention to specific zoological families, and it is no other than two bird families, namely the family *Columbidae*, known as the Pigeons and Doves,' and the family *Corvidae*, known as the Ravens and Crows. In Chapter 22 it was said of the latter, 'their boldness and sagacity, coupled with their extensive dietary range, have enabled them to adapt completely to a lifestyle of co-existing with man, even where the latter has radically altered the habitat.' A radical change in precipitation patterns in a specific location would result in the habitat being significantly altered, albeit temporarily. It is clear that the narrator was an ornithologist to the extent that he realized that if there was one species that would immediately be able to adapt to the new circumstances out there and survive, it would be *Corvinae*. He observed bird behavior to the extent that he knew that Doves and Pigeons (*Columbiformes*) are generally terrestrial birds, and as long as the dove returned to its perch it would be an indication that the ecosystem had not become suitable for human habitation yet. The Hebrew Canon containing these narratives had fully developed by the time of Aristotle, and the accuracy of the ornithological facts contained in this narrative and other Scriptures was never questioned by him or anyone else to this day."[8]

7. GENESIS 12

BHS	וַיֹּאמֶר יְהוָה אֶל־אַבְרָם	1a
Ltrl	Abram—to—Yahweh—and he said	
KJB	Now the LORD had said unto Abram,	
NASB	Now the LORD said to Abram,	
ESV	Now the LORD said to Abram,	
NLT	The LORD had said to Abram,	
NIV	The LORD had said to Abram,	

1. Some modern English translations (KJB, NLT, NIV) have changed "and he said" into "and he had said" in an attempt to harmonize the verse with Acts 7:2: This is probably because according to Gen 12:1 Yahweh's call to Abram occurred in Haran, but according to Stephen's speech, it occurred in Mesopotamia.

2. In accordance with the MT, the Greek Septuagint has και ειπε κυριος meaning, "and the LORD said."

BHS	וַאֲבָרֲכָה מְבָרְכֶיךָ וּמְקַלֶּלְךָᵃ אָאֹר	3a
Ltrl	I will curse—and he who belittles you—he who blesses you—and I will bless	
KJB	And I will bless them that bless thee, and curse him that curseth thee	
NASB	And I will bless those who bless you, And the one who curses you I will curse	
ESV	I will bless those who bless you, and him who dishonors you I will curse,	
NLT	I will bless those who bless you and curse those who treat you with contempt	
NIV	I will bless those who bless you, and whoever curses you I will curse;	

3ª "Read with Cairo Geniza, a few (3–10) medieval Manuscripts, the Samaritan Pentateuch, the Septuagint, the Syriac Peshitta, and the Vulgate Heb."

1. וּמְקַלֶּלְךָ Waw conjunctive + Pi'el part. m. sg. of the verb קָלַל In the qal binyan, the verb means, "to be slight, swift, trifling." In the pi'el binyan it means, "to curse by making contemptible."

2. In this form we find the prefix *me* that is a characteristic of the pi'el part. However, we do not have the characteristic pi'el doubling of the second radical (Eccl 7:21). If we accept that this is indeed a pi'el form, it is only the suffix that has changed from 2ms to 2mp, and this does not affect the translation substantially.

---

8   Hattingh, Tian (2012), p. 105.

3   The remaining issue then is the translation of the pi'el. There are those who are of the view that we should keep the core meaning of the original root in mind, and translate the pi'el as, "curse by treating someone dismissively, disrespectful, with contempt, etc." This view is manifested here in the translations of ESV, NLT for example. Also refer to Lv 19:14; 1 Sm 2:30, 3:13; 2 Sm 16:5, 19:43.

8. GENESIS 14

BHS	וַיִּתֶּן־לוֹ מַעֲשֵׂר מִכֹּל׃	20c
Ltrl	from all—a tenth part—to him—and he gave	
KJB	And he gave him tithes of all.	
YLT	and he giveth to him a tenth of all.	
NASB	He gave him a tenth of all.	
ESV	And Abram gave him a tenth of everything.	
NIV	Then Abram gave him a tenth of everything.	

1   מַעֲשֵׂר Noun, m. sg. abs. meaning, "tenth part, tithe."

2   A number of modern English translations like ESV and NIV follow the Greek Septuagint reads, "και έδωκεν αυτώ Αβραμ δεκάτην από πάντων" meaning, "and gave to him Abram a tenth from all."

3   In Heb 7:2 we read, "and Abraham gave him a tenth of everything."

4   "and given the context and the fact that this verse is talking about Melchizedek, it is more likely Melchizedek is paying Abram the tribute. However, the premise of Heb 7 requires it to be the other way around, and such a reading would also lend support to the doctrine of tithing,"[9]

9. GENESIS 15

BHS	וַיַּחְשְׁבֶהָ לּוֹ צְדָקָה׃	6
Ltrl	righteousness—to him—and he assigned	
KJB	and He accounted it to him for righteousness.	
NLT	and the LORD counted him as righteous because of his faith.	
NASB	and He credited it to him as righteousness.	
ESV	and he counted it to him as righteousness.	
NIV	and he credited it to him as righteousness	

1   וַיַּחְשְׁבֶהָ Waw consecutive + Qal impf. 3ms + suff. 3fs. meaning, "he imputed (assigned to, attributed to), reckoned."

2   צְדָקָה׃ Noun, f. sg. abs. meaning, "righteousness."

---

9   Hattingh, Tian (2012), p. 105.

10. GENESIS 17

BHS	וְלֹא־יִקָּרֵא עוֹד אֶת־שִׁמְךָ אַבְרָם וְהָיָה שִׁמְךָ אַבְרָהָם	5a
Ltrl	—and it will be—Abram—your name—DDOM—still / again—it will be called—and not Abraham—your name	
KJB	Neither shall thy name any more be called Abram, but thy name shall be Abraham;	
NASB	"No longer shall your name be called Abram, But your name shall be Abraham;	
ESV	No longer shall your name be called Abram, but your name shall be Abraham,	
NLT	It will no longer be Abram. Instead, you will be called Abraham,	
NIV	No longer will you be called Abram; your name will be Abraham,	

5ᵃ "Lacks material (in) several (11–20) Manuscripts (and) Samaritan Pentateuch."

1. In the MT it is clear that "your name" is the direct object of the verb "to be called."

2. The new name "Abraham" is seen as meaning, "father of many" as the result of a contraction of אַבְרָם meaning, "exalted father," and הֲמוֹן (see verse 5b below) which means, amongst others, "multitude," "crowd," "great number," and "abundance."

BHS	כִּי אַב־הֲמוֹן גּוֹיִם נְתַתִּיךָ:	5b
Ltrl	I made you—nations—multitude—father of—because	
KJB	for a father of many nations have I made thee.	
NASB	For I will make you the father of a multitude of nations.	
ESV	for I have made you the father of a multitude of nations.	
NLT	for you will be the father of many nations.	
NIV	for I have made you a father of many nations.	

1. The phrase אַב־הֲמוֹן meaning, "father of a multitude" refers directly to the possible meaning of the new name mentioned above.

BHS	וְקָרָאתָ אֶת־שְׁמוֹ יִצְחָק	19b
Ltrl	Isaac—his name—DDOM—and you will call	
KJB	and thou shalt call his name Isaac:	
NASB	and you shall call his name Isaac;	
ESV	and you shall call his name Isaac.	
NLT	You will name him Isaac,	
NIV	and you will call him Isaac.	

1. In Gen 17:17 Abraham laughed. In Gen 17:19 God gives Isaac his name and in so doing uses the verb צָחַק which means, "to laugh." In Gen 18:12–15 Sarah laughed. In Gen 21:6 Sarah foresees that everyone will laugh.

BHS	בְּהִמֹּלוֹ בְּשַׂר עָרְלָתוֹ׃	24b
Ltrl	his foreskin—the flesh of—when it was circumcised	
KJB	when he was circumcised in the flesh of his foreskin.	
NASB	when he was circumcised in the flesh of his foreskin.	
ESV	when he was circumcised in the flesh of his foreskin.	
NLT	when he was circumcised,	
NIV	when he was circumcised,	

1 בְּהִמֹּלוֹ Prep. + niph'al inf. cstr. of the verb מוּל meaning, "to circumcise." The niph'al binyan is used to express a simple passive or reflexive (to oneself) meaning (Chapter 24.8.1 in Vol. 1). Therefore, here the niph'al could mean either, "was circumcised (by someone else)" (passive), or "circumcised himself" (reflexive).

2 בְּשַׂר Noun, m. sg. cstr. of בָּשָׂר meaning, "flesh of." In a construct chain, the construct noun is definite if the absolute noun is definite. Here "his foreskin" is definite (Chapter 14.1.7 in Vol. 1).

11. GENESIS 18

BHS	וַיֹּאמֶר יְהוָה זַעֲקַת סְדֹם וַעֲמֹרָה כִּי־רָבָּה	20a
Ltrl	it is great—because—and Gomorrah—Sodom—outcry of—Yahweh—and he said	
KJB	And the LORD said, Because the cry of Sodom and Gomorrah is great,	
NASB	And the LORD said, "The outcry of Sodom and Gomorrah is indeed great,	
ESV	Then the LORD said, "Because the outcry against Sodom and Gomorrah is great	
NLT	So the LORD told Abraham, "I have heard a great outcry from Sodom and Gomorrah	
NIV	Then the LORD said, "The outcry against Sodom and Gomorrah is so great	
YLT	And Jehovah saith, 'The cry of Sodom and Gomorrah—because great;	

20[a] "SP Heb compare (verse) 21."

1 This footnote suggests that because of the SP we should look at the noun צְעָקָה in verse 21. However, this noun conveys the same core meaning as the verb in verse 20, and would thus not affect a translation.

2 Christians prefer to understand that Sodom had totally fallen into sexual perversion. Therefore, save for the more literal translations like KJB and YLT, most modern English translations have "cry against." This is incorrect, as the noun is in the construct form meaning, "a cry of Sodom." Even in the Talmudic tradition, the term used for "outcry" describes the lamentations of oppressed people, and that actually these cries came from the people within the condemned cities themselves.

12. GENESIS 23

BHS	נְשִׂיא אֱלֹהִים אַתָּה	6a
Ltrl	you—God—prince of	
KJB	thou art a mighty prince among us:	
NASB	you are a mighty prince among us;	
ESV	you are a prince of God among us.	
NLT	you are a prince of God	
NIV	You are a mighty prince	
YLT	a prince of God art thou	

1. A number of modern English translations (KJB, NASB, NIV) hide the fact that these local people recognized Abraham as a servant of God.

13. GENESIS 25

BHS	וַיִּקְרָא שְׁמוֹ יַעֲקֹב	26b
Ltrl	Jacob—his name—and she called	
KJB	and his name was called Jacob:	
NASB	so his name was called Jacob;	
ESV	so his name was called Jacob.	
NLT	So they named him Jacob.	
NIV	so he was named Jacob.	

26ᵃ "Targum, SP Heb."

1. The Targums and Samaritan Pentateuch have the verb in the plural.

2. In verse 25 we have the verb in the plural, with a footnote referring to this verse where the verb is in the singular.

3. עָקַב means, "to follow at the heel," or "to assail insidiously (attack violently in a gradual, subtle way, but with harmful effects)."

14. GENESIS 31

BHS	אֱלֹהֵי אַבְרָהָם וֵאלֹהֵי נָחוֹר יִשְׁפְּטוּᵃ בֵּינֵינוּ אֱלֹהֵי אֲבִיהֶם	53a
Ltrl	between us—they will judge—Nahor—and the gods of—Abraham—the gods of their father—the gods of	
YLT	the God of Abraham and the God of Nahor, doth judge between us— the God of their father,'	
NASB	"The God of Abraham and the God of Nahor, the God of their father, judge between us."	
NIV	May the God of Abraham and the God of Nahor, the God of their father, judge between us."	

53ᵃ "SP LXX Heb."

1. The footnote states that the Samaritan Pentateuch and the Greek Septuagint have the verb in the singular.

2. יִשְׁפְּטוּ Qal impf. 3cp of the verb שָׁפַט meaning, "to judge, govern."

3. אֱלֹהֵי Noun, m. pl. cstr. Literally this means, "gods of," but it also means, "God of" as in "the God of Israel" in Gen 33:20. Because the above verb has a plural form, some scholars believe that it refers to "gods" and not "God."

15. GENESIS 32

BHS	וַיֹּאמֶר לֹא יַעֲקֹב יֵאָמֵר עוֹד שִׁמְךָ כִּי אִם־יִשְׂרָאֵל	29a
Ltrl	Israel—but—your name—anymore—it will be called—Jacob—not—and he said	
KJB	And he said, Thy name shall be called no more Jacob, but Israel:	
NASB	He said, "Your name shall no longer be Jacob, but Israel;	
ESV	Then he said, "Your name shall no longer be called Jacob, but Israel,	
NLT	"Your name will no longer be Jacob," the man told him.	
NIV	Then the man said, "Your name will no longer be Jacob, but Israel."	

1. יִשְׂרָאֵל is the combination of the verb "to persist" in verse 29b below, and the basic Hebrew word for "God" (Chapters 85.1 and 85.4.1 in this volume).

BHS	כִּי־שָׂרִיתָ עִם־אֱלֹהִים וְעִם־אֲנָשִׁים וַתּוּכָל׃	29b
Ltrl	and you prevailed—men—and with—God—with—you persevered—because	
KJB	for as a prince hast thou power with God and with men, and hast prevailed.	
NASB	for you have striven with God and with men and have prevailed."	
ESV	for you have striven with God and with men, and have prevailed."	
NLT	because you have fought with God and with men and have won."	
NIV	because you have struggled with God and with humans and have overcome.	

1 שָׂרִיתָ Qal perf. 2ms of the verb שָׂרָה "to persist, persevered, exert oneself."

2 וַתּוּכָל Hoph'al impf. 2ms of the verb יָכֹל "to prevail, endure, be able."

16. GENESIS 37

BHS	וַיִּשְׁמַע רְאוּבֵן וַיַּצִּלֵהוּ מִיָּדָם	21a
Ltrl	their hand—and rescue him—Ruben—and he heard	
KJB	And Reuben heard it, and he delivered him out of their hands;	
NASB	But Reuben heard this and rescued him out of their hands	
ESV	But when Reuben heard it, he rescued him out of their hands,	
NLT	But when Reuben heard of their scheme, he came to Joseph's rescue.	
NIV	When Reuben heard this, he tried to rescue him from their hands.	

21ᵃ "It has been proposed Heb compare (verse) 26."

1 The proposal is to change the name to "Judah" as in verse 26.

2 וַיַּצִּלֵהוּ Waw conversive + Hiph'il impf. 3ms + suffix 3ms of the verb נָצַל which in the hiph'il binyan means, "to deliver, rescue from."

3 In an attempt to smooth over an apparent inconsistency in the story, the NIV inserts the word "tried," which has the effect of implying the opposite of what the MT says.

BHS	וַיִּמְשְׁכוּ וַיַּעֲלוּ אֶת־יוֹסֵף	28b
Ltrl	Joseph—DDOM—and they lifted—and they pulled up	
KJB	and they drew and lifted up Joseph	
NASB	so they pulled him up and lifted Joseph	
ESV	And they drew Joseph up and lifted him out	
NLT	Joseph's brothers pulled him out	
NIV	his brothers pulled Joseph up out	

1 וַיִּמְשְׁכוּ Waw conversive + qal impf. 3mp of the verb מָשַׁךְ meaning, "to draw, drag."

2 וַיַּעֲלוּ Waw conversive + Hiph'il impf. 3mp of the verb עָלָה which in the hiph'il binyan means, "to bring up (from a place), to cause to ascend."

3 As can be seen above, the NLT and NIV have completely changed the narrative found in the MT. This is done to harmonize it with the narrative in verse 27 wherein his brothers sell him to Ishmaelites. This change obscures the well-known fact that Gen 37 contains two variant traditions.

BHS	לְפוֹטִיפַר סְרִיס פַּרְעֹה	36b
Ltrl	Pharaoh—an officer of—to Potiphar	
KJB	unto Potiphar, an officer of Pharaoh's,	
NASB	to Potiphar, Pharaoh's officer,	
ESV	to Potiphar, an officer of Pharaoh,	
NLT	to Potiphar, an officer of Pharaoh,	
NIV	to Potiphar, one of Pharaoh's officials,	

1. סָרִיס Noun, m. sg. cstr. meaning, "eunuch, head, chief, officer." This noun, is used 42 times in the Hebrew Bible. It is translated 17 times as "eunuch," 13 times as "chamberlain," and 12 times as "officer."

2. Some of the most noticable uses are as follows:

   a) סָרִיסֵי הַמֶּלֶךְ Chamberlain / officer (an officer who manages the household of a monarch or noble) of the king: 2 Kgs 23:11; Est 2:3, 14, 15, 21; 4:5; 6:2, 14; Is 39:7; Jer 29:2, 34:19

   b) הַסָּרִיסִים Eunuchs: Est 1:10, 12, 15; 7:9; Is 56:3, 4; Jer 38:7, 41:16

   c) סְרִיס פַּרְעֹה Pharaoh's officer: Gen 37:36, 39:1, 40:7.

   d) שַׂר הַסָּרִיסִים Commander of the officials: Dn 1:3, 7, 8, 9, 10, 11, 18.

   e) רַב־סָרִיס High-ranking military officer: 2 Kgs 18:17; Jer 39:3, 13; Dn 1:3

17. GENESIS 47

BHS	וַיִּשְׁתַּחוּ יִשְׂרָאֵל עַל־רֹאשׁ הַמִּטָּה׃ פ	31c
Ltrl	the bed—the head of—on—Israel—and he bowed in homage	
KJB	And Israel bowed himself upon the bed's head.	
NASB	Then Israel bowed in worship at the head of the bed.	
ESV	Then Israel bowed himself upon the head of his bed.	
NLT	and Jacob bowed humbly at the head of his bed.	
NIV	and Israel worshiped as he leaned on the top of his staff.	

31ª "LXX (Syr) Grk = Heb compare Hebrews 11:21."

1. This footnote refers us to a text in the Christian New Testament.

2. וַיִּשְׁתַּחוּ From the form וַיִּשְׁתַּחֲוֶה which is: waw conversive + hithpa'lel impf 3ms of the verb שָׁחָה meaning, "to bow down, prostrate oneself in homage."

3. הַמִּטָּה Definite article + noun, f. sg. meaning, "the bed."

4. הַמַּטֶּה Definite article + noun, m. sg. meaning, "the staff, rod, shaft."

5   As the above footnote states, the Greek Septuagint indeed has τῆς ῥάβδου αὐτοῦ which means, "his staff." The Hebrew equivalent of the Greek mentioned in this footnote has the same consonants as the Hebrew word for "bed," but not the same vowels.

6   The Septuagint uses the same word (staff) in Heb 11:21, which prompted the NIV to opt for this spelling and meaning and so harmonize the two texts. As the vocalization (adding vowel points) of the original consonantal text was undertaken by the Masoretes in later times, and while valuable as representing a very ancient tradition, these points are nevertheless not of final authority. This then leaves the interpretation of the word open to debate.

18. GENESIS 48

BHS	וְהָיָה אֱלֹהִים עִמָּכֶם וְהֵשִׁיב אֶתְכֶם	21b
Ltrl	you (pl.)—and he will bring—with you (pl.)—God—and he will be	
KJB	but God shall be with you, and bring you again unto the land of your fathers.	
NASB	but God will be with you, and bring you back to the land of your fathers.	
ESV	but God will be with you and will bring you again to the land of your fathers.	
NLT	but God will be with you and will take you back to Canaan, the land of your ancestors.	
NIV	but God will be with you and take you back to the land of your fathers.	

1   עִמָּכֶם Independent preposition עִם with Type I second person plural suffix (Chapter 17.7.9 in Vol. 1).

2   אֶתְכֶם Object pronoun, second person plural (Chapter 16.4.2 in Vol. 1).

3   Some languages have different forms to distinguish between the singular and plural in the second person. In the case of the personal pronouns for example,0

Language	Singular	Plural
Biblical Hebrew	אַתָּה	אַתֶּם
English (archaic)	thou	ye
Spanish (informal)	o tu	o vosotros
German (informal)	du	ihr
Mandarin Chinese	ni3	ni3 men
Afrikaans (informal)	jy	julle

but

English (modern)	you	you
Dutch	U	U

4   Thus, the only way to correctly distinguish between the second person singular and second person plural in an English translation would be to use the archaic English forms.

5   In this verse, even the original KJB of 1611 does not make any distinction between the singular and plural forms found in the MT.

19. GENESIS 49

BHS	אֲבִיר יַעֲקֹב ׳מִשָּׁם רֹעֵה אֶבֶן׳ יִשְׂרָאֵל	24c
Ltrl	Israel—stone of—shepherd—from where—Jacob—mighty one of	
KJB	the mighty God of Jacob; (from thence is the shepherd, the stone of Israel:)	
NASB	the Mighty One of Jacob (From there is the Shepherd, the Stone of Israel),	
ESV	the Mighty One of Jacob (from there is the Shepherd, the Stone of Israel),	
NLT	the Mighty One of Jacob, by the Shepherd, the Rock of Israel.	
NIV	the Mighty One of Jacob, because of the Shepherd, the Rock of Israel,	

24^{c-c} "It has been proposed Heb (compare Syriac Targum) or Heb."

1. This footnote suggests a radical change from what is found in the MT.

2. מִשָּׁם Directional adverb, "from there / thence?" Refer to Chapter 19.1.3 in Vol. 1.

3. מִשָּׁם עֹזֵר Literally meaning, "from there helping." This would be a radical change from the original MT text.

4. מִשְׁמֶר אֶבֶן Literally meaning, "from protecting the stone of." This option implies that there has been an error, and that the two words, "from where" and "shepherd" should be one word meaning, "from protecting."

5. The Greek Septuagint has εκείθεν ο κατισχύσας Ισραήλ meaning, "from there the one strengthening Israel."

82.6 EXODUS

1. EXODUS 2

BHS	וַיִּקַּח ׳אֶת־בַּת־לֵוִי׳	1b
Ltrl	Levi—daughter of—DDOM—and he took in marriage	
KJB	and took to wife a daughter of Levi.	
NASB	and married a daughter of Levi.	
ESV	and took as his wife a Levite woman.	
NIV	married a Levite woman,	

1^{b-b} "LXX Grk."

1. The Greek Septuagint has των θυγατέρων meaning, "daughters of."

2. וַיִּקַּח Waw conversive + qal impf. 3ms of the verb לָקַח meaning, "to take (in marriage)."

3. The chronology makes it impossible for this to be a daughter in the literal sense, and should rather be understood to be a woman of the same tribe as himself, as a descendant of Levi.

4   Many modern English translations (NIV, ESV) remove or diminish the suggestion of close family ties between Moses and Levi.

BHS	וַתִּקַּֽח־לוֹ תֵּבַת גֹּמֶא	3b
Ltrl	bulrushes—an ark of—for him—and she took	
KJB	she took for him an ark of bulrushes,	
NASB	she got him a papyrus basket	
ESV	she took for him a basket made of bulrushes	
NLT	she got a basket made of papyrus reeds	
NIV	she got a papyrus basket for him	

1   וַיִּקַּח Waw conversive + qal impf. 3fs of the verb לָקַח meaning, "to take."

2   תֵּבַת Noun, f. sg. cstr. This is probably an Egyptian loan-word from t-b-t, meaning, "chest, coffin." In the Hebrew Bible it has the more generic meaning of, "vessel." This noun apears 28 times in the Hebrew Bible. In Gen 6–9 it apears 26 times and is translated there as, "ark." Here in Ex 2:3 and 2:5, the same word is used to describe the vessel that Moses was placed in by his mother.

3   In the case of Noah we have substantive details of the size of the vessel. In the case of Moses, the purpose of the vessel as well as the material used gives us an indication of the size of the vessel. This context prompted translators to call the vessel a "basket."

BHS	וַתִּקְרָא שְׁמוֹ מֹשֶׁה וַתֹּאמֶר כִּי מִן־הַמַּיִם מְשִׁיתִֽהוּ׃	10b
Ltrl	I drew him out—the water—from—because—and she said—Moses—his name—and she called	
KJB	And she called his name Moses: and she said, Because I drew him out of the water.	
NASB	And she named him Moses, and said, "Because I drew him out of the water."	
ESV	She named him Moses, "Because," she said, "I drew him out of the water."	
NLT	The princess named him Moses, for she explained, "I lifted him out of the water."	
NIV	She named him Moses, saying, "I drew him out of the water."	

1   מְשִׁיתִֽהוּ Qal perf. 1cs with a 3ms pronominal suffix meaning, "I drew him" (Chapter 41.1 in Vol. 2, and Chapter 61.2.1 in Vol. 3).

2   This name is most likely derived from Egyptian *mes* meaning, "son, child," but could also possibly mean, "to deliver" in Hebrew. The meaning suggested Ex 2:10 of "drew out" from the Hebrew מֹשֶׁה is probably an invented etymology.

3   This name occurs 766 times in the Hebrew Bible.

2. EXODUS 3

BHS	וַיֹּאמֶר אֱלֹהִים אֶל־מֹשֶׁה ᵃאֶהְיֶה אֲשֶׁר אֶהְיֶהᵃ	14a
Ltrl	I will be—what—I will be—Moses—to—God—and he said	
KJB	And God said unto Moses, I AM THAT I AM:	
NIV	God said to Moses, "I AM WHO I AM.	

14ᵃ⁻ᵃ "LXX Grk."

1. The Greek Septuagint indeed has ἐγώ εἰμι ὁ ὤν meaning, "I am the one being." This explains the MT, rather than translating it, but is otherwise unobjectionable.

2. אֶהְיֶה Qal impf. 1cs of the verb הָיָה which literally means, "I will be." Because it is an impf. form it is often rendered as, "I will become." The imperfect "tense" in Hebrew indicates that the action is incomplete (as apposed to the perfect "tense" which indicates that the action has been completed).

3. The Latin Vulgate has *sum qui sum*, which literally means, "I am who I am," leading to most English translations.

3. EXODUS 12

BHS	וַאֲכַלְתֶּם אֹתוֹ בְּחִפָּזוֹן	11d
Ltrl	in trepidation—it—and you shall eat	
KJB	and ye shall eat it in haste:	
NASB	and you shall eat it in a hurry	
ESV	And you shall eat it in haste.	
NLT	Eat the meal with urgency,	
NIV	Eat it in haste;	

1. בְּחִפָּזוֹן Prep. + noun, m. sg. abs. meaning, "trepidation, hurried flight."

2. This noun occurs only three times in the Hebrew Bible (Ex 12:11, Dt 16:3, Is 52:12).

3. The noun as well as the accompanying verb conveys more of a feeling of fear or agitation about something that may happen, than a feeling of haste. Modern English translations have neglected to show this. The NLT does to some extent indicate the core meaning.

BHS	פֶּסַח הוּא לַיהוָה:	11d
Ltrl	for Yahweh—it—Passover	
KJB	it is the LORD'S Passover.	
NASB	It is the LORD'S Passover.	
ESV	It is the LORD'S Passover.	
NLT	for this is the LORD'S Passover.	
NIV	it is the LORD'S Passover.	

1. פֶּסַח Noun, m. sg. meaning:

   a) The animal victim of the Passover (Ex 12:21: "and kill the Passover").

   b) The festival of the Passover (Ex 34:25: "the feast of the Passover").

   c) The sacrifice of Passover (Ex 12:27. The special feature lay in the Passover sacrifice to the application of the blood to the doorframe of a house to consecrate it. "It is the LORD, who passed over the houses of the Israelites in Egypt when He struck down the Egyptians and spared our homes."

2. פֶּסַח In Ex 12:27 the verb is used to explain the origin and meaning of the Passover celebration. Refer to Dt 16:3 as well.

4. EXODUS 13

BHS	דֶּרֶךְ הַמִּדְבָּר יַם־סוּף	18a
Ltrl	reed—sea of—the desert—way of	
KJB	through the way of the wilderness of the Red sea:	
ISV	way of the desert toward the Reed Sea.	
NLT	through the wilderness toward the Red Sea.	
NIV	the desert road toward the Red Sea.	

1. סוּף Noun, m. sg. abs. meaning, "reeds, rushes."

2. The Greek Septuagint has ἐρυθράν, and the Latin Vulgate has *mare Rubrum*, which in both cases means, "red sea." Almost all English translations have followed these two sources.

3. After the 10th plague (Ex 12:29–30), Israel headed southeast from Rameses in the region of Goshen. Rameses has been identified by archaeologists with Tell ed-Daba, a site located 62 miles northeast of Cairo.

4. The on the first night, the Israelites made camp at Succoth (12:37), whose location is uncertain.

5. God intended for them to not travel to the Canaan directly, but by a detour in the direction of the Sea of Reeds (13:18). They went on to spend the next night at Etham (13:20), a fort near the eastern edge of the Nile Delta. It was here at Etham that God told Moses to change the direction Israel would take to Canaan.

6   The Israelites turned back, and on the third night camped near Pi-hahiroth (14:2). This location is uncertain. The area located west of the modern-day Suez Canal near the Bitter Lakes on the western shores of the Reed Sea has been suggested. To this day the the narrow mountain valley through which Israel approached the Bitter Lakes is called by the locals, "Tiah ben Israel," or "the way of the children of Israel." So, the exact location is debated by historians to this day.

7   Some theories speculate it could be a reference to the Gulf of Eliat, which is also mentioned in the Book of Kings. Another theory suggests that it is the Lake of Tanis near the coast of Egypt.

BHS	וַחֲמֻשִׁים֙ עָל֥וּ בְנֵֽי־יִשְׂרָאֵ֖ל מֵאֶ֥רֶץ מִצְרָֽיִם׃	18b
Ltrl	Egypt—from the land of—Israel—the sons of—they came up—and in battle array	
KJB	and the children of Israel went up harnessed out of the land of Egypt.	
NASB	and the sons of Israel went up in martial array from the land of Egypt.	
ESV	And the people of Israel went up out of the land of Egypt equipped for battle.	
NLT	Thus the Israelites left Egypt like an army ready for battle.	
NIV	The Israelites went up out of Egypt ready for battle.	

18ᵃ "SP Manuscripts Heb, LXX Grk."

1   This footnote states that the Samaritan Pentateuch has the form וַחֲמִישִׁים which means, "and fifty." It further correctly states that the Greek Septuagint has Πέμπτη δε γενεά meaning, "and in the fifth generation."

2   וַחֲמֻשִׁים Waw consecutive + adj. pl. meaning, "and in battle array."

3   It is widely agreed that the text does not suggest that the Israelites were "ready for battle" (NIV, NLT). The adjective should rather be seen as an indication that to prevent confusion, a military order had been adopted for the Exodus to have taken place, as it seems to have done, without serious confusion or entanglement.

5. EXODUS 20

BHS	וַיְדַבֵּ֣ר אֱלֹהִ֔ים אֵ֛ת כָּל־הַדְּבָרִ֥ים הָאֵ֖לֶּה לֵאמֹֽר׃ ס	1
Ltrl	saying—the these—the words—all—DDOM—God—and he spoke	
KJB	And God spake all these words, saying,	
NASB	Then God spoke all these words, saying,	
ESV	And God spoke all these words, saying,	
NLT	Then God gave the people all these instructions:	
NIV	And God spoke all these words:	

1ᵃ "LXX (Vulgate) Grk."

1   This footnote states that the Greek Septuagint uses the word κύριος which is usually translated as "LORD," as apposed to θεός which is the Greek for "God."

2. This footnote is correct in mentioning the Latin Vulgate as supplementary evidence as it uses the word *Dominus* meaning, "Master" or "Lord." The consonants in the Aleppo Codex are as in the MT.

3. The Ten Commandments are also known as the "Decalogue."

BHS	אָנֹכִי יְהוָה אֱלֹהֶיךָ אֲשֶׁר הוֹצֵאתִיךָ מֵאֶרֶץ מִצְרַיִם מִבֵּית עֲבָדִים׃	2
Ltrl	—Egypt—from the land of—brought you out—that—your God—Yahweh—I (am) bondage—from a house of	
KJB	I am the LORD thy God, which have brought thee out of the land of Egypt, out of the house of bondage.	
NASB	"I am the LORD your God, who brought you out of the land of Egypt, out of the house of slavery.	
ESV	"I am the LORD your God, who brought you out of the land of Egypt, out of the house of slavery.	
NLT	"I am the LORD your God, who rescued you from the land of Egypt, the place of your slavery.	
NIV	I am the LORD your God, who brought you out of Egypt, out of the land of slavery.	

1. הוֹצֵאתִיךָ is the hiph'il perf. 1cs of the verb יָצָא which in the qal binyan means, "to go out" or "to come out." The hiph'il binyan being causative, then means, "cause to go out" or "lead out" or "bring out from (a place)."

BHS	לֹא יִהְיֶה־לְךָ אֱלֹהִים אֲחֵרִים עַל־פָּנָֽיַ׃ ᵃ ᵇᵃ	3
Ltrl	my face—on—others—gods—for you—it will be—not	
KJB	Thou shalt have no other gods before me.	
NASB	"You shall have no other gods before Me.	
ESV	"You shall have no other gods before me.	
NLT	"You must not have any other god but me.	
NIV	You shall have no other gods before me.	

3ᵃ⁻ᵃ "LXX (SyP Targum Targum) Grk."

1. This footnote correctly states that the Greek Septuagint has πλην εμού meaning, "besides me." The Syriac Peshitta and several of the Targums are mentioned as supplementary evidence. The MT literally has "upon my face," which could be taken to imply "in my presence."

3ᵇ "Thus Leningrad Codex, multiple (20–60) Manuscripts Editions."

1. It seems that this footnote is confirming the previous note by mentioning further witnesses that are in agreement with the sources of footnote 3ᵃ⁻ᵃ.

2. In most English translations this sentence forms the last part of verse two. This is resulting in a discrepancy in the verse numbers further on when compared to the MT.

4a	לֹא תַעֲשֶׂה־לְךָ פֶסֶל וְכָל־תְּמוּנָה אֲשֶׁר בַּשָּׁמַיִם מִמַּעַל	BHS
Ltrl	above—in the heavens—that—likeness—or any—an idol—for you—you will make—not	
KJB	Thou shalt not make unto thee any graven image, or any likeness of any thing that is in heaven above,	
NASB	"You must not make for yourself an idol of any kind or an image of anything in the heavens	
ESV	"You shall not make for yourself a carved image, or any likeness of anything that is in heaven above,	
NLT	"You must not make for yourself an idol of any kind or an image of anything in the heavens	
NIV	You shall not make for yourself an image in the form of anything in heaven above	

1 פֶסֶל Noun, m. sg. abs. meaning, "idol" or "image." The verb פָסַל is from the same stem and means, "to hew into a shape." Many English translations have opted to be more explicit (KJB, "graven image," NKJV, "carved image") and include what is implied in the MT.

4b	וַאֲשֶׁר בָּאָרֶץ מִתָּחַת וַאֲשֶׁר בַּמַּיִם מִתַּחַת לָאָרֶץ׃	BHS
Ltrl	—from under—in the water—and that (is)—from under—in the earth—or that (is) for the earth	
KJB	or that is in the earth beneath, or that is in the water under the earth:	
NASB	or on the earth beneath or in the water under the earth.	
ESV	or that is in the earth beneath, or that is in the water under the earth.	
NLT	or on the earth or in the sea.	
NIV	or on the earth beneath or in the waters below.	

4a "Compare (footnote) 3b."

1 Here one would expect to find only the definite article, but an inseparable preposition has been added. This footnote is confirming that this is the case in the mentioned sources as well.

5a	לֹא־תִשְׁתַּחֲוֶה לָהֶם וְלֹא תָעָבְדֵם	BHS
Ltrl	you will serve them—and not—to them—you will bow yourself down—not	
KJB	Thou shalt not bow down thyself to them, nor serve them:	
NASB	"You shall not worship them or serve them;	
ESV	You shall not bow down to them or serve them,	
NLT	You must not bow down to them or worship them,	
NIV	You shall not bow down to them or worship them;	

1 The first verb in this line is the hithpa'lel impf. 2ms of the verb שָׁחָה which is found almost exclusively in the reflexive hithpa'lel and then means, "to bow down" or "to prostrate oneself before a monarch or superior in homage."

Selected Passages

BHS	כִּי אָנֹכִי יְהוָה אֱלֹהֶיךָ אֵל קַנָּא פֹּקֵד עֲוֺן אָבֹת	5b
Ltrl	fathers—iniquity of—attending to—jealous—a God—your God—YHWH—I—for	
KJB	for I the LORD thy God am a jealous God, visiting the iniquity of the fathers	
NASB	for I, the LORD your God, am a jealous God, visiting the iniquity of the fathers	
ESV	for I the LORD your God am a jealous God, visiting the iniquity of the fathers	
NIV	for I, the LORD your God, am a jealous God, punishing the children for the sin of the parents	

5ᵃ "Nash Papyrus Heb."

1. The Nash Papyrus has the form קַנּוֹא which is an adj. and found in Js 24:9 and Na 1:2, and simply means, "jealous." However, here in the MT, and also in Dt 5:9, we find that the adjective קַנָּא conveys the expanded meaning of "to be jealous and as a result punishing those who hate me." In addition, in Ex 34:14, Dt 4:24, and Dt 6:15, we find the latter form of the adj. to mean, "to be jealous and therefore demanding exclusive loyalty."

BHS	עַל־בָּנִים עַל־שִׁלֵּשִׁים וְעַל־רִבֵּעִים לְשֹׂנְאָי׃	5c
Ltrl	for those who hate me—fourth—and on—third—on—the sons—on	
KJB	upon the children unto the third and fourth generation of them that hate me;	
NASB	on the third and the fourth generations of those who hate Me,	
ESV	on the children to the third and the fourth generation of those who hate me,	
NLT	the entire family is affected—even children in the third and fourth generations of those who reject me.	
NIV	to the third and fourth generation of those who hate me,	

BHS	וְעֹשֶׂה חֶסֶד לַאֲלָפִים לְאֹהֲבַי וּלְשֹׁמְרֵי מִצְוֺתָי׃ ס	6
Ltrl	—and the keeping of—for those who love me—to thousands—mercy—but making my commandments	
KJB	And showing mercy unto thousands of them that love me, and keep my commandments.	
NASB	but showing loving-kindness to thousands, to those who love Me and keep My commandments.	
ESV	but showing steadfast love to thousands of those who love me and keep my commandments.	
NLT	But I lavish unfailing love for a thousand generations on those who love me and obey my commands.	
NIV	but showing love to a thousand generations of those who love me and keep my commandments.	

1. The translations that have opted to change the literal "thousands" to "thousands of generations" probably had instances like Dt 7:9 in mind.

7a	לֹא תִשָּׂא אֶת־שֵׁם־יְהוָה אֱלֹהֶיךָ לַשָּׁוְא	BHS
	in vain—your God—YHWH—the name of—DDOM—you will take—not	Ltrl
	Thou shalt not take the name of the LORD thy God in vain;	KJB
	"You shall not take the name of the LORD your God in vain,	NASB
	"You shall not take the name of the LORD your God in vain,	ESV
	"You must not misuse the name of the LORD your God.	NLT
	You shall not misuse the name of the LORD your God,	NIV

1 שָׁוְא Noun, m. sg. abs. meaning, "emptiness" or "vanity." So לַשָּׁוְא literally means, "to the emptiness" or "to no good purpose." See Dt 5:11; Ps 24:4, 139:20.

7b	כִּי לֹא יְנַקֶּה יְהוָה אֵת אֲשֶׁר־יִשָּׂא אֶת־שְׁמוֹ לַשָּׁוְא׃ פ	BHS
	in vain—His name—DDOM—takes—who—DDOM—YHWH—he will acquit—not—because	Ltrl
	for the LORD will not hold him guiltless that taketh his name in vain.	KJB
	for the LORD will not leave him unpunished who takes His name in vain.	NASB
	for the LORD will not hold him guiltless who takes his name in vain.	ESV
	The LORD will not let you go unpunished if you misuse his name.	NLT
	for the LORD will not hold anyone guiltless who misuses his name.	NIV

7a "Nash Papyrus Heb."

1. This footnote states that the Nash Papyrus has the consonants שמה among others, be pointed (given vowels) as שְׁמָהּ meaning, "her name."

2. The verb נָקָה means, "emptiness" or "vanity," but יְנַקֶּה is the pi'el impf. and means, "to hold innocent" or "to acquit," or "to leave unpunished."

8	זָכוֹר אֶת־יוֹם הַשַּׁבָּת לְקַדְּשׁוֹ׃	BHS
	to keep it holy—the Sabbath—the day of—DDOM—remember	Ltrl
	Remember the Sabbath day, to keep it holy.	KJB
	"Remember the sabbath day, to keep it holy.	NASB
	"Remember the Sabbath day, to keep it holy.	ESV
	"Remember to observe the Sabbath day by keeping it holy.	NLT
	Remember the Sabbath day by keeping it holy.	NIV

8a "Samaritan Pentateuch Heb."

1. This footnote states that the SP has the consonants שמור that could be pointed (given vowels) as שָׁמוֹר which is the qal infinitive absolute of the verb meaning, "to keep" or "preserve."

The verb in the MT is also in the infinitive absolute form, and would therefore mean, "remember" or "observe."

8ᵇ "Compare (footnote) 3ᵇ."

1   It seems that this footnote is confirming the previous note by mentioning that further witnesses like the Leningrad Codex and multiple (20–60) Manuscripts and Editions are in agreement with the Samaritan Pentateuch.

BHS	שֵׁ֤שֶׁת יָמִים֙ תַּֽעֲבֹ֔ד וְעָשִׂ֖יתָ כָּל־מְלַאכְתֶּ֑ךָ׃	9
Ltrl	your work—all—and you will do—you will work—days—six	
KJB	Six days shalt thou labor, and do all thy work:	
NASB	"Six days you shall labor and do all your work,	
ESV	Six days you shall labor, and do all your work,	
NLT	You have six days each week for your ordinary work,	
NIV	Six days you shall labor and do all your work,	

9ᵃ "Compare (footnote) 3ᵇ."

1   Footnote 3ᵃ stated that the Greek Septuagint, the SyP, and some (11–20) Targums agreed with the MT. Footnote 3ᵇ added the Leningrad Codex and multiple (20–60) Manuscripts and Editions as witnesses agreeing with the MT.

BHS	וְי֨וֹםᵃ הַשְּׁבִיעִ֜י שַׁבָּ֣ת ׀ לַיהוָ֣ה אֱלֹהֶ֗יךָ	10a
Ltrl	your God—for YHWH—a Sabbath—the seventh—but day	
KJB	but the seventh day is the Sabbath of the LORD your God.	
NASB	but the seventh day is a sabbath of the LORD your God;	
ESV	but the seventh day is a Sabbath to the LORD your God.	
NLT	but the seventh day is a Sabbath day of rest dedicated to the LORD your God.	
NIV	but the seventh day is a Sabbath to the LORD your God.	

10ᵃ "Nash Papyrus a few (3–10) Manuscripts LXX Vulgate Heb."

1   The sources mentioned in this footnote have the form וּבַיּוֹם meaning, "but in the day."

2   As seen in Ru 3:15 for example, we find in many other sources the tendency to make what has been implied in the MT, more explicit. This is especially the case in the Greek Septuagint. Here, the MT makes perfect sense, and a more explicit form is not needed.

BHS	לֹא־תַעֲשֶׂה֮ כָל־מְלָאכָ֒ה אַתָּ֣ה וּבִנְךָ֣־וּבִתֶּ֗ךָ	10b
Ltrl	and your daughter—and your son—you—work—any—you will do—not	
KJB	In it you shall do no work: you, nor your son, nor your daughter,	
NASB	in it you shall not do any work, you or your son or your daughter,	
ESV	On it you shall not do any work, you, or your son, or your daughter,	
NLT	On that day no one in your household may do any work. This includes you, your sons and daughters,	
NIV	On it you shall not do any work, neither you, nor your son or daughter,	

10b "Nash Papyrus LXX SyP Vulgate add Heb."

1   The Hebrew בה added to the MT by the sources mentioned in this footnote could be pointed (given vowels) as בָּהּ and mean, "in her" and referring to the Sabbath which is implied in the MT (See 10ª above).

BHS	עַבְדְּךָ֣ וַאֲמָתְךָ֣ וּבְהֶמְתֶּ֣ךָ וְגֵרְךָ֣ אֲשֶׁ֖ר בִּשְׁעָרֶֽיךָ׃	10c
Ltrl	and your stranger—and your livestock—and your maidservant—your manservant in your gates—who—	
KJB	nor your male servant, nor your female servant, nor your cattle, nor your stranger who is within your gates.	
NASB	your male or your female servant or your cattle or your sojourner who stays with you.	
ESV	your male servant, or your female servant, or your livestock, or the sojourner who is within your gates.	
NLT	your male and female servants, your livestock, and any foreigners living among you.	
NIV	nor your male or female servant, nor your animals, nor any foreigner residing in your towns.	

10c "Cairo Geniza multiple (20–60) Manuscripts LXX SyP Targums Heb compare Targum."

1   This footnote states that these sources have a waw conjunctive before this reading, and וְעַבְדְּךָ meaning, "and your manservant."

10d "Nash Papyrus LXX according to Dt 5:14."

1   The MT has the same word here in Ex 20:10 and in Dt 5:14.

10e "Samaritan Pentateuch Heb; lacks material Targum."

1   This footnote states that the SP and the Targum of Jonathan does not have the conjunction as found in the MT.

10^(f-f) "LXX Grk."

1. The Greek Septuagint has *ο παροικών εν σοι* meaning, "the one sojourning among you."

2. The meaning of "sojourn" points to a temporary stay. The masculine noun in the MT is שַׁעַר which, other than "gate," also means, "the area inside the gate as a public meeting place."

10^g "Compare (footnote) 3^b."

1. Refer to footnotes 4^a, 8^b, and 9^a.

BHS	כִּי שֵׁשֶׁת־יָמִים עָשָׂה יְהוָה אֶת־הַשָּׁמַיִם וְאֶת־הָאָרֶץ	11a
Ltrl	the earth—and DDOM—the heavens—DDOM—YHWH—he made—days—six—for	
KJB	For in six days the LORD made the heavens and the earth,	
NASB	"For in six days the LORD made the heavens and the earth,	
ESV	For in six days the LORD made heaven and earth,	
NLT	For in six days the LORD made the heavens, the earth,	
NIV	For in six days the LORD made the heavens and the earth,	

BHS	אֶת־הַיָּם וְאֶת־כָּל־אֲשֶׁר־בָּם וַיָּנַח בַּיּוֹם הַשְּׁבִיעִי	11b
Ltrl	—in the day—and he rested—in them—that—all—and DDOM—the sea—DDOM the seventh	
KJB	the sea, and all that is in them, and rested the seventh day.	
NASB	the sea and all that is in them, and rested on the seventh day;	
ESV	the sea, and all that is in them, and rested on the seventh day.	
NLT	the sea, and everything in them; but on the seventh day he rested.	
NIV	the sea, and all that is in them, but he rested on the seventh day.	

11^a "Multiple (20–60) Manuscripts LXX SyP Targum Vulgate Heb."

1. All these sources have added a waw conjunctive before the DDOM.

2. וַיָּנַח Waw consecutive + qal impf. 3ms of the verb נוּחַ meaning, "to rest." The first time this verb appears is in referring to Noah's ark in Gen 8:4. It is not used in the creation narrative of Gen 2.

BHS	עַל־כֵּן בֵּרַךְ יְהוָה אֶת־יוֹם הַשַּׁבָּת וַיְקַדְּשֵׁהוּ׃ ס	11c
Ltrl	and he consecrated it—the Sabbath—day—DDOM—YHWH—he blessed—therefore	
KJB	Therefore the LORD blessed the Sabbath day and hallowed it.	
NASB	therefore the LORD blessed the sabbath day and made it holy.	
ESV	Therefore the LORD blessed the Sabbath day and made it holy.	
NLT	That is why the LORD blessed the Sabbath day and set it apart as holy.	
NIV	Therefore the LORD blessed the Sabbath day and made it holy.	

11ᵇ "The Nash Papyrus LXX SyP Heb."

1. This footnote has a form that can be pointed (given vowels) as הַשְּׁבִיעִי meaning, "the seventh." The Greek Septuagint indeed has τὴν ἑβδόμην (the seventh) instead of σάββατα ("a Sabbath") as found in verse 10.

11ᶜ "The Nash Papyrus Heb."

1. The form mentioned in this footnote contains an alternative form of the suffix to the suffix that is found in the MT. Refer to the notes on Gen 2:2b.

BHS	כַּבֵּד אֶת־אָבִיךָ וְאֶת־אִמֶּךָ לְמַעַן יַאֲרִכוּן יָמֶיךָ	12a
Ltrl	they will be long—that—your mother—and DDOM—your father—DDOM—honor! your days—	
KJB	Honor thy father and thy mother: that thy days may be long	
NASB	"Honor your father and your mother, that your days may be prolonged	
ESV	"Honor your father and your mother, that your days may be long	
NLT	"Honor your father and mother. Then you will live a long, full life	
NIV	Honor your father and your mother, so that you may live long	

12ᵃ "Nash Papyrus LXX additional Heb."

1. The Hebrew in this footnote could be pointed (given vowels) as וּלְמַעַן יִיטַב לָךְ meaning, "it will be good for you and that." This footnote is agreeing with the Greek Septuagint which adds ἵνα εὖ σοι γένηται καὶ ἵνα meaning, "that good may happen to you and that...."

2. כַּבֵּד Pi'el imp. m. sg. of the verb כָּבֵד which in the qal binyan means, "to be heavy, weighty, burdensome, honored." The pi'el binyan is the intensive mood of the verb and the imperative is the form used to express a command.

3. יַאֲרִכוּן Hiph'il impf. 3mp of the verb אָרַךְ which in the qal binyan means, "to be long," and it is almost always used to express time. Here a paragogic nun is added to the conjugated form (Chapter 1.3 in Vol. 1).

Selected Passages

BHS	עַל הָאֲדָמָ֔ה אֲשֶׁר־יְהוָ֥ה אֱלֹהֶ֖יךָ נֹתֵ֥ן לָֽךְ׃ ס	12b
Ltrl	to you—giving—your God—YHWH—that—the land—upon	
KJB	upon the land which the LORD thy God giveth thee.	
NASB	in the land which the LORD your God gives you.	
ESV	in the land that the LORD your God is giving you.	
NLT	in the land the LORD your God is giving you.	
NIV	in the land the LORD your God is giving you.	

12b "LXX adds Grk."

1. The added Greek της αγαθής means, "the good," and refers to the earth. It is unclear why the authors of the Greek Septuagint deemed this necessary.

BHS	לֹ֥א תִּרְצָֽח׃ ס ᵃ	13
Ltrl	you will murder—not	
KJB	Thou shalt not kill.	
NASB	"You shall not murder.	
ESV	"You shall not murder.	
NLT	"You must not murder.	
NIV	You shall not murder.	

13ᵃ "Original LXX it arranges 14, 15, 13 and Nash Papyrus Philo (De Decalogo 12) Lc 18:20 Rm 13:9 it arranges 14, 13, 15."

1. According to this footnote, the original Greek Septuagint and the Nash Papyrus have placed verse 13 in different positions compared to the MT.

2. תִּרְצָח Qal impf. 2ms of the verb רָצָח meaning, "murder, slay."

3. The verb is not in the imperative, so it is not a command. It appears in Dt 5:17 as well.

4. Murder: the unlawful premeditated killing of one human being by another. Kill: cause the death of (a person, animal, or other living thing).

BHS	לֹא תִּנְאָף׃ ס	14
Ltrl	you will commit adultery—not	
KJB	Thou shalt not commit adultery.	
NASB	"You shall not commit adultery.	
ESV	"You shall not commit adultery.	
NLT	"You must not commit adultery.	
NIV	You shall not commit adultery.	

1. תִּנְאָף Qal impf. 2ms. of the verb נָאַף usually referring to the act committed by a man with the wife of another man. The same verb is used in Dt 5:18.

2. The verb is not in the imperative, so it is not a command.

BHS	לֹא תִּגְנֹב׃ ס	15
Ltrl	you will steal—not	
KJB	Thou shalt not steal.	
NASB	"You shall not steal.	
ESV	"You shall not steal.	
NLT	"You must not steal.	
NIV	You shall not steal.	

1. תִּגְנֹב Qal impf. 2ms. of the verb גָּנַב. The three verbs used in verses 13, 14, and 15, are used together in Hos 4:2.

BHS	לֹא־תַעֲנֶה בְרֵעֲךָ עֵד שָׁקֶר׃ ס	16
Ltrl	false—witness—against your neighbor—you shall bear—not	
KJB	Thou shalt not bear false witness against thy neighbor.	
NASB	"You shall not bear false witness against your neighbor.	
ESV	"You shall not bear false witness against your neighbor.	
NLT	"You must not testify falsely against your neighbor.	
NIV	You shall not give false testimony against your neighbor.	

16ᵃ "Nash Papyrus Heb."

1. This footnote states that the Nash Papyrus uses the same form here as the form found in Dt 5:20 in the MT. Footnote 20ᵇ in Dt 5:20 in turn correctly informs us that "several (11–20) Manuscripts as Ex 20:16." The form used here is the pausal form of the masculine noun שֶׁקֶר which means, "deception, falsehood" or "an injurious falsehood in testimony, especially in a court of law."

Selected Passages

BHS	לֹא תַחְמֹד בֵּית־רֵעֶךָ לֹא־תַחְמֹד אֵשֶׁת רֵעֶךָ[d]	17a
Ltrl	your neighbor—wife of—you will covet—not—your neighbor—house of—you will covet—not	
KJB	Thou shalt not covet thy neighbor's house, thou shalt not covet thy neighbor's wife,	
NASB	"You shall not covet your neighbor's house; you shall not covet your neighbor's wife	
ESV	"You shall not covet your neighbor's house; you shall not covet your neighbor's wife,	
NLT	"You must not covet your neighbor's house. You must not covet your neighbor's wife.	
NIV	You shall not covet your neighbor's house. You shall not covet your neighbor's wife,	

17a "LXX has [a] and [c] in reverse order, likewise Nash Papyrus? Compare Dt 5:21."

1. This footnote states that these two words appear in reverse order in the mentioned sources and correctly refers to Dt 5:21 where the neighbor's wife is mentioned first and then his house.

17b "Nash Papyrus Heb compare Dt."

1. The Nash Papyrus adds a definite direct object marker (DDOM) before the next noun.

17c "Compare (footnote) [a]."

1. This footnote completes the statement made in footnote [a].

17d "Nash Papyrus a few (3–10) Manuscripts Samaritan Pentateuch LXX adds Heb."

1. The masculine noun שָׂדֶה means, "cultivated field" or "pasture land," and is found as τον αγρόν αυτού meaning, "his field" in the Greek Septuagint.

2. תַחְמֹד Qal impf. 2ms. of the verb חָמַד meaning, "to desire (in the bad sense of inordinate, ungoverned, selfish desire), take pleasure in."

BHS	וְעַבְדּוֹ וַאֲמָתוֹ שׁוֹרוֹ וַחֲמֹרוֹ וְכֹל אֲשֶׁר לְרֵעֶךָ׃ פ[e]	17b
Ltrl	nor anything—nor his donkey—nor his ox—nor his maidservant— nor his manservant to your neighbor—that—	
KJB	nor his manservant, nor his maidservant, nor his ox, nor his ass, nor anything that is thy neighbor's.	
NASB	or his male servant or his female servant or his ox or his donkey or anything that belongs to your neighbor."	
ESV	or his male servant, or his female servant, or his ox, or his donkey, or anything that is your neighbor's."	
NLT	male or female servant, ox or donkey, or anything else that belongs to your neighbor."	
NIV	or his male or female servant, his ox or donkey, or anything that belongs to your neighbor.	

17e "Samaritan Pentateuch Heb, Heb."

1. Here one footnote is used to refer to two words. This is quite unusual. This footnote wants to draw our attention to the fact that in the SP both of these words appear without the waw-conjunctive.

17ᶠ "LXX additional information added according to Dt."

1   This footnote states that the Greek Septuagint adds οὔτε παντός κτήνους αυτού meaning, "nor any of his beasts."

17ᵍ "Samaritan Pentateuch additional information added."

1   The SP adds a lengthy paragraph before going on to verse 18:
    "And when it so happens that LORD God brings you to the land of Canaan, which you are coming to posses, you shall set-up there for you great stones and plaster them with plaster and you write on the stones all words of this law. And it becomes for you that across the Jordan you shall raise these stones, which I command you today, in Mount Grizim. And you build there the altar to the LORD God of you. Altar of stones. Not you shall wave on them iron. With whole stones you shall build the altar to LORD God of you. And you bring on it ascend offerings to LORD God of you, and you sacrifice peace offerings, and you eat there and you rejoice before the face of the LORD God of you. The mountain this is across the Jordan behind the way of the rising of the sun, in the land of Canaan who is dwelling in the desert before the Galgal, beside Alvin-Mara, before Sechem."[10]

6. EXODUS 34

BHS	לֹא־יָדַע כִּי קָרַן עוֹר פָּנָיו	29c
Ltrl	his face—skin of—it shone—that—he knew—not	
KJB	Moses wist not that the skin of his face shone	
NASB	Moses did not know that the skin of his face shone	
ESV	Moses did not know that the skin of his face shone	
NLT	he wasn't aware that his face had become radiant	
NIV	he was not aware that his face was radiant	

1   Refer to verse 35.

BHS	וְהִנֵּה קָרַן עוֹר פָּנָיו	30b
Ltrl	his face—skin of—it shone—and behold	
KJB	behold, the skin of his face shone;	
NASB	behold, the skin of his face shone,	
ESV	and behold, the skin of his face shone,	
NLT	the radiance of Moses' face,	
NIV	his face was radiant	

30ᵇ "Cairo Geniza Heb compare (verse) 29."

1   Refer to verse 35.

---
10   Hattingh, Tian (2012), p. 121.

BHS	אֶת־פְּנֵי מֹשֶׁה כִּי קָרַן עוֹר פְּנֵי מֹשֶׁה	35
Ltrl	Moses—face of—skin of—it shone—that—Moses—face of—DDOM	
KJB	the face of Moses, that the skin of Moses' face shone,	
NASB	that the skin of Moses' face shone.	
ESV	that the skin of Moses' face was shining.	
NLT	the radiant glow of his face.	
NIV	that his face was radiant	

1. The word קָרַן appears four times in the Hebrew Bible.

   a) In Ps 69:31 we find מַקְרִן which is a denominative verb (a verb that is derived from a noun) in the hiph'il meaning, "which has horns," indicating an animal that has grown (displaying) horns as a sign of maturity.

   b) Here in Exodus 34 the word appears in verses 29, 30, 35. In this instance it is a denominative verb in the qal meaning, "to shine, to send out rays."

2. The depiction of a horned Moses stems from the description of Moses' face as "cornuta" ("horned") in the Latin Vulgate translation of the passage. The Douay-Rheims Bible translates the Vulgate as, "and he knew not that his face was horned." This was Jerome's effort to faithfully translate the difficult original Hebrew text, which uses the term קָרַן (based on the feminine noun קֶרֶן which often means, "horn"). The term is now interpreted to mean, "shining" or "emitting rays" (somewhat like a horn). Although some historians believe that Jerome made an outright error, Jerome himself appears to have seen קָרַן as a metaphor for "glorified," based on other commentaries he wrote, including one on Ezekiel, where he wrote that Moses' face had "become glorified," or as it says in the Hebrew, "horned." The Greek Septuagint, which Jerome also had available, translated the verse as "Moses knew not that the appearance of the skin of his face was glorified."

3. In general, medieval theologians and scholars understood that Jerome had intended to express a glorification of Moses' face, by his use of the Latin word for "horned." The understanding that the original Hebrew was difficult and was not likely to mean, "horns" persisted into and through the Renaissance.

4. Although Jerome completed the Latin Vulgate in the late 4th century, the first known applications of the literal language of the Vulgate in art are found in an English illustrated book written in the vernacular, that was created around 1050: the *Aelfric Paraphrase of the Pentateuch and Joshua.* For the next 150 years or so, evidence for further images of a horned Moses is sparse. Afterward, such images proliferated and can be found, for example, in the stained glass windows at the Chartres Cathedral, Sainte-Chapelle, and Notre Dame, even as Moses continued to be depicted many times without horns. In the 16th century, the prevalence of depictions of a horned Moses steeply diminished.[11]

---

11 Hattingh, Tian (2012), p. 121.

82.7 LEVITICUS

1. LEVITICUS 2

BHS	אָבִיב קָלוּי בָּאֵשׁ	14b
Ltrl	in the fire—roasted—ears of grain	
KJB	green ears of corn dried by the fire,	
NASB	fresh heads of grain roasted in the fire,	
ESV	fresh ears, roasted with fire,	
NLT	fresh grain . . . roasted on a fire.	
NIV	new grain roasted in the fire.	

1   אָבִיב This noun appears eight times in the Hebrew Bible:

      a)   Six times as the name of the month in which the Passover and Exodus took place (Ex 13:4, 23:15, 34:18, 34:18; Dt 16:1, 16:1). It is therefore the name of the first month in the Jewish calendar, and since Ezra's time known as "Nisan."

      b)   Twice as a noun, m. collective meaning, "ears of grain" (Ex 9:31, Lv 2:14).

2   Taking the noun to mean, "green, fresh, immature grain," enables the justification to place the start of the first month of the Jewish calendar very early in the seasonal cycle, in fact frequently even before the end of winter.

3   However, the phrases following the noun namely, "dried by fire" and "corn beaten out of full ears" (KJV), contradict the notion that the grain was immature and green.

2. LEVITICUS 11

BHS	וְאֶת־אֵלֶּה תְּשַׁקְּצוּ מִן־הָעוֹף לֹא יֵאָכְלוּ שֶׁקֶץ הֵם	13a
Ltrl	—they will be eaten—not—the birds—from—you will detest—these—and DDOM	
Ltrl	they—an abomination	
KJB	And these *are they which* ye shall have in abomination among the fowls; they shall not be eaten, they *are* an abomination:	
NASB	These, moreover, you shall detest among the birds; they are abhorrent, not to be eaten:	
ESV	"And these you shall detest among the birds; they shall not be eaten; they are detestable:	
NLT	"These are the birds that are detestable to you. You must never eat them:	
NIV	These are the birds you are to regard as unclean and not eat because they are unclean	

13a "Samaritan Pentateuch Heb."

1   In the MT the form of the verb is the niph'al impf. 3mp ("they will be eaten"), but in the SP the form can be pointed (given vowels) as qal impf. 2mp ("you will eat"), which would be

acceptable in this context, or as the niph'al impf. 2mp ("you will be eaten"), which does not make sense in this context (Chapter 30.2 in Vol 2).

2 תְּשַׁקְּצוּ Pi'el denominative (a verb derived from a noun) impf. 2mp from the noun שֶׁקֶץ meaning, "detestable thing, abomination" that is regarded as ceremonially unclean and unacceptable for human consumption.

3 הָעוֹף Definite article + collective noun, m. sg. meaning, "fowl, insects, flying creatures." It occurs 71 times in the Hebrew Bible. צִפּוֹר which occurs 40 times in a number of forms, is also used to name birds in general.[12]

| BHS | אֶת־הַנֶּשֶׁר וְאֶת־הַפֶּרֶס וְאֵת הָעָזְנִיָּה׃ | 13b |

1 Refer to Chapter 83.8 for a discussion of the so-called "unclean" birds that are listed here in verses 13b–19 and also in Dt 14:12b–18.

3. LEVITICUS 16

BHS	לַעֲזָאזֵל׃	8c
Ltrl	for Azazel	
ESV	for Azazel.	
KJB	for the scapegoat.	
NIV	for the scapegoat.	
YLT	for a goat of departure;	
CSB	for an uninhabitable place,	
NLT	to the wilderness of Azazel.	
CEV	to the demon Azazel.	

1 עֲזָאזֵל This word appears four times in the Hebrew Bible, all of which are in this chapter. Here in verse 8, in verse 10 (twice), and in verse 26. It has two possible meanings.

   a) "An evil spirit of the wilderness to which a scapegoat was sent by the ancient Hebrews in a ritual of atonement."[13]

   b) "In the Bible, the proper name Azazel appears in association with the scapegoat rite; the name represents a desolate place where a scapegoat bearing the sins of the Jews during Yom Kippur was sent."[14]

2 Some Jewish scholars take it as a proper noun, and regard it as the name of a place about 12 miles east of Jerusalem, into the wilderness.

---

12 Hirsch, Emil G., Casanowicz, I. M., Jacobs, J., Schloessinger. Hapax legomena. Retrieved from http://www.jewishencyclopedia.com/ (2002–2011).
13 Main source: Wikipedia contributors. "*Parashah*." Wikipedia, The Free Encyclopedia, 26 August, 2019. Web: 20 September, 2019. Slightly edited.
14 Brown, F., et al. (1906), p. 417.

3   Others take it to be the name of an evil spirit, or even of Satan. The latter view is based on the notion that the word has two parts, with the first part meaning, "the strong and obstinate one," describing Satan's character, and the second part meaning, "the one who is destined to disappear." describing Satan's fate as he is destined to be driven away into everlasting darkness.

4   Others see the two goats together forming a type of Christ, on whom the Lord "laid the iniquity of us all." The root meaning of this word is "entire removal, separation," and they then interpret the goat "for YHWH" as representing the atonement made, and the goat "for Azazel" as representing the effect of the great work of atonement namely the complete removal of sin.

4. LEVITICUS 18

BHS	וְאִשָּׁה אֶל־אֲחֹתָהּ לֹא תִקָּח לִצְרֹר	18b
Ltrl	to rival—you shall take—not—to her sister—and a wife	
YLT	And a woman unto another thou dost not take, to be an adversary,	
KJB	Neither shalt thou take a wife to her sister, to vex her	
NASB	And you shall not marry a woman in addition to her sister as a second wife	
ESV	And you shall not take a woman as a rival wife to her sister,	
NLT	While your wife is living, do not marry her sister . . . , for they would be rivals.	
NIV	Do not take your wife's sister as a rival wife	

1   לִצְרֹר Preposition + qal inf. cstr. of the verb צרר meaning, "to bind, tie up, be restricted, narrow, scant, or cramped."

2   We find this meaning of the verb in 1 Sm 1:6 as well.

3   However, in Gen 42:35 it has the meaning, "to string together," like beads on a necklace or like coins confined in a purse. So it could mean that a man with multiple wives has a "string" of wives. Support for this translation is found in 2 Sm 20:3.

BHS	וְאֶת־זָכָר לֹא תִשְׁכַּב מִשְׁכְּבֵי אִשָּׁה	22
Ltrl	women—lying down of—you will lie—not—male—and with	
KJB	Thou shalt not lie with mankind, as with womankind:	
NASB	You shall not lie with a male as one lies with a female;	
ESV	You shall not lie with a male as with a woman;	
NLT	"Do not practice homosexuality, having sex with another man as with a woman.	
NIV	"'Do not have sexual relations with a man as one does with a woman;	

1   וְאֶת Waw consecutive + DDOM. The DDOM or "mark of the accusative," per definition is a mark that indicates the direct definite object (accusative) in a sentence and at its core then means, "with something / somebody."

2   תִּשְׁכַּב Qal impf. 2ms of the verb שָׁכַב which simply means, "to lie down," but also means, "to have a sexual relationship." This form is also used in Lv 20:13 to convey this meaning.

3   מִשְׁכְּבֵי Noun, m. pl. cstr. meaning, "place / act of lying, couch."

5. LEVITICUS 20

BHS	חֶסֶד הוּא	17e
Ltrl	it is—a shame	
KJB	it is a wicked thing;	
NLT	it is a shameful disgrace.	
NIV	it is a disgrace	

1   חֶסֶד Noun, m. sg. absolute. The noun occurs in the Hebrew Bible 247 times.

2   Only here and in Prv 14:34 does it mean, "a shameful (thing), a disgrace."

3   In all the other cases it basically means, the "loving-kindness" of mankind and of God.

4   In the case of mankind it means,

    a)   the kindness of men towards men. Gen 47:29, "kindly," 1 Sm 15:6, "kindness."

    b)   the kindness extended to the lowly, needy, and miserable. 1 Sm 20:8, "kindly."

    c)   the affection / piety towards God. Jer 2:2, "devotion."

4   In the case of God it means the loving-kindness of God in condescending to the needs of his creatures.

    a)   Specific loving-kindness,

        i)   in redemption from enemies and troubles. Gen 19:19, "your loving-kindness."

        ii)   in preservation of life from death. Ps 6:5, "thy mercies."

        iii)   in quickening of spiritual life. Ps 109:26, "your loving-kindness."

        iv)   in redemption from sin. Ps 25:7, "your loving kindnesses."

        v)   in keeping the covenants. Ps 18:50, "loving-kindness."

    b)   Grouped with other divine attributes.

        i)   Loving-kindness and fidelity. Gen 24:27, "his mercy and truth."

        ii)   Loving-kindness and justice in Ps 101:1.

        iii)   Goodness and mercy in Ps 23:6.

    c)   The kindness of God is:

        i)   Abundant. Nm 14:18, "abundant in loving-kindness."

        ii)   Great in extent. Nm 14:19, "the greatness of Your loving-kindness."

iii) Everlasting. Jer 33:11, "his loving-kindness is everlasting."

iv) Good. Ps 69:17, "your loving-kindness is good."

d) The mercies (plural) and deeds (plural) of kindness.

i) In general. Ps 17:7, "marvelous loving-kindness."

ii) Shown to David. Is 55:3, "mercies shown to David."

iii) Shown to Jacob. Gen 32:11, "all the mercies."

6. LEVITICUS 21

BHS	וְאִשָּׁה גְּרוּשָׁה מֵאִישָׁהּ	7b
Ltrl	from her husband—driven out—and a woman	
KJB	a woman put away from her husband:	
NASB	a woman divorced from her husband;	
ESV	a woman divorced from her husband,	
NLT	a woman who is divorced from her husband,	
NIV	divorced from their husbands,	

1 גְּרוּשָׁה Qal part. passive f. sg of the verb גָּרַשׁ which means, "to drive out, cast out." This verb occurs 47 times in the Hebrew Bible, but only here, and in 21:14, 22:13, in Nm 30:9, and in Ez 44:22 is it used to describe a man driving his wife away (divorcing her).

7. LEVITICUS 25

BHS	עַד שְׁנַת הַיּוֹבֵל	28b
Ltrl	the ram's horn—year of—until	
KJB	until the year of jubilee:	
CEV	until the Year of Celebration,	
ESV	until the year of jubilee.	
NLT	until the next Year of Jubilee.	
NIV	until the Year of Jubilee.	

1 הַיּוֹבֵל Noun, m. sg. meaning, "ram, ram's horn, cornet." A designation of the 50th year, marked by the blowing of the cornets.

2 In the Latin Vulgate it reads *usque ad annum jubilæum*, giving rise to the English term "Jubilee Year."

82.8 NUMBERS

1. NUMBERS 6

BHS	יְבָרֶכְךָ יְהוָה וְיִשְׁמְרֶֽךָ׃ ס	24
Ltrl	and he will keep / protect you—YHWH—he will bless you abundantly	
KJB	The LORD bless you and keep you;	
NASB	The LORD bless you, and keep you;	
ESV	The LORD bless you and keep you;	
NLT	'May the LORD bless you and protect you.	
NIV	The LORD bless thee, and keep thee:	

1 The first word in this verse is the pi'el impf. 3ms form of the verb בָּרַךְ which has two meanings:

   a) "to kneel" or "adore with bended knees," which usually describes an action of a human being directed toward God, and

   b) "to bless," which is used to describe an action of God directed toward a human being, or an action of a human to a fellow human (Chapter 36.3.2b in Vol. 2).

2 In addition, a 2ms pronominal suffix is attached to the verb (Chapters 10.8 in Vol. 1, and 61.3 in Vol. 3).

3 The pi'el binyan is known as the intensive active form of the qal (Chapters. 25.1 and 25.8 in Vol. 1). Per this definition, the literal translation of the form in this verse then could be, "he will intensely / abundantly bless you."

4 Refer to Gen 1:1 above, concerning the Hebrew letter samek after the verse.

BHS	יָאֵר יְהוָה פָּנָיו אֵלֶיךָ וִיחֻנֶּֽךָ׃ ס	25
Ltrl	and be gracious to you—upon you—his face—YHWH—it will shine	
KJB	The LORD make his face shine upon thee, and be gracious unto thee:	
NASB	The LORD make His face shine on you, And be gracious to you;	
ESV	the LORD make his face to shine upon you and be gracious to you;	
NLT	May the LORD smile on you and be gracious to you.	
NIV	the LORD make his face shine on you and be gracious to you;	

25[a] "Samaritan Pentateuch Heb."

1 The form in the SP is only a variant spelling of the form in the MT. Both forms are the hiph'il impf. 3ms of the biconsonantal verb אוֹר which in the qal binyan means, "to be light" or "to become light," and thus in the hiph'il binyan means, "to give light, to light up, to cause to shine, to make shine" (Chapter 45.6 in Vol. 2).

25ᵇ "SyP Syrian = Heb."

1. This footnote shows the form from the SyP.
2. The form in the MT is the qal impf. 3ms, with a 2ms suffix, of the geminate verb חָנַן which means, "to show favor, to be gracious" (Chapter 57.1 in Vol. 2).
3. In Ps 44:3 we are told the meaning of the phrase "the LORD make his face shine on you." When Yahweh shines (directs) his face (character / personality) toward one, this loving and merciful action becomes the source of life and salvation for the person(s) involved.

BHS	יִשָּׂא יְהוָה פָּנָיו אֵלֶיךָ וְיָשֵׂם לְךָ שָׁלוֹם׃ ס	26
Ltrl	peace—to you—and put / set—upon you—his face—YHWH—he will lift up	
KJB	The LORD lift up his countenance upon thee, and give thee peace.	
NASB	The LORD lift up His countenance on you, And give you peace.'	
ESV	the LORD lift up his countenance upon you and give you peace.	
NLT	May the LORD show you his favor and give you his peace.'	
NIV	the LORD turn his face toward you and give you peace.	

1. The first word in this verse is the qal impf. 3ms form of the verb נָשָׂא which means, "to lift, carry, take" (Chapter 55.1 in Vol. 3).
2. The second verb in this verse is the qal impf. 3ms form of the verb שׂוּם meaning, "to put, set." This is the apocryphal (uncanonical) form, derived from the normal יָשִׂים.

2. NUMBERS 28

BHS	עֹלָה תָמִיד׃	3c
Ltrl	regular—a burnt-offering	
NASB	a continual burnt offering	
NLT	daily burnt offering.	
NIV	a regular burnt offering	
DRB	for the perpetual holocaust	

3ᵇ "Read with a few (3–10) Manuscripts SP Heb as (in verses) 6 and 15."

1. This footnote states that a few sources have the noun in the construct form meaning, "burnt-offering of" as indeed found in the mentioned verses.
2. עֹלָה Noun, f. sg. abs. meaning, "whole burnt-offering." All of the offering (a beast or a fowl) is laid on the altar except the hide and such parts that could not be washed clean. The offering is completely consumed by the fire and goes up in flames and smoke from the altar to God expressing the ascent of the soul in worship.
3. תָמִיד Noun, m. sg. abs. meaning, "continuity." It is often used as the adverb, "continually / continuously."

4   The Douay-Rheims Bible (Chapter 69.5 in Vol. 4 of this series) translates this phrase as, "for the perpetual holocaust."

5   The term holocaust, first used in 1895 by the New York Times to describe the massacre of Armenian Christians by Ottoman Muslims. It comes from the Greek: ὁλόκαυστος meaning, "whole burnt offering" which is coupled to the Hebrew term עָלָה.

6   Yiddish is the language used by Jews in central and eastern Europe before the Holocaust. It was originally a German dialect with words from Hebrew and several modern languages and is today spoken mainly in the USA, Israel, and Russia.

7   Yiddish-speaking Jews and survivors in the years immediately following their liberation called the murder of the Jews the *churban*, the word used to describe the destruction of the First Temple in Jerusalem by the Babylonians in 586 BCE and the destruction of the Second Temple by the Romans in 70 CE.

8   The biblical term שׁוֹאָה meaning, "devastation, ruin, waste, catastrophe" is the term preferred by Israelis and the French and it became the standard Hebrew term for the murder of the European Jews. This term is preferred by people who speak Hebrew and by those who want to be more particular about the Jewish experience or who are uncomfortable with the religious connotations of the word *Holocaust. Yom HaShoah* became Israel's Holocaust Remembrance Day in 1951.

82.9 DEUTERONOMY

1. DEUTERONOMY 6

BHS	שְׁמַ֖עᵃ יִשְׂרָאֵ֑ל יְהוָ֥ה אֱלֹהֵ֖ינוּ יְהוָ֥ה ׀ אֶחָֽד׃	4
Ltrl	one—YHWH—our God—YHWH—Israel—hear!	
KJB	Hear, O Israel: The LORD our God is one LORD:	
NASB	"Hear, O Israel! The LORD is our God, the LORD is one!	
ESV	"Hear, O Israel: The LORD our God, the LORD is one.	
NLT	"Listen, O Israel! The LORD is our God, the LORD alone.	
NIV	Hear, O Israel: The LORD our God, the LORD is one.	

4ᵃ "LXX put before some verb."

1   This footnote is not clear, as the word order in the Greek Septuagint is the same as the MT namely, ἄκουε Ισραηλ.

2   Rabbinic Judaism teaches that the Tetragrammaton YHWH, is the ineffable and actual name of God, and as such is not read aloud in the Shema but is traditionally replaced with *Adonai* ("LORD"). For that reason, the Shema is recited aloud as:

   Sh'ma Yisrael Adonai Eloheinu Adonai Eḥad.
   "Hear, O Israel: the LORD is our God, the LORD is One."

3   There are two larger-print letters in the first sentence ('ayin and dalet) which, when combined, spell "ad." In Hebrew this means, "witness." The idea thus conveyed is that through the recitation or proclamation of the Shema one is a living witness testifying to the truth of its message.

5a	וְאָהַבְתָּ אֵת יְהוָה אֱלֹהֶיךָ בְּכָל־לְבָבְךָ	BHS
	your heart—with all—your God—Yahweh—DDOM—and you shall love	Ltrl
	And thou shalt love the LORD thy God with all thine heart,	KJB
	"You shall love the LORD your God with all your heart	NASB
	You shall love the LORD your God with all your heart	ESV
	And you must love the LORD your God with all your heart,	NLT
	Love the LORD your God with all your heart	NIV

1 וְאָהַבְתָּ Waw conversive + Qal perf. 2ms of the verb אָהֵב meaning, "to love."

2 לְבָבְךָ Noun, m. sg. + suffix 2ms meaning, "your heart, mind, inner man."

3 Because of the waw conversive, this verse is a continuation of the commandment in the previous verse, rather than a separate commandment. Refer to Chapter 23.6 in Volume 1.

5b	וּבְכָל־נַפְשְׁךָ וּבְכָל־מְאֹדֶךָ׃	BHS
	your strength—and with all—your soul—and with all	Ltrl
	and with all thy soul, and with all thy might.	KJB
	and with all your soul and with all your might.	NASB
	and with all your soul and with all your might.	ESV
	all your soul, and all your strength.	NLT
	and with all your soul and with all your strength.	NIV

1 מְאֹדֶךָ Noun, m. sg. + suffix 2ms meaning, "might, force."

2. DEUTERONOMY 14

12a	וְזֶה אֲשֶׁר לֹא־תֹאכְלוּ מֵהֶם הַנֶּשֶׁר וְהַפֶּרֶס וְהָעָזְנִיָּה׃	BHS
	—the bearded vulture—the eagle—from them—you will eat—not—that—and this the lapped-faced vulture	Ltrl
	But these are they of which ye shall not eat: the eagle, and the ossifrage, and the ospray,	KJB
	"But these are the ones which you shall not eat: the eagle and the vulture and the buzzard,	NASB
	But these are the ones that you shall not eat: the eagle, the bearded vulture, the black vulture,	ESV
	These are the birds you may not eat: the griffon vulture, the bearded vulture, the black vulture,	NLT
	But these you may not eat: the eagle, the vulture, the black vulture,	NIV

12ª "In (verses) 12–18 SP Vulgate Heb before all names birds (except Heb 18) as Lv 11:13."

1 This footnote states that the SP and Latin Vulgate employ the direct definite object marker before each bird name in the lists.

2   In Lv 11:13–19 and Dt 14:12–18 the so-called "unclean birds" are listed. Hattingh (2012), p. 232-233 shows the alternative translations found in six Bibles for each one of the birds mentioned in these two lists.

3   Refer to Chapter 83.8 for a discussion of the so-called "unclean" birds that are listed here in verses 14:12b–18 and in Lv 11:13b–19.

3. DEUTERONOMY 24

BHS	וְכָתַב לָהּ סֵפֶר כְּרִיתֻת	1d
Ltrl	divorcement—a writing of—for her—and he will write	
KJB	then let him write her a bill of divorcement,	
NASB	that he writes her a certificate of divorce,	
ESV	and he writes her a certificate of divorce	
NLT	he writes a document of divorce,	
NIV	and he writes her a certificate of divorce,	

1   כְּרִיתֻת Noun, f. sg. abs. meaning, "divorcement." The root is כרת which means, "to cut off, cut down."

2   The Hebrew Bible is predominantly a patriarchal (male dominated) document from a patriarchal age. Therefore there is a great contrast between the women of the present day and those of the Hebrew Bible times.

3   Woman in the Hebrew Bible is subject to the Chinese rule of the three obediences. "When young she must obey her father; when married, she must obey her husband; and when her husband is dead, she must obey her son." They were severely restricted in their rights. For example, they were granted only limited freedom of movement and choice of relationships. To pursue an education or fully participate in society was unthinkable.

4   In ancient times, women's roles and functions were limited to the home. The most important role of woman in early society was that of being a wife and a tool for reproduction. In ancient Israel the influence of a man was measured by the numbers in his family rather than by riches in lifestock, slaves, or land.

5   Not only does the law permit polygamy (Dt 21), the Song of Songs celebrates it (6:8). A number of wives was a sign of wealth and social distinction, especially that of royalty. Monogamy, on the other hand, was the badge of poverty.

6   In traditional agrarian (cultivation of land) societies, a woman's role in the economic well-being of the household was an essential one. Ancient Israel had no developed market economy for most of the Iron Age (c. 1200–300 BCE), so a woman's role in commodity production was essential for survival.

7   Legally the wife was the property of her husband. He was her master, or owner; she was his chattel (a personal possession). She is listed with his ox and ass (Ex 20:17; Dt 5:21), and ranked after his children. As chattel, she may be surrendered for the protection of a guest (Jgs 19),

be made to serve the commercial advantage of her owner (Gen 12), be disposed of with the ancestral estates (Ru 4), be brutally punished (Gen 38:24; Lv 21:9), or be expelled at will from the home (Dt 24:1). A husband could divorce a wife if he chose to, but a wife could not divorce a husband without his consent. The law said a woman could not make a binding vow without the consent of her male authority, so she could not legally marry without male approval.

8   The man alone had the right of divorce. This is partly due to the commercial form of marriage, whereby the woman belongs absolutely to the man. Her economic value is his; her love and fidelity are his due.

9   In spite of all the above, it should also be noted that the Hebrew Bible often portrays women as victors, leaders, and heroines with qualities Israel should emulate. Women such as Hagar, Tamar, Miriam, Rahab, Deborah, Esther, and Yael, are among many female "saviors" of Israel.

10 Refer to Mal 2:16.

BHS	וְנָתַן בְּיָדָהּ וְשִׁלְּחָהּ מִבֵּיתוֹ׃	1e
Ltrl	from his house—and he will send her away—in her hand—and he will give	
KJB	and give it in her hand, and send her out of his house.	
NASB	puts it in her hand, and sends her away from his house,	
ESV	and puts it in her hand and sends her out of his house,	
NLT	hands it to her, and sends her away from his house.	
NIV	gives it to her and sends her from his house,	

1[b] "LXX plural, the same (as verse) 3; Targum Jonathan otherwise; SyP (Vulgate) Syr = Heb."

1   The footnote makes two suggestions, both of which are of no real consequence.

2   וְשִׁלְּחָהּ Waw consecutive + pi'el perf. 3ms + suffix 3fs of the root שׁלח meaning, "to send" in the qal, and "to send off, send away, to dismiss" in the pi'el.

3   There is no word in the Hebrew Bible for "divorce." In light of this passage, and the background information below, it is clear that in the societies in which the narratives of the Hebrew Bible took place, men could, without much effort, rid themselves of a spouse. Because of their position in society, women were never given an equal opportunity.

4   In the Hebrew Bible, three verbs are used in 15 instances to describe the action of a man "divorcing" his wife. These instances can be tabulated as follows:

גרשׁ	שׁלח	כרת
to drive out	**to send away**	**to cut off**
Lv 21:7, 14	Mal 2:16	Dt 24:1, 3
Lv 22:13	Dt 22:19, 29	Is 50:1
Nm 30:10	Dt 24:1, 3	Jer 3:8
Ez 44:22	Jer 3:1	

4. DEUTERONOMY 32

BHS	בְּהַנְחֵל‎ᵃ עֶלְיוֹן גּוֹיִם בְּהַפְרִידוֹ בְּנֵי אָדָם	8a
Ltrl	Adam—sons of—when he separated it—nations—Most High—when he divided	
KJB	When the most High divided to the nations their inheritance, when he separated the sons of Adam,	
NASB	"When the Most High gave the nations their inheritance, When He separated the sons of man,	
ESV	When the Most High gave to the nations their inheritance, when he divided mankind,	
NLT	When the Most High assigned lands to the nations, when he divided up the human race,	
NIV	When the Most High gave the nations their inheritance, when he divided all mankind,	

8ᵃ "Two Manuscripts Samaritan Pentateuch Heb."

1. Two Manuscripts of the MT and various codices of the Samaritan Pentateuch have a Hebrew form that confirms the verb is in the MT is in the hiph'il binyan.

2. The verb mentioned in this footnote can safely be parsed as being an inseparable preposition *beit* before the hiph'il infinitive construct of the verb נָחַל which in the qal binyan means, "to get or take as a possession," and in the hiph'il means, "to cause to inherit" or "to give as an inheritance."

BHS	יַצֵּב‎ᶜ גְּבֻלֹת עַמִּים לְמִסְפַּר‎ᵈ בְּנֵי יִשְׂרָאֵל‎ᵈ:	8b
Ltrl	Israel—sons of—to a number—people boundaries of—he will set	
KJB	he set the bounds of the people according to the number of the children of Israel.	
NASB	He set the boundaries of the peoples According to the number of the sons of Israel.	
ESV	he fixed the borders of the peoples according to the number of the sons of God.	
NLT	he established the boundaries of the peoples according to the number in his heavenly court.	
NIV	he set up boundaries for the peoples according to the number of the sons of Israel.	

8ᵇ "Samaritan Pentateuch Heb."

1. The form יַצֵּב in the MT is the apocopated form of יַצִּיב which is the hiph'il impf. 3ms of the verb נצב and mentioned in this footnote as appearing in a codex of the Samaritan Pentateuch.

8ᶜ "Targum of Jonathan adds 70."

1. This targum adds a specific number to the generic term found in the MT.

8ᵈ⁻ᵈ "Qumran LXX (Grk) Symmachus Old Latin probably correctly Heb or Heb."

1. The Greek Septuagint indeed has αγγέλων θεού which means, "the angels of God." Both the suggested Hebrew phrases mean, "sons of God."

BHS	כְּנֶ֙שֶׁר֙ יָעִ֣יר ᵃ קִנּ֔וֹ עַל־גּוֹזָלָ֖יו יְרַחֵ֑ף	11a
Ltrl	he will hover—his eaglets—over—his nest—he will stir—as an eagle	
KJB	As an eagle stirreth up her nest, fluttereth over her young,	
NASB	"Like an eagle that stirs up its nest, That hovers over its young,	
ESV	Like an eagle that stirs up its nest, that flutters over its young,	
NLT	Like an eagle that rouses her chicks and hovers over her young,	
NIV	like an eagle that stirs up its nest and hovers over its young,	

11ᵃ "Varied selection by B. Kennicott Manuscripts SP Heb, LXX Grk = Heb? compare Targums."

1. The word in the MT is the hiph'il impf. 3ms of the biconsonantal verb עוֹר meaning, "to rouse" and "to stir up." The Hebrew in the first part of this footnote can be pointed (given vowels) as יָעַר / יָעֵר which is the apocopated and conversive form of the MT form. The Greek Septuagint has σκεπάσαι meaning, "sheltering," and which would back-translate to יִצֹּר the qal impf. 3ms of the verb נָצַר meaning, "to watch, guard, keep," as in Prv 3:1.

11ᵇ "Varied selection by B. Kennicott Manuscripts SP LXX SyP Targum Vulgate Heb (by haplography)."

1. This footnote suggests that by haplography (single writing), a waw conjunctive was omitted in the MT but does occur in a wide selection of other sources.

2. "The Hebrew word נֶשֶׁר is often translated as 'eagle,' but this is as much a generic term as is the English. As many of the references are used figuratively, it does not give many clues as to the specific species, and could include any large raptor. Dictionaries therefore mention that it could without difficulty be translated as 'vulture.' Micah 1:16 is a case in point."¹⁵

3. The Hebrew word גּוֹזָל is a masculine noun that appears only twice in the Hebrew Bible. In Gen 15:9 it means, "pigeon chick," and here it has the 3ms suffix that is used for plural nouns, and therefore means, "his eaglets."

4. Refer to Gen 1:2b for a discussing of the verb רחף meaning, "to hover."

5. "Eagle chicks have long post-nestling dependence periods, but it is well known that the chicks exercise their wings extensively while still in the nest, and are quite capable of flying when leaving the nest. This description of bird behavior can therefore not be taken taken literally."¹⁶

---

15 Kushner, Aviya (2015), audiobook section 31.
16 Nelte, Frank, W. (2009). *80 Mistranslations in the Bible and Their Significance*. Sourced on 12 Feb. 2021. https://www.franknelte.net/article.php?article_id=236

BHS	יִפְרֹשׂ כְּנָפָיו יִקָּחֵהוּ יִשָּׂאֵהוּ עַל־אֶבְרָתוֹ׃	11b
Ltrl	his wings—on—he will carry it—he will take it up—his wings—he will spread	
KJB	spreadeth abroad her wings, taketh them, beareth them on her wings:	
NASB	He spread His wings and caught them, He carried them on His pinions.	
ESV	spreading out its wings, catching them, bearing them on its pinions,	
NLT	so he spread his wings to take them up and carried them safely on his pinions.	
NIV	that spreads its wings to catch them and carries them aloft.	

11c "SP Heb; Syriac Peshitta suffix 3(rd person) plural."

11d "Syriac Peshitta suffix 3(rd person) plural."

1. These two footnotes mention those sources which have preferred to use plural object suffixes attached to these two verbs, and thus implying that the eagles had more than one chick in the brood under their care.

2. Siblicide is the killing of an infant individual by its close relatives. Siblicide has mainly, but not only, been observed in birds. It may occur directly between siblings or be mediated by the parents. Siblicide is used as a unifying term for fratricide (killing one's brother) and sororicide (killing one's sister) in the human species; but unlike these more specific terms siblicide leaves the sex of the victim unspecified.

3. Siblicidal behavior can be either obligate or facultative. Obligate siblicide is when a sibling almost always ends up being killed. Facultative siblicide means that siblicide may or may not occur, based on environmental conditions. Obligate siblicidal behavior is common among eagle species and results in the stronger chick killing the other chick(s) at an early age.

4. With all the above in mind, it is significant that the MT has opted to use the suffix in the singular. This might be an indication of the author observing that the eagle parents, although starting of with a number of chicks in the brood, inevitably end up with raising only one chick to adulthood.

5. "The Hebrew Canon, as expounded in the Mosaic Law, the Prophets and the Writings, contains the origin of Ornithology, and the biblical authors concerned, and not Aristotle, were the original Ornithologists."[17] Aristotle (384–322 BC) lived at the time when the Hebrew canon was being finalized after a developmental period spanning in the order of ten centuries (Chapter 65.8 in Vol. 4). Evaluating the hypothesis quoted above was the central theme of the publication *Birds and Bibles in History*.

6. "As mentioned above, eagle chicks have long post-nestling dependence periods, but it is well known that the chicks exercise their wings extensively while still in the nest, and are quite capable of flying when leaving the nest. The description in Dt 32:11 can therefore not be taken literally."[18]

---

17 Hattingh, Tian (2012), p. 186.
18 Davidson, Paul, *Genesis 14:20*, "isthatinthebible.wordpress.com," 12/25/2020. https://isthatinthebible.wordpress.com/articles-and-resources/deliberate-mistranslation-in-the-new-international-version-niv/

BHS	הַרְנִינוּ גוֹיִם‎ᵃ עַמּוֹ‎ᵇ	43a
Ltrl	his people—nations—rejoice!	
KJB	Rejoice, O ye nations, *with* his people:	
NASB	"Rejoice, you nations, *with* His people;	
ESV	"Rejoice with him, O heavens;	
NLT	"Rejoice with him, you heavens,	
NIV	Rejoice, you nations, with his people,	

43ᵃ "Perhaps read with Qumran LXX Heb."

1. This footnote suggests that we follow the Qumran texts and the Greek Septuagint and change "nations" to "heavens." The ESV and NIV have implemented this suggestion.

43ᵇ "A Manuscript put before Heb; LXX Grk = Heb; perhaps read Heb; Qumran LXX and H 1:6 adds Heb or Heb."

1. This footnote contains four suggestions:

    a) That we add a Direct Definite Object Marker (DDOM) before the third word.

    b) That we take note of the Greek Septuagint which has ἁμα αυτώ meaning, "together with him."

    c) That we should read the second and third words as "with his people."

    d) That we should take note that three sources add another phrase here.

1. הַרְנִינוּ Hiph'il imp. 3mp of the verb רָנַן which in the qal binyan means, "to give a ringing cry," but in the hiph'il binyan means, "cause to ring out for joy, ring out a cry of joy" (Ps 32:11, 81:2).

2. A number of modern English translations have subtly altered the meaning by adding "with" into the text. A likely reason for this insertion is to harmonize the verse with its quotation in Rom 15:10. "For the NIV, removing polytheistic language seemingly takes priority over accuracy."[19]

3. In the NIV there is a footnote which translates the Qumran text as saying "let all the angels worship him." However the text of the Qumran scroll 4QDeutq actually reads "let all the gods worship him."

---

19   Stepbible.org. (2019). *Samaritan Pentateuch in English*. Exodus 20:17. Accessed 19 October 2019.

82.10 JOSHUA

1. JOSHUA 1

BHS	וַיֹּאמֶר יְהוָה אֶל־יְהוֹשֻׁעַ[b]	1b
Ltrl	Joshua—unto—Yahweh—and he said	
KJB	the LORD spake unto Joshua	
NASB	the LORD spoke to Joshua	
ESV	the LORD said to Joshua	
NLT	the LORD spoke to Joshua	
NIV	the LORD said to Joshua	

1[b] "Dt 3:21, Jgs 2:7 Heb."

1. This footnote mentions the two verses where, for the "u" vowel in the name, a shureq is used instead of the usual qibbuts.

2. יֵשׁוּעַ is the short Aramaic form of יְהוֹשֻׁעַ (Joshua). Aramaic was the *lingua franca* (the commonly spoken language) in Palestine at the time when the virgin Mary gave birth to her firstborn son. As instructed to Joseph by the angel, they gave their son this Aramaic name. It was translated in the Greek Septuagint as Ἰησοῦς and from that into English as, "Jesus."

3. The name "Joshua" appears 218 times in the Hebrew Bible.

BHS	רַק חֲזַק וֶאֱמַץ מְאֹד[a] לִשְׁמֹר לַעֲשׂוֹת[b] כְּכָל[c]־הַתּוֹרָה	7a
Ltrl	the law—like all (of)—to do—to keep—very—and be alert / bold!—be strong!—surely	
KJB	Only be thou strong and very courageous, that thou mayest observe to do according to all the law,	
NASB	"Only be strong and very courageous; be careful to do according to all the law	
ESV	Only be strong and very courageous, being careful to do according to all the law	
NLT	Be strong and very courageous. Be careful to obey all the instructions	
NIV	"Be strong and very courageous. Be careful to obey all the law	

7[a] "Lacking (in) original Septuagint."

1. This is indeed the case as can be seen in the ABP[20] Greek version for example.

---

[20] Main source: Wikipedia contributors. *"Moses (Michelangelo)."* Wikipedia, The Free Encyclopedia, 20 August, 2019. Web: 10 September, 2019. Slightly edited.

BHS	אֲשֶׁר c צִוְּךָ מֹשֶׁה עַבְדִּי אַל־e תָּסוּר מִמֶּנּוּ	7b
Ltrl	from it—you will turn aside—not—my servant—Moses—he commanded you—which	
KJB	which Moses my servant commanded thee: turn not from it	
NASB	which Moses My servant commanded you; do not turn from it	
ESV	that Moses my servant commanded you. Do not turn from it	
NLT	Moses gave you. Do not deviate from them,	
NIV	my servant Moses gave you; do not turn from it	

7b "Several (11–20) Manuscripts the original Septuagint Vulgate Heb."

1   These sources add a waw consecutive here.

BHS	יָמִין וּשְׂמֹאול לְמַעַן תַּשְׂכִּיל בְּכֹל אֲשֶׁר תֵּלֵךְ׃	7c
Ltrl	you produce—that—in all—you will prosper—in order that—or to the left—to the right	
KJB	to the right hand or to the left, that thou mayest prosper whithersoever thou goest.	
NLT	turning either to the right or to the left. Then you will be successful in everything you do.	
NIV	to the right or to the left, that you may be successful wherever you go.	

1   יָמִין Noun, f. sg. "right hand," but also indicating direction toward, "to the right," or indicating the situation of something, "on the right hand of."

2   וּשְׂמֹאול Waw consecutive + noun, m. sg. meaning, "left (hand) side."

3   לְמַעַן Preposition or conjunctive meaning, "for the sake of, on account of, to the intent, in order that."

4   תַּשְׂכִּיל Hiph'il impf. 2ms of the verb שָׂכַל meaning, "to act prudently, prosper, have success."

5   תֵּלֵךְ Qal impf. 2ms of the verb יָלַד meaning, "to bear, bring forth, beget."

7c-c "Septuagint Grk, read Heb (compare Heb)."

1   The Greek Septuagint indeed has καθότι meaning, "in so far as." Then this footnote suggests that we read כַּאֲשֶׁר meaning, "like which," or "according to that which."

7d "A few (3–10) Manuscripts Arabic versions Heb, two Manuscripts SyP Vulgate Heb."

1   The suggested form בְּכֹל makes sense, and should be considered.

2   רַק An adverb with restrictive force meaning, "only, altogether, surely."

3   חֲזַק Qal imp. m. sg. of the verb חָזַק meaning, "be strong, grow strong / firm."

4   וֶאֱמָץ Waw consecutive + Qal imp. m. sg. of the verb אָמַץ meaning, "be strong, bold, alert, stout" (also in verse 6).

5 לִשְׁמֹר Refer to Chapters 23.13.5.4.3 and 17.4.6 in Vol. 1.

6 לַעֲשׂוֹת Refer to Chapters 23.13.5.4.3 and 17.4.7 in Vol. 1.

7e "Original Septuagint put before Grk."

1 In the Greek Septuagint we find και ουκ meaning, "and do not."

2 צִוְּךָ Pi'el perf. 3ms + suffix 2ms of the verb צָוָה meaning, "to command, order."

3 תָסוּר Qal impf. 2ms of the verb סוּר meaning, "to turn aside."

2. JOSHUA 4

BHS	וּשְׁתֵּים עֶשְׂרֵה אֲבָנִים הֵקִים יְהוֹשֻׁעַ בְּתוֹךְ הַיַּרְדֵּן	9a
Ltrl	the Jordan—in the middle of—Joshua—he set up—stones—ten—and two	
KJB	And Joshua set up twelve stones in the midst of Jordan,	
NASB	Then Joshua set up twelve stones in the middle of the Jordan	
ESV	And Joshua set up twelve stones in the midst of the Jordan,	
NLT	Joshua also set up another pile of twelve stones in the middle of the Jordan,	
NIV	Joshua set up the twelve stones that had been in the middle of the Jordan	

1 It is well known by scholars that this account of events stands in contrast to the account in Jos 4:20 in which the stones are set up at Gilgal.

2 The NIV attempts to harmonize these two accounts by changing this verse to say that Joshua set up the twelve stones that "had been" in the middle of the Jordan. However, the past-tense verb that the NIV has inserted does not appear in the Hebrew.

3 To their credit, the NIV does offer an alternate translation in a footnote, which is almost correct, but adds "also" to imply a second set of 12 stones.

82.11 JUDGES

1. JUDGES 4

BHS	וּדְבוֹרָה אִשָּׁה נְבִיאָה	4a
Ltrl	a prophetess—a woman—And Deborah	
KJB	And Deborah, a prophetess,	
NASB	Now Deborah, a prophetess,	
ESV	Now Deborah, a prophetess,	
NIV	Now Deborah, a prophet,	

1 The name "Deborah" is a feminine noun meaning, "bee."

2 The name appears 10 times in the Hebrew Bible. In Gen 35:8, and nine times in the Book of Judges.

2. JUDGES 6

BHS	וְגִדְעוֹן בְּנוֹ חֹבֵט חִטִּים בַּגַּת	11c
Ltrl	in the winepress—wheat—threshed—his son—and Gideon	
KJB	and his son Gideon threshed wheat by the winepress	
NASB	his son Gideon was beating out wheat in the wine press	
ESV	his son Gideon was beating out wheat in the winepress	
NIV	where his son Gideon was threshing wheat in a winepress	

1 The name "Gideon" stems from the verb גָּדַע meaning, "to hew, cut down."

2 The name appears 39 times in the Book of Judges in the Hebrew Bible.

3. JUDGES 12

BHS	וַיֹּאמְרוּ לוֹ אֱמָר־נָא שִׁבֹּלֶת וַיֹּאמֶר סִבֹּלֶת	6a
Ltrl	sibbolet—and he said—shibbolet—please—say—to him—and they said	
KJB	Then said they unto him, Say now Shibboleth: and he said Sibboleth:	
NASB	then they would say to him, "Say now, 'Shibboleth.'" But he said, "Sibboleth,"	
ESV	they said to him, "Then say Shibboleth," and he said, "Sibboleth,"	
NLT	they would tell him to say "Shibboleth." . . . . , he would say "Sibboleth,"	
NIV	they said, "All right, say 'Shibboleth.'" If he said, "Sibboleth,"	

1 שִׁבֹּלֶת Noun, f. sg. abs. meaning, "flowing stream" (here and in Ps 69:3). The construct form is found in Ps 69:16, and in Is 27:12. Elsewhere it is found to mean, "ear of grain." In the abs. sg. in Jb 24:24. In the abs. pl. in Gen 41:5–27; Is 17:5, 5; Ru 2:2. In the pl. cstr in Zec 4:12.

2 סִבֹּלֶת Noun, f. sg. abs. This is an example of a *hapax legomenon* (a word that is found only once in a body of work like the Hebrew Bible). It has no connection to any other root, making it impossible to ascertain with certainty what the original author meant.

3 One only has to know the Hebrew alphabet to be able to see how the difference in pronunciation of the same word in different dialects was used by Jephthah as a code word to identify Ephraimites masquerading as Gileadites.

82.12 RUTH

1. RUTH 1

BHS	וְשֵׁם הַשֵּׁנִית רוּת	4b
Ltrl	Ruth—the second—and the name of	
KJB	and the name of the other Ruth:	
NASB	and the name of the other Ruth.	
ESV	and the name of the other Ruth.	
NLT	and the other a woman named Ruth.	
NIV	and the other Ruth	

1   The name "Ruth" was derived from the Hebrew word רְעוּת meaning, "fellow, fellow-woman," or "friend(ship)."

2. RUTH 4

BHS	הוּא אֲבִי־יִשַׁי אֲבִי דָוִד׃ פ	17b
Ltrl	David—father of—Jesse—father of—he	
KJB	he is the father of Jesse, the father of David.	
NASB	He is the father of Jesse, the father of David.	
ESV	He was the father of Jesse, the father of David.	
NLT	He became the father of Jesse and the grandfather of David.	
NIV	He was the father of Jesse, the father of David.	

1   The name "David" occurs 1075 times in the Hebrew Bible.

2   Towards the end of the book of Ruth, David is mentioned for the first time in the Hebrew Bible, when it is pointed out that David was the great-grandson of Boaz and his Moabite wife Ruth.

3   The name "David" was probably derived from דּוֹד meaning, "beloved" or "uncle," which some scholars believe has its origins in *Dodo*, the title given to the sun-god who was worshipped in the region at the time.

82.13   1 SAMUEL

1.   1 SAMUEL 1

BHS	עַל־מְזוּזַת־הֵיכַל֭ יְהוָה׃	9b
Ltrl	YHWH—the temple of—the doorpost of—by	
KJB	by a post of the temple of the LORD.	
NASB	by the doorpost of the temple of the LORD.	
ESV	beside the doorpost of the temple of the LORD.	
NLT	beside the entrance of the Tabernacle.	
NIV	by the doorpost of the LORD'S house.	

9c "Cited plural compare LXX Targums Vulgate."

1   This footnote states that three major sources have the plural form. The Greek Septuagint indeed has τῶν φλιῶν meaning, "the doorposts."

9d "One manuscript Heb, SyP Codex Leningradensis Syr compare footnote 3:3a."

1   This footnote states that one Manuscript has "house of YHWH." It also refers us to 3:3 where similar footnote is found. The NIV for example, follows this suggestion.

2   מְזוּזַת Noun, f. sg. cstr. meaning, "doorpost of, gatepost of." Today, to fulfill the *mitzvah* (Biblical commandment) in Dt 6:9, a "mezuzah" (a small parchment inscribed with religious texts and attached in a case to the doorpost of a Jewish home as a sign of faith).

3   The Tabernacle remained stationary at Shiloh for 369 years. It is therefore reasonable to summize that numerous buildings of a more solid nature grew up around it. The Hebrew word used here, and the expression "doors of the house" (1Sm 3:15), seem to suggest that by the time of this narrative, a permanent structure or building, possibly of stone, and surrounding the Tabernacle, had been built.

BHS	וַתִּקְרָא אֶת־שְׁמוֹ שְׁמוּאֵל כִּי מֵיְהוָה שְׁאִלְתִּיו׃	20b
Ltrl	I asked him—from Yahweh—because—Samuel—his name—DDOM—and she called	
KJB	and called his name Samuel, saying, Because I have asked him of the LORD.	
NASB	and she named him Samuel, saying, "Because I have asked him of the LORD."	
ESV	and she called his name Samuel, for she said, "I have asked for him from the LORD."	
NLT	She named him Samuel, for she said, "I asked the LORD for him."	
NIV	She named him Samuel, saying, "Because I asked the LORD for him."	

1   Hannah explains the origin of the name "Samuel" by referring to the Hebrew verb שָׁאַל which means, "to ask, inquire."

2   There is a person called "Samuel" mentioned in Nm 34:20. The prophet Samuel is mentioned 139 times in the two books bearing his name.

2. 1 SAMUEL 2

BHS	וְהִבַּטְתָּ צַר מָעוֹן בְּכֹל אֲשֶׁר־יֵיטִיב אֶת־יִשְׂרָאֵלa	32a
Ltrl	Israel—DDOM—it will be good—which—in all—dwelling—enemy—and you will see	
KJB	And thou shalt see an enemy in my habitation, in all the wealth which God shall give Israel:	
NASB	You will see the distress of My dwelling, in spite of all the good that I do for Israel;	
ESV	Then in distress you will look with envious eye on all the prosperity that shall be bestowed on Israel,	
NLT	You will watch with envy as I pour out prosperity on the people of Israel.	
NIV	and you will see distress in my dwelling. Although good will be done to Israel,	

32a-a "This material is lacking in the LXX."

1 A large part of the MT verse does not appear in the Greek Septuagint.

2 וְהִבַּטְתָּ Waw conversive + Hiph'il perfect 2 m. sg. of the root נבט which means, "to look upon." The hiph'il has a causative (causes something to happen) meaning, and would then mean, "cause (yourself) to see."

3 יֵיטִיב Hiph'il imperfect 3 m. sg. of the verb יָטַב which is a stative verb (he will be good) in the qal, but in the hiph'il becomes, "he will do good."

4 צַר מָעוֹן From the wide range of interpretations displayed in translations, it is obvious that this phrase is found to be highly problematic.

BHS	וְלֹא־יִהְיֶה זָקֵן בְּבֵיתְךָ כָּל־הַיָּמִים׃	32b
Ltrl	the days—all—in your house—an old man—there will be—and not	
KJB	and there shall not be an old man in thine house for ever.	
NASB	and an old man will not be in your house forever.	
ESV	and there shall not be an old man in your house forever.	
NLT	But no members of your family will ever live out their days.	
NIV	no one in your family line will ever reach old age.	

32b "Qumran adds Heb, LXX adds Grk."

1 "Both Qumran and the Greek septuagint adds, 'for you.'"

32c "Qumran LXX suffix first person singular."

1 The above footnotes do not substantially influence the meaning of the verse.

2 כָּל־הַיָּמִים "All the days." In other words, "forever."

BHS	וְכָל־מַרְבִּית בֵּיתְךָ יָמוּתוּ אֲנָשִׁים׃	33c
Ltrl	men—they will die—your house—increase / great number—and all	
KJB	and all the increase of thine house shall die in the flower of their age.	
NASB	and all the increase of your house will die in the prime of life.	
ESV	and all the descendants of your house shall die by the sword of men.	
NLT	and their children will die a violent death.	
NIV	and all your descendants will die in the prime of life.	

33ᵇ "Qumran adds material Heb, LXX adds material Grk."

1. εν ρομφαία "the broadsword." The Greek Septuagint does indeed add this term to what is found in the MT.

2. בחרב The Qumran Texts add this word. It means, "by a / the sword."

3. The MT states that the descendants will die as men, implying that they will not die in old age, but rather in the prime of their lives. The additions made in the Qumran Texts and the Septuagint does not focus on the time of their demise, but rather on the manner in which they will die, namely a violent death by the sword.

3. 1 SAMUEL 3

BHS	וְאָמַרְתָּ דַּבֵּר יְהוָה כִּי שֹׁמֵעַ עַבְדֶּךָ	9b
Ltrl	your servant—listening—because—Yahweh—speak—and you will say	
KJB	thou shalt say, Speak, LORD; for thy servant heareth.	
NASB	you shall say, 'Speak, LORD, for Your servant is listening.'"	
ESV	you shall say, 'Speak, LORD, for your servant hears.'"	
NLT	say, 'Speak, LORD, your servant is listening.'"	
NIV	say, 'Speak, LORD, for your servant is listening.'	

4. 1 SAMUEL 14

BHS	ᵃכְּבַחֲצִי מַעֲנָה צֶמֶדᵇ שָׂדֶה׃	14b
Ltrl	land—square—a field for ploughing—as in half	
KJB	as it were an half acre of land, *which* a yoke *of oxen might plow*.	
NASB	within about half a furrow in an acre of land.	
ESV	within as it were half a furrow's length in an acre of land.	
NLT	and their bodies were scattered over about half an acre.	
NIV	in an area of about half an acre.	

14ᵃ⁻ᵃ "LXX Grk (Heb) (LXX manuscripts Grk) Grk (Heb) Grk, Old Latin Version 115 Lat, Old Latin Versions 93, 94 Lat, SyP Syr (plural, a Heb) Syr (plural) Syr (plural) Syr."

1. Instead of the MT sentence, the Greek Septuagint has εν βολίσι και εν πετροβόλοις και εν κόχλαξι του πεδίου meaning, "by arrows and by rock slinging and by pebbles of the plain."

2. The Old Latin Versions quoted by this footnote also has a sentence similar to the LXX.

3. The Syriac Peshitta has some words in the plural.

14ᵇ "Two Manuscripts add Heb compare Targums Vulgate."

1. The two Manuscripts add בָּקָר changing the meaning to the more specific, "a span of oxen."

2. כְּבַחֲצִי Preposition + preposition + noun, m. sg. meaning, "half (of anything)."

3. מַעֲנָה Noun, f. sg. literally meaning, "a place for a task." Here, and in Ps 129:3 it takes on the meaning, "a field for ploughing."

4. צֶמֶד Noun, m. sg. meaning, "couple, pair, span of oxen." In addition, it has the meaning of an area and is the only square measure in the Hebrew Bible. It was defined as "the area that a span of oxen could plough in one day."

5. שָׂדֶה Noun, m. sg. (ordinary contracted form) meaning, "open field, pasture-land, cultivated land." Refer to 2 Kgs 5:17.

82.14 2 SAMUEL

1. 2 SAMUEL 3

BHS	וּמַחֲזִיק בַּפֶּלֶךְ	29c
Ltrl	on a crutch—and one who leans on	
KJB	that leaneth on a staff,	
NASB	who takes hold of a distaff,	
ESV	who holds a spindle	
NLT	who walks on crutches	
NIV	who leans on a crutch	

1. וּמַחֲזִיק Waw consecutive + hiph'il part. ms of the verb חָזַק which in the qal binyan means, "to be / grow strong / firm; to strengthen." In the hiph'il binyan it means, among others, "to cling to."

2. בַּפֶּלֶךְ Prep. + noun, m. sg. meaning, "district" eight times in Neh 3, but here and in Prv 31:19 is means, "whirl of a weaving spindle."

3. There are two ways in which the above noun could be used to describe this curse.

   a) This noun has now been identified from Ugaritic and Akkadian as the word for "spindle" or "distaff" (a stick or spindle onto which wool or flax is wound for spinning). The phrase used here was the common description of a woman involved in menial tasks. Should a Hittite soldier break his oath, it would result in the loss of his manhood. The oath describes this penalty in terms of the violator holding the spindle and mirror. This second curse in this verse then threatens Joab's house with decreased virility.

b) The second interpretation is that "distaff" is a derogatory euphemism for a cripple who requires a crutch. This is consistent with word "agad" ("staff") used to translate the noun in the Aramaic Targum attributed to Onkelos.

BHS	וַיֵּבְךְּ אֶל־קֶבֶר אַבְנֵר	32b
Ltrl	Abner—the grave of—at—and he wept	
KJB	and wept at the grave of Abner;	
NASB	and wept at the grave of Abner,	
ESV	and wept at the grave of Abner,	
NLT	and the king . . . . wept at his graveside.	
NIV	and the king wept aloud at Abner's tomb.	

32c "A few (3–10) manuscripts cited Heb compare Syriac Peshitta Targums and 1:24ª."

1. The alternative preposition does not affect the translation.

2. וַיֵּבְךְּ Waw conversive + Qal imperfect 3ms of the verb בָּכָה meaning, "weep, bewail (in a loud voice)."

3. קֶבֶר Noun, m. sg. cstr. meaning, "grave, sepulchre (a small room or monument, cut in rock or built of stone, in which a dead person is laid or buried), tomb, gravesite, memorial."

4. One could say that the grave (qever) refers of the place where physical corpses are laid to rest, and that the place where the immaterial part of the deceased goes would then be "Sheol."

5. Refer to Is 5:14 concerning the word "Sheol."

2. 2 SAMUEL 13

BHS	וְיוֹנָדָב אִישׁ חָכָם מְאֹד׃	3d
Ltrl	very—shrewd—man—and Jonadab	
KJB	and Jonadab was a very subtil man.	
NASB	and Jonadab was a very shrewd man.	
ESV	And Jonadab was a very crafty man.	
NIV	Jonadab was a very shrewd man.	

1. חָכָם Adjective m. sg. It is commonly known to mean, "to be wise," but actually has a wide range of meanings.

    a) As "wise" in the administration of affairs (Gen 33, Dt 1:13), etc.

    b) As "skillful" at technical work in many fields. Artificers (Is 3:3), sailors (Ez 27:8), mourning women (Jer 9:16), women in spinning (Ex 35:25), etc.

    c) As "shrewd, crafty, cunning" (2 Sm 13:3), intelligent animals (Prv 30:24), etc.

d) As a class of "learnerd and shrewd" men, including magicians from Egypt (Gen 41:8), from Babylon (Is 44:25), from Persia (Est 1:13, 6:13), etc.

e) As "prudent," (Prv 11:29, 16:14, 29:8).

f) As ethically and religiously "wise of mind," (Prv 10:8, 16:21).

3. 2 SAMUEL 18

BHS	וַיֶּחֱזַק רֹאשׁוֹ בָאֵלָה	9d
Ltrl	in the terebinth—his head—and it caught firm	
KJB	and his head caught hold of the oak,	
NASB	Then his head caught firmly in the oak,	
ESV	and his head caught fast in the oak,	
NLT	his hair got caught in the tree.	
NIV	hair got caught in the tree.	

1   וַיֶּחֱזַק Waw conversive + qal impf. 3ms of the verb חָזַק meaning, "to be or grow firm, to be strong, to be caught firm."

2   בָאֵלָה Prep. + noun, f. sg. meaning, "terebinth, oak." In Hebrew there is a distinction between the Palestine Oak and the terebinth.

3   This phrase dispels the popular legend that Absalom was caught by his hair, inspired by a reference to his coiffure (a person's hairstyle, typically an elaborate one) as described in 2 Sm 14:26.

4. 2 SAMUEL 23

BHS	וְאֵלֶּה דִּבְרֵי דָוִד הָאַחֲרֹנִים	1a
Ltrl	the last—David—the words of—and these	
KJB	Now these *be* the last words of David.	
NASB	Now these are the last words of David.	
ESV	Now these are the last words of David:	
NLT	These are the last words of David:	
NIV	These are the last words of David:	

1   הָאַחֲרֹנִים Definite article + adjective m. pl. meaning, "behind, hindermost, last."

BHS	נְאֻם דָּוִד בֶּן־יִשַׁי וּנְאֻם הַגֶּבֶר הֻקַם עָל	1b
Ltrl	up—be raised up—the man—and utterance—Jesse—son of—David—utterance of	
KJB	David the son of Jesse said, and the man *who was* raised up on high,	
NASB	David the son of Jesse declares, The man who was raised on high declares,	
ESV	The oracle of David, the son of Jesse, the oracle of the man who was raised on high,	
NLT	"David, the son of Jesse, speaks—David, the man who was raised up so high,	
NIV	The inspired utterance of David son of Jesse, the utterance of the man exalted by the Most High,	

1ᵃ "A Manuscript cited LXX Leningradensis Old Latin Versions 93, 94 (Lat a Heb) Syriac Peshitta Heb."

1. This footnote mentions the root אָמַן which (unlikely) can be pointed (given vowels) as the verb אָמַן which means, "to confirm, support," but could also be pointed as אָמֵן which is the adverb meaning, "verily, truly." It is also pointed as אֹמֶן which is a noun, m. sg. meaning, "faithfulness" which is alluded to by the Latin word *fidelis* in this footnote.

1ᵇ⁻ᵇ "Qumran Scrolls Heb."

1. In the Qumran Scrolls we find הקים אל which can be pointed (given vowels) as the hiph'il perf. 3ms of the verb קוּם followed by the name of God and then meaning, "raised up / exalted (by) God."

2. נְאֻם Qal part. passive m. sg. construct of the root נאם which then becomes a noun, m. sg. meaning, "utterance." Refer to Jer 29:11 in this volume.

3. הֻקַם Hoph'al perf. 3ms of the stem קוּם meaning, "be raised up."

BHS	מְשִׁיחַ אֱלֹהֵי יַעֲקֹב וּנְעִים זְמִרוֹת יִשְׂרָאֵל:	1c
Ltrl	Israel—psalmist of—and sweet—Jacob—the God of—the anointed of	
KJB	the anointed of the God of Jacob, and the sweet psalmist of Israel,	
NASB	The anointed of the God of Jacob, And the sweet psalmist of Israel,	
ESV	the anointed of the God of Jacob, the sweet psalmist of Israel:	
NLT	the man anointed by the God of Jacob, David, the sweet psalmist of Israel.	
NIV	the man anointed by the God of Jacob, the hero of Israel's songs:	

1. מְשִׁיחַ Noun, m. sg. cstr. meaning, "anointed one."

2. וּנְעִים Waw consecutive + adjective meaning, "and sweetly sounding." The phrase is then translated by some as, "Israel's sweet singer of songs."

3. זְמִרוֹת Noun, m. pl. cstr. meaning, "songs of . . ."

82.15   1 KINGS

1.   1 KINGS 19

BHS	וְאַחַר הָאֵשׁ קוֹל דְּמָמָה דַקָּה׃	12b
Ltrl	small / fine—whisper—a voice—the fire—and after	
KJB	and after the fire a still small voice.	
NASB	and after the fire a sound of a gentle blowing.	
ESV	And after the fire the sound of a low whisper.	
NLT	And after the fire there was the sound of a gentle whisper.	
NIV	And after the fire came a gentle whisper.	
CSB	And after the fire there was a voice, a soft whisper.	

12ᵃ "Septuagint Versions (Vulgate Manuscripts) add Grk."

1   The Greek Septuagint does indeed add κακεί κύριος meaning, "there was the LORD."

2   קוֹל Noun, m. sg. meaning, "sound, voice."

3   דְּמָמָה Noun, f. sg. meaning, "a whisper."

4   דַקָּה Adjective f. sg. from the adjective דַּק meaning, "thin, small, fine."

5   The Greek Septuagint has φωνή αὔρας λεπτῆς which literally means, "a sound breeze of a fine." More idiomatic it could mean, "a sound of a fine breeze."

6   There is no reason to believe, as a number of scholars do, that the "voice" is in the construct and coupled to the last two words. This results in, "the voice of a soft whisper."

7   The last two words are a noun followed by an attributive adjective. The correct and more dynamic equivalent of the actual MT would then be, "And after the fire, a voice, a fine whisper," as is found in the CSB translation for example.

BHS	תַּחְתֶּיךָ׃	16b
Ltrl	under you	
KJB	in thy room.	
NASB	in your place.	
ESV	in your place.	
NLT	to replace you	
NIV	to succeed you	

1   תַּחְתֶּיךָ׃ Prep. + suffix 2mp meaning, "under you."

2   Modern English translations imply that Elisha would replace Elijah fairly soon. But there is no indication of that in this verse.

3   In 2 Kgs 3:11 Elisha is identified as Elijah's personal servant.

2. 1 KINGS 20

BHS	וַיִּתְחַפֵּשׂ בָּאֲפֵרᵃ עַל־עֵינָיו:	38b
Ltrl	his eyes—on—with headgear—he disguised himself	
KJB	and disguised himself with ashes upon his face.	
WBT	and disguised himself with ashes upon his face.	
NASB	and disguised himself with a bandage over his eyes.	
ESV	disguising himself with a bandage over his eyes.	
NIV	He disguised himself with his headband down over his eyes.	

38ᵃ "LXX (Targums) Grk = Heb, SyP (Aquila's Greek Version Symmachus's Greek Version Vulgate) Syr = Heb."

1. In this footnote, two groups of external sources are mentioned that have different views on the garment mentioned in the MT.

2. וַיִּתְחַפֵּשׂ Waw conversive + Hithpa'el impf. 3ms of the verb חָפֵשׂ meaning, "to search" in the qal binyan, and "to disguise oneself" (literally, "to let oneself be searched for") in the hithpa'el binyan.

3. בָּאֲפֵר Inseparable preposition + noun, m. sg. meaning, "bandage, covering." In the Hebrew Bible, this noun appears only here and in verse 41.

4. The Greek word τελαμῶνι from the Septuagint as mentioned in this footnote means, "a ligature" (a thing used for tying or binding something tightly). The Hebrew word equated to the Greek in this footnote is the noun פְּאֵר meaning, "head-dress, headgear, turban" worn by men of position like priests (Ez 44:18). This garment is easily pulled over one's eyes, and could be removed quickly (verse 41).

5. The second group of sources mentioned in this footnote have בָּאֵפֶר which means, "with ashes." Only the KJB and WBT follow these sources.

82.16 2 KINGS

1. 2 KINGS 3

BHS	עָשֹׂה הַנַּחַל הַזֶּה גֵּבִים גֵּבִים:	16b
Ltrl	ditch—ditch—the this—the wadi—making	
KJB	Make this valley full of ditches.	
NASB	'Make this valley full of trenches.'	
ESV	'I will make this dry streambed full of pools.'	
NLT	This dry valley will be filled with pools of water!	
NIV	I will fill this valley with pools of water.	

1   "Wadi" (pl. wadis) is the Arabic term traditionally referring to a valley, ravine, channel or riverbed that is dry for almost all of the time. After heavy rains in their catchment areas, storm water will rush down them for a very short period of time, after which they will return to their dry state.

2   From the southern shores of the Sea of Galilee, southwards up to and including the shores of the Dead Sea, wadis are common in the mountains on the west bank of the river Jordan. Typically, they carry rainwater in the form of flash floods from their catchment areas on the highlands of Galilee, Samaria, and Judea down into the river Jordan.

3   The above-mentioned wadis are relatively narrow and steep and do not fit into the circumstances described in this passage. However, as the definition above indicates, a so-called "wadi" could be wide enough to be called a dry river. The areas known as Moab and Edom at the time of this incident, are situated on the east bank of the river Jordan opposite to Samaria and Judea. The mountains there are significantly lower than on the west bank, resulting in much more gradual gradients and as a result much wider wadis. This type of wadi would perfectly fit the circumstances described here. In addition, this latter location correlates well with the areas from where the warring parties in this narrative originated from.

4   Like rivers, in many instances wadis are also named locations. Some scholars are of the opinion that this incident took place at Wadi el-Aksy. Situated east of the Jordan, in the region of Moab and Edom, it runs into the Dead Sea near its extreme southeast corner. It is mentioned in Nm. 21:12 and Dt. 2:14 by the name Zered. In Is 15:7 it is called the "brook of the willows," and in Amos 6:14 the "river of the wilderness."

5   In this incident, the ditches were to gather the water, which otherwise would soon have run away in the torrent (Jer. 14:3–4). As was often the case with the miracles performed by Jesus, this miracle was accomplished by God utilizing commonly known natural phenomena, backed up by the originality of historic facts. However, the people had to take action and dig the trenches for the wonder to take place.

2. 2 KINGS 5

BHS	מַשָּׂא צֶמֶד־פְּרָדִים אֲדָמָה[b]	17b
Ltrl	earth—mules—pair of—loads	
KJB	two mules' burden of earth	
NASB	two mules' load of earth;	
ESV	two mule loads of earth,	
NLT	two of my mules with earth from this place,	
NIV	as much earth as a pair of mules can carry,	

17[b] "Lacking in the original Septuagint."

1   This footnote draws our attention to the text of the Greek Septuagint.

1   צֶמֶד Noun, m. sg. meaning, "couple, pair, span of oxen." In addition, it has the meaning of an area and is the only square measure in the Hebrew Bible. It was defined as "the area that a span of oxen could plough in one day."

2   פְּרָדִים Noun, m. pl. meaning, "mules." Refer to 1 Sm 14:14.

82.17 1 CHRONICLES

1. 1 CHRONICLES 4

BHS	וַיְהִ֣י יַעְבֵּ֔ץ נִכְבָּ֖ד מֵאֶחָ֑יו וְאִמּ֗וֹ קָרְאָ֨ה שְׁמ֤וֹ יַעְבֵּץ֙	9a
Ltrl	—and his mother—than his brothers—more honorable—Jabez—and he was Jabez—his name—she called	
KJB	And Jabez was more honorable than his brethren: and his mother called his name Jabez,	
NASB	Jabez was more honorable than his brothers, and his mother named him Jabez	
ESV	Jabez was more honorable than his brothers; and his mother called his name Jabez,	
NLT	Jabez who was more honorable than any of his brothers. His mother named him Jabez	
NIV	Jabez was more honorable than his brothers. His mother had named him Jabez,	

BHS	לֵאמֹ֔ר כִּ֥י יָלַ֖דְתִּי בְּעֹֽצֶב׃ᵃ	9b
Ltrl	in sorrow—I gave birth—because—saying	
KJB	saying, Because I bare him with sorrow.	
NASB	saying, "Because I bore him with pain."	
ESV	saying, "Because I bore him in pain."	
NLT	because his birth had been so painful.	
NIV	saying, "I gave birth to him in pain."	

9ᵃ "LXX Grk."

1 As the Greek words in this footnote do not appear in the Greek Septuagint, it is not clear what is meant.

BHS	וַיִּקְרָ֣א יַעְבֵּ֗ץ לֵאלֹהֵ֤י יִשְׂרָאֵל֙ לֵאמֹ֔ר	10a
Ltrl	saying—Israel—to the God(s) of—Jabez—and he called	
KJB	And Jabez called on the God of Israel, saying,	
NASB	Now Jabez called on the God of Israel, saying,	
ESV	Jabez called upon the God of Israel, saying,	
NLT	He was the one who prayed to the God of Israel,	
NIV	Jabez cried out to the God of Israel,	

Selected Passages

BHS	אִם־בָּרֵךְ תְּבָרֲכֵנִי וְהִרְבִּיתָ אֶת־גְּבוּלִי	10b
Ltrl	my border—DDOM—and you will enlarge—you will bless me—indeed bless—that	
KJB	Oh that thou wouldest bless me indeed, and enlarge my coast,	
NASB	"Oh that You would bless me indeed and enlarge my border,	
ESV	"Oh that you would bless me and enlarge my border,	
NLT	"Oh, that you would bless me and expand my territory!	
NIV	"Oh, that you would bless me and enlarge my territory!	

BHS	וְהָיְתָה יָדְךָ עִמִּי וְעָשִׂיתָ מֵּרָעָהᵇ	10c
Ltrl	from evil—and you will keep (me)—with me—your hand—and it will be	
KJB	and that thine hand might be with me, and that thou wouldest keep me from evil,	
NASB	and that Your hand might be with me, and that You would keep me from harm	
ESV	and that your hand might be with me, and that you would keep me from harm	
NLT	Please be with me in all that I do, and keep me from all trouble	
NIV	Let your hand be with me, and keep me from harm	

10ᵃ "Insert Heb (haplography)? compare Is 26:18."

1. This footnote states that we should insert the word that was probably omitted erroneously as a result of a haplography. The word is יְשׁוּעָתִי which is a noun, f. sg. with a 1cs pronominal suffix meaning, "my salvation, deliverance" (see also Ps 62:2).

10ᵇ "Thus Leningradensis, multiple (20–60) Manuscripts Editions Heb."

1. This footnote mentions many sources that do not have the DF in the mem. This is a reasonable suggestion as there is no need for the DF here.

BHS	לְבִלְתִּי עָצְבִּי וַיָּבֵא אֱלֹהִים אֵת אֲשֶׁר־שָׁאָל׃	10d
Ltrl	he asked—what—DDOM—God—and he granted—that it may pain me—that not	
KJB	that it may not grieve me! And God granted him that which he requested.	
NASB	that it may not pain me!" And God granted him what he requested.	
ESV	so that it might not bring me pain!" And God granted what he asked.	
NLT	and pain!" And God granted him his request.	
NIV	so that I will be free from pain." And God granted his request.	

1. עָצְבִּי Qal infinitive construct + 1cs suffix of the verb עָצַב meaning, "to hurt, pain, grieve."

82.18 2 CHRONICLES

1. 2 CHRONICLES 6

1	אָז אָמַר שְׁלֹמֹה יְהוָה אָמַר לִשְׁכּוֹן בָּעֲרָפֶֽל׃ªֿ	BHS
	in the heavy cloud—to dwell—he said—Yahweh—Solomon—he said—then	Ltrl
	Then said Solomon, The LORD hath said that he would dwell in the thick darkness.	KJB
	Then Solomon said, "The LORD has said that He would dwell in the thick cloud.	NASB
	Then Solomon said, "The LORD has said that he would dwell in thick darkness.	ESV
	Then Solomon prayed, "O LORD, you have said that you would live in a thick cloud of darkness.	NLT
	Then Solomon said, "The LORD has said that he would dwell in a dark cloud;	NIV

1ª⁻ª "Thus compare 1 Kgs 8:12."

1 Actually, large parts of 2 Chr 1–6 are repetitions of parts of 1 Kgs 5–8.

2 לִשְׁכּוֹן Inseparable preposition + qal infinitive absolute of the verb שָׁכַן / שָׁכֵן meaning, "to settle down, abide, dwell."

3 בָּעֲרָפֶל Inseparable preposition + definite article + noun, m. sg. meaning, "cloud, heavy cloud."

2	וַאֲנִיª בָּנִיתִי בֵית־זְבֻל לָךְ וּמָכוֹן לְשִׁבְתְּךָ עוֹלָמִֽים׃	BHS
	forever—for you to dwell—and a place—for you—exalted—a house of—I built—and I	Ltrl
	But I have built an house of habitation for thee, and a place for thy dwelling for ever.	KJB
	"I have built You a lofty house, And a place for Your dwelling forever."	NASB
	But I have built you an exalted house, a place for you to dwell in forever."	ESV
	Now I have built a glorious Temple for you, a place where you can live forever!"	NLT
	I have built a magnificent temple for you, a place for you to dwell forever."	NIV

2ª "1 Kgs 8:13 Heb."

1 1 Kgs 8:13 starts with the words בָּנֹה בָנִיתִי and a footnote that points out that here the original Greek Septuagint is similar to the MT. The words are the qal infinitive absolute followed by the qal perf. 1cs of the same verb בָּנָה and together means, "I will surely build," as apposed to the "And I built" in the MT.

2 עוֹלָמִים From the singular noun meaning, "long duration, antiquity," this plural form means, "forever, always."

2. 2 CHRONICLES 36

BHS	בֶּן־שְׁמוֹנֶהˣ שָׁנִים יְהוֹיָכִין בְּמָלְכוֹ	9a
Ltrl	when his reign (began)—Jehoiachin—years—eight—son (old)	
KJB	Jehoiachin was eight years old when he began to reign,	
NASB	Jehoiachin was eighteen years old when he became king,	
ESV	Jehoiachin was eighteen years old when he became king,	
NLT	Jehoiachin was eighteen years old when he became king,	
NIV	Jehoiachin was eighteen years old when he became king,	

9a "Insert with one Manuscript LXX and 2 Kgs 24:8 and 3 Ezr 1:41 LXX Heb compare with c-c."

1 This footnote suggest that we insert עֶשְׂרֵת which means, "ten." This would then agree with some versions of the LXX, and also with 2 Kgs 24:8 which has בֶּן־שְׁמֹנֶה עֶשְׂרֵה שָׁנָה meaning, "son (old) eight ten year."

2 Except for KJV, all other major English translations follow the footnote's suggestion.

3 To motivate this they refer to 2 Kgs 24:15 which states that he had "wives," and to Jer 22:38 which states that he had "seed."

82.19 EZRA

1. EZRA 6

BHS	וְשֵׁיצִיאˣ בַּיְתָה דְנָה עַד יוֹם תְּלָתָהˣ לִירַח אֲדָר	15a
Ltrl	Adar—for month of—three—day—on—this—house—and it was finished	
KJB	And this house was finished on the third day of the month Adar,	
NASB	This temple was completed on the third day of the month Adar;	
ESV	and this house was finished on the third day of the month of Adar,	
NLT	The Temple was completed on March 12,	
NIV	The temple was completed on the third day of the month Adar,	

15a "LXX 7:5 correctly (verse) 23."

1 This footnote is not at all clear.

2 וְשֵׁיצִיא This is an Aramaic (Chaldean) word. Chaldean is an old name for the Aramaic language, particularly Biblical Aramaic. Chaldean has a binyan called *shapel* in which the consonant shin and a vowel is prefixed onto the verb. The Chaldean verb is close to the Hebrew verb יָצָא meaning, "go / come out" and here means, "bring out (to an end), = finish."

3 דְנָה Chaldean demonstrative pronoun emphatic, "this."

4 תִּלְתָה Chaldean cardinal number m. sg. from the f.sg. תְּלָת.

5 לִירַח Inseparable preposition + noun, m. sg.

BHS	דִּי־הִיא שְׁנַת־שֵׁת לְמַלְכוּת דָּרְיָוֶשׁ מַלְכָּא׃ פ	15b
Ltrl	king—Darius—the reign of—six—year—it—which	
KJB	which was in the sixth year of the reign of Darius the king.	
NASB	it was the sixth year of the reign of King Darius.	
ESV	in the sixth year of the reign of Darius the king.	
NLT	during the sixth year of King Darius's reign.	
NIV	in the sixth year of the reign of King Darius.	

1 דִּי Chaldean particle of relation meaning, "who, which."

1 מַלְכָּא Chaldean noun, m. sg. meaning, "king."

2. EZRA 7

BHS	הוּא עֶזְרָא עָלָה מִבָּבֶל	6
Ltrl	from Babylon—he went up—Ezra—this	
KJB	This Ezra went up from Babylon;	
NASB	This Ezra went up from Babylon,	
ESV	this Ezra went up from Babylonia.	
NIV	this Ezra came up from Babylon.	

1 עָזַר This verb means, "to help, succor (assist in time of distress)."

2 The name "Ezra" appears 22 times in the Ezra-Nehemiah book in the Hebrew Bible.

82.20 NEHEMIAH

1. NEHEMIAH 1

BHS	דִּבְרֵי נְחֶמְיָה בֶּן־חֲכַלְיָה[a]	1
Ltrl	Hacaliah—son of—Nehemiah—the words of	
KJB	The words of Nehemiah the son of Hachaliah.	
NASB	The words of Nehemiah the son of Hacaliah.	
ESV	The words of Nehemiah the son of Hacaliah.	
NLT	These are the memoirs of Nehemiah son of Hacaliah.	
NIV	The words of Nehemiah son of Hakaliah:	

1[a] "LXX[BL] (SyP Vulgate) Grk."

1   These versions have a name that differs from the standard Greek Septuagint.

2   The verb root נחם means, "to be sorry" or "to console oneself." It appears only in the niph'al and pi'el binyamin. In the pi'el binyan it means, "to comfort, console."

3   Keeping the above verb in mind, the literal translation of the name "Nehemiah" would then be, "Yah comforts" (Chapter 87.3.1).

2. NEHEMIAH 2

BHS	וָאֶתְפַּלֵּל אֶל־אֱלֹהֵי הַשָּׁמָיִם׃	4
Ltrl	the heavens—God of—to—and I prayed	
KJB	So I prayed to the God of heaven.	
NASB	So I prayed to the God of heaven.	
ESV	So I prayed to the God of heaven.	
NLT	With a prayer to the God of heaven,	
NIV	Then I prayed to the God of heaven,	

1   וָאֶתְפַּלֵּל Waw conversive + hithpa'el impf. 1cs of the verb פלל meaning, "to intervene, interpose, intercede," and in the hithpa'el, "to pray." The Hithpa'el paradigm is used to express an intensive type of action with a reflexive (or sometimes passive) voice.

2   Afrikaans has two major Bible translations. The first was published in 1933 and revised in 1953. This was, for the most part, a literal translation of the Leningrad Codex of the MT. It was deliberately translated in old-fashioned language that resembled the Old Dutch *Statenvertaling* (1637), to prevent it from being rejected by Christians who were used to using the Dutch translation. In order to mark the 50th anniversary of the original 1933 translation and provide much needed revision, a more dynamic equivalence translation was published in 1983, which, in addition to the MT, also took additional sources, like the Greek Septuagint and the Qumran scrolls for example, into account. To this day, this translation is being rejected by the more conservative Afrikaans-speaking public and academics.

3   Here in Neh 2:4 for example, the 1933 translation follows the MT literally (as does the KJB and most English translations) and translates the verb simply as, "I prayed." However, in the 1983 translation it uses the Afrikaans word "skietgebed" which describes a spontaneous prayer, made out of desperation in an emergency. The prayer is most often not spoken out aloud, and the hithpa'el form of the verb might have contributed to the view that this was more of a prayer to oneself. In English, the New English Translation (NET) (2005) is notable as it uses "I quickly prayed."

3. NEHEMIAH 4

BHS	אֵין־אֲנַחְנוּ פֹשְׁטִים בְּגָדֵינוּ אִישׁ שִׁלְחוֹ הַמָּֽיִם׃[b]	17d
Ltrl	the water—his weapon—a man—our clothes—strip off—us—none of	
KJB	none of us put off our clothes, saving that every one put them off for washing.	
NASB	none of us removed our clothes, each took his weapon even to the water.	
ESV	none of us took off our clothes; each kept his weapon at his right hand.	
NIV	took off our clothes; each had his weapon, even when he went for water.	

17[b] "Dubious; it has been proposed Heb, the original LXX omits Heb."

1. The editors of BHS are of the opinion that this form is dubious, and therefore deemed it necessary to include this footnote. The Greek Septuagint does not support this view.

2. הֵימִינוּ This form that is suggested in this footnote, would be the hiph'il infinitive construct of the verb יָמַן with a 1cp suffix which then means, "we choose / use the right hand."

3. The Apostolic Bible Polyglot (ABP)[21] does not omit the last two words as—according to this footnote—the original Greek Septuagint does. The ABP reads, ανήρ και όπλον αυτού εις το ύδωρα meaning, "a man and his weapons into the water."

82.21 ESTHER

1. ESTHER 2

BHS	וַיְהִי אֹמֵן אֶת־הֲדַסָּה הִיא אֶסְתֵּר בַּת־דֹּדוֹ[a]	7a
Ltrl	his uncle—daughter of—Esther—she—Hadassah—DDOM—he supported—and it was	
KJB	And he brought up Hadassah, that is, Esther, his uncle's daughter:	
NASB	He was bringing up Hadassah, that is Esther, his uncle's daughter,	
ESV	He was bringing up Hadassah, that is Esther, the daughter of his uncle,	
NIV	Mordecai had a cousin named Hadassah, whom he had brought up	

7[a] "LXX additional information Grk refer to (verse) 15 (and) 9:29."

1. The word Αμιναδάβ mentioned in this footnote does appear in Ru 4:19 for example, but not in any of the verses mentioned by the footnote. However, in those verses (2:15 and 9:29) of the Greek Septuagint, we do find the word Αβιχάϊλ but not here in this verse.

2. אֹמֵן Qal part. active m. sg. of אָמַן meaning, "to support, nourish."

3. הֲדַסָּה This was the Hebrew name of the girl who was known as "Esther" in the city Shushan, the capital of Persia. It stems from הֲדַס meaning, "myrtle tree."

---

21 Hattingh, Tian (2012), p. 210.

4   The name "Esther" possibly means, "star" in Persian. Alternatively it could be a derivative of the name of the Near Eastern goddess Ishtar.

5   The name "Esther" occurs 55 times in this book, and nowhere else in the Hebrew Bible.

2. ESTHER 4

BHS	וּמִי יוֹדֵעַ אִם־לְעֵת כָּזֹאת הִגַּעַתְּ לַמַּלְכוּת׃	14c
Ltrl	to the kingdom—you arrived—as this—for a time—if—knows—and who	
KJB	and who knoweth whether thou art come to the kingdom for such a time as this?	
NASB	And who knows whether you have not attained royalty for such a time as this?"	
ESV	And who knows whether you have not come to the kingdom for such a time as this?"	
NLT	Who knows if perhaps you were made queen for just such a time as this?"	
NIV	And who knows but that you have come to your royal position for such a time as this?"	

1   יוֹדֵעַ Qal part. active m. sg. Of the verb יָדַע meaning, "to know."

2   לְעֵת Inseparable preposition + noun, f. sg. meaning, "time."

3   הִגַּעַתְּ Hiph'il perf. 2fs of the verb נָגַע which in the hiph'il binyan means, "to cause to touch, to reach, to approach, to arrive."

82.22 JOB

1. JOB 1

BHS	אִישׁ הָיָה בְאֶרֶץ־עוּץ אִיּוֹב שְׁמוֹ	1
Ltrl	his name—Job—Uz—in the land of—he was—a man	
KJB	There was a man in the land of Uz, whose name was Job;	
NASB	There was a man in the land of Uz whose name was Job;	
ESV	There was a man in the land of Uz whose name was Job,	
NLT	There once was a man named Job who lived in the land of Uz.	
NIV	In the land of Uz there lived a man whose name was Job.	

1   The meaning of the name "Job" is unknown.

2. JOB 9

BHS	כְּנֶשֶׁר יָטוּשׂ עֲלֵי־אֹכֶל׃	26b
Ltrl	prey—on—he swoops—as an eagle	
KJB	as the eagle that hasteth to the prey.	
NASB	Like an eagle that swoops on its prey.	
ESV	like an eagle swooping on the prey.	
NLT	like an eagle swooping down on its prey.	
NIV	like eagles swooping down on their prey.	

1. יָטוּשׂ Qal impf. 3ms of the root טושׂ meaning, "to rush, dart." This is the only occurrence of this root in the Hebrew Bible (Chapter 83.3.2).

3. JOB 10

BHS	וְכַגְּבִנָּה תַּקְפִּיאֵנִי׃	10b
Ltrl	curdle me—and like cheese	
KJB	and curdled me like cheese?	
NASB	And curdle me like cheese;	
ESV	and curdle me like cheese?	
NLT	and formed me in the womb.	
NIV	and curdle me like cheese,	

1. תַּקְפִּיאֵנִי Hiph'il impf. 2ms + 1cs suffix of the verb קָפָא which in the qal banyan means, "to thicken, condense, congeal," and in the hiph'il means, "curdle" (cause something to separate into curds or lumps).

2. וְכַגְּבִנָּה Waw consecutive + prep. + noun, f. sg. The word has become extremely common in modern Hebrew where it means, "cheese." However, in the MT it does not say what the end product of the curding would be.

3. This is an example of a *hapax legomenon* (a word that is found only once in a body of work like the Hebrew Bible). It has no connection to any other verb root, making it impossible to ascertain with certainty what the original author meant.

4. JOB 15

BHS	נֹדֵד הוּא לַלֶּחֶם אַיֵּה	23a
Ltrl	where—for bread—he—a wanderer	
KJB	He wandereth abroad for bread,	
NASB	"He wanders about for food,	
ESV	He wanders abroad for bread,	
NIV	He wanders about for food like a vulture;	

1   The word אַיֵּה meaning, "where," is similar to the word אַיָּה found in Job 28:7 and meaning, "hawk, falcon, kite." KJB has translated it as a "vulture" which does not seem correct when compared to other occurrences in the Hebrew Bible (Chapter 83.3.4).

5. JOB 16

BHS	יָרֻץ עָלַי כְּגִבּוֹר:	14b
Ltrl	like a mighty man of valour—unto me—he will run	
KJB	he runneth upon me like a giant.	
WEB	He runs on me like a giant.	
NASB	He runs at me like a warrior.	
ESV	he runs upon me like a warrior.	
NIV	he rushes at me like a warrior.	
NLT	charging at me like a warrior.	

1   יָרֻץ Qal impf. 3ms of the verb רוּץ meaning, "to run."

2   כְּגִבּוֹר Prep. + noun, m. sg. abs. meaning, "a strong and valiant man." It does not mean, "giant." Also refer to Is 9:5a.

6. JOB 20

BHS	כְּגֶלֲלוֹ לָנֶצַח יֹאבֵד	7a
Ltrl	he will perish—forever—as his excrement	
KJB	Yet he shall perish for ever like his own dung:	
NASB	He perishes forever like his refuse;	
ESV	he will perish forever like his own dung;	
NLT	yet they will vanish forever, thrown away like their own dung.	
NIV	he will perish forever, like his own dung;	

1   כְּגֶלֲלוֹ Prep. + noun, m. sg. There are two spellings of the noun namely גָּלָל and גֵּל. It appears only four times in the Hebrew Bible, with different meanings determined by the context.

   a)   In Zep 1:17 as, "animal dung" or "rubbish, refuse."

   b)   In 1 Kgs 14:10 as, "rubbish, refuse."

   c)   Refer to Ez 4:12 in Chapter 82.29.

   d)   Refer to Ez 4:15 in Chapter 82.29.

7. JOB 24

BHS	מַדּוּעַ מִשַּׁדַּי לֹא־נִצְפְּנוּ עִתִּים	1a
Ltrl	times—they are stored up—not—from Shaddai—wherefore	
KJB	Why, seeing times are not hidden from the Almighty	
NASB	"Why are times not stored up by the Almighty,	
ESV	"Why are not times of judgment kept by the Almighty,	
NLT	"Why doesn't the Almighty bring the wicked to judgment?	
NIV	"Why does the Almighty not set times for judgment?	

1 מַדּוּעַ It is possible that this could consist of מַה־יָדוּעַ literally meaning, "what being known?" in other words, "from what motive?"

2 נִצְפְּנוּ Niph'al perf. 3mp of the root צפן which in the qal binyan means, "to hide," or "to treasure up." In the niph'al binyan it means, "to be stored up."

3 עֵת A feminine noun with the basic meaning, "time." Here it has an irregular plural as found in 1 Chr 12:33. This noun is often used to indicate a time of judgment (end), as in for example, the end of Babylon in Is 13:22, the end of a city or the city of Jerusalem in Ez 22:3, the end of a land in Jer 27:7, of the final punishment of a man in Ez 21:30, 34.

4 Refer to Chapter 85.3.1 for a discussion of the name Shaddai

8. JOB 28

BHS	נָתִיב לֹא־יְדָעוֹ עָיִט וְלֹא שְׁזָפַתּוּ עֵין אַיָּה׃	7
Ltrl	falcon—eye of—he has seen it—and not—bird of prey—he knows it—not—a path	
KJB	There is a path which no fowl knoweth, and which the vulture's eye hath not seen:	
NASB	"The path no bird of prey knows, Nor has the falcon's eye caught sight of it.	
ESV	"That path no bird of prey knows, and the falcon's eye has not seen it.	
NLT	These are treasures no bird of prey can see, no falcon's eye observe.	
NIV	No bird of prey knows that hidden path, no falcon's eye has seen it.	

1 עִיט Qal impf. 3ms meaning, "to scream, shriek." This verb occurs only in 1 Sm 25:14 and is closely related to עַיִט which is used as a generic term for "birds of prey," and occurs four other times namely, Gen 15:11, Jer 12:9, Is 18:6, and Ez 39:4 (Chapter 83.3.4).

BHS	לֹא־יַעַרְכֶנָּה זָהָב וּזְכוֹכִית	17a
Ltrl	and crystal—gold—it will compare with—not	
KJB	The gold and the crystal cannot equal it:	
NASB	"Gold or glass cannot equal it,	
ESV	Gold and glass cannot equal it,	
NLT	Wisdom is more valuable than gold and crystal.	
NIV	Neither gold nor crystal can compare with it,	

1 יַעַרְכֶנָּה Qal impf. 3fs of the verb עָרַךְ meaning, "to compare, arrange, set in order."

2 וּזְכוֹכִית Waw conjunctive + noun, f. sg. The word derives from the verb root זָכָה meaning, "to be clear, clean, pure." This has led many to translate it as "glass" as in modern Hebrew. However, this is an example of a *hapax legomenon* (a word that is found only once in a body of work like the Hebrew Bible). It has no connection to any other verb root, making it impossible to ascertain with certainty what the original author meant.

9. JOB 30

BHS	אָח הָיִיתִי לְתַנִּים וְרֵעַ לִבְנוֹת יַעֲנָה:	29
Ltrl	an ostrich—to daughters of—and a companion—to ostriches—I am—a brother	
KJB	I am a brother to dragons, and a companion to owls.	
NASB	"I have become a brother to jackals And a companion of ostriches.	
ESV	I am a brother of jackals and a companion of ostriches.	
NLT	Instead, I am considered a brother to jackals and a companion to owls.	
NIV	I have become a brother of jackals, a companion of owls.	

1 לְתַנִּים This is often seen as an erroneous form of תַּנִּין meaning, "serpent, dragon, sea-monster." However, from many instances like Mi 1:8 and Is 13:22 it clearly means a well-know animal known for its mournful howling.[22]

2 לִבְנוֹת In this form, this word occurs only here and in Nm 36:6, and Is 34:13.

3 Refer to Chapter 83.2.1.

---

22 Merriam-Webster.com Dictionary, s.v. "Azazel," accessed February 13, 2021, https://www.merriam-webster.com/dictionary/Azazel.

10. JOB 38

BHS	מִי־שָׁת בַּטֻּחוֹת חָכְמָה אוֹ מִי־נָתַן לַשֶּׂכְוִי בִינָה:	36
Ltrl	—he gave—who—or—wisdom—in the inner parts—he has placed–who understanding—to the rooster	
KJB	Who hath put wisdom in the inward parts? or who hath given understanding to the heart?	
NASB	"Who has put wisdom in the innermost being Or given understanding to the mind?	
ESV	Who has put wisdom in the inward parts or given understanding to the mind?	
NLT	Who gives intuition to the heart and instinct to the mind?	
NIV	Who gives the ibis wisdom or gives the rooster understanding?	

1. שָׁת Qal perf. 3ms of the verb שִׁית "to put, set (Chapter 83.4.4)."

2. The mentioning of an "ibis" in the NIV is probably because of the mentioning of the "rooster" in the second part of the verse. The Egyptians worshipped the sacred ibis as the god Thoth, which was responsible for maintaining the universe, judging the dead, and overseeing systems of magic, writing, and science. It was seen as wise in that it could forecast the annual flooding of the Nile (Hattingh [2012], p. 179).

3. Refer to Ps 51:8.

BHS	מִי יָכִין לָעֹרֵב צֵידוֹ	41a
Ltrl	his prey—for the raven—he will provide—who	
KJB	Who provideth for the raven his food?	
NASB	"Who prepares for the raven its nourishment	
ESV	Who provides for the raven its prey,	
NLT	Who provides food for the ravens	
NIV	Who provides food for the raven	

1. יָכִין Hiph'il impf. 3ms of the root כּוּן which means, "to provide for" in the hiph'il binyan (Chapter 83.7.3).

2. From the verb צוּד "to hunt," we find the masculine noun צַיִד "hunting, game." Here we have the construct form of the noun with a 3ms suffix meaning, "his hunt." We could paraphrase the implication by saying, "Who will provide the food needed by him when the raven is hunting?"

11. JOB 39

BHS	כְּנַף־רְנָנִים נֶעֱלָסָה	13a
Ltrl	she flaps joyously—female ostrich—a wing	
NKJV	The wings of the ostrich wave proudly	
NASB	"The ostriches' wings flap joyously	
ESV	"The wings of the ostrich wave proudly,	
NLT	"The ostrich flaps her wings grandly,	
NIV	The wings of the ostrich flap joyfully,	

1 נֶעֱלָסָה Niph'al perf. 3fs of the verb עָלַס meaning, "to rejoice" in the qal binyan. It occurs only here and in Jb 20:18 and Prv 7:18. In the niph'al binyan and in this context it takes on the meaning, "to flap joyously" (Chapter 83.2.1.3).

BHS	הֲמִבִּינָתְךָ יַאֲבֶר־נֵץ	26a
Ltrl	a hawk—he will fly—does by your wisdom	
KJB	Doth the hawk fly by thy wisdom,	
NASB	"Is it by your understanding that the hawk soars,	
ESV	"Is it by your understanding that the hawk soars	
NLT	"Is it your wisdom that makes the hawk soar	
NIV	Does the hawk take flight by your wisdom	

1 יַאֲבֶר This verb only occurs here in the Hebrew Bible and is derived from the m. noun אֵבֶר meaning, "pinions," which is the outer part of a bird's wing. It includes the flight feathers that essentially enables a bird to fly (Chapter 83.3.5).

BHS	אִם־עַל־פִּיךָ יַגְבִּיהַּ נָשֶׁר וְכִי יָרִים קִנּוֹ׃	27
Ltrl	his nest—make on high—and thus—an eagle—he will soar—your command—at	
KJB	Doth the eagle mount up at thy command, and make her nest on high?	
NASB	"Is it at your command that the eagle mounts up And makes his nest on high?	
ESV	Is it at your command that the eagle mounts up and makes his nest on high?	
NLT	Is it at your command that the eagle rises to the heights to make its nest?	
NIV	Does the eagle soar at your command and build its nest on high?	

1 יַגְבִּיהַּ Hiph'il impf. 3ms of the root גבה which in the qal binyan means, "to be high," or "to be exalted." In the hiph'il binyan it takes on the meaning of "soar aloft," or "make their flight high" (Chapter 83.3.2).

82.23 PSALMS

1. PSALM 1

BHS	אַשְׁרֵי־הָאִישׁ אֲשֶׁר לֹא הָלַךְ בַּעֲצַת־רְשָׁעִים	1a
Ltrl	wicked ones—in the council of—he walks—not—that—the man—blessedness of	
KJB	Blessed is the man that walketh not in the counsel of the ungodly	
NASB	How blessed is the man who does not walk in the counsel of the wicked,	
ESV	Blessed is the man who walks not in the counsel of the wicked,	
NLT	Oh, the joys of those who do not follow the advice of the wicked,	
NIV	Blessed is the one who does not walk in step with the wicked	

1ª "Numerous lacking information Leningrad Codex."

1   According to the footnote, this word does not appear in the Leningrad Codex,.and the word mentioned in footnote 1ᵇ and this one are in reverse order.

2   עֲצַת is the construct form of the feminine noun עֵצָה meaning, "council," "advice" from the verb יָעַץ meaning, "to advise" or "to counsel." The root meaning also contains something like, "machinations" or "plottting," "conspire," "syncing up with."

BHS	וּבְדֶרֶךְ חַטָּאִים לֹא עָמָד וּבְמוֹשַׁב לֵצִים לֹא יָשָׁב׃	1b
Ltrl	and in the sitting company—he stands,—not—sinful ones—and in the path of he sits—not—scornful ones	
KJB	nor standeth in the way of sinners, nor sitteth in the seat of the scornful.	
NASB	Nor stand in the path of sinners, Nor sit in the seat of scoffers!	
ESV	nor stands in the way of sinners, nor sits in the seat of scoffers;	
NLT	or stand around with sinners, or join in with mockers.	
NIV	or stand in the way that sinners take or sit in the company of mockers,	

1ᵃ·ᵇ "SyP in reverse order."

1   In the SyP the word marked in footnote ᵃ and this word are in reverse order. This is not the case in the Greek Septuagint, the Aleppo Codex or the Latin Vulgate.

BHS	כִּי אִם בְּתוֹרַת יְהוָה חֶפְצוֹ	2a
Ltrl	his delight / pleasure—YHWH—in the law of—but	
KJB	But his delight is in the law of the LORD;	
NASB	But his delight is in the law of the LORD,	
ESV	but his delight is in the law of the LORD	
NLT	But they delight in the law of the LORD,	
NIV	but whose delight is in the law of the LORD,	

BHS	וּבְתוֹרָתוֹ יֶהְגֶּה יוֹמָם וָלָיְלָה:	2b
Ltrl	and night—day—he will muse / meditate—and in his law	
KJB	and in his law doth he meditate day and night.	
NASB	And in His law he meditates day and night.	
ESV	and on his law he meditates day and night.	
NLT	meditating on it day and night.	
NIV	and who meditates on his law day and night.	

1   יֶהְגֶּה Qal impf. 3ms of the verb הָגָה meaning, "to moan, growl, utter, speak, muse, consider something thoughtfully." In Is 31:4 it is used to describe the growling of a lion over its prey. Some scholars associate the protective stance of the lion at its prey to the attitude of the man meditating on the Law.

2   יוֹמָם is a Chaldean (Neo-Aramaic) term, that resembles the Hebrew word for "day" with a 3mp pronominal suffix. It is used in biblical Hebrew as the singular absolute noun.

BHS	וְהָיָה כְּעֵץ שָׁתוּל עַל־פַּלְגֵי מָיִם	3a
Ltrl	water—canals of—on—transplanted—like a tree—and he will be	
KJB	He is like a tree planted beside flowing streams	
NASB	He will be like a tree firmly planted by streams of water,	
ESV	He is like a tree planted by streams of water	
NLT	They are like trees planted along the riverbank,	
NIV	That person is like a tree planted by streams of water,	
LXX	An he will be as the tree being planted by the outlet of the waters	
Vulg	And he shall be like a tree which is planted near the running waters	

1   שָׁתוּל Qal part. pass. of the verb שָׁתַל meaning, "to transplant." This verb occurs 10 times in the Hebrew Bible, and is always (incorrectly) translated as "plant" in modern English translations.

2   Refer to Ps 92:13; Jer 17:8; Ez 17:8, 10, 22, 23, 19:10, 13; Hos 9:13.

3   The Segholate noun פֶּלֶג literally means, "channel" or "artificial canal" and appears 10 times in the Hebrew Bible. In this metaphor, a stream would emphasize the abundance of water, whereas the image of a man-made irrigating canal or channel would add the concept of a reliant source. In Ps 46:5 we find "a river whose streams," suggesting an irrigation canal that was dug by a farmer (God) and leading from a river to his fields.

4   Refer to Jb 29:6; Ps 46:4, 65:9, 119:136; Prv 5:16, 21:1; Is 30:25, 32:2; Lam 3:48.

BHS	אֲשֶׁ֤ר פִּרְיֽוֹ ׀ יִתֵּ֬ן בְּעִתּ֗וֹ וְעָלֵ֥הוּ לֹֽא־יִבּ֑וֹל	3b
Ltrl	it will wither—not—and it's leaf—in his usual time—he will give—his fruit—that	
KJB	that bears its fruit in its season and whose leaf does not wither.	
NASB	Which yields its fruit in its season And its leaf does not wither;	
ESV	that yields its fruit in its season, and its leaf does not wither.	
NLT	bearing fruit each season. Their leaves never wither,	
NIV	which yields its fruit in season and whose leaf does not wither—	

3ª "Lacking information (in the) Targumim." The MT makes perfect sense.

1   יִבּוֹל The qal impf. 3ms of the verb נָבֵל meaning, "to sink down, drop down, fall, fade, languish, wither."

BHS	וְכֹ֖ל אֲשֶׁר־יַעֲשֶׂ֣ה יַצְלִֽיחַ׃	3c
Ltrl	it will prosper / be successful—he will do,—that—all—and	
KJB	Whatever he does prospers.	
NASB	And in whatever he does, he prospers.	
ESV	In all that he does, he prospers.	
NLT	and they prosper in all they do.	
NIV	whatever they do prospers.	

3ᵇ⁻ᵇ "Gloss, compare Js 1:8."

1   This footnote is of the opinion that this sentence is a gloss that was meant to expand on the previous sentence. In Js 1:8 it literally states, "for then you will make prosperous your way, then you will have good success."

2   **gloss**: A foreign word or sentence, in Hebrew characters, inserted in Hebrew writings. In order to convey to the reader the exact meaning of a Biblical word or sentence not easily explained in Hebrew.

BHS	לֹא־כֵ֥ן הָרְשָׁעִ֑ים כִּ֥י אִם־כַּ֝מֹּ֗ץ אֲֽשֶׁר־תִּדְּפֶ֥נּוּ רֽוּחַ׃	4a
Ltrl	the wind—she will drive away us—that—like chaff—but—the wicked ones—so—not	
KJB	The ungodly are not so: but are like the chaff which the wind driveth away.	
NASB	The wicked are not so, But they are like chaff which the wind drives away.	
ESV	The wicked are not so, but are like chaff that the wind drives away.	
NLT	But not the wicked! They are like worthless chaff, scattered by the wind.	
NIV	Not so the wicked! They are like chaff that the wind blows away.	

4ª "Insert Heb, compare the LXX."

1   This footnote is correct in stating that the Septuagint does repeat the phrase לֹא־כֵן.

4ᵇ "LXX adds Grk."

1   The Greek Septuagint does indeed add *ἀπὸ προσώπου τῆς γῆς* meaning, "from the face of the earth."

BHS	עַל־כֵּן לֹא־יָקֻמוּ רְשָׁעִים בַּמִּשְׁפָּט	5a
Ltrl	in the judgment—wicked (ones)—they will stand—not—so—upon	
KJB	Therefore the ungodly shall not stand in the judgment,	
NASB	Therefore the wicked will not stand in the judgment,	
ESV	Therefore the wicked will not stand in the judgment,	
NLT	They will be condemned at the time of judgment.	
NIV	Therefore the wicked will not stand in the judgment,	

BHS	וְחַטָּאִים בַּעֲדַת צַדִּיקִים׃	5b
Ltrl	the righteous—in the assembly of—and sinful (ones)	
KJB	nor sinners in the congregation of the righteous.	
NASB	Nor sinners in the assembly of the righteous.	
ESV	nor sinners in the congregation of the righteous;	
NLT	Sinners will have no place among the godly.	
NIV	nor sinners in the assembly of the righteous.	

5ᵃ "LXX Grk compare (verse) 1."

1   This footnote is correct, as the Greek Septuagint does indeed use *εν βουλή* ("in the council") in verse one as well as here in verse five. The MT in contrast uses בַּעֲצַת ("in the council") in verse one, but בַּעֲדַת ("in the assembly") here in verse five.

BHS	כִּי־יוֹדֵעַ יְהוָה דֶּרֶךְ צַדִּיקִים	6a
Ltrl	the righteous (ones)—the road of—YHWH—he knows—because	
KJB	For the LORD watches over the way of the righteous,	
NASB	For the LORD knows the way of the righteous,	
ESV	for the LORD knows the way of the righteous,	
NLT	For the LORD watches over the path of the godly,	
NIV	For the LORD watches over the way of the righteous,	

BHS	וְדֶרֶךְ רְשָׁעִים תֹּאבֵד׃	6b
Ltrl	it will perish—wicked (ones)—and the road of	
KJB	but the way of the wicked leads to ruin.	
NASB	But the way of the wicked will perish.	
ESV	but the way of the wicked will perish.	
NLT	but the path of the wicked leads to destruction.	
NIV	but the way of the wicked leads to destruction.	

2. PSALM 2

BHS	תְּרֹעֵם בְּשֵׁבֶט בַּרְזֶל	9a
Ltrl	iron—with a rod of—you will break them	
KJB	Thou shalt break them with a rod of iron;	
BSV	You will break them with an iron scepter;	
NLT	You will break them with an iron rod	
NIV	You will break them with a rod of iron;	
NHEB	You shall rule them with an iron scepter.	

9ᵃ "LXX (Syr) Grk = Heb."

1. The Greek Septuagint does indeed have ποιμανεῖς meaning, "you shall tend, take care of."

2. תְּרֹעֵם Qal impf. + suffix 3mp of the verb רָעַע meaning, "to break."

3. בְּשֵׁבֶט Prep. + noun, m. sg. cstr. meaning, "rod, staff, club, sceptre."

4. בַּרְזֶל Noun, m. sg. abs. meaning, "iron."

5. Some English translations like NHEB changes "break" to "rule": This apparently is an attempt to Christianize the MT and so bring it in line with Revelation 2:27.

3. PSALM 6

BHS	כִּי אֵין בַּמָּוֶת זִכְרֶךָ[a]	6a
Ltrl	remembers / names you—in death—there are not—because	
KJB	For in death there is no remembrance of thee:	
NLT	For the dead do not remember you.	
NIV	Among the dead no one proclaims your name	

6a "LXX Grk = Heb."

1. The Greek Septuagint does (in verse five) indeed have ο μνημονεύων σου meaning, "remembering you." This footnote equates this to זִכְרֶךָ the qal part. m. sg. active + suffix 2ms of the verb זָכַר meaning, "to remember, to name, to mention."

2. בַּמָּוֶת Prep. + definite article + noun, m. sg. meaning, "in the state / place of the death."

3. The NIV has been criticized for its translation, but it is justified as the verb does not only mean, "remember" but could also contain the nuance of "naming / referring to someone" or "proclaiming someone's name."

4. PSALM 8

BHS	לַמְנַצֵּחַ עַל־הַגִּתִּית[a] מִזְמוֹר לְדָוִד:	1
Ltrl	of David—a Psalm—the Gittite—upon—for the Chief Musician	
KJB	To the chief Musician upon Gittith, A Psalm of David.	
NASB	For the choir director; on the Gittith. A Psalm of David.	
NIV	For the director of music. According to gittith. A psalm of David.	

1a "LXX Symmachus's Greek Version (Hieronymus) plural, those 81:1a 84:1a."

1. In the Greek Septuagint we find the plural υπέρ των ληνών meaning, "to the wine-presses," which can be regarded as a song for the Feast of the Booths (also called the Feast of the Tabernacles, or by its Hebrew name *Sukkot*) (Gen 33:17, Lv 23:34).

2. This word occurs only in this phrase, and is found only here and in Ps 81:1, 84:1.

3. Several English translations, like NLT, ESV, CSB, and GNT, completely omit verse one.

BHS	יְהוָה אֲדֹנֵינוּ מָה־אַדִּיר שִׁמְךָ בְּכָל־הָאָרֶץ	2a
Ltrl	the earth—in all—your name—excellent—how—our God—YHWH	
KJB	O LORD our Lord, how excellent is thy name in all the earth!	
NASB	O LORD, our Lord, How majestic is Your name in all the earth,	
ESV	O LORD, our Lord, how majestic is your name in all the earth!	
NLT	O LORD, our Lord, your majestic name fills the earth!	
NIV	LORD, our Lord, how majestic is your name in all the earth!	

BHS	אֲשֶׁר תְּנָהᵃ הוֹדְךָ עַל־הַשָּׁמָיִם:	2b
Ltrl	the heavens—upon—your splendor—you will set—that / who	
KJB	who hast set thy glory above the heavens.	
NASB	Who have displayed Your splendor above the heavens!	
ESV	You have set your glory above the heavens.	
NLT	Your glory is higher than the heavens.	
NIV	You have set your glory in the heavens.	

2ᵃ⁻ᵃ "Corrupt. LXX Grk, SyP (Targum) Syr which you have given, Symmachus's Greek Version (Hieronymus) Grk; read Heb, proposed Heb or Heb."

1. This footnote starts by stating that the verb in the MT is corrupt. The MT form תְּנָה is parsed as the qal imp. m. sg. of the root נתן meaning, "to give" or "to bestow upon." The phrase thus reads, "which you bestow upon." This footnote further states:

2. The word επήρθη used in the Greek Septuagint means, "to lift up."

3. The Syriac Peshitta has *djhbt* meaning, "which you have given."

4. Symmachus's Greek Version (Hieronymus) has ος έταζας, meaning, "oh my gosh."

5. Read: אֲשֶׁר נָתַתָּה the qal perf. 2ms, then meaning, "which you gave."

6. Proposed: אֲשֶׁר נִתָּן the niph'al perf. 3ms, then meaning, "which he set."

7. Proposed: אֲשֶׁר נָתְנָה the qal perf. 2ms, then meaning, "which she gave."

BHS	מִפִּי עוֹלְלִים וְיֹנְקִים יִסַּדְתָּ עֹז[a]	3a
Ltrl	strength—you have ordained—and nursing infants—babies—from the mouth of	
KJB	Out of the mouth of babes and sucklings hast thou ordained strength	
NASB	From the mouth of infants and nursing babes You have established strength	
ESV	Out of the mouth of babies and infants, you have established strength	
NLT	You have taught children and infants to tell of your strength	
NIV	Through the praise of children and infants you have established a stronghold	

3[a] "SyP Syr glory your."

1. The SyP makes that which is implied in the MT more exact. It is noteworthy that this noun has the additional meaning of "a stronghold" which makes sense in light of the next phrase.

2. This text is referred to by Jesus in Mt 21:16.

BHS	לְמַעַן צוֹרְרֶיךָ[b] לְהַשְׁבִּית אוֹיֵב וּמִתְנַקֵּם:	3b
Ltrl	and avenge yourself—the enemy—that you may destroy—your harassers—because	
KJB	because of thine enemies, that thou mightiest still the enemy and the avenger.	
NASB	Because of Your adversaries, To make the enemy and the revengeful cease.	
ESV	because of your foes, to still the enemy and the avenger.	
NLT	silencing your enemies and all who oppose you.	
NIV	against your enemies, to silence the foe and the avenger.	

3[b] "Hieronymus suffix 1 singular."

1. It is unclear why Hieronymus would opt for this suffix as the MT makes perfect sense.

2. צוֹרְרֶיךָ Qal part. active m. pl. with 2ms object suffix of the verb צרר meaning, "to show hostility towards, treat with enmity." The literal translation will be, "your harassers."

3. לְהַשְׁבִּית Preposition *le* with hiph'il infinitive construct of the verb שבת which in the qal binyan means, "to rest, cease, desist, abstain," but in the hiph'il binyan means, "to cause to cease, put an end to, exterminate, destroy."

4. וּמִתְנַקֵּם: Waw consecutive with hithpa'el part. active m. sg. of the verb נקם meaning, "to avenge, take vengeance."

BHS	כִּי־אֶרְאֶהa שָׁמֶיךָb מַעֲשֵׂיc אֶצְבְּעֹתֶיךָ	4a
Ltrl	your fingers—the deeds of—your heavens—I will consider—when	
KJB	When I consider thy heavens, the work of thy fingers,	
NASB	When I consider Your heavens, the work of Your fingers,	
ESV	When I look at your heavens, the work of your fingers,	
NLT	When I look at the night sky and see the work of your fingers—	
NIV	When I consider your heavens, the work of your fingers,	

4ᵃ "SyP 3 plural."

1. The verb form in the MT is parsed as qal impf. 1cs of the verb רָאָה meaning, "I see, perceive, observe, pay attention to" (Chapter 58.1 in Vol. 3). It is not clear why the Syriac Peshitta opted to us the 3mp "they will."

4ᵇ "LXX it omits suffix."

1. The Greek Septuagint indeed has τους ουρανούς, "the heavens."

4ᶜ "Cairo Geniza multiple (20–60) Manuscripts SyP Heb."

1. In the MT we find the plural construct form of the noun meaning, "deeds of." This footnote states that the sources mentioned have the singular absolute form, "deed" of the same noun namely מַעֲשֶׂה.

BHS	יָרֵחַ וְכוֹכָבִים אֲשֶׁר כּוֹנָנְתָּה:	4b
Ltrl	you established it—which—and stars—moon	
KJB	the moon and the stars, which thou hast ordained;	
NASB	The moon and the stars, which You have ordained;	
ESV	the moon and the stars, which you have set in place,	
NLT	the moon and the stars you set in place—	
NIV	the moon and the stars, which you have set in place,	

1. כּוֹנָנְתָּה Polel perf. 2ms with 3fs object suffix of the verb כּוּן "to be firm," and with the meaning in the polel, "to set up, establish, constitute." (Chapter 63.2.3.1 in Vol. 3).

BHS	מָה־אֱנוֹשׁ כִּי־תִזְכְּרֶנּוּ וּבֶן־אָדָם כִּי תִפְקְדֶנּוּ:	5
Ltrl	you visit him—that—man—and son of—you remember him—is man—what	
KJB	What is man, that thou art mindful of him?and the son of man, that thou visitest him?	
NASB	What is man that You take thought of him, And the son of man that You care for him?	
ESV	what is man that you are mindful of him, and the son of man that you care for him?	
NLT	what are mere mortals that you should think about them, human beings that you should care for them?	
NIV	what is mankind that you are mindful of them, human beings that you care for them?	

1   תִּזְכְּרֶנּוּ Qal impf. 2ms with pronominal suffix 1cs of the verb זָכַר "to remember, call to mind, recall."

2   תִפְקְדֶנּוּ: Qal impf. 2ms with pronominal suffix 1cs of the verb פָּקַד "to visit, to attend to, muster, appoint."

BHS	וַתְּחַסְּרֵהוּ מְּעַט מֵאֱלֹהִים	6a
Ltrl	from God—a little—and you made him lack	
KJB	For thou hast made him a little lower than the angels,	
NASB	Yet You have made him a little lower than God,	
ESV	Yet you have made him a little lower than the heavenly beings	
NLT	Yet you made them only a little lower than God	
NIV	You have made them a little lower than the angels	

1   וַתְּחַסְּרֵהוּ Waw conversive + pi'el impf. 2ms + suffix 3ms of the verb חָסַר meaning in the qal binyan, "to lack, need, be lacking, decrease." In the pi'el binyan it means, "to cause to lack."

2   מְּעַט Adj. m. sg. meaning, "a little, a few."

3   מֵאֱלֹהִים Prep. + noun, m. pl. that has a number of meanings:

4   Some English translations (NIV, KJB) have changed "God" to "the angels" to match the quotation in Heb 2:6, which is based on the Greek *αγγέλους* in the Greek Septuagint.

5. PSALM 18

BHS	כִּי־בְךָ אָרֻץ גְּדוּד וּבֵאלֹהַי אֲדַלֶּג־שׁוּר׃	30
Ltrl	a wall—I can jump over—and with my God—a band / troop—I can run to meet—with you—for	
KJB	For by thee I have run through a troop; and by my God have I leaped over a wall.	
NASB	For by You I can run upon a troop; And by my God I can leap over a wall.	
ESV	For by you I can run against a troop, and by my God I can leap over a wall.	
NLT	In your strength I can crush an army; with my God I can scale any wall.	
NIV	With your help I can advance against a troop; with my God I can scale a wall.	

LXX	ὅτι	ἐν	σοι	ῥυσθήσομαι	ἀπό	πειρατηρίου
Ltrl	For	by	you	I shall be rescued	from	the band of marauders

30ᵃ "LXX Grk."

1. In verse 30 of the MT we find אָרֻץ which is the qal impf. 1cs of the root רוּץ meaning, "I will run." In verse 29 of the ABP Septuagint[23] we find ῥυσθήσομαι meaning, "I shall be rescued."

30ᵇ "LXX Grk; read probably Heb compare 2 Sm 22:30 LXXᴸ Grk = Heb."

1. This footnote makes three points namely,

   a) The ABP[24] version of the Greek Septuagint has πειρατηρίου meaning, "a band (of marauders)" which corresponds with the MT.

   b) 2 Sm 22:30 has the same word as here in the MT, but this footnote suggests that we should probably read גָּדֵר meaning, "wall."

   c) The LXXᴸ version of the Greek Septuagint has πεφραγμένος which equals the Hebrew גָּדוּר meaning, "band / troop."

30ᶜ "2 Sm 22:30 Heb."

1. In 2 Sm 22:30 the waw conjunctive is indeed absent. Otherwise these two verses are amazingly similar.

2. In conclusion, it seems that we do not have to question the MT.

---

23 Main source: Wikipedia contributors. "*Azazal.*" Wikipedia, The Free Encyclopedia, 31 August, 2021. Web: 14 February, 2021. Slightly edited.

24 Hattingh, Tian (2012), p. 104.

BHS	מְשַׁוֶּה רַגְלַי֮ כָּאַיָּל֗וֹת וְעַ֥ל בָּ֝מֹתַ֗י יַעֲמִידֵֽנִי׃	34
Ltrl	—my high places—and upon—like young female antelopes—my feet—he places he will cause me to stand firm	
KJB	He maketh my feet like hinds' feet, and setteth me upon my high places.	
NASB	He makes my feet like hinds' feet, And sets me upon my high places.	
ESV	He made my feet like the feet of a deer and set me secure on the heights.	
NLT	He makes me as surefooted as a deer, enabling me to stand on mountain heights.	
NIV	He makes my feet like the feet of a deer; he causes me to stand on the heights.	
LXX	The one readying my feet as a stag, and upon the high places setting me,	

34ª "2 Sm 22:34 (Ketiv) Heb."

1   This footnote suggests the plural pronominal suffix, which makes common sense.

34ᵇ "LXX SyP Hieronymus and 2 Sm 22:34 (LXX Vulgate) they omit suffix."

1   In 2 Sm 22:34 there is also a footnote concerning the suffix. Omitting the suffix does make sense in this context.

2   מְשַׁוֶּה Pi'el part. active m. sg. of the root שׁוה meaning, "to place" or "to set."

3   כָּאַיָּלוֹת Inseparable preposition + noun, f. pl. of אַיָּלָה meaning, "hind (female red deer), doe" which comes from אַיִל which is a noun m. sg. meaning, "ram" (for sacrificial purposes) as in Ex 29:22.

4   יַעֲמִידֵנִי׃ Hiph'il impf. 3ms of the root עמד meaning in the qal binyan, "to take one's stand," but in the hiph'il binyan has a causative meaning.

5   The phrase "He makes my feet like the feet of a deer; he causes me to stand firm on high places" occurs in three locations in the Hebrew Bible namely 2 Sm 22:34, Hb 3:19, and here in Ps 18:34.

6   "The Nubian ibex (*Capra nubiana*) is a desert-dwelling goat species found in mountainous areas of northern and northeast Africa, and the Middle East. Its range is within Egypt, Israel, Jordan, Lebanon, etc. In Israel, the historically dense ibex population, described in the Hebrew Bible (Psalm 104:18), was decimated in the wake of the First World War. The Biblical heroine Yael's name means 'Ibex' in Hebrew (Jgs. 4:18–22). The sudden availability of rifles enabled Bedouin to hunt them to near extinction. After the establishment of the state of Israel, when hunting was outlawed and nature reserves were created in which they were protected, the ibex population rebounded. Three ibex populations have been discovered in Israel: in the Judean Desert, the Negev mountains and Eilat."[25]

7   "The klipspringer (*Oreotragus oreotragus*) is a small antelope found in eastern and southern Africa. The vernacular name 'klipspringer' is a compound of the Afrikaans words 'klip' (rock) and 'springer' (leaper). The klipspringer inhabits places characterized by rocky terrain and

---

25   Hattingh, Tian (2012), p. 105.

sparse vegetation. A klipspringer's hooves are cylindrical and downward-pointing, giving it a tiptoe walk and provide an amazing sure-footed agility on the rocks."[26]

BHS	מְפַלְטִ֑י מֵאֹיְבָ֥י אַ֣ףᵇ מִן־קָמַ֣יᶜ תְּרוֹמְמֵ֑נִי	49a
Ltrl	—those who rise (against) me—also—from my enemies—he causes me to escape you will lift me up	
KJB	He delivereth me from mine enemies: yea, thou liftest me up above those that rise up against me:	
NASB	He delivers me from my enemies; Surely You lift me above those who rise up against me;	
ESV	who rescued me from my enemies; yes, you exalted me above those who rose against me;	
NLT	and rescues me from my enemies. You hold me safe beyond the reach of my enemies;	
NIV	who saves me from my enemies. You exalted me above my foes;	

49ᵃ "2 Sm 22:49 Heb."

1   In 2 Sm 22:49 we find an almost exact replica of Ps 18:49. All the footnotes in this verse mention the small differences that occur between the two verses. In 2 Sm 22:49 we find וּמוֹצִיאִ֖י for example.

49ᵇ "Lacks this a few (3–10) Manuscripts and 2 Sm 22:49."

1   In addition, the Greek Septuagint does not have this conjunction donating addition, especially of something greater.

49ᶜ⁻ᶜ "Cairo Geniza Manuscripts and 2 Sm 22:49 Heb."

1   The form suggested in this footnote is an alternative way to use the preposition (Chapter 17.5 in Vol. 1).

Ps 18	מְפַלְטִי	Pi'el part. active m. sg. + pronominal suffix 1cs of the verb פָּלַט meaning, "to deliver, bring into security, deliver, cause to escape." This pi'el is a causative (to cause something to happen).
2 Sm	וּמוֹצִיאִי	Waw consecutive + hiph'il part. active m. sg. Of the verb יָצָא meaning, "to go out, come out." The hiph'il binyan is per definition causative thus meaning, "to cause to come = to bring out, lead out, deliver."
Ps 18 2 Sm	קָמַי	Qal part. active m. pl. + 1cs pronominal suffix of the verb קוּם which then means, "those who rise (against) me" (Chapters 10.8 in Vol. 1, and 45.2.2a in Vol. 2). It appears in both texts.
Ps 18 2 Sm	תְּרוֹמְמֵנִי	Pi'lel impf. 2ms + pronominal suffix 1cs of the verb רוּם meaning "to be high, exalted," or "to rise up against." It appears in both texts.

---

26   Hattingh, Tian (2012), p. 186.

BHS	מֵאִישׁ חֲמָסִֽים תַּצִּילֵֽנִי׃	49b
Ltrl	you will deliver me—violent—from a man	
KJB	thou hast delivered me from the violent man.	
NASB	You rescue me from the violent man.	
ESV	you delivered me from the man of violence.	
NLT	you save me from violent opponents.	
NIV	from a violent man you rescued me.	

49ᵈ "Several (11–20) Manuscripts and 2 Sm 22:49 Heb."

1. This footnote suggests that the singular noun could be in the plural or it could be a verb in the qal part. active m. pl. form meaning, "those who treat violently."

2. חָמָס Noun, m. sg. meaning, "violence, wrong." In the context of the previous word it then becomes "a violent man."

3. תַּצִּילֵנִי Hiph'il impf. 2ms + 1cs pronominal suffix of the root נצל meaning, "to take away, snatch away, rescue, deliver from enemies."

6. PSALM 19

BHS	וּֽמַעֲשֵׂ֥ה יָ֝דָ֗יו מַגִּ֥יד הָרָקִֽיעַ׃	2b
Ltrl	the firmament—shows—his hands—and the doing	
KJB	and the firmament sheweth his handywork.	
NASB	And their expanse is declaring the work of His hands.	
ESV	and the sky above proclaims his handiwork.	
NLT	The skies display his craftsmanship.	
NIV	the skies proclaim the work of his hands.	

2ª "Cairo Geniza a few (3–10) Manuscripts Heb, Cairo Geniza Symmachus's Greek Version Targums Vulgate Heb."

1. The first part of this footnote suggests that we drop the waw consecutive.

2. The second part of this footnote suggests that we change the noun to the plural cstr. form. Both of these suggestions are non-consequential.

3. הָרָקִיעַ Definite article + noun, m. sg. meaning, "extended surface" or "(solid) expanse." Also described as the "vault of heaven," this "dome-shaped firmament" was regarded by the ancient Hebrews as a solid part of the cosmos, separating the sky from the "waters" above it.

4. This noun occurs 17 times in the Hebrew Bible. Five times with the article, namely in Gen 1:7, Ps 19:1, Ez 1:23, Ez 10:1, and Dn 12:3.

5. Many modern English translations (NIV, NLT, ESV) avoid mentioning this phenomenon. This trend is found in Ps 150:1 as well.

7. PSALM 22

BHS	כָּאֲרִי֗ יָדַ֥י וְרַגְלָֽי׃	17c
Ltrl	and my feet—my hands—as a lion	
KJB	they pierced my hands and my feet.	
NASB	They pierced my hands and my feet.	
ESV	they have pierced my hands and feet.	
NLT	They have pierced my hands and my feet.	
NIV	they pierce my hands and my feet.	

17[b] "A few (3–10) Manuscripts Editions Heb, two Manuscripts Editions Heb compare LXX (Syr) Grk, Aquila's Greek Version Grk, Symmachus's Greek Version Grk."

1. כָּאֲרִי Prep. + noun, m. sg. meaning, "as a lion." In the context this does not make sense, so this footnote presents a number of alternatives.

2. A few (3–10) Manuscripts and Editions have כארו which points to the verb כור but the spelling with the aleph would then be incorrect.

3. Two Manuscripts and Editions have כָּרוּ which is the correct form of the qal perf. 3ms of the verb כור meaning, "they pierced, bore, dig, hew, etc." However, by the textual-critical principle of *lex difficilior* ("the more difficult variant is to be preferred"), (Chapter 73.3.2 in Vol. 4), this is almost certainly a late Medieval correction to the text.

4. The Greek Septuagint has ὤρυξαν meaning, "they dug into." Many modern English translations follow the Greek Septuagint and use "pierced" in order to read Christ's crucifixion into the text. Other Greek forms meaning, "to bind" are also mentioned in this footnote.

5. Only one fragmentary copy of Psalm 22 has been found among the Dead Sea Scrolls. Unfortunately, this document, known as 4QPsf, becomes illegible at precisely this location in the text. Only the faded remnants of what may be "kr" are visible.

6. A copious amount of literature has been written on this verse, but ultimately we have accept the MT as it is, or concede that we simply do not know what the original text contained.

8. PSALM 23

BHS	מִזְמ֥וֹר לְדָוִ֑ד יְהוָ֥ה רֹ֝עִ֗י לֹ֣א אֶחְסָֽר׃	1
Ltrl	I shall be lacking / needing—not—my shepherd—YHWH—from David—A psalm	
KJB	A Psalm of David. The LORD is my shepherd; I shall not want.	
NASB	A Psalm of David. The LORD is my shepherd, I shall not want.	
ESV	The LORD is my shepherd; I shall not want.	
NLT	The LORD is my shepherd; I have all that I need.	
NIV	A psalm of David. The LORD is my shepherd, I lack nothing.	

1   "Metaphors are particularly difficult to translate, because words have different metaphoric meanings in different cultures. Shepherds in the Hebrew Bible were symbols of might, ferocity and royalty, whereas now they generally represent peaceful guidance and oversight. So the image of the Lord as shepherd in Psalm 23 originally meant that the Lord was mighty, fierce and royal."[27]

BHS	בִּנְאוֹת דֶּשֶׁא יַרְבִּיצֵנִי עַל־מֵי מְנֻחוֹת יְנַהֲלֵנִי:	2
Ltrl	—still—water of—upon—he lets me to lie down—tender grass—in pastures of he will lead me	
KJB	He maketh me to lie down in green pastures: he leadeth me beside the still waters.	
NASB	He makes me lie down in green pastures; He leads me beside quiet waters.	
ESV	He makes me lie down in green pastures. He leads me beside still waters.	
NLT	He lets me rest in green meadows; he leads me beside peaceful streams.	
NIV	He makes me lie down in green pastures, he leads me beside quiet waters,	

2ᵃ "To this place transpose."

1   The term "transpose" means, "to cause two or more things to change places with each other." This footnote does not state from where this verb was transposed.

2   בִּנְאוֹת Prep. + f. pl. cstr. form of the noun נָוֶה meaning, "grassy pasture, meadow." In Am 1:2 we find, "the pastures of the shepherds" (NIV), or, "the habitations of the shepherds" (KJB).

3   דֶּשֶׁא Noun, m. sg. most commonly meaning, "grass." However, in other cases we find it to be more specific. In Prv 27:25 we find, "new growth" (NIV), "tender grass" (KJB), referring to a second crop of grass. In Dt 32:2 we find, "new grass" (NIV), "fresh grass" (NASB), and "tender herb" (KJB).

BHS	נַפְשִׁי יְשׁוֹבֵב יַנְחֵנִי בְמַעְגְּלֵי־צֶדֶק לְמַעַן שְׁמוֹ:	3
Ltrl	—righteousness—in the paths of—he will lead me—he will restore—my soul his name—for sake of	
KJB	He restoreth my soul: he leadeth me in the paths of righteousness for his name's sake.	
NASB	He restores my soul; He guides me in the paths of righteousness For His name's sake.	
ESV	He restores my soul. He leads me in paths of righteousness for his name's sake.	
NLT	He renews my strength. He guides me along right paths, bringing honor to his name.	
NIV	he refreshes my soul. He guides me along the right paths for his name's sake.	

---

27   Hattingh, Tian (2012), p. 105.

BHS	גַּם כִּי־אֵלֵךְ בְּגֵיא צַלְמָוֶת לֹא־אִירָא רָע	4a
Ltrl	evil—I will fear—not—shadow of death—in a valley of—I will walk—though—even	
KJB	Yea, though I walk through the valley of the shadow of death, I will fear no evil:	
NASB	Even though I walk through the valley of the shadow of death, I fear no evil,	
ESV	Even though I walk through the valley of the shadow of death, I will fear no evil,	
NLT	Even when I walk through the darkest valley, I will not be afraid,	
NIV	Even though I walk through the darkest valley, I will fear no evil,	

1. צַלְמָוֶת literally means, "death-shadow." Figuratively it means, "extreme danger," which, if the metaphor were to be expounded, would change the English translation to, "valley of extreme (deadly) danger."

2. Some scholars are of the opinion that צַלְמָוֶת probably consists of the two words צֵל and מָוֶת where the latter is the well-known "death," and the former is from the root צלל meaning, "to quiver in terror," or "to be dark," "to grow dark."

BHS	כִּי־אַתָּה עִמָּדִי שִׁבְטְךָ וּמִשְׁעַנְתֶּךָ הֵמָּה יְנַחֲמֻנִי׃ᵃ	4b
Ltrl	comfort me—they—and your staff—your rod—with me—You—for	
KJB	for thou art with me; thy rod and thy staff they comfort me.	
NASB	for You are with me; Your rod and Your staff, they comfort me.	
ESV	for you are with me; your rod and your staff, they comfort me.	
NLT	for you are close beside me. Your rod and your staff protect and comfort me.	
NIV	for you are with me; your rod and your staff, they comfort me.	

4ᵃ "It has been proposed Heb."

1. The proposed יַנְחֻנִי would be the hiph'il impf. 3mp of the verb נָחָה meaning, "to lead / guide," and with a 1cs ("me") pronominal suffix added. The MT, however, has the pi'el impf. 3mp of the root נחם which means, "to comfort," or "to console" in the pi'el, and a 1cs pronominal suffix ("me").

BHS	תַּעֲרֹךְ לְפָנַי שֻׁלְחָןᵃ נֶגֶד צֹרְרָי	5a
Ltrl	my enemies—presence of—a table—before me—You prepare	
KJB	Thou preparest a table before me in the presence of mine enemies:	
NASB	You prepare a table before me in the presence of my enemies;	
ESV	You prepare a table before me in the presence of my enemies;	
NLT	You prepare a feast for me in the presence of my enemies.	
NIV	You prepare a table before me in the presence of my enemies.	

5ᵃ "It has been proposed Heb (nun dittography)."

1   If in fact, the nun was a case of "double writing," then שֻׁלְחָן which means, "table," could be pointed as (given the vowels) שֶׁלַח which means, "missile" or "weapon." This would make sense in the context of this sentence and fit the character of David as the "warrior king."

2   The phenomenon of dittography (abbreviated in *BHS* as: dttg), literally meaning, "double writing," is the accidental repetition by a copyist of a letter, a group of letters, a word, or a group of words. For example: In Is 30:30 the first word in the verse is duplicated in 1QIs^a.

BHS	דִּשַּׁנְתָּ בַשֶּׁמֶן רֹאשִׁי כּוֹסִי רְוָיָה׃	5b
Ltrl	runs over—my cup—my head—with oil—You anoint	
KJB	thou anointest my head with oil; my cup runneth over.	
NASB	You have anointed my head with oil; My cup overflows.	
ESV	you anoint my head with oil; my cup overflows.	
NLT	You honor me by anointing my head with oil. My cup overflows with blessings.	
NIV	You anoint my head with oil; my cup overflows.	

5^b "Original Septuagint Grk = Heb."

1   The Greek και το ποτήριόν σου, mentioned in the footnote, does indeed appear in the Septuagint, and would then be וְכוֹסְךָ meaning, "and your cup" in Hebrew, just as in the Greek.

BHS	אַ֤ךְ ט֖וֹב וָחֶ֣סֶד יִרְדְּפ֑וּנִי כָּל־יְמֵ֣י חַיָּ֑י	6a
Ltrl	my life—the days of—all—it will follow me—and mercy—goodness—surely	
KJB	Surely goodness and mercy shall follow me all the days of my life:	
NASB	Surely goodness and loving-kindness will follow me all the days of my life,	
ESV	Surely goodness and mercy shall follow me all the days of my life	
NLT	Surely your goodness and unfailing love will pursue me all the days of my life,	
NIV	Surely your goodness and love will follow me all the days of my life,	

6^{a-a} "Septuagint they connect with (verse) 5."

1   This footnote is correct, and verse 5 in the Greek Septuagint ends with, και το ποτήριόν σου μεθύσκον με ωσεί κράτιστον, "and your cup is intoxicating me as most excellent."

6^b "Septuagint SyP add suffix second person singular."

1   The Septuagint has και το έλεός σου, "and your mercy."

BHS	וְשַׁבְתִּי בְּבֵית־יְהוָה לְאֹרֶךְ יָמִים׃	6b
Ltrl	days—for ever—YHWH—in the house of—and I will dwell	
KJB	and I will dwell in the house of the LORD forever.	
NASB	And I will dwell in the house of the LORD forever.	
ESV	and I shall dwell in the house of the LORD forever.	
NLT	and I will live in the house of the LORD forever.	
NIV	and I will dwell in the house of the LORD for ever.	

6ᶜ "LXX (Symmachus's Greek Version) Grk = Heb compare (Psalm) 27:4, SyP Syr—Heb?"

1. In Ps 27:4 we find the form 1cs שִׁבְתִּי which is the qal infinitive construct with suffix of the verb יָשַׁב meaning, "to sit, remain, dwell." This is the form (with a conjunctive added), that is mentioned (correctly) in this footnote as appearing in the Greek LXX as καὶ τὸ κατοικεῖν με, and is translated as, "and my dwelling." This footnote further states that in the SyP we find the questionable form וְיֵשֵׁב "and he will dwell." However, in the MT we find וְשַׁבְתִּי which is the more obvious qal perf. 1cs of the verb שׁוּב meaning, "and I will return," but could also stand for יָשַׁבְתִּי which is the qal perf. 1cs of the verb יָשַׁב meaning, "to sit, remain, dwell." This last option is the form that most English translations have accepted.

9. PSALM 37

BHS	וְדַרְכּוֹ יֶחְפָּץ׃	23b
Ltrl	he will delight—and his way / manner	
KJB	and he delighteth in his way.	
NASB	And He delights in his way.	
ESV	when he delights in his way;	
NLT	He delights in every detail of their lives.	
NIV	the one who delights in him;	

1. וְדַרְכּוֹ Waw consecutive + noun, m. sg. + suffix 3ms meaning, "and his manner."

2. יֶחְפָּץ Qal impf. 3ms of the verb חָפֵץ meaning, "to delight in."

3. There are two possible meanings of the phrase.

   a) God delights in the path of the righteous man.

   b) Man delights in his own path.

   c) Man delights in the path of God.

4. The Hebrew itself is inherently ambiguous and does not give us any clue as to which one of the above are meant.

10. PSALM 42

BHS	כְּאַיָּל˙ תַּעֲרֹג עַל־אֲפִיקֵי־מָיִם	2a
Ltrl	water—channels of—to—she will long for—as the hart	
KJB	As the hart panteth after the water brooks,	
NASB	As the deer pants for the water brooks	
ESV	As a deer pants for flowing streams,	
NLT	As the deer longs for streams of water,	
NIV	As the deer pants for streams of water,	

2ª "Read Heb (haplography)."

1. This footnote states that we should insert the letter tav that was probably omitted erroneously because of a haplography. This would change the deer from a male (as presently in the MT) to a female which would then correspond to the female gender expressed in the following verb.

2. כְּאַיֶּלֶת Prep. + noun, f. sg. cstr. form of אַיָּלָה meaning, "hind, doe."

3. Hart is an archaic word for "stag" (from Old English heorot, "deer"—compare with modern Dutch *hert*, medieval French *hart*, German *hirsch*). A hind (also doe) is a female deer, especially a Red Deer (*Cervus elaphus*), and the males are stags.

4. תַּעֲרֹג Qal impf. 3fs of the verb עָרַג meaning, "she will long for."

5. אֲפִיקֵי Noun, m. pl. cstr. meaning, "channels of, streams of." The verb אָפַק means, "to hold." This has lead to the view that the noun actually is indicating the bank of the channel or stream that is holding the water. The deer is longing to reach the bank from where he can get to the water.

11. PSALM 46

BHS	הַרְפּוּ וּדְעוּ, כִּי־אָנֹכִי אֱלֹהִים	11a
Ltrl	God—I (am)—that—and know—keep calm!	
KJB	Be still, and know that I am God:	
NASB	"Stop striving and know that I am God;	
ESV	"Be still, and know that I am God.	
NLT	"Be still, and know that I am God!	
NIV	He says, "Be still, and know that I am God;	
CSB	"Stop fighting, and know that I am God,	
LSV	Desist, and know that I [am] God,	
YLT	Desist, and know that I am God,	

1. הַרְפּוּ Hiph'il imp 3mp of the root רפה

2. The core meaning of this root is, "to drop your hands (from whatever you are doing)."

3. In the Hiph'il it takes on the meaning of, "to cease doing something," "to keep calm," "to relax," "to let go," "to desist."

12. PSALM 51

BHS	כִּי־פְשָׁעַיˣ אֲנִי אֵדָע וְחַטָּאתִי נֶגְדִּיˣ תָּמִיד:	5
Ltrl	always—before me—and my sins—I know—I—my transgressions—because	
KJB	For I acknowledge my transgressions: and my sin is ever before me.	
NASB	For I know my transgressions, And my sin is ever before me.	
ESV	For I know my transgressions, and my sin is ever before me.	
NLT	For I recognize my rebellion; it haunts me day and night.	
NIV	For I know my transgressions, and my sin is always before me.	

5ᵃ "Compare (footnote) 3ᶜ."

1. Footnote 3ᶜ states, "LXX singular, likewise (footnote) 5ᵃ." In this context, the plural of the MT makes more sense.

5ᵇ "A few (3–10) Manuscripts Heb."

1. Adding the inseparable preposition does not change the meaning ("before, in front of"), as the adverb often has prepositions prefixed to it.

2. אֵדָע Qal impf. 1cs of the verb יָדַע "to know" (Chapter 52.1 in Vol. 3).

BHS	הֵן־אֱמֶת חָפַצְתָּ בַטֻּחוֹתˣ	8a
Ltrl	in the inner parts—you delight in—truth—look!	
KJB	Behold, thou desirest truth in the inward parts:	
NASB	Behold, You desire truth in the innermost being,	
ESV	Behold, you delight in truth in the inward being,	
NLT	But you desire honesty from the womb,	
NIV	Yet you desired faithfulness even in the womb;	

8ᵃ "LXX it connects with following; material lacking in Syr."

1. חָפַצְתָּ Qal perf. 2ms of the verb חָפֵץ meaning, "to delight in."

2. בַטֻּחוֹת Prep. + article + noun, f. pl. meaning, "inward parts." This noun appears only twice in the Hebrew Bible, namely here and in Jb 38:36. In Job the "inner parts" or "heart" is seen as the seat of "wisdom." This wisdom is associated with the obedience of the ibis bird to the laws of nature in predicting the flooding of the Nile. Although tempting, there is no reason for changing the MT as was done by the NIV for example.

3. The word "womb" in the NLT and NIV are certainly not found in the MT.

Selected Passages

BHS	זִבְחֵי־אֱלֹהִים רוּחַ נִשְׁבָּרָה	19a
Ltrl	she is broken—a spirit—God—the sacrifices of	
KJB	The sacrifice pleasing to God is a broken spirit.	
NASB	The sacrifices of God are a broken spirit;	
ESV	The sacrifices of God are a broken spirit;	
NLT	The sacrifice you desire is a broken spirit.	
NIV	My sacrifice, O God, is a broken spirit	

19ª "Read probably Heb."

1   This form in the MT is the masculine plural construct of the noun זֶבַח meaning, "a sacrifice." This footnote suggests that we change it to the absolute form with a 1cs pronominal suffix then meaning, "my sacrifice."

BHS	לֵב־נִשְׁבָּר וְנִדְכֶּה אֱלֹהִים לֹא תִבְזֶה:	19b
Ltrl	you will despise—not—God—and she is contrite—it is broken—a heart	
KJB	a broken and a contrite heart, O God, thou wilt not despise.	
NASB	A broken and a contrite heart, O God, You will not despise.	
ESV	a broken and contrite heart, O God, you will not despise.	
NLT	You will not reject a broken and repentant heart, O God.	
NIV	a broken and contrite heart you, God, will not despise.	

19ᵇ "Lacking (in) SyP, probably delete."

1   The MT makes perfect sense and it is not known why the SP would want to delete this word.

19ᶜ "SyP omits conjunction, probably read Heb."

1   The MT makes perfect sense and it is not known why the SP would want to omit the conjunction.

19ᵈ "LXX SyP 3 singular."

1   The present form is the qal impf. 2ms ("you will despise"). This footnote does not stipulate the gender of the third person singular. In the impf. the 3fs has the same prefix as the 2ms. The MT does make sense in this context, and therefore no change is needed.

2   וְנִדְכֶּה Niph'al part. active m. sg. of the verb דָּכָה which in the niph'al binyan means, "to be crushed," "to be broken," "to be contrite" (a feeling or expression of remorse or penitence; affected by guilt). This verb is found only in the Psalms.

13. PSALM 81

BHS	לְיוֹם חַגֵּנוּ׃	4
Ltrl	our feast—to a day of	
KJB	on our solemn feast day.	
ESV	on our feast day.	
NIV	on the day of our festival;	

1. חַגֵּנוּ Noun, m. sg. abs. + suffix 1cp meaning, "festival-gathering, feast, pilgrim feast."

2. There is no reason to depict it as a solemn feast day (KJV).

14. PSALM 85

BHS	חֶסֶד־וֶאֱמֶת נִפְגָּשׁוּ צֶדֶק וְשָׁלוֹם נָשָׁקוּ׃	11
Ltrl	have kissed—and peace—righteousness—they meet—and truth—kindness	
KJB	Mercy and truth are met together; righteousness and peace have kissed each other.	
NASB	Loving-kindness and truth have met together; Righteousness and peace have kissed each other.	
ESV	Steadfast love and faithfulness meet; righteousness and peace kiss each other.	
NLT	Unfailing love and truth have met together. Righteousness and peace have kissed!	
NIV	Love and faithfulness meet together; righteousness and peace kiss each other.	

1. נִפְגָּשׁוּ Niph'al perfect 3 mp of the verb פָּנַשׁ meaning, "to meet" or "to encounter." In the Hebrew Bible, this verb occurs in the niph'al binyan only here and in Prv 22:2, 29:13.

2. נָשָׁקוּ Qal perfect 3 mp of the verb נָשַׁק meaning, "to kiss."

BHS	אֱמֶת מֵאֶרֶץ תִּצְמָח וְצֶדֶק מִשָּׁמַיִם נִשְׁקָף׃	12
Ltrl	—from the heavens—righteousness—it shall spring—from the earth–truth it shall look down	
KJB	Truth shall sprout out of the earth; and righteousness shall look down from heaven.	
NASB	Truth springs from the earth, And righteousness looks down from heaven.	
ESV	Faithfulness springs up from the ground, and righteousness looks down from the sky.	
NLT	Truth springs up from the earth, and righteousness smiles down from heaven.	
NIV	Faithfulness springs forth from the earth, and righteousness looks down from heaven.	

1. תִּצְמָח Qal imperfect 2 fs of the verb צָמַח meaning, "to sprout" or "to spring up."

2. נִשְׁקָף Niph'al perfect 3 ms of the verb שָׁקַף meaning, "to look down."

3. Although the latter verb is in the perfect, it is translated as an imperfect. Refer to Chapter 23.3 in Vol. 1 for details on translating the perfect.

15. PSALM 95

BHS	אַרְבָּעִים שָׁנָה אָקוּט	10a
Ltrl	I loathed—years—forty	
KJB	Forty years long was I grieved	
NASB	"For forty years I loathed	
ESV	For forty years I loathed	
NLT	For forty years I was angry	
NIV	For forty years I was angry	

1. אָקוּט Qal impf. 1cs of the verb קוּט possibly meaning, "feel a loathing, feel intense dislike or disgust for."

2. This is an example of a *hapax legomenon* (a word that is found only once in a body of work like the Hebrew Bible). It has no connection to any other verb root, making it impossible to ascertain with certainty what the original author meant.

16. PSALM 96

BHS	כִּי כָּל־אֱלֹהֵי הָעַמִּים אֱלִילִים	5a
Ltrl	worthless gods—the nations—the gods of—all—for	
KJB	For all the gods of the nations are idols:	
NASB	For all the gods of the peoples are idols,	
ESV	For all the gods of the peoples are worthless idols,	
NLT	The gods of other nations are mere idols,	
NIV	For all the gods of the nations are idols,	

1. אֱלִילִים The m. pl. abs. form of the noun אֱלִיל meaning, "worthless / naught gods" from the unused root אלל "to be weak or insufficient."

17. PSALM 104

BHS	בָּרֲכִי נַפְשִׁי אֶת־יְהוָהᵃ	1a
Ltrl	Yahweh—my soul—bless	
KJB	Bless the LORD, O my soul.	
NASB	Bless the LORD, O my soul!	
ESV	Bless the LORD, O my soul!	
NLT	Let all that I am praise the LORD.	
NIV	Praise the Lord, my soul.	

1ᵃ "Qumran LXX put before Heb."

1. The Qumran Scrolls and the Greek Septuagint identify the author by inserting לְדָוִד "From David" before the start of the first verse.

2. The verb in this line is the pi'el imp. f. sg. form of בָּרַךְ which has two meanings,

   a) "to kneel" or "adore with bended knees," which usually describes an action by a human being directed toward God, and

   b) "to bless," which is used to describe an action by God directed toward a human being, or an action of a human to a fellow human (Chapter 36.3.2b in Vol. 2).

3. The imperative is used mainly to express direct commands. These verbs will demand an immediate action from the person or thing that is being addressed. Therefore the literal translation here will be, "You, my soul, are commanded to adore YHWH with bended knees."

4. The verb בָּרַךְ occurs 330 times in the Hebrew Bible, and בָּרְכִי occurs five times namely in the previous Ps 103 in verses 1, 2, and 22, and here in Ps 104 in verses 1 and 35.

BHS	יְהוָה אֱלֹהַי גָּדַלְתָּ מְּאֹד	1b
Ltrl	very—you are great—my God—Yahweh	
KJB	O LORD my God, thou art very great;	
NASB	O LORD my God, You are very great;	
ESV	O LORD my God, you are very great!	
NLT	O LORD my God, how great you are!	
NIV	Lord my God, you are very great;	

1ᵇ "Lacking (in) a few (3–10) Manuscripts."

1. A few medieval Manuscripts omit the duplication of the Tetragrammaton YHWH.

1ᶜ "Qumran Heb."

1. The Qumran Scrolls have the pronominal suffix as the 1cp (our God), as apposed to the MT that has the suffix as 1cs (my God).

BHS	הוֹד וְהָדָר לָבָשְׁתָּ:	1c
Ltrl	you are clothed with—and majesty—honor	
KJB	thou art clothed with honor and majesty.	
NASB	You are clothed with splendor and majesty,	
ESV	You are clothed with splendor and majesty,	
NLT	You are robed with honor and majesty.	
NIV	you are clothed with splendor and majesty.	

Selected Passages

BHS	עֹטֶה־אוֹר כַּשַּׂלְמָה	2a
Ltrl	as a garment—light—cover	
KJB	Who coverest thyself with light as with a garment:	
NASB	Covering Yourself with light as with a cloak,	
ESV	covering yourself with light as with a garment,	
NLT	You are dressed in a robe of light.	
NIV	The Lord wraps himself in light as with a garment;	

BHS	נוֹטֶה שָׁמַיִם כַּיְרִיעָה:	2b
Ltrl	like a curtain—heavens—stretch out	
KJB	who stretchest out the heavens like a curtain:	
NASB	Stretching out heaven like a tent curtain.	
ESV	stretching out the heavens like a tent.	
NLT	You stretch out the starry curtain of the heavens;	
NIV	he stretches out the heavens like a tent	

BHS	הַמְקָרֶה בַמַּיִם עֲלִיּוֹתָיו	3a
Ltrl	his upper chambers—in the water—the one who lays the beams	
KJB	Who layeth the beams of his chambers in the waters:	
NASB	He lays the beams of His upper chambers in the waters;	
ESV	He lays the beams of his chambers on the waters;	
NLT	you lay out the rafters of your home in the rain clouds.	
NIV	and lays the beams of his upper chambers on their waters.	

BHS	הַשָּׂם־עָבִים רְכוּבוֹ	3b
Ltrl	his chariot—clouds—he makes	
KJB	who maketh the clouds his chariot:	
NASB	He makes the clouds His chariot;	
ESV	he makes the clouds his chariot;	
NLT	You make the clouds your chariot;	
NIV	He makes the clouds his chariot	

BHS	הַֽמְהַלֵּ֗ךְ עַל־כַּנְפֵי־רֽוּחַ׃	3c
Ltrl	the wind—the wings of—on—the one who walks	
KJB	who walketh upon the wings of the wind:	
NASB	He walks upon the wings of the wind;	
ESV	he rides on the wings of the wind;	
NLT	you ride upon the wings of the wind.	
NIV	and rides on the wings of the wind.	

BHS	עֹשֶׂ֣ה מַלְאָכָ֣יו רוּח֑וֹת	4a
Ltrl	spirits—his angels—he makes	
KJB	Who maketh his angels spirits;	
NASB	He makes the winds His messengers,	
ESV	he makes his messengers winds,	
NLT	The winds are your messengers	
NIV	He makes winds his messengers,	

BHS	מְ֝שָׁרְתָ֗יו אֵ֣שׁ לֹהֵֽט׃	4b
Ltrl	flame—fire of—his ministers	
KJB	his ministers a flaming fire:	
NASB	Flaming fire His ministers.	
ESV	his ministers a flaming fire.	
NLT	flames of fire are your servants.	
NIV	flames of fire his servants.	

BHS	יָֽסַד־אֶ֭רֶץ עַל־מְכוֹנֶ֑יהָ	5a
Ltrl	her foundations—on—earth—he laid	
KJB	Who laid the foundations of the earth,	
NASB	He established the earth upon its foundations,	
ESV	He set the earth on its foundations,	
NLT	You placed the world on its foundation	
NIV	He set the earth on its foundations;	

BHS	בַּל־תִּמּוֹט עוֹלָם וָעֶד׃	5b
Ltrl	and forever—forever—it will be moved—not	
KJB	that it should not be removed for ever.	
NASB	So that it will not totter forever and ever.	
ESV	so that it should never be moved.	
NLT	so it would never be moved.	
NIV	it can never be moved.	

18. PSALM 121

BHS	שִׁיר לַמַּעֲלוֹת אֶשָּׂא עֵינַי אֶל־הֶהָרִים מֵאַיִן יָבֹא עֶזְרִי׃	1
Ltrl	—from where—the mountains—to—my eyes—I will lift up—to the ascents—a song my help—it will come	
KJB	A Song of degrees. I will lift up mine eyes unto the hills, from whence cometh my help.	
NASB	A Song of Ascents. I will lift up my eyes to the mountains; From where shall my help come?	
ESV	I lift up my eyes to the hills. From where does my help come?	
NLT	I look up to the mountains—does my help come from there?	
NIV	A song of ascents. I lift up my eyes to the mountains—where does my help come from?	

1ª "LXX several (11–20) Manuscripts Heb as 122:1."

1 The literal translation in Ps 122 would then be, "A song for the Ascents."

1ᵇ "SyP Syr = Heb."

1 The vowel pointing suggested in this footnote would change the noun in the MT to the particle of the verb with the same root as the noun. This is an alternative way to convey the same meaning.

2 מַעֲלוֹת Absolute plural of the feminine noun מַעֲלָה meaning, "step, stair, or ascent."

3 Song of Ascents: Any one of the 15 Psalms in the series Ps 120 through Ps 134 sung by Hebrew pilgrims on their way to Jerusalem or possibly while ascending Mount Zion or the steps of the Temple. It is also called a Gradual Psalm, Pilgrim Psalm, or Psalm of Ascents.

19. PSALM 136

BHS	הוֹד֣וּ לַיהוָ֣ה כִּי־ט֑וֹב כִּ֖י לְעוֹלָ֣ם חַסְדּֽוֹ׃	1
Ltrl	his loving-kindness—forever—because—good—because—to Yahweh—give thanks	
KJB	O give thanks unto the LORD; for he is good: for his mercy endureth for ever.	
NASB	Give thanks to the LORD, for He is good, For His loving-kindness is everlasting.	
ESV	Give thanks to the LORD, for he is good, for his steadfast love endures forever.	
NLT	Give thanks to the LORD, for he is good! His faithful love endures forever.	
NIV	Give thanks to the LORD, for he is good. His love endures forever.	

1   הוֹדוּ Hiph'il imp. m. sg. of the verb יָדָה which in the qal binyan means, "to throw, cast," but in the hiph'il binyan takes on the meaning, "to give thanks, laud, praise." This specific form appears 16 times in the Hebrew Bible (Ps 33:2, 100:4, 105:1, 106:1, etc.), and the verb root appears 114 times.

2   חַסְדּוֹ׃ Refer to Lv 20:17.

20. PSALM 139

BHS	גָּלְמִ֤י ׀ רָ֘א֤וּ עֵינֶ֗יךָ וְעַֽל־סִפְרְךָ֮ כֻּלָּ֪ם יִכָּ֫תֵ֥בוּ יָמִ֥ים יֻצָּ֑רוּ וְלֹ֖א אֶחָ֣ד בָּהֶֽם׃	16
Ltrl	—them all—your book—and upon—your eyes—they saw—my embryo in them—one—and not—they were fashioned—days—they were written	
KJB	Thine eyes did see my substance, yet being unperfect; and in thy book all my members were written, which in continuance were fashioned, when as yet there was none of them.	
NASB	Your eyes have seen my unformed substance; And in Your book were all written The days that were ordained for me, When as yet there was not one of them.	
ESV	Your eyes saw my unformed substance; in your book were written, every one of them, the days that were formed for me, when as yet there was none of them.	
NLT	You saw me before I was born. Every day of my life was recorded in your book. Every moment was laid out before a single day had passed.	
NIV	Your eyes saw my unformed body; all the days ordained for me were written in your book before one of them came to be.	

16[a-a] "Perhaps delete and to this place transfer Heb according to 16a."

1   This footnote suggests that we delete the first three words and replace them with the first two words from the next line in the Hebrew text that mean, "the days were."

16[b] "It has been proposed Heb compare SyP."

1   This footnote suggests that we replace גָּלְמִי "my embryo" with גְּמָלַי "my dealings."

16[c] "It has been proposed Heb."

1   The suggestion does not have any merit.

16ᵈ "It has been proposed Heb."

1   This footnote suggests that we change the verb from 3mp to 3ms.

16ᵉ "It has been proposed Heb."

1   The suggestion that we change it to "all my days" makes sense in the context.

16ᶠ "A few (3–10) Manuscripts as the Qere."

1   The Qere reads וְלִי meaning, "and for me" and makes sense in this context.

16ᵍ "A few (3–10) Manuscripts Heb."

1   This footnote suggests an alternative preposition, but with the same suffix.

2   גָּלְמִי Noun, m. sg. abs. meaning, "embryo, imperfect substance." This is an example of a *hapax legomenon* (a word that is found only once in a body of work like the Hebrew Bible). It has no connection to any other verb root, making it impossible to ascertain with certainty what the original author meant.

3   יֻצָּרוּ Pu'al perfect 3cp of the verb יָצַר which in the qal binyan means, "to form, fashion" and in the pu'al binyan means, "to be pre-ordained (in the divine purpose)."

4   The ESV translation seems to be the closest to the original, especially if we implement the two footnotes 16ᶠ and 16ᵍ.

BHS	וְעוֹדִי עִמָּךְ:	18c
Ltrl	with you—and I am still	
KJB	I am still with thee.	
NASB	I am still with You.	
ESV	and I am still with you.	
NLT	you are still with me!	
NIV	I am still with you.	

1   עִמָּךְ Preposition + pronominal suffix 2ms pausal.

2   Words containing an atnach or silluq, are said to be in pause because of the break in the recitation flow of the text (Chpt 64.1.6 in Vol. 3).

3   The pausal form of the 2ms pronominal suffix has the same spelling as the normal 2fs pronominal suffix. Therefore, God is seen as masculine here, and not as feminine as stated in some sources like Biblehub.com for example.

82.24 PROVERBS

1. PROVERBS 24

BHS	מְעַט שֵׁנוֹת מְעַט תְּנוּמוֹת מְעַט חִבֻּק יָדַיִם לִשְׁכָּב׃	33
Ltrl	to lie down—hands—folding of—little—slumber—little—sleep—little	
KJB	Yet a little sleep, a little slumber, a little folding of the hands to sleep:	
NASB	"A little sleep, a little slumber, A little folding of the hands to rest,"	
ESV	A little sleep, a little slumber, a little folding of the hands to rest,	
NLT	A little extra sleep, a little more slumber, a little folding of the hands to rest—	
NIV	A little sleep, a little slumber, a little folding of the hands to rest	

1 שֵׁנוֹת The plural of the feminine noun שֵׁנָה from the verb יָשֵׁן "to sleep."

2 תְּנוּמוֹת The plural of the feminine noun תְּנוּמָה from the verb נוּם "to be drowsy," "to slumber."

3 חִבֻּק The masculine noun meaning, "clasping, folding," from the verb חָבַק "to clasp, embrace."

4 לִשְׁכָּב׃ Qal infinitive construct of the verb שָׁכַב "to lie down."

BHS	וּבָא־מִתְהַלֵּךְᵃ רֵישֶׁךָ וּמַחְסֹרֶיךָᶜ כְּאִישׁ מָגֵן׃ פ	34
Ltrl	armed—like a man—and your need—your poverty—like a prowler—and it will come	
KJB	So shall thy poverty come as one that travelleth; and thy want as an armed man.	
NASB	Then your poverty will come as a robber And your want like an armed man.	
ESV	and poverty will come upon you like a robber, and want like an armed man.	
NLT	then poverty will pounce on you like a bandit; scarcity will attack you like an armed robber.	
NIV	and poverty will come on you like a thief and scarcity like an armed man.	

34ᵃ "Bomberg edition here it begins Chapter 25."

1 This footnote is clear and simple.

34ᵇ "Read with a multitude (20–60) Manuscripts Vulgate Heb compare 6:11."

1 The Hebrew that is suggested here and also found in Chapter 6 verse 11, is the inseparable preposition *ke* with the pi'el part. active m. sg. of the verb הָלַךְ "to go, come, walk," and translated as "like one walking." The form in the MT is the hithpa'el part. active m. sg. of the same verb and meaning, "walking to and fro."

34ᶜ "Read with several (11–20) Manuscripts Versions Heb."

1 The form in this footnote has the 2ms suffix as apposed to the 2mp suffix in the MT.

2   When an ᵃ appears before (to the right of) the first word of a verse and is then never repeated within the same verse, it indicates that the footnote should be made applicable to the entire verse (Chapter 75.2.4 in Vol. 4).

2. PROVERBS 30

BHS	שְׁלֹשָׁה הֵמָּה נִפְלְאוּ מִמֶּנִּי וְאַרְבָּעָה לֹא יְדַעְתִּים׃	18
Ltrl	I understand them—not—and four—to me—they are wonderful—they—three	
KJB	There be three things which are too wonderful for me, yea, four which I know not:	
NASB	There are three things which are too wonderful for me, Four which I do not understand:	
ESV	Three things are too wonderful for me; four I do not understand:	
NLT	There are three things that amaze me—no, four things that I don't understand:	
NIV	There are three things that are too amazing for me, four that I do not understand:	

18ᵃ "Ketiv Heb, Qere Heb."

1   The Qere is logical, as it shows the correct form of the numeral (Chapter 18.4 in Vol. 1).

2   הֵמָּה Pronoun 3mp. It is used incorrectly for the feminine in Ru 1:22, Sg 6:8 and Zec 5:10.

3   נִפְלְאוּ Niph'al perf. 3mp of the denominative (from a noun) verb פָּלָא meaning, "to be surpassing, to be extraordinary, to be wonderful," from the noun, m. sg.

4   יְדַעְתִּים Qal perf. 1cs + suffix 3mp of the verb יָדַע "to know."

BHS	דֶּרֶךְ הַנֶּשֶׁר בַּשָּׁמַיִם דֶּרֶךְ נָחָשׁ עֲלֵי צוּר	19a
Ltrl	rock—on—a serpent—a way of—in the air—the eagle—the way of	
KJB	The way of an eagle in the air; the way of a serpent upon a rock;	
NASB	The way of an eagle in the sky, The way of a serpent on a rock,	
ESV	the way of an eagle in the sky, the way of a serpent on a rock,	
NLT	how an eagle glides through the sky, how a snake slithers on a rock,	
NIV	the way of an eagle in the sky, the way of a snake on a rock,	

1   צוּר Noun, m. sg. with a variety of meanings like, "rock, cliff, rocky wall, block of stone, boulder," but here, and in 2 Sm 21:10, more specifically, "a rock with a flat surface."

BHS	דֶּרֶךְ־אֳנִיָּה בְלֶב־יָם וְדֶרֶךְ גֶּבֶר בְּעַלְמָה׃	19b
Ltrl	with a virgin—a man—and the way of—the sea—in the midst of—a ship—the way of	
KJB	the way of a ship in the midst of the sea; and the way of a man with a maid.	
NASB	The way of a ship in the middle of the sea, And the way of a man with a maid.	
ESV	the way of a ship on the high seas, and the way of a man with a virgin.	
NLT	how a ship navigates the ocean, how a man loves a woman.	
NIV	the way of a ship on the high seas, and the way of a man with a young woman.	

1   בְּעַלְמָה Inseparable preposition + noun, f. sg. meaning, "a young woman (sexually ripe, a maid, or newly married)," and thus not specifically a virgin as used in a few English translations (ESV, NKJV).

3. PROVERBS 31

BHS	אֵשֶׁת־חַיִל מִי יִמְצָא וְרָחֹק מִפְּנִינִים מִכְרָהּ׃	10
Ltrl	—and far beyond—he will find—who—efficiency—a woman / wife of her value—more than corals	
KJB	Who can find a virtuous woman? for her price is far above rubies.	
NASB	An excellent wife, who can find? For her worth is far above jewels.	
ESV	An excellent wife who can find? She is far more precious than jewels.	
NLT	Who can find a virtuous and capable wife? She is more precious than rubies.	
NIV	A wife of noble character who can find? She is worth far more than rubies.	

10ᵃ "Verses 10–31 in LXX after 29:27."

1   The ABP[28] has followed the MT and verses 10–31 are part of Chapter 31.

2   חַיִל Noun, m. sg. meaning, "strength, efficiency, ability, wealth, army."

3   וְרָחֹק Waw consecutive + adjective meaning, "far, distant." With the preposition it takes on the meaning of, "far beyond."

BHS	וַתִּתֵּן טֶרֶףᵃ לְבֵיתָהּ	15b
Ltrl	to her house—food—and she will give	
KJB	and giveth meat to her household,	
NASB	And gives food to her household	
ESV	and provides food for her household	
NLT	to prepare breakfast for her household	
NIV	she provides food for her family	

15ᵃ "It has been proposed Heb compare Heb."

---

28 Davidson, Paul, Deuteronomy 32:43, isthatinthebible.wordpress.com. Accessed 4 January 2021. https://isthatinthebible.wordpress.com/articles-and-resources/deliberate-mistranslationin-the-new-international-version-niv/

1. טֶרֶף Noun, m. sg. meaning, "prey, food, leaf." The corresponding verb is טָרַף meaning, "to tear, rend (tear something into two or more pieces), pluck." The adjective טָרָף means, "freshly plucked."

2. The translation of טֶרֶף depends on the context in which it is used.

    2.1 In Am 3:4, Jb 4:11, Jb 38:39, Ps 104:21, etc. it refers to the "prey" of a lion.

    2.2 But in Jb 24:5 it refers to the "food" of the wild donkeys. In Ps 111:5 the "food" for people, and here in Proverbs the "food" for her household is meant.

    2.3 In Ez 17:9 we find it translated as, "leaves" (KJB), or "sprouting leaves" (NASB), or "fresh sprouting leaves" (ESV).

3. There are some who are of the opinion that the noun cannot be translated with the generic term "food." They believe that one should keep in mind a) the core meaning of the verb (to tear / divide something into parts), and b) the meaning of חֹק (something that is needed for the sustentation of animals and people). This brings them to a nuance translated as, "a sustainable portion to her household."

82.25 ECCLESIASTES

1. ECCLESIASTES 1

BHS	דִּבְרֵי קֹהֶלֶת בֶּן־דָּוִד מֶלֶךְ בִּירוּשָׁלָ͏ִם׃	1
Ltrl	in Jerusalem—king—David—son of—a preacher—words of	
KJB	The words of the Preacher, the son of David, king in Jerusalem.	
NASB	The words of the Preacher, the son of David, king in Jerusalem.	
ESV	The words of the Preacher, the son of David, king in Jerusalem.	
NLT	These are the words of the Teacher, King David's son, who ruled in Jerusalem.	
NIV	The words of the Teacher, son of David, king in Jerusalem:	

1ª "LXX additional information Grk."

1. The Greek Septuagint has, βασιλέως Ισραήλ εν Ιερουσαλήμ, "the king of Israel in Jerusalem."

2. קֹהֶלֶת Noun, m. sg. meaning, "collector (of sentences), preacher."

BHS	וְהָאָרֶץ לְעוֹלָם עֹמָדֶת׃	4b
Ltrl	abides—for ever—but the earth	
KJB	but the earth abideth for ever.	
NASB	But the earth remains forever.	
ESV	but the earth remains forever.	
NLT	but the earth never changes.	
NIV	but the earth remains forever.	

1. עֹמֶדֶת Qal part. fs of the verb עָמַד meaning, "to stand" or "to take one's stand" or "remain standing."

2. עוֹלָם This noun has a wide variety of contextual meanings including, "long duration, antiquity, indefinite futurity, for ever, always, continuous existence."

3. The word does not necessarily mean, "for ever and ever" in the sense of "infinity" or "unending time." This is illustrated by its use with a number of nouns which clearly do not last forever. For example, it used of a slave serving his master forever: Dt 15:17, 1 Sm 27:12, Jb 40:28, Ex 21:6, Lv 25:46, etc. In these contexts, "forever" means as long as the slave (or master) lives. A finite time span. In other words, the meaning depends on how long the noun to which it is attached lasts, or, the situation does not change as long as the noun exists. More examples are,

   3.1 Is 32:14—the destruction of Jerusalem. The city (a noun) was rebuilt many years later and exists to this day.

   3.2 1 Kgs 1:31—David lives forever. It is hoped that David (a noun) will live for a long time, but it does not mean, "forever."

   3.3 Ps 115:18—I will praise forever. In other words, "as long as I (a noun) live."

   3.4 Is 63:9, 11—days of old. The number and duration of the days (a noun) are finite.

   3.5 Eccl 1:4, Ps 78:69, 104:5—as long as the earth exists. Here it also means, "continuous existence" as long as the noun (the earth) lasts.

4. However, when the noun in the above argument is Yahweh or El, the sense becomes unambiguously "forever without end" because God is immortal and unending. For example,

Gen 21:33	everlasting God	אֵל עוֹלָם
Is 40:28	the everlasting God	אֱלֹהֵי עוֹלָם
Ex 15:18	Yahweh will reign for ever and ever	יְהוָה יִמְלֹךְ לְעֹלָם וָעֶד׃

BHS	הַכֹּל הֶבֶל וּרְעוּת רוּחַ׃	14b
Ltrl	wind/breath—and longing—vanity / worthless—all	
KJB	all is vanity and vexation of spirit.	
NASB	all is vanity and striving after wind.	
ESV	all is vanity and a striving after wind.	
NLT	it is all meaningless—like chasing the wind.	
NIV	all of them are meaningless, a chasing after the wind.	

1. הֶבֶל Noun, m. sg. literally meaning, "vapor, breath," and figuratively meaning, "worthless, vanity, unsubstantial."

2. וּרְעוּת Waw consecutive + noun, f. sg. cstr. meaning, "longing for, striving for."

2. ECCLESIASTES 5

BHS	וְיִתְר֥וֹן אֶ֖רֶץ בַּכֹּ֣ל הִ֑יא מֶ֥לֶךְ לְשָׂדֶ֖ה נֶעֱבָֽד׃	8
Ltrl	is tilled—from a field—a king—he—for all—earth—and the profit	
KJB	Moreover the profit of the earth is for all: the king himself is served by the field.	
NASB	After all, a king who cultivates the field is an advantage to the land.	
ESV	But this is gain for a land in every way: a king committed to cultivated fields.	
NLT	Even the king milks the land for his own profit!	
NIV	The increase from the land is taken by all; the king himself profits from the fields.	

1ª "Cairo Geniza (and) two Manuscripts (and) SyP as Qere Heb; Ketiv Heb."

1   This footnote points out that the pronoun should be 3ms as in the Qere, and not 3fs as it is written (Chapters 16.4.1 in Vol. 1, and 70.4.2d in Vol. 4).

2   וְיִתְרוֹן This masculine noun is found only here in Ecclesiastes, and means, "profit, advantage."

3   נֶעֱבָד Niph'al perf. 3ms of the verb עָבַד which in the qal binyan means, "to work, serve," but in the niph'al binyan means, "to be tilled, cultivated."

4   Scholars admit that it is a difficult verse, especially the latter part, to translate.

3. ECCLESIASTES 11

BHS	שַׁלַּ֥ח לַחְמְךָ֖ עַל־פְּנֵ֣י הַמָּ֑יִם כִּֽי־בְרֹ֥ב הַיָּמִ֖ים תִּמְצָאֶֽנּוּ׃	1
Ltrl	—the days—in many—because—the waters—the face of—on—your bread–throw you will find it	
KJB	Cast thy bread upon the waters: for thou shalt find it after many days.	
NASB	Cast your bread on the surface of the waters, for you will find it after many days.	
ESV	Cast your bread upon the waters, for you will find it after many days.	
NLT	Send your grain across the seas, and in time, profits will flow back to you.	
NIV	Ship your grain across the sea; after many days you may receive a return.	

1   שַׁלַּח Pi'el imp. m. sg. of the verb שָׁלַח meaning in the pi'el, "send off, send away, send out; let go, set free, let loose."

2   תִּמְצָאֶנּוּ Qal impf. 2ms + suffix 3ms of the verb מָצָא meaning, "to find."

3   The definitive meaning of this passage is uncertain, but there are several plausible interpretations. Some English translations go to great lengths in changing the original MT to project their specific point of view. The NIV, for example, takes great liberties in rewriting the text to be about shipping and investments.

4. ECCLESIASTES 12

BHS	עֲשׂוֹת סְפָרִים הַרְבֵּה אֵין קֵץ	12b
Ltrl	end—no—many—books—making of	
KJB	of making many books there is no end;	
NASB	the writing of many books is endless,	
ESV	Of making many books there is no end,	
NLT	for writing books is endless,	
NIV	Of making many books there is no end,	

BHS	וְלַהַג הַרְבֵּה יְגִעַת בָּשָׂר׃	12c
Ltrl	the flesh—wearying of—much—and study	
KJB	and much study is a weariness of the flesh.	
NASB	and excessive devotion to books is wearying to the body.	
ESV	and much study is a weariness of the flesh.	
NLT	and much study wears you out.	
NIV	and much study wearies the body.	

1 וְלַהַג Noun, m. sg. meaning, "study, devotion to books."
2 יְגִעַת Noun, f. sg. construct of יְגִעָה meaning, "wearing."

82.26 SONG OF SOLOMON

1. SONG OF SOLOMON 1

BHS	שִׁיר הַשִּׁירִים אֲשֶׁר לִשְׁלֹמֹה׃	1
Ltrl	to Solomon—which—the songs—the song of	
KJB	The song of songs, which is Solomon's.	
NASB	The Song of Songs, which is Solomon's.	
ESV	The Song of Songs, which is Solomon's.	
NLT	This is Solomon's song of songs,	
NIV	Solomon's Song of Songs.	

2. SONG OF SOLOMON 4

BHS	עֵינַיִךְ יוֹנִים מִבַּעַד לְצַמָּתֵךְ	1b
Ltrl	behind your woman's veil—inside—doves—your eyes	
KJB	thou hast doves' eyes within thy locks:	
NASB	Your eyes are like doves behind your veil;	
ESV	Your eyes are doves behind your veil.	
NLT	Your eyes are like doves behind your veil.	
NIV	Your eyes behind your veil are doves.	

1. לְצַמָּתֵךְ Preposition + f. sg. cstr. form of the noun צַמָּה meaning, "for your woman's veil." This noun appears here, in Sg 4:3; 6:7, and Is 47:2.

2. יוֹנָה in Hebrew means, "dove" (Chapter 81, 83.6).

3. "The Hebrew word *jonah* is a generic term usually translated as 'dove.' It is derived from the stem *anah* which means 'to mourn,' probably applied to the dove because of the call of some species like the Laughing Dove (*Streptopelia senegalensis*), for example."[29]

BHS	שַׂעְרֵךְ כְּעֵדֶר הָעִזִּים שֶׁגָּלְשׁוּ מֵהַר גִּלְעָד:	1c
Ltrl	Gilead—from mount—they are going down—goats—like a flock of—your hair	
KJB	thy hair is as a flock of goats, that appear from mount Gilead.	
NASB	Your hair is like a flock of goats That have descended from Mount Gilead.	
ESV	Your hair is like a flock of goats leaping down the slopes of Gilead.	
NLT	Your hair is like a flock of goats descending from the hills of Gilead.	
NIV	Your hair is like a flock of goats descending from the hills of Gilead.	

1a "LXX Grk Symmachus's Greek Version Grk."

1. The Greek Septuagint indeed has αι απεκαλύφθησαν meaning, "the ones who were revealed."

1b-b "Cairo Geniza some Manuscripts LXX Heb compare 6:5."

1. In Sg 6:5 of the MT we do find מִן־הַגִּלְעָד and in the Greek Septuagint it has ἀπό τοῦ Γαλαάδ which also means, "from Gilead."

2. שֶׁגָּלְשׁוּ Relative pronoun (Chapter 16.6.3 in Vol. 1) + qal perf. 3mp of the verb גָּלַשׁ meaning, "to sit, sit up." It only appears here and in 6:5 in the Hebrew Bible where it possibly means, "to recline," rather awkwardly simulating a woman's hair.

---

29 The Apostolic Bible Polyglot (ABP), originally published in 2003 is a Bible translation by Charles Vander Pool. The ABP is an English translation with a Greek interlinear gloss and is keyed to a concordance.

BHS	שִׁנַּיִךְ֙ כְּעֵ֣דֶר הַקְּצוּב֔וֹת	2a
Ltrl	shorn—like a flock of sheep—your teeth	
KJB	Thy teeth are like a flock of sheep that are even shorn,	
NASB	"Your teeth are like a flock of newly shorn ewes	
ESV	Your teeth are like a flock of shorn ewes	
NLT	Your teeth are as white as sheep, recently shorn	
NIV	Your teeth are like a flock of sheep just shorn,	

2ª "Cairo Geniza Heb."

1. The Cairo Geniza has the suffix in the plural.

2ᵇ "Cairo Geniza Heb."

1. The Cairo Geniza has a different vowel to indicate the construct form, which makes sense in this context.

2. הַקְּצוּבוֹת Qal part. Passive of the verb קָצַב meaning, "to cut off, to shear." The verb is found only here and in 2 Kgs 6:6.

BHS	כְּח֤וּט הַשָּׁנִי֙ שִׂפְתוֹתַ֔יִךְ וּמִדְבָּרֵ֖ךְ נָאוֶ֑ה	3a
Ltrl	lovely—and your mouth—your lips—the scarlet—like a strand of	
KJB	Thy lips are like a thread of scarlet, and thy speech is comely:	
NASB	"Your lips are like a scarlet thread, And your mouth is lovely	
ESV	Your lips are like a scarlet thread, and your mouth is lovely.	
NLT	Your lips are like scarlet ribbon; your mouth is inviting.	
NIV	Your lips are like a scarlet ribbon; your mouth is lovely.	

3ª "Ketiv Cairo Geniza Heb, Qere Heb."

1. The Qere form seems to be the correct one in this context.

2. שִׂפְתוֹתַיִךְ Dual sg. of the noun שָׂפָה + suffix 2fs meaning, "your pair of lips."

3. וּמִדְבָּרֵךְ Waw consecutive + preposition + noun, m. sg. מִדְבָּר meaning, "mouth (as an organ of speech)," + suffix 2fs. This noun is a *hapax legomenon* (a word that is found only once in a body of work like the Hebrew Bible).

BHS	כְּפֶלַח הָרִמּוֹן רַקָּתֵךְ מִבַּעַד לְצַמָּתֵךְ:	3b
Ltrl	to your veil—from behind—your temples—the pomegranate—like a slice	
KJB	thy temples are like a piece of a pomegranate within thy locks.	
NASB	Your temples are like a slice of a pomegranate Behind your veil.	
ESV	Your cheeks are like halves of a pomegranate behind your veil.	
NLT	Your cheeks are like rosy pomegranates behind your veil.	
NIV	Your temples behind your veil are like the halves of a pomegranate.	

1 כְּפֶלַח Inseparable preposition + noun, f. sg. from the verb פָּלַח which means, "to cleave, split." The noun could then mean, "a slice," or in the case of a fruit, "a piece."

2 The NIV translation is notable here, as it displays an accurate understanding of the MT.

BHS	כְּמִגְדַּל דָּוִיד צַוָּארֵךְ בָּנוּי לְתַלְפִּיּוֹת	4a
Ltrl	for an armory—built—your neck—David—like the tower of	
KJB	Thy neck is like the tower of David builded for an armory,	
NASB	"Your neck is like the tower of David, Built with rows of stones	
ESV	Your neck is like the tower of David, built in rows of stone;	
NIV	Your neck is like the tower of David, built with courses of stone;	

4ª "LXX Grk, LXX Aquila's Greek Version Grk compare SyP Vulgate, Symmachus's Greek Version Grk, Origen's Greek revision Grk."

1 The Greek Septuagint agrees with the MT.

2 בָּנוּי Qal part. Passive (Chapter 41.1 in Vol 2).

3 לְתַלְפִּיּוֹת Preposition + noun, f. pl. This noun is a *hapax legomenon* (a word that is found only once in a body of work like the Hebrew Bible). The meaning is unclear but in this context could mean, "weapons."

BHS	שְׁנֵי שָׁדַיִךְ כִּשְׁנֵי עֳפָרִים תְּאוֹמֵי צְבִיָּה הָרוֹעִים בַּשּׁוֹשַׁנִּים:	5
Ltrl	in the lilies—which graze—a gazelle—twins of—fawns—like two—your breasts—two	
KJB	Thy two breasts are like two young roes that are twins, which feed among the lilies.	
NASB	"Your two breasts are like two fawns, Twins of a gazelle Which feed among the lilies.	
ESV	Your two breasts are like two fawns, twins of a gazelle, that graze among the lilies.	
NLT	Your breasts are like two fawns, twin fawns of a gazelle grazing among the lilies.	
NIV	Your breasts are like two fawns, like twin fawns of a gazelle that browse among the lilies.	

5ª "Cairo Geniza Heb."

1 Both spellings are acceptable (Sg 2:9, 17; 7:4; 8:14).

5ᵇ⁻ᵇ "Addition compare 2:16."

1   This footnote is of the opinion that this clause was added because it appears in Sg 2:16 as well.

2   עֲפָרִים Noun, m. pl. meaning, "young hart," used here as a simile. A simile is a figure of speech where the comparison of one thing with another thing of a different kind is used to make a description more emphatic or vivid. The definition of a "hart" is, "an adult male European Red Deer. An example of a hart is a stag."

3   תְּאוֹמֵי Noun, m. pl. construct meaning, "twins of," and used in the construct for animals.

4   הָרוֹעִים Definite article + qal part. active m. pl. of the verb רָעָה meaning, "to tend, graze, pasture." The translation could then be, "those who are grazing," or "the ones who are grazing," or "which are grazing," or "which graze."

3. SONG OF SOLOMON 6

BHS	לֹא יָדַעְתִּי נַפְשִׁי שָׂמַתְנִיᵃ מַרְכְּבוֹת ᵇעַמִּי־נָדִיבᵇ׃	12
Ltrl	Amminadib—the chariots of—it set me—my soul—I knew—Before
KJB	Or ever I was aware, my soul made me like the chariots of Amminadib.
NASB	"Before I was aware, my soul set me Over the chariots of my noble people."
ESV	Before I was aware, my desire set me among the chariots of my kinsman, a prince.
NLT	Before I realized it, my strong desires had taken me to the chariot of a noble man.
NIV	Before I realized it, my desire set me among the royal chariots of my people.

12ᵃ "Perhaps read Heb."

1   The footnote suggests the form שִׂמְּחַתְנִי which is the pi'el perf 2fs + suff 1pc of the stem שׂמח which in the pi'el means, "to cause to rejoice, to gladden."

2   In the MT שָׂמַתְנִי is the qal perf 2ms + suff 1pc of the root שׂום meaning, "to put, place, set."

12ᵇ⁻ᵇ "A few (3–10) Manuscripts LXX Vulgate Heb."

1   The footnote notes that the Greek Septuagint and the Latin Vulgate were translating from a vorlage that did not have the maqqeph connecting the last two words. This then results in translating these two words as one proper noun, "Amminadab." The words found in the MT would not typically be connected by a maqqeph, which makes the suggestion a possible alternative.

2   From the above it seems that it is impossible to find a dynamic equivalent of this sentence. It is therefore generally accepted that the MT as we have it had been corrupted in some way or another.

82.27 ISAIAH

1. ISAIAH 1

BHS	חֲזוֹן יְשַׁעְיָהוּ בֶן־אָמוֹץ	1
Ltrl	Amoz—the son of—Isaiah—the vision	
KJB	The vision of Isaiah the son of Amoz,	
NASB	The vision of Isaiah the son of Amoz	
ESV	The vision of Isaiah the son of Amoz,	

1 יָשַׁע In the hiph'il binyan this verb means, "to save, deliver."

  יָהּ is a m. sg. noun meaning, "Lord." It is commonly regarded as an abbreviated form of Yahweh.

2 In combination the two parts would then mean, "Yahweh is salvation" (Chapter 87.3).

BHS	אִם־יִהְיוּ חֲטָאֵיכֶם כַּשָּׁנִים כַּשֶּׁלֶג יַלְבִּינוּ	18b
Ltrl	they will be made white—as snow—like scarlet—your sins—they are—though	
KJB	though your sins be as scarlet, they shall be as white as snow;	
NASB	"Though your sins are as scarlet, They will be as white as snow;	
ESV	though your sins are like scarlet, they shall be as white as snow;	
NLT	"Though your sins are like scarlet, I will make them as white as snow.	
NIV	Though your sins are like scarlet, they shall be as white as snow;	

18ᵃ "Read compare Isaiah Scroll of St. Mark's Monastery a few (3–10) Manuscripts Heb compare LXX SyP Vulgate."

1 The form suggested in this footnote is the noun in the singular, כַּשָּׁנִי whereas the MT has the plural form of the noun.

2 יַלְבִּינוּ Hiph'il impf. 3mp of לָבֵן which in the hiph'il means, "make white, purify."

BHS	אִם־יַאְדִּימוּ כַתּוֹלָע כַּצֶּמֶר יִהְיוּ׃	18c
Ltrl	they will be—like wool—like crimson—they are glaring—though	
KJB	though they be red like crimson, they shall be as wool.	
NASB	Though they are red like crimson, They will be like wool.	
ESV	though they are red like crimson, they shall become like wool.	
NLT	Though they are red like crimson, I will make them as white as wool.	
NIV	though they are red as crimson, they shall be like wool.	

1 יַאְדִּימוּ Hiph'il impf. 3mp of the verb אָדֹם / אָדַם meaning, "to be red" in the qal, and "to be glaring, flagrant" in the hiph'il.

2 כַּתּוֹלָע Inseparable prep. + definite article + noun, m. sg. meaning, "scarlet stuff."

3 *Kermes* (previously named *Coccus*), is a genus of scale insects that feed on the sap of evergreen oaks. The females, of primarily the species *Kermes vermilio*, produce a red dye, also called "kermes," that is the source of natural crimson. The word "kermes" is derived from the Arabic word *qirmiz* meaning, "crimson" (both the color and the dyestuff).

2. ISAIAH 5

BHS	לָכֵן הִרְחִיבָה שְׁאוֹל נַפְשָׁהּ	14a
Ltrl	herself—Sheol—she enlarged—therefore	
KJB	Therefore hell hath enlarged herself,	
NASB	Therefore Sheol has enlarged its throat	
ESV	Therefore Sheol has enlarged its appetite	
NLT	The grave is licking its lips in anticipation,	
NIV	Therefore Death expands its jaws,	

1 לָכֵן Inseparable preposition + adverb meaning, "therefore" or "that being so" or "according to such conditions."

2 הִרְחִיבָה Hiph'il perfect 3fs of the verb רחב meaning, "be, or grow wide, large."

3 שְׁאוֹל There is no English word that conveys the precise sense of this Hebrew word. At the time when this was written, the word referred simply to the abode of the dead and suggested no moral distinctions. The word "hell" as it is understood today, is therefore not an accurate translation. It is therefore correct to simply transliterate the word into English as "Sheol." Refer to 2 Sm 3:32 for notes on *qever* meaning, "grave."

We should note the following about *Sheol*:

a) *Sheol* is never used in the plural but "grave" is used in the plural 29 times in the Hebrew Bible. For example, Ex 14:11, Jer 26:23.

b) *Sheol* is never used to say corpses (or even bones) go there.

c) *Sheol* is never said to be near the surface of the ground, as is a grave.

d) *Qever* is always used to refer to a person's resting place.

e) Corpses are always placed in a *qever* (1 Kings 13:30).

f) *Sheol* is never described as being dug, as is a grave. But *qever* is used in this way six times in the Hebrew Bible (Gen. 50:5).

4 נַפְשָׁהּ Noun, f. sg. construct + suffix 3fs meaning, "herself."

3. ISAIAH 7

BHS	הִנֵּה הָעַלְמָה הָרָה וְיֹלֶדֶת בֵּן וְקָרָאת שְׁמוֹ עִמָּנוּ אֵל:	14b
Ltrl	—a son—and she will bear—she will become pregnant—the young woman–behold God—with us—his name—and she will call	
KJB	Behold, a virgin shall conceive, and bear a son, and shall call his name Immanuel.	
NASB	Behold, a virgin will be with child and bear a son, and she will call His name Immanuel.	
ESV	Behold, the virgin shall conceive and bear a son, and shall call his name Immanuel.	
NLT	Look! The virgin will conceive a child! She will give birth to a son and will call him Immanuel	
NIV	The virgin will conceive and give birth to a son, and will call him Immanuel.	

14ᵇ "LXX LXX Heb."

1   In the MT there is a suffixed tav, indicating 2fs ("she"), but in these two versions of the Greek Septuagint the *tav* is absent, indicating 3ms ("he").

2   הָעַלְמָה Definite article + noun, f. sg. meaning, "young woman."

3   Here in Is 7:14 the Septuagint has η παρθένος, "the virgin."
    The Christian New Testament was written in Greek, and in Mt 1:23 the Septuagint duplicates the term "virgin" it used in Is 7:14. Some hold the opinion that because most young women in antiquity were virgins and most virgins were young women, the Greek Septuagint wasn't concerned and did not distinguish between the words for "virgin" and "young woman" when translating the Hebrew.

4   As can be seen from the MT, the English name Immanuel is in fact the transliteration of two separate Hebrew words meaning, "with us" (Chapter 17.7.9 in Vol. 1) and "God" (Chapter 85 in this volume).

5   This name occurs only twice in the Hebrew Bible namely here and in Is 8:8.

6   Some English translations changed the word "young woman" in the MT to "virgin" in an attempt to harmonize the MT with the quotation of the text in Mt 1:23.

4. ISAIAH 9

BHS	הָעָם הַהֹלְכִים בַּחֹשֶׁךְ רָאוּ אוֹר גָּדוֹל	1a
Ltrl	great—a light—they saw—in darkness—who walked—the people	
KJB	The people that walked in darkness have seen a great light:	
NASB	The people who walk in darkness Will see a great light;	
ESV	The people who walked in darkness have seen a great light;	
NLT	The people who walk in darkness will see a great light.	
NIV	The people walking in darkness have seen a great light;	

1ᵃ "Perhaps delete on account of the metre."

1 הַהֹלְכִים Definite article + qal part. m. pl. active of the verb הָלַךְ "to walk, come, go" (Chapter 33.1 in Vol. 2). Translations include, "those who walk," and "which walked."

2 רָאוּ Qal perf. 3mp of the verb רָאָה "to see" (Chapter 58.1 in Vol. 3).

BHS	יֹשְׁבֵי בְּאֶרֶץ צַלְמָוֶת אוֹר נָגַהּ עֲלֵיהֶם׃	1b
Ltrl	upon them—it shined—a light—the shadow of death—in the land of—those who dwelt	
KJB	they that dwell in the land of the shadow of death, upon them hath the light shined.	
NASB	Those who live in a dark land, The light will shine on them.	
ESV	those who dwelt in a land of deep darkness, on them has light shone.	
NLT	For those who live in a land of deep darkness, a light will shine.	
NIV	on those living in the land of deep darkness a light has dawned.	

1 צַלְמָוֶת Noun, m. sg. meaning, "death-shadow, deep shadow, deep darkness." Literally it means, "shadow of death."

2 נָגַהּ Qal perf. 3ms meaning, "to shine."

BHS	אֵל גִּבּוֹר	פֶּלֶא יוֹעֵץ	5a
Ltrl	God mighty / Messiah	marvel of a counselor	
KJB	The mighty God	Wonderful, Counselor	
NASB	Mighty God,	Wonderful Counselor,	
ESV	Mighty God,	Wonderful Counselor,	
NLT	Mighty God,	Wonderful Counselor,	
NIV	Mighty God	Wonderful Counselor	

BHS	שַׂר־שָׁלוֹם׃	אֲבִיעַד	5b
Ltrl	captain / general of peace	father for ever	
KJB	The Prince of Peace	The everlasting Father	
NASB	Prince of Peace.	Eternal Father,	
ESV	Prince of Peace.	Everlasting Father	
NLT	Prince of Peace.	Everlasting Father	
NIV	Prince of Peace.	Everlasting Father	

1 Morphologically there should actually be a space between *father* and *everlasting*, but here is no footnote in *BHS* to indicate this, and lexicons list this as one word.

2 The construct masculine noun שַׂר is possibly a military term. We could think of God here as a captain or general in the present-day UN Peacekeeping Force.

3 The last six of the eight words in this verse obviously fall into three couplets, and some scholars are of the opinion the first two should probably also be taken together. These scholars then go on to point out that we then actually have four elements of one compound name.

5. ISAIAH 14

BHS	אֵיךְ נָפַלְתָּ מִשָּׁמַיִם הֵילֵלᵃ בֶּן־שָׁחַר	12a
Ltrl	morning—son of—shining one—from heaven—you fell—how	
KJB	"How you are fallen from heaven, O Lucifer, son of the morning!	
NASB	"How you have fallen from heaven, You star of the morning, son of the dawn!	
ESV	"How you are fallen from heaven, O Day Star, son of Dawn!	
NLT	"How you are fallen from heaven, O shining star, son of the morning!	
NIV	How you have fallen from heaven, morning star, son of the dawn!	

12ᵃ "Read Heb *luna crecens* (new moon)."

1   As the word in the MT is clear, there is no need to consider the alternative mentioned.

2   הֵילֵל Noun, m. sg. abs. from the verb הָלַל meaning, "to shine." Here it is used as an appellation (name, title). It is a *hapax legomenon* (a word that is found only once in a body of work like the Hebrew Bible). It has no connection to any other verb root, making it impossible to ascertain with certainty what the original author meant.

6. ISAIAH 16

BHS	שִׁלְחוּ־כַרᵇ מֹשֵׁל־ᶜאֶרֶץ	1a
Ltrl	a land—a ruler of—lamb—send (pl.)!	
KJB	Send ye the lamb to the ruler of the land	
NASB	Send the tribute lamb to the ruler of the land,	
ESV	Send the lamb to the ruler of the land,	
NIV	Send lambs as tribute to the ruler of the land,	
LXX	I will send a male lamb lording over the land;	

1ᵃ "Perhaps read Heb compare Targum."

1   This footnote suggests that a waw consecutive be inserted at the beginning of the verse.

1ᵇ "Perhaps Heb compare Targum."

1   This footnote suggests that the word כַּר meaning, "pasture, lamb" should be in the plural.

1ᶜ "Perhaps Heb."

1   The suggested Hebrew means, "to the rulers of . . ."

2   שִׁלְחוּ Qal imp. m. sg. of the verb שָׁלַח "to send." (Chapter 40.1 in Vol. 2).

3   מֹשֵׁל Qal part. active m. sg. of the verb מָשַׁל "to rule, reign."

4 We should remember that before the Masoretes came along, the original Hebrew texts consisted of consonants only, and there were no spaces between words. In the Dead Sea Scrolls (which did have spaces) for example, the second and third words are one word namely כרמֹשל and thought to be a place name.

BHS	מִסֶּלַע מִדְבָּרָהִ אֶל־הַר בַּת־צִיּוֹן:	1b
Ltrl	Zion—daughter of—a mountain—to—from a wilderness—from Sela	
KJB	from Sela to the wilderness, unto the mount of the daughter of Zion.	
NASB	From Sela by way of the wilderness to the mountain of the daughter of Zion.	
ESV	from Sela, by way of the desert, to the mount of the daughter of Zion.	
NIV	from Sela, across the desert, to the mount of Daughter Zion.	
LXX	not rock desolate is the mountain of the daughter of Zion?	

1ᵈ "SyP (Vulgate) Syr = Heb compare LXX."

1 The sources have a definite article. This does not have any affect on the meaning of the phrase.

2 In the Dead Sea scrolls מסלע is spelt מסלה meaning, "raised / paved way, highway, public road (never a street in a city)" which frequently appears in Isaiah (7:3, 11:18, 19:23, 33:8, 49:11, 59:7, and the well-known 40:3). This led to the translation, "send the lamb to rule the land through the highway in the desert."

7. ISAIAH 19

BHS	וְאֶל־הָאֹבוֹת וְאֶל־הַיִּדְּעֹנִים:	3d
Ltrl	the sorcerers—and to—the mediums—and to	
KJB	and to them that have familiar spirits, and to the wizards.	
NASB	And to mediums and spiritists.	
ESV	and the mediums and the necromancers;	
NLT	mediums, and those who consult the spirits of the dead.	
NIV	the mediums and the spiritists.	

1 הָאֹבוֹת Definite article + noun, m. pl. This noun has four meanings.

   a) Ghost. This meaning is found in Is 29:4. The "chirping speech" might refer to the sounds made by a necromancer as in Is 8:19.

   b) Necromancy: In 1 Sm 28:7, 7, 8 and 1 Chr 10:13 this seems to be referring to the ghost or familiar spirit dwelling in the necromancer.

   c) Skin-bottle: This meaning is found only once in Jb 32:19, and is in the plural. The hollow sound produced by a skin-bottle, leads us to the next meaning.

   d) Necromancer: When practicing their art of seeking the dead for instruction, the chirping & muttering of the necromancers, probably in the form of ventriloquism, is reminicent of the sound of a skin-bottle (Is 8:19, 29:4).

2 הַיִּדְּעֹנִים: Noun, f. abs. pl. from the stem ידע meaning, "to know." This noun then literally means, "those who know," and then more specically in a particular context like here, "the who know (are familiar with) the secrets of the unseen world of the dead and the future" (Dt 18:11).

3 necromancy: The supposed practice of communicating with the dead, especially in order to predict the future; sorcery or black magic in general (Lv 20:27).

4 *sorcerer*: a person who can perform sorcery—witchcraft or magic (often black magic—magic used for evil purposes). A female performing sorcery, is called a sorceress.

8. ISAIAH 28

BHS	כִּי בְּלַעֲגֵי שָׂפָה וּבְלָשׁוֹן אַחֶרֶת	11a
Ltrl	another—and with language—speech—with stammerings of—so	
KJB	For with stammering lips and another tongue	
NASB	Indeed, ... Through stammering lips and a foreign tongue,	
ESV	For by people of strange lips and with a foreign tongue	
NLT	So . . . . through foreign oppressors who speak a strange language!	
NIV	Very well then, with foreign lips and strange tongues	

1 בְּלַעֲגֵי Prep. + noun, m. pl. cstr. meaning, "stammerings of."

2 שָׂפָה Noun, f. sg. abs. meaning, "speech, lip."

3 וּבְלָשׁוֹן Waw conjunctive + prep + noun, m. sg. abs. meaning, "language, tongue."

4 אַחֶרֶת Adjective f. sg. meaning, "another."

5 Some English translations changed the wording in an attempt to harmonize the MT with the quotation of the text in 1 Corinthians 14:21.

9. ISAIAH 34

BHS	וִירֵשׁוּהָ קָאַת וְקִפּוֹד וְיַנְשׁוֹף וְעֹרֵב יִשְׁכְּנוּ־בָהּ	11a
Ltrl	—and short-eared owl—little owl—and they take possession in it—they will dwell—and a raven—and a Northern long-eared owl	
KJB	But the cormorant and the bittern shall possess it; the owl also and the raven shall dwell in it:	
NASB	But pelican and hedgehog will possess it, And owl and raven will dwell in it;	
ESV	But the hawk and the porcupine shall possess it, the owl and the raven shall dwell in it.	
NLT	It will be haunted by the desert owl and the screech owl, the great owl and the raven.	
NIV	The desert owl and screech owl will possess it; the great owl and the raven will nest there.	

1 וִירֵשׁוּהָ Waw conjunctive + qal perf. 3mp + suffix 3ms for וִירֵשׁוּהָ of the verb יָרַשׁ meaning, "to take possession of, inherit."

2. קָאַת Noun, f. sg. abs. meaning, "little owl." Hattingh (2012) states, "and the subspecies *Athene noctua lilith*, with the Hebrew word *qa'ath* in Lev 11:18, Dt 14:17, Ps 102:7, Is 34:11, and Zeph 2:14."[30] Refer to Chapter 83.5 in this volume.

3. וְקִפּוֹד Waw consecutive + noun, m. sg. abs meaning, "short-eared owl."[31]

4. וְיַנְשׁוֹף Waw consecutive + noun, m. sg. abs meaning, "Northern long-eared owl."[32]

5. וְעֹרֵב Waw consecutive + noun, m. sg. abs meaning, "raven."[33]

6. This text is an excellent example of the difficulties in identifying which bird and animal species the biblical authors are referring to.

7. Hattingh (2012) states, "The Hebrew Canon, as expounded in the Mosaic Law, the Prophets and the Writings, contains the origin of Ornithology, and the biblical authors concerned, and not Aristotle, were the original Ornithologists."[34] However, throughout this publication he maintains that these authors knew birds by their generic names only. It is safe to presume that this would be the situation with biblical animals as well (verse 14a below).

BHS	וּפָגְשׁוּ צִיִּים אֶת־אִיִּים	14a
Ltrl	jackals—desert-dwellers—and they will meet	
KJB	The wild beasts of the desert shall also meet with the wild beasts of the island,	
NASB	The desert creatures will meet with the wolves,	
ESV	And wild animals shall meet with hyenas;	
NLT	Desert animals will mingle there with hyenas,	
NIV	Desert creatures will meet with hyenas	

1. וּפָגְשׁוּ Waw conversive + qal perf. 3mp of the verb פָּנַשׁ meaning, "to meet."

2. צִיִּים Noun, m. pl. abs. meaning, "desert dweller, wild beast."

3. אִיִּים Noun, m. pl. abs. meaning, "jackal, howler, wolf."

4. Some translators seem to be uneasy with biblical texts mentioning imaginary creatures, and they would attempt, like here, to demythologize such texts.

---

30. The Apostolic Bible Polyglot (ABP), originally published in 2003 is a Bible translation by Charles Vander Pool. The ABP is an English translation with a Greek interlinear gloss and is keyed to a concordance.
31. Hattingh, Tian (2012), p. 96.
32. The Apostolic Bible Polyglot (ABP), originally published in 2003 is a Bible translation by Charles Vander Pool. The ABP is an English translation with a Greek interlinear gloss and is keyed to a concordance.
33. Main source: Wikipedia contributors. "*Nubian ibex.*" Wikipedia, The Free Encyclopedia, 30 December, 2019. Web: 22 December, 2019. Slightly edited.
34. Main source: Wikipedia contributors. "*Klipspringer.*" Wikipedia, The Free Encyclopedia, 19 December, 2019. Web: 22 December, 2019. Slightly edited.

BHS	אַךְ־שָׁם הִרְגִּיעָה לִילִית	14c
Ltrl	Little Owl—she will rest—there—also	
KJB	the screech owl also shall rest there,	
NASB	Yes, the night monster will settle there	
ESV	there the night bird settles	
NLT	and night creatures will come there to rest.	
NIV	there the night creatures will also lie down	

1. הִרְגִּיעָה Hiph'il perf. 3fs of the verb רָגַע meaning, "to be at rest, repose" in the qal binyan, and "to rest" in the hiph'il.

2. לִילִית Noun, f. proper transliterated as "Lilith."

3. This is an example of a *hapax legomenon* (a word that is found only once in a body of work like the Hebrew Bible). It has no connection to any other verb root, making it impossible to ascertain with certainty what the original author meant.

4. "The Little Owl is a semi-desert dweller. The subspecies *Athene noctua lilith* is common in the Middle East. Stories about whom and what Lilith was are plentiful. She was purportedly a female demon of the night that supposedly flied around searching for newborn children either to kidnap or strangle them. Alan G. Hefner in his article in *Encyclopedia Mythica* states that one story is that God created Adam and Lilith as twins joined together at the back. She demanded equality with him, refusing to lie beneath him during sexual intercourse. She left him in anger and hurried to her home at the Red Sea, became a lover to demons and produced a hundred babies per day. Adam complained to God who then created Eve from Adam's rib, making her submissive to male dominance. In another version Adam supposedly had become tired of coupling with animals (a common Middle-Eastern herdsman practice, [declared a sin in Dt 27:21]), and married Lilith. Refer to the Wikipedia article on 'Lilith' for some interesting reading."[35] Also refer to Chapter 83.5.3 in this volume.

BHS	שָׁמָּה קִנְּנָה קִפּוֹז... אַךְ־שָׁם נִקְבְּצוּ דַיּוֹת	15
Ltrl	—they will be gathered—also there . . . . a tawny owl—make a neat nest–there griffon vultures	
KJB	There shall the great owl make her nest, ... there shall the vultures also be gathered	
NASB	The tree snake will make its nest . . . . Yes, the hawks will be gathered there,	
ESV	There the owl nests . . . . indeed, there the hawks are gathered,	
NLT	There the owl will make her nest . . . . And the buzzards will come	
NIV	The owl will nest there . . . . there also the falcons will gather,	

1. קִנְּנָה Pi'el perf. 3fs of the verb קנן which is associated with the noun קֵן meaning, "nest."

---

35 1 Hoffman, Dr. Joel M. (8 February, 2012). *Five Mistakes in Your Bible Translation.* Retrieved from https://www.huffpost.com/entry/five-mistakes-bible-translation_b_1129620 on 21 September 2020.

2 קִפּוֹז Noun, f. sg. meaning, "tawny owl."[36]

3 נִקְבָּצוּ Niph'al perf. 3mp of the verb קָבַץ meaning, "to gather, collect."

4 דַּיּוֹת Noun, f. pl. meaning, "griffon vultures."[37]

10. ISAIAH 40

BHS	יַשְּׁרוּ בָּעֲרָבָה מְסִלָּה לֵאלֹהֵינוּ:	3c
Ltrl	for our God—a highway—in the desert—make straight	
KJB	Make straight in the desert A highway for our God.	
NASB	Make smooth in the desert a highway for our God.	
ESV	make straight in the desert a highway for our God.	
NLT	Make a straight highway through the wasteland for our God!	
NIV	make straight in the desert a highway for our God.	

1 יַשְּׁרוּ Pi'el imp. m. pl. of יָשַׁר meaning in the pi'el, "make smooth, make straight."

2 בָּעֲרָבָה a) Preposition + article + noun, f. sg. meaning, "desert-plain, arid steppe."

b) The Arabah, or Arava / Aravah (Hebrew: *HaAravah*, literally, "desolate and dry area"), as it is known by its respective Arabic and Hebrew names, is a geographic area 166 km (103 mi) in length, south of the Dead Sea basin, which forms part of the border between Israel to the west and Jordan to the east.

2 מְסִלָּה See a discussion in the notes to Is 16:1b in Chpt 82.25.4 above.

BHS	כְּצִיץ הַשָּׂדֶה:	6
Ltrl	the field—like the blossom of	
KJB	like the flower of the field.	
NASB	as the flower of the field:	
ESV	like the flower of the field.	
NLT	as the flowers in a field.	
NIV	like the flowers of the field.	

1 כְּצִיץ Prep. + noun, m. sg. cstr. This noun has two meanings,

2 a) "blossom, flower." Modern English translations do not pay attention to the fact that it might not refer to a "flower" (1 Kgs 6:18, 29, 32, 35), but rather to a "blossom" (Nm 17:8).

b) "shining thing, plate of gold." This object was part of the headdress of the High Priest and is mentioned three times (Ex 28:9, 39:30; Lv 8:9).

3 In Jer 48:9 this noun takes on the meaning of, "wings."

---

36 The Apostolic Bible Polyglot (ABP), originally published in 2003 is a Bible translation by Charles Vander Pool. The ABP is an English translation with a Greek interlinear gloss and is keyed to a concordance.

37 Hattingh, Tian (2012), p. 158.

BHS	יַעֲלוּ אֵבֶר כַּנְּשָׁרִים	31b
Ltrl	like eagles—wing—they will cause to ascend	
KJB	they shall mount up with wings as eagles;	
NASB	They will mount up with wings like eagles,	
ESV	they shall mount up with wings like eagles;	
NLT	They will soar high on wings like eagles.	
NIV	They will soar on wings like eagles;	

1 יַעֲלוּ Hiph'il impf. 3ms (Chapter 48.5 in Vol. 3) of the verb עָלָה meaning, "to go up, ascend, climb" in the qal. Here the verb is in the causative.

2 אֵבֶר Noun, m. sg. meaning, "pinions." In the Hebrew Bible it appears here and in Ps 55:7 as אֵבֶר כַּיּוֹנָה "wings of a dove," and in Ez 17:3 as אֶרֶךְ הָאֵבֶר "long pinions."

3 כַּנְּשָׁרִים Preposition + article + noun, m. pl. Refer to Dt 32:11 (Chapter 82.7), and Chapter 83.3.2.

11. ISAIAH 43

BHS	אַל־תִּירָא כִּי גְאַלְתִּיךָ קָרָאתִי בְשִׁמְךָ לִי־אָתָּה:	1b
Ltrl	you—for me—by your name—I called—I redeemed you—for—you will fear—not	
KJB	Fear not: for I have redeemed thee, I have called thee by thy name; thou art mine.	
NASB	"Do not fear, for I have redeemed you; I have called you by name; you are Mine!	
ESV	"Fear not, for I have redeemed you; I have called you by name, you are mine.	
NLT	"Do not be afraid, for I have ransomed you. I have called you by name; you are mine.	
NIV	Do not fear, for I have redeemed you; I have summoned you by name; you are mine.	

1ᵃ "All or most of the Versions add suffix 2 m. sg. read Heb."

1 The adding of the suffix makes perfect sense in this context because קְרָאתִיךָ means, "I called you."

1ᵇ "Read Heb compare (verse) 7."

1 בְשִׁמְי means, "in my name." This would then change the core meaning of the MT sentence.

2 תִּירָא Qal impf. 2ms of יָרֵא "to fear" (Chapter 52.1 in Vol. 3).

3 גְאַלְתִּיךָ Qal perf. 1cs + suffix 2ms of גָּאַל "to redeem, act as kinsman."

4 A "kinsman-redeemer" is a male relative who, according to various laws of the Pentateuch, had the privilege or responsibility to act on behalf of a relative who was in trouble, danger, or need. It could be one who delivers or rescues (Gen 48:16; Ex 6:6) or redeems property or person (Lv 27:9–25, 25:47–55). A kinsman who redeems or vindicates a relative is illustrated most clearly in the book of Ruth, where the kinsman-redeemer is Boaz.

12. ISAIAH 50

BHS	אֵי זֶה סֵפֶר כְּרִיתוּת	1a
Ltrl	divorcement—letter / deed / certificate of—it—where	
KJB	Where is the bill of your mother's divorcement,	
NASB	"Where is the certificate of divorce	
ESV	"Where is your mother's certificate of divorce,	
NLT	"Was your mother sent away because I divorced her?	
NIV	"Where is your mother's certificate of divorce	

1. כְּרִיתוּת Noun, f. sg. meaning, "divorcement." This noun ocuurs only four times in the Hebrew Bible. Here, in Dt 24:1, 3, and in Jer 3:8.

13. ISAIAH 53

BHS	נִבְזֶה וַחֲדַל אִישִׁים אִישׁ מַכְאֹבוֹת וִידוּעַ ᵃ חֹלִי	3a
Ltrl	sickness—and knowing—sorrows—a man of—men—and rejected—he is despised	
KJB	He is despised and rejected of men; a man of sorrows, and acquainted with grief:	
NASB	He was despised and forsaken of men, A man of sorrows and acquainted with grief;	
ESV	He was despised and rejected by men, a man of sorrows and acquainted with grief;	
NLT	He was despised and rejected—a man of sorrows, acquainted with deepest grief.	
NIV	He was despised and rejected by mankind, a man of suffering, and familiar with pain	

3ᵃ "Qumran Isaiah Scroll 1QIsa LXX SyP Vulgate Heb Qumran Isaiah Scroll 1QIsb Heb; read Masoretic Texts."

1. This footnote draws attention to the two most famous Dead Sea Scrolls (DSS) from Qumran (Chapter 68 in Vol. 4):

    a) Qumran Isaiah Scroll 1QIsᵃ, also known as the Isaiah Scroll of St. Mark's Monastery (Chapter 68.2.2.1 in Vol. 4). This scroll has וְיוֹדֵעַ which is the qal part. active m. sg. meaning, "and knows."

    b) Qumran Isaiah Scroll 1QIsᵇ, also known as the Isaiah Scroll of the Hebrew University (Chapter 68.2.2.2 in Vol. 4). This scroll has וְיָדַע which is a waw conversive + qal perf. 3ms meaning, "and he will know."

2. נִבְזֶה Niph'al part. active m. sg, from the verb בָּזָה "to despise, regard with contempt."

3. וַחֲדַל Waw conjunctive + construct of the adjective meaning, "forbearing (restrained), lacking." The phrase "lacking of men" then means, "forsaken or rejected by people."

4. מַכְאֹבוֹת Noun, m. pl. meaning, "pain."

5   חֳלִי Noun, m. sg. meaning, "sickness," from the verb חָלָה meaning, "to be weak, to be sick." The noun appears 24 times in the Hebrew Bible and always translated as, "sickness, illness." However, here in this and the next verse, it is often translated as, "grief."

BHS	וְהוּא מְחֹלָלֽ מִפְּשָׁעֵנוּ מְדֻכָּא מֵעֲוֹנֹתֵינוּ	5a
Ltrl	our iniquities—bruised—our transgressions—wounded—but he	
KJB	But he was wounded for our transgressions, he was bruised for our iniquities:	
NASB	But he was pierced for our rebellion, crushed for our sins.	
ESV	But he was pierced for our transgressions; he was crushed for our iniquities;	
NLT	But he was pierced for our rebellion, crushed for our sins.	
NIV	But he was pierced for our transgressions, he was crushed for our iniquities;	

5ᵃ "Proposed Heb."

1. The proposed form מְחֹלָל can be found in Ez 36:23. There it is the pu'al part. m. sg. active of חָלַל meaning, "be profaned." It is also found in Ez 32:26 with the same parsing, but meaning, "be pierced by the sword."

2. מְחֹלָל Po'al part. m. sg. active of the verb חָלַל meaning, "pierced, wounded" (Chapter 63.3.4.3 in Vol. 3).

3. מִפְּשָׁעֵנוּ Preposition + noun, m. pl. + suffix 1cs meaning, "our transgressions."

4. מְדֻכָּא Pu'al part. m. sg. active of דָּכָא meaning, "crushed, broken in pieces, shattered."

5. מֵעֲוֹנֹתֵינוּ Preposition + m. pl. + suffix 1cp of the noun עָוֹן meaning, "our iniquities."

BHS	מֵעֲמַל נַפְשׁוֹ יִרְאֶה יִשְׂבָּע	11a
Ltrl	he will be satisfied—he will see—his soul—from the trouble of	
KJB	He shall see of the travail of his soul, and shall be satisfied:	
NASB	As a result of the anguish of His soul, He will see it and be satisfied;	
ESV	Out of the anguish of his soul he shall see and be satisfied;	
NLT	When he sees all that is accomplished by his anguish, he will be satisfied.	
NIV	After he has suffered, he will see the light of life and be satisfied;	

11ᵃ "Qumran LXX adds Heb, but Heb = Heb."

1. In this verse the Greek Septuagint differs substantially from the MT. This footnote is correct as the LXX does contain the phrase δεῖξαι αὐτῷ φως meaning, "to show to him light."

2. מֵעֲמַל Prep. + noun, m. sg. abs. meaning, "from the labour, toil, trouble."

3. Some translations like NIV, CSB and ISV incorporate the additional phrase from the Greek Septuagint into their translations even though it does not appear in the MT.

14. ISAIAH 55

BHS	הוֹי כָּל־צָמֵא לְכוּ לַמַּיִם וַאֲשֶׁר אֵין־לוֹ ᵃכֶּסֶף לְכוּᵃ	1a
Ltrl	come—money—for him—not—and what—to the waters—come—thirsty—all—ho	
KJB	Ho, every one that thirsteth, come ye to the waters, and he that hath no money; come ye,	
NASB	"Ho! Every one who thirsts, come to the waters; And you who have no money come,	
ESV	"Come, everyone who thirsts, come to the waters; and he who has no money, come,	
NLT	"Is anyone thirsty? Come and drink—even if you have no money!	
NIV	Come, all you who are thirsty, come to the waters; and you who have no	

1ᵃ⁻ᵃ "Read Heb."

1. The suggested כֶּסֶף לְכוּ is a noun + an alternate form of the qal imp. m. pl. of the same verb as in the MT.

2. לְכוּ Qal imp. m. pl. of הָלַךְ "to go, come, walk."

3. אֵין־לוֹ Refer to Chapter 17.9.3 in Vol. 1 for the ways to express (lack of) possession.

BHS	שִׁבְרוּ וֶאֱכֹלוּ ᵇוּלְכוּ שִׁבְרוּ בְּלוֹא־כֶסֶף וּבְלוֹא מְחִיר יַיִן וְחָלָב׃	1b
Ltrl	and milk—wine—price—and without—money—without—buy—and come—and eat—buy	
KJB	buy, and eat; yea, come, buy wine and milk without money and without price.	
NASB	buy and eat. Come, buy wine and milk Without money and without cost.	
ESV	buy and eat! Come, buy wine and milk without money and without price.	
NLT	Come, take your choice of wine or milk—it's all free!	
NIV	buy and eat! Come, buy wine and milk without money and without cost.	

1ᵇ "Proposed Heb."

1. וֶאֱכֹלוּ is an alternative spelling of the qal imp. m. pl. of the MT word.

1ᶜ⁻ᶜ "Lacks this material (in) Qumran Isaiah Scroll 1QIsa LXX SyP, delete."

1. Although the MT repeats itself here, it is still perfectly acceptable.

2. בְּלוֹא The inseparable preposition + the negative forms the preposition or adverb, "without."

3. מְחִיר Noun, m. sg. meaning, "price."

15. ISAIAH 63

BHS	וַיִּזְכֹּר יְמֵי־עוֹלָם ᵃמֹשֶׁה עַמּוֹᵃᵇ	11a
Ltrl	his people—Moses—antiquity—days of—and he remembered	
KJB	Then he remembered the days of old, Moses, and his people,	
NASB	Then His people remembered the days of old, of Moses.	
ESV	Then he remembered the days of old, of Moses and his people.	
NLT	Then they remembered those days of old when Moses led his people out of Egypt.	
NIV	Then his people recalled the days of old, the days of Moses and his people	

11ᵃ⁻ᵃ "This material is lacking in LXX."

11ᵇ "It has been proposed Heb (compare Syrohexapla Vulgate) or (compare a few Manuscripts Syriac Peshitta) Heb."

1 עַבְדּוֹ Meaning, "his slave / servant."

2 Refer to Eccl 1:4 for a discussion of the meaning of עוֹלָם

82.28 JEREMIAH

BHS	דִּבְרֵי יִרְמְיָהוּᵃ בֶּן־חִלְקִיָּהוּ	1
Ltrl	Hilkiah—son of—Jeremiah—the words of	
KJB	The words of Jeremiah the son of Hilkiah,	
NASB	The words of Jeremiah the son of Hilkiah,	
ESV	The words of Jeremiah, the son of Hilkiah,	
NLT	These are the words of Jeremiah son of Hilkiah,	
NIV	These are the words of Jeremiah son of Hilkiah,	

1ᵃ "LXX Grk."

1 This footnote correctly states that the Greek Septuagint differs from the MT and has the following text, "The saying of God which came to Jeremiah."

2 The verb רוּם means, "to be high" or "to be exalted."

3 Keeping the above verb in mind, the literal translation of the name "Jeremiah" would then be, "Yah exalts" (Chapters 86.4.1 and 87.3.1). Refer to Jer 27:1.

2. JEREMIAH 13

BHS	הֲיַהֲפֹךְ כּוּשִׁי עוֹרוֹ, וְנָמֵר חֲבַרְבֻּרֹתָיו	23a
Ltrl	his marks—or a leopard—his skin—a Cushite—can he alter?	
KJB	Can the Ethiopian change his skin, or the leopard his spots?	
NASB	"Can the Ethiopian change his skin, Or the leopard his spots?	
ESV	Can the Ethiopian change his skin, or the leopard his spots?	
NLT	Can an Ethiopian change the color of his skin? Can a leopard take away its spots?	
NIV	Can an Ethiopian change his skin or a leopard its spots?	

1   הֲיַהֲפֹךְ Interrogative hey + qal impf. 3ms of the verb הָפַךְ meaning, "to turn, turn into, transform, change, alter."

2   וְנָמֵר Waw consec. + noun m. sg. The meaning of the stem נמר is not clear. It could be from the Assyrian *namaru* meaning, "shine, gleam." The Latin *pardus* (which is the species name of the leopard) means, "clear, bright," referring to the leopard's glossy coat.

3   חֲבַרְבֻּרֹתָיו Noun, f. pl. + suffix 3mp. meaning, "his stripes" or "his marks." Because we are dealing with a leopard here, modern English translations took the liberty of calling it "spots."

3. JEREMIAH 18

BHS	הֲכַיּוֹצֵר הַזֶּה לֹא־אוּכַל לַעֲשׂוֹת לָכֶם בֵּית יִשְׂרָאֵל נְאֻם־יְהוָה	6a
Ltrl	Yahweh—says—Israel—house of—with you—to do—I am able—not—this—as a potter?	
KJB	O house of Israel, cannot I do with you as this potter? saith the LORD.	
NASB	"Can I not, O house of Israel, deal with you as this potter does?" declares the LORD.	
ESV	"O house of Israel, can I not do with you as this potter has done? declares the LORD.	
NLT	"O Israel, can I not do to you as this potter has done to his clay?	
NIV	He said, "Can I not do with you, Israel, as this potter does?" declares the LORD.	

6a-a "Lacking (in) original Septuagint."

1   The phrase does, however, appear in the Apostolic Bible Polyglot (ABP).[38]

2   הֲכַיּוֹצֵר Interrogative hey + inseparable preposition + qal part. active m. sg. of the verb יָצַר meaning, "to form, fashion," and in the part. it then means, "potter, creator" (Chapter 21.7 in Vol 1).

3   אוּכַל Hoph'al impf. 1cs of the verb יָכֹל / יָכוֹל meaning, "to be able, have power, prevail, endure."

---

38 Hattingh, Tian (2012), p.148.

Selected Passages

BHS	הִנֵּה כַחֹמֶר בְּיַד הַיּוֹצֵר כֵּן־אַתֶּם בְּיָדִי בֵּית יִשְׂרָאֵל׃ ס	6b
Ltrl	Israel—house of—in my hand—you—so—the potter—in the hand of—like the clay—look	
KJB	Behold, as the clay *is* in the potter's hand, so *are* ye in mine hand, O house of Israel.	
NASB	"Behold, like the clay in the potter's hand, so are you in My hand, O house of Israel.	
ESV	Behold, like the clay in the potter's hand, so are you in my hand, O house of Israel.	
NLT	As the clay is in the potter's hand, so are you in my hand.	
NIV	"Like clay in the hand of the potter, so are you in my hand, Israel.	

1 חֹמֶר Noun, m. sg. meaning, "clay, mortar, cement."

4. JEREMIAH 23

BHS	יְהוָה צִדְקֵנוּ	6b
Ltrl	our righteousness—Yahweh	
NASB	The LORD our righteousness.'	
NLT	'The LORD Is Our Righteousness.'	
NIV	The LORD Our Righteous Savior.	

1 Refer to Chapter 86.3.10 in this volume.

2 The NIV is an exception in that it has added the noun "savior" despite it not appearing in the MT. This significantly affects the interpretation and is an obvious case of an effort to Christianize the MT text.

5. JEREMIAH 27

BHS	יִרְמְיָה	1c

1 From Chapter 1–26 the name in Hebrew is spelt יִרְמְיָהוּ but here in 27:1 and in and in 28:5, 6, 10, 11, 12, 15; and 29:1 the alternate form is used. In 29:27 the original spelling resumes and is continued to the end. Refer to Jer 1:1.

2 During Babylonian exile, Hebrews were forced to speak Aramaic which abbreviated names like this. Pronunciation often changed when translating from Hebrew into Greek and Latin and centuries later into English.

6. JEREMIAH 29

BHS	כִּי אָנֹכִי ªיָדַעְתִּי אֶת־הַמַּחֲשָׁבֹת אֲשֶׁר אָנֹכִי חֹשֵׁב עֲלֵיכֶם נְאֻם־יְהוָה	11a
Ltrl	Yahweh—utterance—on you—think—I—that—the thoughts—DDOM—know—I—for	
KJB	For I know the thoughts that I think toward you, saith the LORD,	
NASB	For I know the plans that I have for you,' declares the LORD,	
ESV	For I know the plans I have for you, declares the LORD,	
NLT	For I know the plans I have for you," says the LORD.	
NIV	For I know the plans I have for you," declares the LORD,	

11a-a "Lacking (in) original Septuagint (homoioteleuton)."

1. The phrase ends with the word "I," which appears directly before the phrase involved.

2. Homoioteleuton, abbreviated "homtel," occurs when something is accidentally omitted because the ending of two words / phrases are similar/the same.

3. הַמַּחֲשָׁבֹת Definite article + noun, f. pl. meaning, "thought, device."

4. חֹשֵׁב Qal part. active m. sg. of the verb חָשַׁב meaning, "to think, account."

5. נְאֻם Qal part. passive m. sg. construct of the root נאם which then becomes a noun, m. sg. meaning, "utterance." Refer to 2 Sm 23:1 in this volume.

BHS	מַחְשְׁבוֹת שָׁלוֹם וְלֹא לְרָעָה לָתֵת לָכֶם ªאַחֲרִית וְתִקְוָהª:	11b
Ltrl	and a hope—a future—for you—to give—of evil—and not—peace—thoughts of	
KJB	thoughts of peace, and not of evil, to give you an expected end.	
NASB	plans for welfare and not for calamity to give you a future and a hope.	
ESV	plans for welfare and not for evil, to give you a future and a hope.	
NLT	"They are plans for good and not for disaster, to give you a future and a hope.	
NIV	"plans to prosper you and not to harm you, plans to give you hope and a future.	

11b-b "The original Septuagint Grk, Septuagint codices Grk."

1. The original Septuagint has, "give you these (things)." The other codices have, "give you this after all."

2. אַחֲרִית Noun, f. sg. meaning, "end, after-part, future." In other words, "a happy close of a life," suggesting the idea of a posterity, that is promised to the righteous.

3. וְתִקְוָה Waw consecutive + noun, f. sg. meaning, "outcome, things hoped for."

JEREMIAH 31

BHS	נָתַתִּי אֶת־תּוֹרָתִי בְּקִרְבָּם וְעַל־לִבָּם אֶכְתֲּבֶנָּה	33b
Ltrl	I will write it—their hearts—and on—in their minds—my Law—DDOM—I will put	
KJB	I will put my law in their inward parts, and write it in their hearts;	
NASB	"I will put My law within them and on their heart I will write it;	
ESV	I will put my law within them, and I will write it on their hearts.	
NLT	"I will put my instructions deep within them, and I will write them on their hearts.	
NIV	I will put my law in their minds and write it on their hearts.	

33b "Multiple (20–60) Manuscripts Heb."

1. The manuscripts add a waw conversive to the verb.

2. Without the waw, the verb is in the qal perf. meaning, "I had put," but with the waw it becomes, "I will put," which fits in with the tenses of the other verbs in the verse.

3. בְּקִרְבָּם Inseparable preposition + noun, m. sg. + pronominal suffix 3mp meaning, "in the inward parts of their physical body."

4. אֶכְתֲּבֶנָּה Qal impf. 1cs + pronominal suffix 3fs meaning, "I will write it."

82.29 LAMENTATIONS

1. LAMENTATIONS 1

BHS	שָׂחֲקוּ עַל מִשְׁבַּתֶּהָ: ס	7d
Ltrl	her annihilation—upon—they laughed	
KJB	did mock at her sabbaths.	
DRB	have mocked at her sabbaths.	
NASB	They laughed at her ruin.	
ESV	they mocked at her downfall.	
NLT	laughed as she fell.	
NIV	laughed at her destruction.	

1. מִשְׁבַּתֶּהָ Noun, m. sg. cstr. + suffix 3fp meaning, "cessation, annihilation."

2. The Greek Septuagint has ἐπί τῇ μετοικεσίᾳ αὐτῆς correctly meaning, "upon her displacement."

3. The source of the incorrect translation in the KJB and DRB is Jerome's Latin Vulgate, which translated the noun as *sabbata eius*, Latin for "her Sabbaths." This is an example of the powerful influence the Latin Vulgate had on the early English translators.

2. LAMENTATIONS 4

BHS	גַּם־תַּנִּין֙ חָ֣לְצוּ שַׁ֔ד הֵינִ֖יקוּ גּוּרֵיהֶ֑ן	3a
Ltrl	their young—to nurse—breast—they present—jackals—even	
KJB	Even the sea monsters draw out the breast, they give suck to their young ones:	
NASB	Even jackals offer the breast, They nurse their young;	
ESV	Even jackals offer the breast; they nurse their young;	
NLT	Even the jackals feed their young, but not my people Israel.	
NIV	Even jackals offer their breasts to nurse their young,	

3ª "Two Manuscripts Qere Heb."

1   The correct plural form of the noun is seen in the Qere.

2   שַׁד Noun, m. sg. meaning, "female breast." The term is used for both humans and animals alike.

הֵינִיקוּ Hiph'il perf. 3mp of the verb יָנַק meaning, "to suck." In the hiph'il binyan it then means, "to cause to suck, give suck to = to nurse."

3   גּוּרֵיהֶן Noun, m. pl. + suffix 3fp. of the Noun, גּוּר meaning, "whelp, young."

BHS	בַּת־עַמִּי֙ לְאַכְזָ֔ר כִּ֥י עֵנִ֖ים בַּמִּדְבָּֽר׃ ס	3b
Ltrl	in the wilderness—like ostriches—to be cruel—my people—daughter of	
KJB	the daughter of my people *is become* cruel, like the ostriches in the wilderness.	
NASB	But the daughter of my people has become cruel Like ostriches in the wilderness.	
ESV	but the daughter of my people has become cruel, like the ostriches in the wilderness.	
NLT	But the daughter of my people has become cruel Like ostriches in the wilderness.	
NIV	but my people have become heartless like ostriches in the desert.	

3ᵇ "Grk read Heb."

1   The Greek Septuagint indeed has θυγατέρας "daughters," and this footnote urges us to accept the Hebrew equivalent.

3ᶜ⁻ᶜ "Many (20–60) Manuscripts and Versions as Qere Heb; Ketiv doubtful."

1   The form in the Qere makes sense as a Hebrew word for "ostrich" is the masculine noun יָעֵן which in the plural and with the inseparable preposition results in כִּיְעֵנִים which in turn has the same consonants as כִּי עֵנִים in the current MT text.

82.30 EZEKIEL

1. EZEKIEL 1

BHS	הָיֹה הָיָהᵃ דְבַר־יְהוָה אֶל־יְחֶזְקֵאל	3
Ltrl	Ezekiel—to—Yahweh—the word of—it was—indeed	
KJB	The word of the LORD came expressly unto Ezekiel	
NASB	the word of the LORD came expressly to Ezekiel	
ESV	the word of the LORD came to Ezekiel	
NLT	The LORD gave this message to Ezekiel	
NIV	the word of the LORD came to Ezekiel	

1ᵃ⁻ᵃ "Probably read Heb (dittography refer to Versions)."

1 The construction הָיֹה הָיָה in the MT consists of the qal infinitive absolute followed by the qal perf. 3ms of the verb meaning, "to be." As seen in Chapter 23.12.6.1, the infinitive absolute has an emphatic function. In order to emphasize the certainty of the verbal meaning, the infinitive absolute will immediately precede a perf. or impf. verb of the same root. The English translation will often require the use of adverbs such as, "surely," "certainly," and "indeed."

2 The verb חָזַק means, "to be firm / strong" or "to grow firm / strong."

3 Keeping the above verb in mind, the literal translation of the name "Ezekiel" would then be, "God will strengthen" (Chapters 85.4 and 87.2).

2. EZEKIEL 4

BHS	בְּגֶלְלֵי צֵאַת הָאָדָם	12b
Ltrl	the mankind—human excrement of—with dung of	
KJB	with dung that cometh out of man,	
NASB	over human dung."	
ESV	on human dung."	
NLT	using dried human dung as fuel	
NIV	using human excrement for fuel."	

1 בְּגֶלְלֵי In Jb 20:7 we dealt with alternative meanings, but here and in verse 15, the context determines that we are dealing specifically with human excrement.

2 צֵאַת Noun, f. sg. cstr. meaning, "filth" and specifically "human excrement." It only appears here and in Dt 23:14 in the Hebrew Bible.

3 See verse 15 below.

BHS	אֶת־צְפוּעֵיᵃ הַבָּקָר תַּחַת גֶּלְלֵי הָאָדָם	15b
Ltrl	the human—excrement of—instead of—the cow—dung of—DDOM	
KJB	cow's dung for man's dung,	
NASB	cow's dung in place of human dung	
ESV	cow's dung instead of human dung,	
NLT	cow dung instead of human dung."	
NIV	cow dung instead of human excrement."	

15ᵃ "Ketiv Heb, some (11–20) Manuscripts as Qere."

1. צְפוּעֵי This is the form in the MT, but this footnote suggests that the Ketiv (written form) should be צְפוּעֵי and that the Qere (to be read) form should be צְפִיעֵי which is the plural construct form of the noun צָפִיעַ which appears only here in the Hebrew Bible and means, "cattle dung."

2. See verse 12 above.

3. EZEKIEL 14

BHS	וְהַנָּבִיא כִי־יְפֻתֶּה וְדִבֶּר דָּבָר	9a
Ltrl	a word—and he will speak—if—and the prophet	
KJB	And if the prophet be deceived when he hath spoken a thing,	
NASB	But if the prophet is prevailed upon to speak a word,	
ESV	And if the prophet is deceived and speaks a word,	
NLT	And if a prophet is deceived into giving a message,	
NIV	And if the prophet is enticed to utter a prophecy,	

1. יְפֻתֶּה Pu'al impf. 3ms of the verb פָּתָה which in the qal binyan means, "to be simple, foolish." In the pu'al (which is a passive voice) the meaning is, "to be persuaded" or, "to be deceived." It is when this second meaning is used in translations (ESV, NLT) that it becomes controversial. A more nuanced translation could be, "to foolishly give in to temptation."

2. Those that use the second meaning subscribe to the idea called the "Divine Passive." It states that God is held responsible (because He is omnipotent) for that which He does not prevent. The LORD is not the deceiver but He takes responsibility for it, because He allows those who foolishly gives in to temptation the opportunity to pursue it.

3. In the Hebrew Bible this root appears 28 times, but the pu'al form occurs only here and in Jer 20:10 and Prv 25:15.

4. EZEKIEL 20

BHS	וְגַם־אֲנִי נָתַתִּי לָהֶם חֻקִּים לֹא טוֹבִים	25a
Ltrl	good—not—statutes—to them—I gave—I—and also	
KJB	Wherefore I gave them also statutes that were not good,	
NASB	"I also gave them statutes that were not good	
ESV	Moreover, I gave them statutes that were not good	
NLT	I gave them over to worthless decrees	
NIV	So I gave them other statutes that were not good	

1. Most English translations follow the MT correctly. Some, like the NIV for example, attempt to obscure the embarrassing fact that the author thinks the statutes given to the Israelites in the wilderness were not good: To achieve this, the NIV added "other."

5. EZEKIEL 28

BHS	וָאַבֶּדְךָᵈ כְּרוּב הַסֹּכֵךְᵉ	16c
Ltrl	the covering—cherub—and he will destroy you	
KJB	and I will destroy thee, O covering cherub,	
NASB	And I have destroyed you, you covering cherub,	
ESV	and I destroyed you, O guardian cherub,	
NLT	I expelled you, O mighty guardian,	
NIV	and I expelled you, guardian cherub,	

16ᵈ "LXX Grk, perhaps read Heb; others propose Heb."

1. The Greek Septuagint does indeed have καὶ ἤγαγέ σε meaning, "and led you." The second proposal is to add a waw conversive, and the third proposal states that other sources have the pi'el form meaning, "to cause to perish, to destroy, to kill."

16ᵉ "Lacks this material in the Original Septuagint."

1. וָאַבֶּדְךָ Waw conversive + qal perf. 3ms of the verb אָבַד meaning, "to perish, to be ruined, to destroy" + pronominal suffix 2ms.

2. The above verb is used 184 times in the Hebrew Bible. In addition to the common meaning mentioned above, it could also mean,

   a) "to drive out" (Dt 9:3; Jer 27:10, 15).

   b) "to be wandering" (Dt 26:5).

   c) In Jeremiah and Ezekiel it often has the meaning of "to be lost" (Jer 18:18, 48:36, 49:38, 50:6) and (Ezk 7:26, 19:5, 34:16, 37:11).

3. The meaning is often coupled to the ceremony that was enacted every year on the Day of Atonement. The goat was driven away into the wilderness; it was not killed (Lv 16:22).

6. EZEKIEL 37

BHS	וַיֹּאמֶר אֵלַי בֶּן־אָדָם הֲתִחְיֶינָה הָעֲצָמוֹת הָאֵלֶּה	3a
Ltrl	the these—the bones—can live?—man—son of—to me—and he said	
KJB	And he said unto me, Son of man, can these bones live?	
NASB	He said to me, "Son of man, can these bones live?"	
ESV	And he said to me, "Son of man, can these bones live?"	
NLT	Then he asked me, "Son of man, can these bones become living people again?"	
NIV	He asked me, "Son of man, can these bones live?"	

1 הֲתִחְיֶינָה Interrogative hey + Qal impf. 3fp of the verb חָיָה meaning, "will they live?" (Chapters 50.1.1 in Vol. 3, and 21.7 in Vol. 1).

2 הָעֲצָמוֹת Definite article (Chapter 12.2 in Vol. 1) + noun, f. pl. of עֶצֶם "bone, self, substance" (Chapter 10.11.B.1.1 in Vol. 1).

7. EZEKIEL 39

BHS	וְשֹׁבַבְתִּיךָ וְשִׁשֵּׁאתִיךָᵃ	2a
Ltrl	and I will lead you on—I will turn you around	
KJB	And I will turn thee back, and leave but the sixth part of thee,	
NASB	and I will turn you around, lead you on a rope	
ESV	And I will turn you about and drive you forward,	
NLT	I will turn you around and drive you	
NIV	I will turn you around and drag you along.	
YLT	And have turned thee back, and enticed thee,	

2ᵃ "Targum Heb = Heb?"

1 The footnote mentions that a Targum has the form וְהִשֵּׁאתִיךָ which is the hiph'il perf. 1cs of the root נשא meaning, "and I will beguile (deceive) you."

2 וְשִׁשֵּׁאתִיךָ Waw consecutive + Pi'el perf. 1cs + suffix 2ms of the root ששא apparently meaning, "to lead on," or "to annihilate," or "leave by the sixth part." The latter translation is confusing it with שָׁסָה meaning, "to plunder, spoil."

3 This is the only occurrence of this word in the Hebrew Bible (a *hapax legomenon*), and therefore we cannot be sure what it means.

82.31 DANIEL

1. DANIEL 1

BHS	וַיְהִי בָהֶם מִבְּנֵי יְהוּדָה דָּנִיֵּאל[b] [a]	6
Ltrl	Daniel—Judah—from the sons of—in them—and it was	
KJB	Now among these were of the children of Judah, Daniel,	
NASB	Now among them from the sons of Judah were Daniel,	
NIV	Among those who were chosen were some from Judah: Daniel,	

6[a] "Sebir Heb."

1. In this Sebir (marginal notes by the Masoretes to indicate an unusual word or usage in the text), the form is וַיִּהְיוּ which is the qal impf. 3mp of the verb "to be," meaning, "and they were," as apposed to the qal impf. 3ms in the MT which means, "and he was."

2. The plural form makes more sense in this context and the Masoretes correctly decided to add a Sebir here.

6[b] "Cairo Geniza here and here and there Heb, likewise Ez 14:14, 20."

1. The form דָּנִיאֵל is indeed found in Ezekiel, and is an alternative form of the one found here.

2. Both the above-mentioned forms of the name "Daniel" can be translated as, "God is my judge." The verb דִּין means, "to judge," and אֵל is used 247 times in the Hebrew Bible as the name of the God of the Hebrew people (Chapter 85.1.2).

2. DANIEL 2

BHS	וּלְדָנִיֵּאל סְגִד	46b
Ltrl	he paid homage—and to Daniel	
KJB	and worshipped Daniel,	
NASB	and did homage to Daniel,	
ESV	and paid homage to Daniel,	
NLT	before Daniel and worshiped him,	
NIV	before Daniel and paid him honor	

1. סְגִד Pe'al perf. 3ms of the Aramaic verb meaning, "pay homage." Hebrew has an identical verb meaning, "prostrate oneself in worship; be lowly, submissive; prostrate oneself in prayer."

2. The portions of the Hebrew Bible that were written in Aramaic include Ezra 4:8–6:18 and 7:12–26 (67 verses), and Daniel 2:4b–7:28 (200 verses). Various proper names and single words and phrases in Aramaic are scattered throughout the Hebrew Bible (Gen 31:47, Jeremiah 10:11).

3. This specifically religious veneration by the king of Daniel and Daniel's apparent acceptance of it seems to have been an embarrassment for some translators and they therefore opted to weaken the religious overtones of the verb that is used.

3. DANIEL 5

BHS	וּדְנָה כְתָבָא דִּי רְשִׁים מְנֵא מְנֵא תְּקֵל וּפַרְסִין׃	25
Ltrl	*uparsin-tekeil—menei—menei*—it was inscribed—that—inscription—and this	
KJB	And this *is* the writing that was written, MENE, MENE, TEKEL, UPHARSIN.	
NASB	"Now this is the inscription that was written out: 'MENE, MENE, TEKEL, UPHARSIN.'	
ESV	And this is the writing that was inscribed: Mene, Mene, Tekel, and Parsin.	
NLT	"This is the message that was written: Mene, Mene, Tekel, and Parsin	
NIV	"This is the inscription that was written: mene, mene, tekel, parsin	

25ᵃ "Lacks material LXX (likewise LXX in summary before read compare 17) Vulgate Josephus Antiquities (Vol.) X 11:3, addition? Compare (verse) 26."

1. The Greek Septuagint has only three words namely μανή θεκέλ φαρές (*mene tekel Peres*).

25ᵇ "LXX (LXX in the same place) Vulgate Hieronymus Josephus Antiquities Grk, probably read Heb."

1. This footnote suggests an alternative form of the Chaldean verb with the same meaning.

2. Chaldean is an old name for the Aramaic language, particularly biblical Aramaic.

3. וּדְנָה Waw consecutive + Chaldean demonstrative pronoun emphatic, "this."

4. כְתָבָא Chaldean noun, m. sg. emphatic from the root כתב meaning, "writing, inscription."

5. דִּי Chaldean relative pronoun, "which."

6. רְשִׁים Chaldean Pa'el part. passive m. sg of the root רשם meaning, "to inscribe."

7. מְנֵא Chaldean Pa'el perf. 3ms of the root מנא meaning, "to number, reckon." In this context then meaning, "God has numbered (the days of) your kingdom." In other words, "God has put an end to your kingdom."

8. תְּקֵל Chaldean Pa'el part. passive m. sg. of the root תקל meaning, "to weigh."

9. וּפַרְסִין Waw consecutive + Chaldean Pe'il perf. 3fs of the root פָּרַס meaning, "to break in two."

4. DANIEL 8

BHS	עַד עֶרֶב בֹּקֶר אַלְפַּיִם וּשְׁלֹשׁ מֵאוֹת וְנִצְדַּק קֹדֶשׁ׃	14b
Ltrl	—and it will be cleaned—hundred—and three—two thousand—morning—evening—up to sanctuary	
KJB	Unto two thousand and three hundred days; then shall the sanctuary be cleansed.	
NASB	"For 2,300 evenings and mornings; then the holy place will be properly restored."	
ESV	"For 2,300 evenings and mornings. Then the sanctuary shall be restored to its rightful state."	
NLT	"It will take 2,300 evenings and mornings; then the Temple will be made right again."	
NIV	It will take 2,300 evenings and mornings; then the sanctuary will be reconsecrated.	

1   עַד This preposition has a vast array of meanings. It is found with various adverbs of time and then meaning, "even to, until, towards the end of."

2   אַלְפַּיִם Refer to Chapter 18.8 in Vol. 1 for an explanation of the numbers larger than 99.

3   וְנִצְדַּק Waw conversive + Niph'al perf. 3ms of the verb צָדַק / צְדֹק meaning in the niph'al binyan, "and it will be justified (put right, put in a right condition)," or "its cause vindicated (cleared of blame / suspicion, proved to be right or justified)."

4   קֹדֶשׁ Noun, m. sg. meaning, "apartness, sacredness." Of places it means among others, "the sanctuary." Generally this means, "a place set apart as sacred by God's presence." More specifically is refers to the temple and its precincts, or the tabernacle and its courts.

5. DANIEL 11

BHS	וּבָנָיו^a יִתְגָּרוּ^b וְאָסְפוּ^b	10a
Ltrl	and they will assemble—they will wage war—and his sons	
KJB	But his sons shall be stirred up, and shall assemble	
NASB	"And his sons will mobilize and assemble	
ESV	"His sons shall wage war and assemble	
NIV	His sons will prepare for war and assemble	

10[a] "LXX Syr Vulgate as Qere Heb; read with Ketiv LXX Heb."

1   This footnote points us to the Qere form, which makes sense as the verbs are in the plural.

10[b-b] "LXX singular, read Heb."

1   When the Qere form above is accepted, this footnote does not apply.

2   וּבָנָיו This is the Qere form which consists of the noun with the plural suffix meaning, "his sons."

3   יִתְגָּרוּ Hithpa'el impf. 3mp of the verb גָּרָה meaning, "engage in strife." Only here in Daniel does it take on the meaning of, "attack, wage war."

82.32 HOSEA

1. HOSEA 1

BHS	דְּבַר־יְהוָה אֲשֶׁר הָיָה אֶל־הוֹשֵׁעַ	1
Ltrl	Hosea—toward—it was—that—Yahweh—the word of	
KJB	The word of the LORD that came unto Hosea,	
NASB	The word of the LORD which came to Hosea	
ESV	The word of the LORD that came to Hosea,	
NLT	The LORD gave this message to Hosea	
NIV	The word of the LORD that came to Hosea	

1 The verb יָשַׁע means, "to deliver, be saved, be liberated."

2 Keeping the above verb in mind, the literal translation of the name "Hosea" would then be, "deliverer."

3 A number of people in the Hebrew Bible are called "Hosea."

  1 The prophet in the Book of Hosea.

  2 According to Nm 13:8 and Dt 32:44, this was the original name of Joshua.

  3 According to 2 Kgs 15:30 and 17:1, the last king of the northern kingdom of Israel was called "Hosea."

  4 According to 1 Chr 27:20, an Ephraimite chief under David was called "Hosea."

  5 According to Neh 10:24, a chief under Nehemiah was called "Hosea."

2. HOSEA 6

BHS	כִּי חֶסֶד חָפַצְתִּי וְלֹא־זָבַח וְדַעַת אֱלֹהִים מֵעֹלוֹת׃	6
Ltrl	—and knowledge of—a sacrifice—and not—I have delight in—loving-kindness–for more than whole burnt offerings—God	
KJB	For I desired mercy, and not sacrifice; and the knowledge of God more than burnt offerings.	
NASB	For I delight in loyalty rather than sacrifice, And in the knowledge of God rather than burnt offerings.	
ESV	For I desire steadfast love and not sacrifice, the knowledge of God rather than burnt offerings.	
NLT	I want you to show love, not offer sacrifices. I want you to know me more than I want burnt offerings.	
NIV	For I desire mercy, not sacrifice, and acknowledgment of God rather than burnt offerings.	

1 חֶסֶד Refer to Lv 20:17 for a complete discussion of this term.

2 חָפַצְתִּי Qal perf. 1 cs meaning, "to have delight in, to have pleasure in."

3   מֵעֹלוֹת Prep. + noun, f. pl. abs. meaning, "more than whole burnt-offerings." Refer to Chapter 17.5.4 in Vol. 1 for the use of the preposition to express a comparative statement.

4   Take note that the NIV replaces "loving-kindness" or "steadfast love" (ESV) with "mercy" to match the LXX-based quotations from Mt 9:13 and 12:7.

5   The NASB is one of the few English translations that display the true meaning of the verb which is more than "I desire."

3. HOSEA 7

BHS	וַיְהִי אֶפְרַיִם כְּיוֹנָה פוֹתָה אֵין לֵב	11a
Ltrl	heart / mind—there is not—simple—like a dove—Ephraim—and he was	
KJB	Ephraim also is like a silly dove without heart:	
NASB	So Ephraim has become like a silly dove, without sense;	
ESV	Ephraim is like a dove, silly and without sense,	
NLT	"The people of Israel have become like silly, witless doves,	
NIV	"Ephraim is like a dove, easily deceived and senseless—	

1   כְּיוֹנָה Prep. + noun, f. sg. meaning, "dove" (Chapter 83.6.2).

2   פוֹתָה Qal part. f. sg. of the verb פָּתָה meaning, "to be simple."

3   אֶפְרַיִם Proper noun, m. sg. The second son of Joseph and Asenath (Gen 41:50–52). The name is associated with the verb פָּרָה meaning, "to bear fruit, be fruitful."

4   After the death of King Solomon, the kingdom of Saul and David was divided in two. The southern kingdom consisted only of the tribes of Judah and Benjamin and thus became known as the kingdom of Judah, with Jerusalem as its capital. The northern kingdom consisted of the remaining ten tribes and was called Israel.

5   Joseph was the eleventh son of Jacob (also called Israel), but died in Egypt. His sons Ephraim and Manasseh were known as "the House of Joseph" and they served as one of the twelve tribes in place of Joseph. Although Manasseh was the eldest, he was not blessed by Jacob, and the tribe was called the tribe of Ephraim.

6   The tribes were named after the twelve sons that Jacob had with four women. They are numbered here in the chronological order that they were born.

Leah	Rachel	Bilha	Zilpa
Gen 29:16	Gen 29:28	Gen 30:3	Gen 30:9
Older sister	Younger sister	A handmaid	A handmaid
Reuben (1)	Joseph (11)	Dan (5)	Gad (7)
Simeon (2)	Benjamin (12)	Naphtali (6)	Asher (8)
Levi (3)			
Judah (4)			
Issachar (9)			
Zebulun (10)			
Dina (a daughter)			

		12b
BHS	אֶפְרוֹשׂ עֲלֵיהֶם רִשְׁתִּי כְּעוֹף הַשָּׁמַיִם אוֹרִידֵם	
Ltrl	the heavens—like birds of—my net—on them—I will spread	
KJB	I will spread my net upon them; I will bring them down as the fowls of the heaven;	
NASB	I will spread My net over them; I will bring them down like the birds of the sky.	
ESV	I will spread over them my net; I will bring them down like birds of the heavens;	
NLT	I will throw my net over them and bring them down like a bird from the sky.	
NIV	I will throw my net over them; I will pull them down like the birds in the sky.	

1. אֶפְרוֹשׂ Qal impf. 1cs of the verb פָּרַשׂ meaning, "to spread out, spread."
2. רִשְׁתִּי Noun, f. sg. + suffix 1cs meaning, "my net."
3. כְּעוֹף Prep. + collective noun, m. sg. cstr. Refer to Hattingh (2012), p. 210.
4. אוֹרִידֵם Hiph'il impf. 1cs +suffix 3mp of the verb יָרַד meaning, "to go down, come down, descend" in the qal binyan, and "to bring down."

4. HOSEA 11

		11a
BHS	יֶחֶרְדוּ כְצִפּוֹר מִמִּצְרַיִם וּכְיוֹנָה מֵאֶרֶץ אַשּׁוּר	
Ltrl	Assyria—from the land of—and like a dove—from Egypt—like a bird—they will tremble	
KJB	They shall tremble as a bird out of Egypt, and as a dove out of the land of Assyria:	
NASB	They will come trembling like birds from Egypt And like doves from the land of Assyria;	
ESV	they shall come trembling like birds from Egypt, and like doves from the land of Assyria,	
NLT	Like a flock of birds, they will come from Egypt. Trembling like doves, they will return from Assyria.	
NIV	They will come from Egypt, trembling like sparrows, from Assyria, fluttering like doves.	

1   כְּצִפּוֹר Noun, f. sg. meaning, "bird," and less often used collectively. Also refer to the second note in Chpt 5.1.1 in Vol. 1. The female form צִפֹּרָה was the name of Moses' wife in Ex 2:21, 4:25, 18:2.

5. HOSEA 12

BHS	וְאָנֹכִי יְהוָה אֱלֹהֶיךָ מֵאֶרֶץ מִצְרָיִם	10a
Ltrl	Egypt—from the land of—your God—Yahweh—and I	
KJB	And I that am the LORD thy God from the land of Egypt	
NASB	But I have been the LORD your God since the land of Egypt;	
ESV	I am the LORD your God from the land of Egypt;	
NLT	"But I am the LORD your God, who rescued you from slavery in Egypt.	
NIV	"I have been the LORD your God ever since you came out of Egypt;	
ISV	"Yet I remain the LORD your God, who brought you out of the land of Egypt.	

1   From the examples above it is clear that some translators finds this description of God's origins objectionable, and made a number of changes in their translations.

6. HOSEA 13

BHS	אֱהִיᵃ דְבָרֶיךָᵇ מָוֶת	14c
Ltrl	death—your plagues—where	
KJB	O death, I will be thy plagues;	
NASB	Death, where are your thorns?	
ESV	O Death, where are your plagues?	
NLT	O death, bring on your terrors!	
NIV	Where, O death, are your plagues?	

14ᵃ "LXX (Syr) Grk, read Heb compare (footnote) 10ᵃ."

1   The Greek Septuagint does indeed have που meaning, "where is?" The suggested אַיֵּה also means, "where?" The same word is found in verse 10.

14ᵇ "Multiple (20–60) Manuscripts Heb (=Heb?); LXX (Syr) Grk."

1   This footnote suggests that the noun should be the singular suffix. The Greek Septuagint does indeed have η δίκη σου meaning the singular, "your punishment."

2   אֱהִי Adverb meaning, "where?" It is found three times in the Hebrew Bible: Once in verse ten, and twice in this verse. This is also the way in which it is quoted in 1 Cor 15:55 in the NT. It is taken by many of the older interpreters (KJV, NKJV, DRB) as the qal impf 1cs of the verb הָיָה with apocope (the loss of a sound or sounds at the end of a word) then meaning, "I would be."

This translation is found ten times in the Hebrew Bible (Neh 1:4, 2:11, 13, 15; Ps 18:23, 38:14, 69:11, 73:14; Job 30:9; Jgs 18:4).

3 Many translations (KJV, ESV, NIV) add the nuance of a redition (contemptuous ridicule or mockery) namely, "O!."

82.33 JOEL

1. JOEL 1

BHS	דְּבַר־יְהוָה אֲשֶׁר הָיָה אֶל־יוֹאֵל	1
Ltrl	Joel—toward—it was—that—Yahweh—the word of	
KJB	The word of the LORD that came to Joel,	
NASB	The word of the LORD that came to Joel,	
ESV	The word of the LORD that came to Joel,	
NLT	The LORD gave this message to Joel	
NIV	The word of the LORD that came to Joel,	

1 It would seem that the name "Joel" is a combination of "YHWH" and "El," but we have no evidence to support this view.

2 We do know that it is the name of several Israelites mentioned in the Hebrew Bible. For example, 1 Sm 8:2, 1 Chr 4:35, 5:4, 5:8, 5:12.

2. JOEL 2

BHS	וּבְעַד הַשֶּׁלַח יִפֹּלוּ ᵃלֹא יִבְצָעוּ:	8b
Ltrl	they will stop—not—they will fall—the sword—and when	
KJB	and when they fall upon the sword, they shall not be wounded.	
NASB	When they burst through the defenses, They do not break ranks.	
ESV	they burst through the weapons and are not halted.	
NLT	They break through defenses without missing a step.	
NIV	They plunge through defenses without breaking ranks.	
ISV	When they fall by the sword they are not injured.	

8ᵃ⁻ᵃ "Corrupt? it has been proposed Heb and compare with Heb 9 (compare 9a); transpose Heb before Heb?"

1 The two alternative verbs are discussed below. No reason is given for the suggestion to move the negative which would drastically change the meaning.

2 יִבְצָעוּ Qal impf 3ms of the verb בָּצַע meaning at its core, "to cut off, to break off, to gain by violence." Here the object namely "their ranks" is ommitted, and it takes on the meaning of,

"breaking off / stopping (their ranks)." This verb occurs 17 times in the Hebrew Bible, with no less than 15 different meanings.

3 יְבַקֵּעוּ Qal impf 3ms of the verb בָּקַע meaning, "to cleave, to break open, to break through." Again the object is ommitted, and the proposal would be acceptable, but seems to be unnecessary, as the current MT also makes perfect sense.

4 The translators of the KJB chose "wounded," and the ISV chose "injured" primarily because for them this was supposed to be a reference to an army of locusts (1:4, 2:3, 25) and not a human army.

3. JOEL 3

BHS	וְנִבְּאוּ בְּנֵיכֶם וּבְנוֹתֵיכֶם זִקְנֵיכֶם חֲלֹמוֹת יַחֲלֹמוּן	1b
Ltrl	—dreams—your old men—and your daughters—your sons—they will prophesy they will dream	
KJB	and your sons and your daughters shall prophesy, your old men shall dream dreams,	
NASB	And your sons and daughters will prophesy, Your old men will dream dreams,	
ESV	your sons and your daughters shall prophesy, your old men shall dream dreams,	
NLT	Your sons and daughters will prophesy. Your old men will dream dreams,	
NIV	Your sons and daughters will prophesy, your old men will dream dreams,	

1 In the Greek Septuagint, Chapter 2 has 32 verses followed by a Chapter 3. Most modern Bibles follow this enumeration. However, in the Hebrew Bible Chapter 2 has only 27 verses. The next five verses are numbered as Chapter 3:1–5, followed by a Chapter 4. This Chapter 4 is then the same as Chapter 3 in the Greek Septuagint and modern translations.

2 Most English translations diligently follow the literal meaning of the MT.

4. JOEL 4

BHS	בְּעֵמֶק הֶחָרוּץ	14a
Ltrl	the strict decision—valley of	
KJB	in the valley of decision!	
NIV	in the valley of decision!	

1 Refer to the notes in Joel 3 above.

2 For this phrase, the Greek Septuagint has εν τη κοιλάδι της δίκης, "in the valley of punishment / justice / righteousness." Jerome's Latin Vulgate renders it as *concisionis*, meaning either "decision" or "destruction."

3 חָרוּץ has three meanings.

   a) an adjective meaning, "sharp, diligent," and is used to describe a threshing instrument (Is 31:15, Am 1:3).

b) a noun meaning, "moat, trench" (Dn 9:25).

c) a noun meaning, "strict decision" and used here in Joel. It is then often linked to a sharp instrument like a sickle that is used in a harvest. The link between "harvest" and "a final decision / determination" is well established (Prv 22:8, Jer 51:33). This can then furthermore be linked to the iconography of Death wielding a scythe (a kind of sickle) in his hands, as a symbol of a final, irrevocable decision, about the life of man.

82.34 AMOS

1. AMOS 1

BHS	דִּבְרֵי עָמוֹס אֲשֶׁר־הָיָה בַנֹּקְדִים מִתְּקוֹעַ	1
Ltrl	from Tekoa—among herdsmen—he was—that—Amos—the words of	
KJB	The words of Amos, who was among the herdsmen of Tekoa,	
NASB	The words of Amos, who was among the sheepherders from Tekoa,	
ESV	The words of Amos, who was among the shepherds of Tekoa,	
NLT	This message was given to Amos, a shepherd from the town of Tekoa	
NIV	The words of Amos, one of the shepherds of Tekoa	

1 עָמַס A verb meaning, "to load" or "to carry a load."

2. AMOS 4

BHS	הָפַכְתִּי בָכֶם כְּמַהְפֵּכַת אֱלֹהִים אֶת־סְדֹם וְאֶת־עֲמֹרָה	11a
Ltrl	and Gomorrah—Sodom—God—as the overthrow of—some of you—I have overthrown	
KJB	I have overthrown some of you, as God overthrew Sodom and Gomorrah,	
NASB	"I overthrew you, as God overthrew Sodom and Gomorrah,	
ESV	"I overthrew some of you, as when God overthrew Sodom and Gomorrah,	
NLT	"I destroyed some of your cities, as I destroyed Sodom and Gomorrah.	
NIV	"I overthrew some of you as I overthrew Sodom and Gomorrah.	

11ᵃ "Compare 10ᵉ."

1 Footnote 10ᵉ suggests that we change the word in verse 10 to וּבְאַפִּי which means, "and in my anger" and then also insert it here at the beginning of the verse.

11ᵇ "It has been proposed Heb."

1 This footnote suggests that we change the word to בָּתֵּיכֶם which means, "your houses." In this context it would make sense, but there is no reason for the change.

2 הָפַכְתִּי Qal perf. 1cs of the verb הָפַךְ meaning, "to turn, overturn, overthrow."

3 כְּמַהְפֵּכַת Prep. + noun, f. sg. cstr. meaning, "overthrow." This form appears six times in the Hebrew Bible, is always in the construct, and is always used when Sodom and Gomorrah is mentioned (Dt 29:23; Is 1:7, 13:19; Jer 49:18, 50:40).

4 It is said that translations like NIV and NLT have changed "Elohim" in the MT to "I" in order to remove any form of polytheistic language from their translations.

3. AMOS 7

BHS	וָאֹמַר אֲנָךְ	8b
Ltrl	a plumb-line—and I said	
KJB	And I said, A plumbline.	
NASB	And I said, "A plumb line."	
ESV	And I said, "A plumb line."	
NLT	I answered, "A plumb line."	
NIV	"A plumb line," I replied.	

1 Plumb line: a line / string with a plumb attached to one end. It is used for determining the depth of water, or determining if an upright structure (like a wall) is perfectly vertical. Structures that are found to be "out of plumb" are deemed unacceptable, and have to be pulled down. Here the plumb line is used figuratively to mean the measure by which a people will be judged (2 Kgs 21:13, Is 34:11, Lam 2:8).

4. AMOS 9

BHS	וְכָל־הַגּוֹיִם אֲשֶׁר־נִקְרָא שְׁמִי עֲלֵיהֶם	12b
Ltrl	upon them—my name—he is called—that—the nations—and all	
KJB	And all the Gentiles who are called by My name,"	
NASB	And all the nations who are called by My name,"	
ESV	and all the nations who are called by my name,"	
NLT	and all the nations I have called to be mine."	
NIV	and all the nations that bear my name,	

1 הַגּוֹיִם Noun, m. pl. The word refers to two groups of people:

   a) Israel. This could be Israel per se, the descendants of the patriarchs (Abraham, Isaac, and Jacob), or Israel and Judah.

   b) Non-Hebrew peoples. Heathens, Gentiles. This meaning is common (Ex 9:24, 34:10; Is 11:10, 12).

2 נִקְרָא Niph'al perf. 3ms. The verb is in the singular and "my name" would then be the subject of the verb. This is then translated as, "on whom my name is called."

82.35 OBADIAH

1. OBADIAH 1

BHS	חֲזוֹן עֹבַדְיָה	1
Ltrl	Obadiah—the vision of	
KJB	The vision of Obadiah.	
NASB	The vision of Obadiah.	
ESV	The vision of Obadiah.	
NLT	This is the vision that the Sovereign LORD revealed to Obadiah	
NIV	The vision of Obadiah.	

1. עָבַד in the Qal binyan means, "to labor, work, do work," and also, "to work for another, serve, serve by labor."

2. Keeping the above verb in mind, the literal translation of the name "Obadiah" would then be, "Servant of Yah" (Chapter 87.3.1).

BHS	אִםᵃ־תַּגְבִּיהַּ כַּנֶּשֶׁר וְאִםᵇ־בֵּין כּוֹכָבִים שִׂיםᵇᶜ קִנֶּךָ	4a
Ltrl	your nest—set—stars—and among—as an eagle—you ascend high—though	
KJB	Though thou exalt *thyself* as the eagle, and though thou set thy nest among the stars,	
NASB	"Though you build high like the eagle, Though you set your nest among the stars,	
ESV	Though you soar aloft like the eagle, though your nest is set among the stars,	
NLT	But even if you soar as high as eagles and build your nest among the stars,	
NIV	Though you soar like the eagle and make your nest among the stars,	

4ᵃ "Jer 49:16 Heb."

1. The two verses are similar but are started with different conjunctions.

4ᵇ⁻ᵇ "Lacking material in Jer 49:16."

1. This phrase does not appear in Jer 49:16.

4ᶜ "Either read Heb (compare Versions) or delete."

1. The alternative proposed by this footnote is the impf. However, the part. passive is perfectly suitable here.

2. שִׂים Qal part. passive m. sg. meaning, "set."

3. תָּשִׂים Qal impf. 2ms meaning, "you will set."

4 כַּנֶּ֫שֶׁר "The Hebrew word *nesher* is often translated as 'eagle', but this is as much a generic word as the English. As many of the references are used figuratively, it does not give many clues as to the specific species, and could include any large raptor (Chpt 83.3)."[39]

82.36 JONAH

1. JONAH 1

BHS	וַיְהִי דְּבַר־יְהוָה אֶל־יוֹנָה	1
Ltrl	Jonah—to—Yahweh—the word of—And it was	
KJB	Now the word of the LORD came unto Jonah	
NASB	The word of the LORD came to Jonah	
ESV	Now the word of the LORD came to Jonah	
NLT	The LORD gave this message to Jonah	
NIV	The word of the LORD came to Jonah	

1 יוֹנָה in Hebrew means, "dove" (Chapter 81, 83.6).

2 "The Hebrew word *jonah* is a generic term usually translated as 'dove.' It is derived from the stem *anah* which means 'to mourn,' probably applied to the dove because of the call of some species like the Laughing Dove, for example."[40]

2. JONAH 2

BHS	וַיְמַן יְהוָה דָּג גָּדוֹל לִבְלֹעַ אֶת־יוֹנָה	1a
Ltrl	Jonah—DDOM—to swallow—great—fish—Yahweh—and he assigned	
KJB	Now the LORD had prepared a great fish to swallow up Jonah.	
NASB	And the LORD appointed a great fish to swallow Jonah,	
ESV	And the LORD appointed a great fish to swallow up Jonah.	
NLT	Now the LORD had arranged for a great fish to swallow Jonah.	
NIV	Now the LORD provided a huge fish to swallow Jonah,	

1 וַיְמַן Pi'el impf. 3ms of מָנָה meaning, "to count, number, reckon, assign, appoint."

---

39 Hattingh, Tian (2012), p.150.
40 Hattingh, Tian (2012), p.148.

BHS	וַיְהִ֤י יוֹנָה֙ בִּמְעֵ֣י הַדָּ֔ג שְׁלֹשָׁ֥ה יָמִ֖ים וּשְׁלֹשָׁ֥ה לֵילֽוֹת׃	1b
Ltrl	nights—and three—days—three—the fish—in the belly—Jonah—and he was	
KJB	And Jonah was in the belly of the fish three days and three nights.	
NASB	and Jonah was in the stomach of the fish three days and three nights.	
ESV	And Jonah was in the belly of the fish three days and three nights.	
NLT	And Jonah was inside the fish for three days and three nights.	
NIV	and Jonah was in the belly of the fish three days and three nights.	

1 בִּמְעֵי Inseparable preposition + noun, m. pl. construct meaning, "in the internal organs, bowels, inward parts, intestines."

3. JONAH 3

BHS	מַהֲלַ֖ךְ שְׁלֹ֥שֶׁת יָמִֽים׃	3c
Ltrl	days—three—a journey	
KJB	of three days' journey.	
NASB	a three days' walk.	
ESV	three days' journey in breadth.	
NLT	it took three days to see it all.	
NIV	it took three days to go through it.	

1 מַהֲלַךְ Noun, m. sg. cstr. meaning, "walk of, journey of."

2 We simply do not know what the author meant with "a walk" or "a journey," and it would therefore be unwise to assume that it literally means, "the distance that a person could walk in three days."

82.37 MICAH

1. MICAH 1

BHS	ᵃדְּבַר־יְהוָ֗ה אֲשֶׁ֤ר הָיָה֙ אֶל־מִיכָ֔ה	1
Ltrl	Micah—to—it was—that—Yahweh—The word of	
KJB	The word of the LORD that came to Micah	
NASB	The word of the LORD which came to Micah	
ESV	The word of the LORD that came to Micah	
NLT	The LORD gave this message to Micah	
NIV	The word of the LORD that came to Micah	

1ᵃ⁻ᵃ "The original LXX Grk."

Selected Passages

1. The beginning of the verse in the Greek Septuagint reads as follows,

και	εγένετο	λόγος	κυρίου	προς	Μιχαίαν
and	it came to pass	the word of	the LORD	to	Micah

2. Footnote 18[b] in Jer 26:18 states that there is a Ketiv (written) form מִיכָיה and a Qere (to be read) form מִיכָה The written form can be seen as consisting of the interrogative pronoun מִי (who), followed by the inseparable preposition כְּ (like) and יָה (Yahweh). Together these three words would then amount up to, "who (is) like Yahweh?" (Chapter 86.4.6,7).

BHS	אֶעֱשֶׂה מִסְפֵּד כַּתַּנִּים וְאֵבֶל כִּבְנוֹת יַעֲנָה:	8b
Ltrl	ostrich—like daughters of—and a mourning—like jackals—a wailing—I will make	
KJB	I will make a wailing like the dragons, and mourning as the owls.	
NKJV	I will make a wailing like the jackals And a mourning like the ostriches,	
NASB	I must make a lament like the jackals And a mourning like the ostriches.	
ESV	I will make lamentation like the jackals, and mourning like the ostriches.	
NLT	I will howl like a jackal and moan like an owl.	
NIV	I will howl like a jackal and moan like an owl.	

1. מִסְפֵּד Noun, m. sg. meaning, "wailing because of a calamity experienced."

2. Refer to Chapter 83.2.1.2 for a discussion of the phrase כִּבְנוֹת יַעֲנָה.

BHS	הַרְחִבִי קָרְחָתֵךְ כַּנֶּשֶׁר	16b
Ltrl	like a vulture—your baldness—enlarge	
KJB	make yourselves as bald as an eagle,	
NASB	Extend your baldness like the eagle,	
ESV	make yourselves as bald as the eagle,	
NLT	Make yourselves as bald as a vulture,	
NIV	make yourself as bald as the vulture,	

1. הַרְחִבִי Hiph'il imp. f. sg. of the verb רָחַב meaning, "to be / grow wide or large." In the hiph'il binyan it then means, "cause to be/grow large = enlarge."

2. קָרְחָתֵךְ Noun, f. sg. + suffix 2fs meaning, "your baldness, your bald spot (made as a sign of mourning)." "A characteristic for which vultures are well known is their almost bare heads and necks, which is covered with short, sparse, downy-like feathers only. This was probably acquired during their evolution as a result of their carrion-feeding habit of reaching deep into carcasses."[41]

---

[41] Hattingh, Tian (2012), p.168.

3 כַּנֶּ֫שֶׁר "The Hebrew word *nesher* is often translated as 'eagle', but this is as much a generic term as the English. As many of the references are used figuratively, it does not give many clues as to the specific species, and could include any large raptor (Chpt 83.3)."[42]

2. MICAH 5

BHS	וְאַתָּה בֵּֽית־לֶ֫חֶם אֶפְרָ֫תָה צָעִיר לִהְיוֹת בְּאַלְפֵ֫י יְהוּדָה	1a
Ltrl	Judah—in thousands—for you are—little—Ephratah—house of Lechem—and you	
KJB	But thou, Bethlehem Ephratah, though thou be little among the thousands of Judah,	
NASB	"But as for you, Bethlehem Ephrathah, Too little to be among the clans of Judah,	
ESV	But you, O Bethlehem Ephrathah, who are too little to be among the clans of Judah,	
NLT	But you, O Bethlehem Ephrathah, are only a small village among all the people of Judah.	
NIV	"But you, Bethlehem Ephrathah, though you are small among the clans of Judah,	

1ᵃ⁻ᵃ "Probably read Heb."

1 אֶפְרָת הַצָּעִיר This Hebrew in this footnote has the same meaning as the MT.

1ᵇ "Probably delete, from ad."

1 לִהְיוֹת is the qal infinitive construct of the verb הָיָה meaning, "to be." From the context there seems no reason to delete the word in the MT.

BHS	מִמְּךָ לִי יֵצֵא לִהְיוֹת מוֹשֵׁל בְּיִשְׂרָאֵל	1b
Ltrl	in Israel—ruler—the one to be—he shall come forth—to me—out of you	
KJB	yet out of thee shall he come forth unto me that is to be ruler in Israel;	
NASB	From you One will go forth for Me to be ruler in Israel.	
ESV	from you shall come forth for me one who is to be ruler in Israel,	
NLT	Yet a ruler of Israel, whose origins are in the distant past, will come from you on my behalf.	
NIV	out of you will come for me one who will be ruler over Israel,	

1ᶜ "Perhaps read Heb compare 2ab; or it has dropped out (the) verb after Heb?"

1 The masculine noun יֶ֫לֶד meaning, "a child, son, boy, youth" will be a much better fit in this context, but we have no evidence that such a sizeable mistake was made.

2 יֵצֵא Qal impf. 3ms of the verb יָצָא meaning, "to go out," or "to come out."

3 מוֹשֵׁל Qal part. active m. sg. of the verb מָשַׁל meaning, "to rule, have dominion, to reign."

---

42 Hattingh, Tian (2012), p. xxii.

BHS	וּמוֹצָאֹתָיו מִקֶּדֶם מִימֵי עוֹלָם׃	1c
Ltrl	everlasting—from—from old—and whose goings are	
KJB	whose goings forth have been from of old, from everlasting.	
NASB	His goings forth are from long ago, From the days of eternity."	
ESV	whose coming forth is from of old, from ancient days.	
NLT	whose origins are in the distant past,	
NIV	whose origins are from of old, from ancient times."	

1   וּמוֹצָאֹתָיו Waw consecutive prefix and 3ms suffix added onto the f. pl. noun. The meaning of this noun is not at all clear. Other than here, it only occurs in 2 Kgs 10:27, and there it is used euphemistically in a Qere to mean, "privy, outhouse" from the literal "places of going out to."

82.38 NAHUM

1. NAHUM 1

BHS	סֵפֶר חֲזוֹן נַחוּם	1
Ltrl	Nahum—the vision of—the book of	
KJB	The book of the vision of Nahum	
NASB	The book of the vision of Nahum	
ESV	The book of the vision of Nahum	
NLT	This message concerning Nineveh came as a vision to Nahum,	
NIV	The book of the vision of Nahum	

1   נַחוּם This name is from the root נחם which in the pi'el binyan means, "to comfort, console."

2. NAHUM 2

BHS	וּמְחַנֵּק לְלִבְאֹתָיו	13b
Ltrl	for his lionesses—and strangeling	
KJB	and strangled for his lionesses,	
NASB	Killed enough prey for his lionesses,	
ESV	and strangled prey for his lionesses;	
NLT	and strangled prey for his mate.	
NIV	and strangled the prey for his mate,	

1   וּמְחַנֵּק Waw consecutive + pi'el part. act. m. sg. of the verb חָנַק meaning, "to strangle." This form occurs only here in the Hebrew Bible. Another form, of the same verb root but in the niph'al binyan is found in 2 Sm 17:23, and also occurs only this once.

2   The use of this Hebrew word is in accordance with the killing strategy of the spotted cats. Instead of attempting to fatally wound their prey, the would rather clamp their powerful jaws around the throat of the prey and so prevent it from breathing. They would then focus on maintaining their grip, and patiently wait for the prey to be suffocated (strangled) to death.

3   לִלְבָאֹתָיו Prep. + noun f. pl. + suffix 3ms meaning, "his lionesses." There are three variations from the stem לָבִא meaning, "lioness." This stem is used 20 times in the Hebrew Bible (Ez19:2, Gen 49:9, Nm 24:9, Jb 4:11).

4   אֲרִי Noun, m. sg. meaning, "lion." This is a generic term for the animal, and used 78 times in the Hebrew Bible (Am 3:12, 2 Sm 23:20, Lam 3:10, Ps 22:17).

5   אַרְיֵה Noun, m. sg. meaning, "lion." This is variation of the above generic term, and used 47 times in the Hebrew Bible (Am 3:4, Jgs 14:8, 8, 9, 1 Kgs 13:24–28).

6   כְּפִיר Noun, m. sg. meaning, "young lion." This noun appears 32 times in the Hebrew Bible (Samson in Jgs 14:5).

7   שַׁחַל Noun, m. sg. meaning, "lion." This noun appears seven times in the Hebrew Bible (Hos 5:14, Jb 4:10).

8   לַיִשׁ Noun, m. sg. meaning, "lion." This noun appears three times in the Hebrew Bible (Jb 4:11, Is 30:5, Prv 30:30).

9   גּוּר Noun, m. sg. meaning, "whelp." This noun appears seven times in the Hebrew Bible (Gen 49:9; Ez 19:2, 3, 5).

10   גּוֹר Noun, m. sg. meaning, "whelp." This variant spelling of the above mentioned noun appears twice in the Hebrew Bible (Jer 51:38, Na 2:13).

11   There has been much debate and controversy among zoologists on the taxonomical classification of lions. For the sake of this discussion we will accept that the lions of the Hebrew Bible are the Barbary Lion (also called North African Lion, Berber Lion, Atlas Lion, and Egyptian Lion).

12   African lion taxonomy

Kingdom:	*Animalia*
Phylum:	*Chordata*
Class:	*Mammalia*
Order:	*Carnivora* (flesh eating)
Family:	*Felidae* (cats)
Sub-family:	*Pantherinae* (spotted cats)
Genus:	*Panthera*, including the tiger (*P. tigris*), lion (*P. leo*), jaguar (*P. onca*), leopard (*P. pardus*), and the snow leopard (*P. uncia*). The latter belongs here, but, unlike the others, cannot roar.
Species:	African lion (*Panthera leo leo*).
Subspecies	*P. leo barbarica*, *P. leo nubica* and *P. leo somaliensis*

13 The Barbary Lion (*P. leo barbarica*), is an extinct population that lived in the Barbary Coast region of the Maghreb from the Atlas Mountains in Morocco to Egypt. They were eradicated following the spread of firearms and bounties for shooting lions. Small groups may have survived in Algeria until the early 1960s, and in Morocco until the mid-1960s. In 19th century hunter accounts, the Barbary Lion was claimed to be the largest lion, with a weight of wild males ranging from 270 to 300 kg (600 to 660 lb).

14 Some modern English translations (NIV, NLT) have changed the plural "lionesses" to the singular "mate." This could be to reflect their belief that, contrary to other African subspecies, these lions did not gather in prides due to a lack of prey in its arid surroundings and therefore ought to be monogamous. As can be seen in many instances elsewhere, the authors of the Hebrew Bible were naturalists (Job 40) and more specifically ornithologists (Gen 6–8, Job 39) par excellence. Therefore, there is no reason to doubt that this author carefully observed the behaviour and social structures of this species and thus deliberately used this particular verb and the plural form of the noun.

2. NAHUM 3

BHS	הִנֵּה עַמְּךָ נָשִׁים בְּקִרְבֵּךְ	13a
Ltrl	in your midst—women—your people—look!	
KJB	Behold, thy people in the midst of thee are women:	
NASB	Behold, your people are women in your midst!	
ESV	Behold, your troops are women in your midst.	
NLT	Your troops will be as weak and helpless as women	
NIV	Look at your troops—they are all weaklings.	

13ᵃ "Perhaps read Heb (=Heb) or Heb compare LXX (Syr Targums) Grk."

1 This footnote suggests that the form should be נָשִׂים which is the qal impf. 1mp of the verb שׂוּם / שִׂים meaning, "they will put, place, set," or maybe כְּנָשִׁים meaning, "as women." It further suggests that we compare the Greek Septuagint which, as it is stated in the note, does indeed have ὡς γυναῖκες meaning, "as women."

2 The NIV hides the embarrassing misogyny (ingrained prejudice against women) in the MT, by changing "women" to "weaklings" (Jer 50:37, 51:30).

82.39 HABAKKUK

1. HABAKKUK 1

BHS	הַמַּשָּׂא אֲשֶׁר חָזָה חֲבַקּוּק הַנָּבִיא:	1
Ltrl	the prophet—Habakkuk—he saw—that—The prophetic utterance	
KJB	The burden which Habakkuk the prophet did see.	
NASB	The oracle which Habakkuk the prophet saw.	
ESV	The oracle that Habakkuk the prophet saw.	
NLT	This is the message that the prophet Habakkuk received in a vision.	
NIV	The prophecy that Habakkuk the prophet received.	

1   This name is from the root חבק meaning, "to embrace."

2. HABAKKUK 3

BHS	ᵃכִּי־תְאֵנָה לֹא־תִפְרָח וְאֵין יְבוּל בַּגְּפָנִים	17a
Ltrl	on the vines—fruit—and there is not—she will blossom—not—a fig tree—when	
KJB	Although the fig tree shall not blossom, neither shall fruit be in the vines;	
NASB	Though the fig tree should not blossom And there be no fruit on the vines,	
ESV	Though the fig tree should not blossom, nor fruit be on the vines,	
NLT	Even though the fig trees have no blossoms, and there are no grapes on the vines;	
NIV	Though the fig tree does not bud and there are no grapes on the vines,	

17ᵃ "The whole verse (was) probably added."

17ᵇ "LXX Grk read Heb."

1   The Greek Septuagint indeed has καρποφορήσει meaning, "to bear fruit."

2   תְאֵנָה Noun, f. sg. meaning, "fig tree." This could be *Ficus carica* know as "common fig," and found throughout the Middle East.

3   תִפְרָח Qal impf. 3fs of the verb פָּרַח meaning, "to bud, sprout, shoot." The alternative Hebrew pointing in this footnote, does not alter the meaning.

4   יְבוּל Noun, m. sg. meaning, "produce of the soil."

5   בַּגְּפָנִים Inseparable preposition + definite article + f. pl. of the noun גֶּפֶן meaning, "vine."

BHS	כִּחֵשׁ מַעֲשֵׂה־זַיִת וּשְׁדֵמוֹת לֹא־עָשָׂה אֹכֶל	17b
Ltrl	food—it yielded—not—and fields—olive—labor of—it failed	
KJB	the labor of the olive shall fail, and the fields shall yield no meat;	
NASB	Though the yield of the olive should fail And the fields produce no food,	
ESV	the produce of the olive fail and the fields yield no food,	
NLT	and there are no grapes on the vines; even though the olive crop fails,	
NIV	though the olive crop fails and the fields produce no food,	

17ᶜ "Read Heb or preferably Heb."

1. The first suggestion in the Hebrew pointing does not alter the meaning, but the second suggestion is the noun with a 3ms pronominal suffix which then means, "his work" (Chapter 17.7.8 in Vol. 1). Because of the maqqeph joining the two words into "work of olive tree," this is not a possibility.

BHS	גָּזַר מִמִּכְלָה צֹאן וְאֵין בָּקָר בָּרְפָתִים׃	17c
Ltrl	in the stalls—a herd—and there is not—a flock—from the enclosure—it was cut off	
KJB	the flock shall be cut off from the fold, and there shall be no herd in the stalls:	
NASB	Though the flock should be cut off from the fold And there be no cattle in the stalls,	
ESV	the flock be cut off from the fold and there be no herd in the stalls,	
NLT	even though the flocks die in the fields, and the cattle barns are empty,	
NIV	though there are no sheep in the pen and no cattle in the stalls,	

17ᵈ "Read Heb."

1. The niph'al form suggested in the footnote would have a passive voice as apposed to the active voice of the qal binyan in the MT (Chapter 24.1.2 in Vol. 1).

2. נִגְזַר Niph'al perf. 3ms of the same verb in the MT. Here it would then mean, "to be cut off, separated, excluded from."

3. מִמִּכְלָה Preposition מִן + noun, m. sg. meaning, "enclosure, fold."

4. בָּרְפָתִים Inseparable preposition + definite article + noun, m. sg. meaning, "stable, stall." This is the only occurrence of this word in the Hebrew Bible (a *hapax legomenon*).

BHS	וַאֲנִי בַּיהוָה אֶעְלוֹזָה אָגִילָה בֵּאלֹהֵי יִשְׁעִי׃	18
Ltrl	my salvation—in the God of—I will rejoice—I will exult—to Yahweh—and (still) I	
KJB	Yet I will rejoice in the LORD, I will joy in the God of my salvation.	
NASB	Yet I will exult in the LORD, I will rejoice in the God of my salvation.	
ESV	yet I will rejoice in the LORD; I will take joy in the God of my salvation.	
NLT	yet I will rejoice in the LORD! I will be joyful in the God of my salvation!	
NIV	yet I will rejoice in the LORD, I will be joyful in God my Savior.	

1. אֶעְלוֹזָה Qal impf. 1cs of the verb עָלַז meaning, "to exult," + paragogic hey.
2. אָגִילָה Qal impf. 1cs of the verb גִּיל meaning, "to rejoice, be excited about."
3. יִשְׁעִי Noun, m. sg. יֵשַׁע meaning, "deliverance, rescue, salvation, safety, welfare," with a 1cs pronominal suffix.

BHS	יְהוִה אֲדֹנָי חֵילִי וַיָּשֶׂם רַגְלַי כָּאַיָּלוֹת	19a
Ltrl	like deer—my feet—and he will make—my strength—the Lord—Yahweh	
KJB	The LORD God is my strength, and he will make my feet like hinds' feet,	
NASB	The Lord GOD is my strength, And He has made my feet like hinds' feet,	
ESV	GOD, the Lord, is my strength; he makes my feet like the deer's;	
NLT	The Sovereign LORD is my strength! He makes me as surefooted as a deer,	
NIV	The Sovereign LORD is my strength; he makes my feet like the feet of a deer,	

19ᵃ "Perhaps they have dropped out hemistich (half of a line)."

1. This seems to be the case as is evident from the large gap in the layout of *BHS*.
2. וַיָּשֶׂם Waw conversive + qal impf. 3ms of the verb שׂוּם / שִׂים meaning, "to put, place, set."
3. כָּאַיָּלוֹת Refer to Chapter 82.21.3.

BHS	וְעַל בָּמוֹתַי יַדְרִכֵנִי לַמְנַצֵּחַ בִּנְגִינוֹתָי׃	19b
Ltrl	—to the Chief Musician—he will make me walk—my high places—and on with my stringed music	
KJB	and he will make me to walk upon mine high places. To the chief singer on my stringed instruments.	
NASB	And makes me walk on my high places. For the choir director, on my stringed instruments.	
ESV	he makes me tread on my high places. To the choirmaster: with stringed instruments.	
NLT	able to tread upon the heights. (For the choir director: This prayer is to be accompanied by stringed instruments.)	
NIV	he enables me to tread on the heights. For the director of music. On my stringed instruments.	

19ᵇ "LXX Grk, perhaps read Heb (yod dittography)."

1	The Greek Septuagint does indeed have τα υψηλά meaning, "high places." In the MT the f. pl. form of the noun בָּמָה seems to be used, but the yod at the end changes it to be the f. pl. noun + 1cs pronominal suffix, with the meaning, "my high places." As this does not make sense in this context, this footnote correctly suggests that this is a case of dittography (the accidental duplication of a letter, word, or phrase by a copyist).

19c "Perhaps read Heb compare Ps 4:1 etc."

1	This footnote suggests that there should not be a pronominal suffix added to the f. pl. noun meaning, "music of stringed instruments." The suggestion makes sense, but there is no reason why the MT would be unacceptable.
2	The phrase "He makes my feet like the feet of a deer; he causes me to stand firm on high places" occurs in three locations in the Hebrew Bible namely 2 Sm 22:34, Hb 3:19, and Ps 18:34.

82.40 ZEPHANIAH

1. ZEPHANIAH 1

BHS	דְּבַר־יְהוָה אֲשֶׁר הָיָה אֶל־צְפַנְיָה	1
Ltrl	Zephaniah—to—it was—that—Yahweh—the word of	
KJB	The word of the LORD which came unto Zephaniah	
NASB	The word of the LORD which came to Zephaniah	
ESV	The word of the LORD that came to Zephaniah	
NLT	The LORD gave this message to Zephaniah	
NIV	The word of the LORD that came to Zephaniah	

1	The name "Zephaniah" is from the root צפן meaning, "to hide, treasure up."
2	With יָה it would then literally mean, "Yahweh has hidden" (Chapter 86.4.8).

2. ZEPHANIAH 3

BHS	יַחֲרִישׁ בְּאַהֲבָתוֹ	17d
Ltrl	with his love—he will cause to be quiet	
KJB	he will rest in his love,	
NASB	He will be quiet in His love	
ESV	he will quiet you by his love;	
NLT	With his love, he will calm all your fears.	
NIV	in his love he will no longer rebuke you,	
WEB	He will calm you in his love.	

17c-c "Probably read Heb compare LXX (Grk) SyP."

1 יַחֲרִישׁ Hiph'il impf. 3ms of the verb חָרַשׁ meaning, "to be silent, dumb, speechless." The ESB and WEB clearly express the causative meaning of the hiph'il binyan.

2 יְחַדֵּשׁ Pi'el impf. 3ms of the root חדשׁ meaning, "to renew, repair." The footnote suggests this form in accordance with the Greek Septuagint which has καινιεῖ σε ἐν meaning, "he shall revive you in (his affection)."

82.41 HAGGAI

1. HAGGAI 1

BHS	הָיָה דְבַר־יְהוָה בְּיַד־חַגַּי הַנָּבִיאᵃ	1b
Ltrl	the prophet—Haggai—by the hand of—Yahweh—the word of—it was	
KJB	came the word of the LORD by Haggai the prophet	
NASB	the word of the LORD came by the prophet Haggai	
ESV	the word of the LORD came by the hand of Haggai the prophet	
NLT	the LORD gave a message through the prophet Haggai	
NIV	the word of the LORD came through the prophet Haggai	

1ᵃ "LXX additional Grk (LXX Mss additional Grk) compare 2:1, 2)."

1 The Greek Septuagint indeed has λέγων εἶπον meaning, ". . . saying. Say . . ." This is in accordance to the end of Hg 2:1 and the beginning of Hg 2:2 in the MT.

2 This name is from the root חגג meaning, "to make a pilgrimage," or "keep a pilgrim-feast."

BHS	בְּבֵית־יְהוָה צְבָאוֹת אֱלֹהֵיהֶם׃ פ	14d
Ltrl	their God—armies—YHWH—on the house of	
KJB	in the house of the LORD of hosts, their God,	
ESV	on the house of the LORD of hosts, their God,	
NASB	on the house of the LORD of armies, their God,	
NLT	on the house of their God, the LORD of Heaven's Armies,	
NIV	on the house of the LORD Almighty, their God,	
GNT	on the Temple of the LORD Almighty, their God,	
ISV	on the house of their God, the LORD of the Heavenly Armies.	

1 צְבָאוֹת Noun, f. pl. form of צָבָא meaning, "army, war, warfare." It occurs 283 times in the Hebrew Bible, and in almost all of these cases, in combination with Yahweh. It is first used in 1 Sm 1:3, and most frequently used in Isaiah (62 times) and Jeremiah (82 times). The most common translation into English is, "LORD of Hosts" (KJB, ESV, ERV), but other alternatives are,

"LORD Almighty" (NIV, GNT), "LORD of Heaven's Armies" (NLT, ISV), "LORD All-Powerful" (CEV), "Yahweh of Armies" (WEB), "Jehovah of hosts" (ASV), "LORD of armies" (NASB).

2 Haggai uses this appelation 14 times (1:2, 5, 7, 9, 14; 2:4, 6, 7, 8, 9, 9, 11, 23, 23).

82.42 ZECHARIAH

1. ZECHARIAH 1

BHS	הָיָה דְבַר־יְהוָה אֶל־זְכַרְיָה	1b
Ltrl	Zechariah—to—Yahweh—the word of—it was	
KJB	came the word of the LORD unto Zechariah,	
NASB	the word of the LORD came to Zechariah	
ESV	the word of the LORD came to the prophet Zechariah,	
NLT	the LORD gave this message to the prophet Zechariah	
NIV	the word of the LORD came to Zechariah	

1 This name is from the root זכר meaning, "to remember."

2 With יָה it would then literally mean, "Yahweh remembers" (Chapter 86.4.9).

2. ZECHARIAH 4

BHS	לֹא בְחַיִל וְלֹא בְכֹחַ כִּי אִם־בְּרוּחִי אָמַר יְהוָה צְבָאוֹת׃	6b
Ltrl	armies—Yahweh—he said—by my spirit—but rather—by power—and not—by force—not	
KJB	Not by might, nor by power, but by my spirit, saith the LORD of hosts.	
NASB	Not by might nor by power, but by My Spirit,' says the LORD of hosts.	
ESV	Not by might, nor by power, but by my Spirit, says the LORD of hosts.	
NLT	It is not by force nor by strength, but by my Spirit, says the LORD of Heaven's Armies.	
NIV	Not by might nor by power, but by my Spirit,' says the LORD Almighty.	

1 חַיִל Noun, m. sg. meaning, "strength, efficiency, wealth, army, force."

2 כֹּחַ Noun, m. sg. meaning, "(human) strength, power."

3 צְבָאוֹת Noun, m. pl. meaning, "armies, wars, warfare."

4 Refer to Chapter 86.3.7 for a discussion of the title יְהוָה צְבָאוֹת.

3. ZECHARIAH 9

BHS	צַדִּ֤יק וְנוֹשָׁ֨ע ה֔וּא עָנִ֕י וְרֹכֵ֥ב עַל־חֲמ֖וֹר וְעַל־עַ֥יִר בֶּן־אֲתֹנֽוֹת׃	9b
Ltrl	—and on—a male donkey—on—and riding—humble—he—and victorious–just female donkeys—a foal of—a beast of burden	
KJB	he is just, and having salvation; lowly, and riding upon an ass, and upon a colt the foal of an ass.	
NASB	He is just and endowed with salvation, Humble, and mounted on a donkey, Even on a colt, the foal of a donkey.	
ESV	righteous and having salvation is he, humble and mounted on a donkey, on a colt, the foal of a donkey.	
NLT	He is righteous and victorious, yet he is humble, riding on a donkey—riding on a donkey's colt.	
NIV	righteous and victorious, lowly and riding on a donkey, on a colt, the foal of a donkey.	

9a "LXX Grk—SyP Syr—Targum Heb—Vulgate Lat."

1 וְנוֹשָׁע The form in the MT is the niph'al part. active m. sg. of the root ישׁע with an active meaning in the hiph'il binyan namely, "to deliver, save," but with a passive meaning in the niph'al binyan namely, "to be victorious, to be liberated." The Greek Septuagint has σώζων meaning, "delivering."

2 עָנִי An adjective meaning, "poor, afflicted, humble."

3 חֲמוֹר Noun, m. sg. from the verb root חמר meaning, "reddish-brown," and used for riding by men and woman alike.

4 עַיִר Noun, m. sg. meaning, "a young and vigorous male donkey, male ass," used for riding and as a beast of burden.

5 אֲתֹנוֹת Noun, f. pl. meaning, "feminine donkeys, she-asses."

4. ZECHARIAH 14

BHS	וְהָיָ֖ה בַּיּ֣וֹם הַה֑וּא לֹֽא־יִהְיֶ֣ה א֔וֹר יְקָר֖וֹת יִקְפָּאֽוּן׃	6
Ltrl	they will contract—splendid—light—it will be—not—the that—in the day—and it will be	
KJB	And it shall come to pass in that day, that the light shall not be clear, nor dark:	
NASB	In that day there will be no light; the luminaries will dwindle.	
ESV	On that day there shall be no light, cold, or frost.	
NLT	On that day the sources of light will no longer shine,	
NIV	On that day there will be neither sunlight nor cold, frosty darkness.	
LXX	And it will be in that day there shall no be light, and chilliness and ice.	

6a "Read Heb compare Gen 8:22."

1   קֹר The reference to Gen 8:22 by this footnote is the only place in the Hebrew Bible where this noun appears, and there it means, "cold." There it is written in the so-called *scriptio defectiva* or defective writing when the vowel point is written without the *mater*, which in this case is a waw.

6ᵇ⁻ᵇ "LXX Grk, read Heb compare Symmachus's Greek Version SyP Targums Vulgate."

1   The second footnote correctly quotes the Greek Septuagint. It suggests that we read וְקָרוֹת וְקִפְאוֹן which consists of the construct form of the feminine noun קָרָה meaning, "a cold day," and the qal perf. 3mp of the verb קָפָא which means, "to thicken, condense, contract, congeal."

2   יְקָרוֹת יִקְפְּאוּן in the MT consists of an adjective f. pl. meaning, "precious, rare, splendid, weighty," followed by the Ketiv form of the Qere יִקְפָּאוּן which is the qal imperfect 3mp with a paragogic nun of the verb קָפָא meaning, "it will thicken, condense, congeal."

3   If we take "splendid" in the MT to mean the stars or the sun and moon, we could get to, "and the luminaries (the stars or the sun and moon) will contract (into darkness)."

BHS	זֹאת תִּהְיֶה חַטַּאת מִצְרָיִם	19a
Ltrl	Egypt—the sin of—it will be—this	
YLT	This is the punishment of the sin of Egypt,	
KJB	This shall be the punishment of Egypt,	
NASB	This will be the punishment of Egypt,	
ESV	This shall be the punishment to Egypt	
NIV	This will be the punishment of Egypt	

1   חַטַּאת Noun, f. sg. cstr. meaning, "sin, sin offering." This noun, stems from the verb חָטָא which means, "to miss a goal, to go wrong, to sin."

2   The Greek Septuagint has η αμαρτία and the Vulgate has *hoc erit peccatum Aegypti*, both of them correctly translating the MT meaning as, "the sin of Egypt."

3   The Geneva Bible introduced the expression "the punishment of Egypt" into this verse. The Bishops Bible rendered this as "the plague of Egypt." The King James translators accepted the wording of the Geneva Bible, and from there it has found almost universal acceptance into the modern English language translations. It should be noted that John Calvin and his aggressively punitive theology, which affected the views of most Protestant religions, had been the driving force behind the Geneva Bible.

82.43 MALACHI

1. MALACHI 1

BHS	מַשָּׂא דְבַר־יְהוָה אֶל־יִשְׂרָאֵל בְּיַד מַלְאָכִי׃ª	1
Ltrl	Malachi—by the hand of—Israel—to—Yahweh—the word of—a revelation	
KJB	The burden of the word of the LORD to Israel by Malachi.	
NASB	The oracle of the word of the LORD to Israel through Malachi.	
ESV	The oracle of the word of the LORD to Israel by Malachi.	
NLT	This is the message that the LORD gave to Israel through the prophet Malachi.	
NIV	A prophecy: The word of the LORD to Israel through Malachi.	

1ª "LXX Grk, additional information Grk from Hg 2:15, 18."

1. The two tables below show that the Greek texts mentioned in this footnote are indeed found in the Septuagint.

LXX	λῆμμα	λόγου	Κυρίου	επί	τον Ισραήλ	εν	χειρί	αγγέλου αυτού
	The concern	of the word	of the LORD	over	Israel	by	the hand	of his messenger.

Hg 2:15	θέσθε	Δη	επί	τας καρδίας υμών
	set it	indeed	upon	your hearts

2. מַשָּׂא A masculine noun meaning amongst others, "a (prophetic) utterance," or "an oracle," or "a revelation."

3. מַלְאָכִי A masculine noun with a 1cs pronominal suffix (Chapter 17.7 in Vol. 1) meaning, "my messenger," or "my angel."

4. This name occurs only this once in the Hebrew Bible.

BHS	כִּי מֶלֶךְ גָּדוֹל אָנִי אָמַר יְהוָה צְבָאוֹת	14b
Ltrl	armies—Yahweh—says—I—great—King—because	
KJB	for I am a great King, saith the LORD of hosts,	
NASB	for I am a great King," says the LORD of hosts,	
ESV	For I am a great King, says the LORD of hosts,	
NLT	For I am a great king," says the LORD of Heaven's Armies,	
NIV	For I am a great king," says the LORD Almighty,	

1. In this case, it is Yahweh of armies (LORD Almighty) that is calling himself a great King. In Ps 47:2, 48:2, 95:3 it is a third person, the Psalmists, calling God by this name.

2. MALACHI 2

BHS	כִּי־שָׂנֵאא שַׁלַּחb אָמַר יְהוָה אֱלֹהֵי יִשְׂרָאֵל	16a
Ltrl	Israel—God of—Yahweh—he said—send away—he hates—because	
KJB	For the LORD, the God of Israel, saith that he hateth putting away:	
NASB	"For I hate divorce," says the LORD, the God of Israel,	
ESV	"For the man who does not love his wife but divorces her, says the LORD, the God of Israel,	
NLT	"For I hate divorce!" says the LORD, the God of Israel.	
NIV	"The man who hates and divorces his wife," says the LORD, the God of Israel,	

16a "Probably read Heb."

1. The verb in the MT is the qal perf. 3ms meaning, "he hates."

2. The footnote suggests the qal perf. 1cs meaning, "I hate." In the context of verses 15 and 16, this is not a quote of what Yahweh is saying, and therefore the third person is in order.

16b-b "Added?"

1. This might be true, but does not change the message of the verse.

2. שַׁלַּח Pi'el infinitive construct of the root שלח meaning, "to send." In the pi'el binyan it takes on the meaning, "send off, send away, cast out, and dismiss." In the context of the last words of the preceding verse 15 namely, "against the wife of your youth," we could conclude the wife is the object of the "sending away" action, which is a description of what happens when a man divorces his wife.

3. This a very common verb, occuring 847 times in the Hebrew Bible. The pi'el is often used to express a command. The most famous example being, "Let my people go!" in Ex 5:1; 7:16; 8:1, 20; 9:1, 13; 10:3.

4. In the pi'el it is also used to express the concept of "divorce." The most famous case being here in Malachi. It is also used as such in Dt 22:11, 19, 29; Dt 24:1, 3; and Jer 3:1.

BHS	וְכִסָּהc חָמָס עַל־לְבוּשׁוֹ אָמַר יְהוָה צְבָאוֹת	16b
Ltrl	armies—Yahweh of—he said—his garment—upon—violence—and it will cover	
KJB	for one covereth violence with his garment, saith the LORD of hosts:	
NASB	"and him who covers his garment with wrong," says the LORD of hosts.	
ESV	covers his garment with violence, says the LORD of hosts.	
NLT	"To divorce your wife is to overwhelm her with cruelty," says the LORD of Heaven's Armies	
NIV	"does violence to the one he should protect," says the LORD Almighty.	

16c "Perhaps read Heb, it has been proposed Heb."

1. וְכִסָּה Pi'el perf. 3ms of the root כסה meaning, "to cover."

2. כַּסֵּה This would then be the pi'el imp. sg. of the same root, with the alternative כְּכַסֵּה being the same form but with an inseparable preposition added.

3 לְבוּשׁוֹ Noun, m. sg. with an 3ms object suffix meaning, "his garment, clothing, raiment."

BHS	וְנִשְׁמַרְתֶּם בְּרוּחֲכֶם וְלֹא תִבְגֹּֽדוּ׃ ס	16c
Ltrl	you will deal treacherously—and not—in your spirit—and you will guard	
KJB	therefore take heed to your spirit, that ye deal not treacherously.	
NASB	"So take heed to your spirit, that you do not deal treacherously."	
ESV	So guard yourselves in your spirit, and do not be faithless."	
NLT	"So guard your heart; do not be unfaithful to your wife."	
NIV	So be on your guard, and do not be unfaithful.	

16^(d-d) "Probably added compare 15ba."

1 This footnote notes that this whole sentence might later have been added onto the original text.

2 וְנִשְׁמַרְתֶּם Niph'al perf. 2mp of the root שמר meaning, "you (pl.) will be on your guard."

3 תִבְגֹּדוּ Qal impf. 2mp of the verb בָּגַד meaning, "to act / deal treacherously."

3. MALACHI 3

BHS	הִנְנִי שֹׁלֵחַ מַלְאָכִי וּפִנָּה־דֶרֶךְ לְפָנָי	1a
Ltrl	before me—a road—and he will prepare—my messenger—sending—behold	
KJB	Behold, I will send my messenger, and he shall prepare the way before me:	
NASB	"Behold, I send my messenger, and he will prepare the way before me.	
ESV	"Behold, I am going to send My messenger, and he will clear the way before Me.	
NLT	"Look! I am sending my messenger, and he will prepare the way before me.	
NIV	"I will send my messenger, who will prepare the way before me.	

1 שֹׁלֵחַ Qal part. active m. sg. meaning, "sending."

2 וּפִנָּה Waw + pi'el perf. 3ms of the root פנה meaning, "to turn" in the qal, but here in the pi'el it means, "to make clear, make free of obstacles, clear away (ground)."

3 This sentence is quoted by Jesus in Mt 11:10.

BHS	כִּי־הִנֵּה הַיּוֹם בָּא בֹּעֵר כַּתַּנּוּר^a	19a
Ltrl	like an oven—burning—it is coming—the day—behold—because	
KJB	For, behold, the day cometh, that shall burn as an oven;	
NASB	"For behold, the day is coming, burning like a furnace;	
ESV	"For behold, the day is coming, burning like an oven,	
NLT	"The day of judgment is coming, burning like a furnace.	
NIV	"Surely the day is coming; it will burn like a furnace.	

19^a "The original LXX adds Grk."

Selected Passages

1. The Greek Septuagint does indeed add the words καὶ φλέξει αυτούς meaning, "and it shall blaze against them."

2. בֹּעֵר Qal part. active m. sg. of the verb בָּעַר "to burn, consume."

3. כַּתַּנּוּר Noun, m. sg. with a prefixed inseparable preposition and definite article meaning, "like an fire-pot, portable stove, oven."

4. In the Greek Septuagint this verse is the first of a new chapter, numbered Chapter 4.

BHS	וְזָרְחָה לָכֶם יִרְאֵי שְׁמִי שֶׁמֶשׁ צְדָקָה	20a
Ltrl	righteousness—a sun of—my name—who fear—to you—but it will rise	
KJB	But unto you that fear my name shall the Sun of righteousness arise	
NASB	"But for you who fear My name, the sun of righteousness will rise	
ESV	But for you who fear my name, the sun of righteousness shall rise	
NLT	"But for you who fear my name, the Sun of Righteousness will rise	
NIV	But for you who revere my name, the sun of righteousness will rise	

1. וְזָרְחָה Waw conversive and qal perf. 3fs of the verb זָרַח "to rise, come forth."

2. יִרְאֵי Qal part. m. pl. construct of the verb יָרֵא "to fear."

BHS	וּמַרְפֵּא בִּכְנָפֶיהָ וִיצָאתֶם וּפִשְׁתֶּם כְּעֶגְלֵי מַרְבֵּק׃	20b
Ltrl	stall-fed—like calves of—and gambol—and you will go out—in his wings—and healing	
KJB	with healing in his wings; and ye shall go forth, and grow up as calves of the stall.	
NASB	with healing in its wings; and you will go forth and skip about like calves from the stall.	
ESV	with healing in its wings. You shall go out leaping like calves from the stall.	
NLT	with healing in his wings. And you will go free, leaping with joy like calves let out to pasture.	
NIV	with healing in its rays. And you will go out and frolic like well-fed calves.	

1. וּמַרְפֵּא Waw consecutive + noun, m. sg. meaning, "and healing."

2. בִּכְנָפֶיהָ Inseparable preposition + dual noun, cstr. of כָּנָף "wing."

   וּפִשְׁתֶּם Waw conversive + qal perf. 2mp of the verb פּוּשׁ meaning, "to spring about playfully, gambol."

3. כְּעֶגְלֵי Inseparable preposition + m. pl. noun in the cstr. of עֵגֶל meaning, "like calves of."

4. מַרְבֵּק Noun, m. sg. meaning, "stall = an individual compartment for an animal in a stable or barn, enclosed on three sides." כְּעֶגְלֵי מַרְבֵּק then means, "like stall-fed, fattened calves."

83 Birds in the Tanakh

83.1 INTRODUCTION

1. "The Hebrew Canon, as expounded in the Mosaic Law, the Prophets and the Writings, contains the origin of Ornithology, and the biblical authors concerned, and not Aristotle, were the original Ornithologists."[1]

2. The hypothesis stated above is from the book *Birds and Bibles in History* by Tian Hattingh. Although we are not concerned with this hypothesis here, the book provides us with a large number of examples where a basic knowledge of Biblical Hebrew and of textual criticism enables the reader of the Hebrew Bible to come to a more accurate dynamic equivalent translation.

3. In the Hebrew Bible there are 343 references to birds. In 174 of these instances there is some degree of certainty regarding the specific species mentioned. In addition, there are 108 references to birds in general, and 61 references to avian terms in general.[2]

4. Chapter 83.8 contains an alphabetical list of the 36 species that are mentioned in the Hebrew Bible. However, in this chapter we will deal with a selection of these species according to their positions in the binominal system of classification. This system uses common features to group the birds (and all other living species on the planet) into "Orders." These are then divided further into "Families" of species who more specifically possess similar features.

83.2 FLIGHTLESS BIRDS

1. OSTRICH

1. "This family consists of five subspecies of which only one, the Southern Ostrich (*Struthio camelus australis*) found in Southern Africa, has survived. The Arabian Ostrich (*Struthio camelus syriacus*), also called the Syrian Ostrich or Middle Eastern Ostrich, lived on the Arabian Peninsula, the same area where the Biblical authors were from. After World War I, the proliferation of firearms, coupled with the availability of motorized transport and the drying-up of the area, led to the devastation of populations and the virtual extinction of the subspecies by 1941. The habitat became increasingly inhospitable and this subspecies finally became extinct in 1966 with the last record of an individual found dying in Jordan."[3]

2. "When the ostrich is mentioned in the Hebrew Bible, the word יַעֲנָה is used, and בַּת־יַעֲנָה meaning, 'daughter of ostrich,' and plural, בְּנוֹת־יַעֲנָה occurring seven times, (Lv 11:16; Dt 14:15; Is 13:21, 34:13, 43:20; Jer 50:39; Mi 1:8), and probably referring to the females of this family. In Is 13:21, Is 34:13 and Jer 50:39, the ostrich is associated with the desolation and loneliness of ruins and death. The voice of the ostrich, which is described as a deep booming sound,

---

1. Hattingh, Tian, Tian (2012), p.147.
2. Hattingh, Tian (2012), p.216.
3. Hattingh, Tian (2012), p.108.

similar to that of a lion at long distance, is used in Mi 1:8 to describe the cry of a mourner in deep distress. In Job 30:29 the author describes his loneliness by stating that the ostriches are his only friends (Chapter 82.22.6). In Job 39:13–18 the behavior of the female ostrich רְנָנִים is described accurately and in fine detail (Chapter 82.22.6,8)."[4]

3   Job 39:13

BHS	כְּנַף־רְנָנִים נֶעֱלָסָה אִם־אֶבְרָה חֲסִידָה וְנֹצָה:
Ltrl	and feather—stork—pinion—but—wave proudly—ostrich—the wings of
NIV	The wings of the ostrich flap joyfully, though they cannot compare with the wings and feathers of the stork
NLT	"The ostrich flaps her wings grandly, but they are no match for the feathers of the stork.
ESV	"The wings of the ostrich wave proudly, but are they the pinions and plumage of love?
KJB	Gavest thou the goodly wings unto the peacocks? or wings and feathers unto the ostrich?
NASB	"The wings of the ostrich flap joyously, With the pinion and feathers of love,

1   pinion: the outer part of a bird's wing including the flight feathers.

2   The Hebrew verb רָנַן means, "to give a ringing / complaining / distressing / mourning cry." The m. pl. noun רְנָנִים then literally means, "ringing (etc.) cries." This distinctive feature was then used to name the ostrich in Biblical Hebrew.

3   Translations like the King James Bible, English Standard Version, and the New American Standard Bible have substantially altered the literal meaning of this verse. One possible reason for this might be that in the East the stork is a symbol of parental love, and the ostrich was known to treat it's young harshly in an attempt to adequately prepare them for the hard realities of their environment (Lam 4:3).

4   Samuel Bochart (1599–1667), the French Protestant biblical scholar wrote, that there is, perhaps, scarce any passage of Scripture which is less understood.

83.3 DIURNAL BIRDS OF PREY

1. INTRODUCTION

1   Diurnal creatures like cows, antelope, and eagles are active mainly during the day, as apposed to nocturnal creatures like hippos, bats, and owls that are active mainly at night.

2   In this order there are three families that do not occur in the Hebrew Bible. They are:

   a)   The New World Vultures from North and South America including the California Condor (*Gymnogyps californianus*) and Andean Condor (*Vultur gryphus*).

   b)   The Secretary Bird (*Sagittarius serpentarius*) from sub-Saharan Africa.

   c)   The Osprey (*Pandion haliaetus*).

---

4   The Apostolic Bible Polyglot (ABP), originally published in 2003 is a Bible translation by Charles Vander Pool. The ABP is an English translation with a Greek interlinear gloss and is keyed to a concordance.

3   Many members of the remaining two families in this order are mentioned in the Hebrew Bible. Here we will look at the following families:

   a)   The "True / Booted" Eagles.

   b)   The Kites.

   c)   The Falcons.

   d)   The Vultures.

2. EAGLES

1   "In both the lists of 'unclean' birds found in Lv. 11:13–19 and Dt 14:12–18, נֶשֶׁר meaning 'eagle,' is the first to be mentioned. The 'clean birds' are not mentioned in detail. As many of the 'unclean birds' are birds of prey, it would seem that a bird would be classified as such purely on account of its diet. Carnivorous birds would not be suitable as food or for sacrificial purposes, and those scavenging on carrion would be especially obnoxious."[5]

2   "In eight of the twenty-five references to eagles in the Hebrew Bible, namely: Dt 28:49, 2 Sam 1:23, Job 9:26, Jer 4:13, Jer 48:40, Jer 49:22, Lam 4:19 and Hab 1:8, the authors are using the exceptional speed with which the eagle swoops down on its prey to illustrate a particular point in their writings (Chapter 82.22.2,8)."[6]

3   Deuteronomy 28:49

BHS	כַּאֲשֶׁר יִדְאֶה[a] הַנָּשֶׁר
Ltrl	the eagle—it will fly swiftly—as
NIV	like an eagle swooping down

49[a] "Samaritan Pentateuch Heb." The verb in the MT means, "to fly swiftly," whereas the one in the SP means, "to see." It seems that the SP incorrectly has a resh in the verb instead of the dalet found in the MT. The letters look very similar and the SP scribe probably made a mistake. This is a very common error (Chapter 72.2.1a in Vol. 4).

4   Jeremiah 48:40

BHS	הִנֵּה כַנֶּשֶׁר יִדְאֶה
Ltrl	he will fly swiftly—as an eagle—behold
NIV	like an eagle swooping down

40[a-a] "Lacks material (in) the original Septuagint, added from 49:22." This footnote states that the Greek Septuagint has a shorter text than the MT, and that we should refer to Jer 49:22 where this phrase does appear.

1   This is one of the eight instances in the Hebrew Bible where the author uses the swiftness of the eagle to illustrate a point.

---

5   Hattingh, Tian (2012), p. 104.
6   Hattingh, Tian (2012), p. 158.

3. VULTURES

1. "To the layman in Biblical times, the vultures were probably the most abhorrent of all the birds. Even to this day they are more often than not associated with the stench and filth of decaying carrion (dead and rotting flesh). Their value as scavengers in preventing the spread of diseases, like Anthrax, especially in undeveloped areas, was not appreciated then, and even to a large extent, today."[7]

2. "For the second bird mentioned in the lists of 'unclean' birds in Lv 11:13 and Dt 14:12, the Hebrew word פֶּרֶס is used. Hebrew dictionaries list this word as *Gypaetus barbatus*, and call it the 'lamb vulture,' derived from the earlier German 'Lammergeier or Lammergeyer,' literally meaning 'lambs vulture'."[8]

3. "Today this species is known as the Bearded Vulture, German: Bartgeier, from the prominent patch of black bristles below the bill, It is occasionally referred to as the 'bone breaker,' from its habit of dropping larger bones from heights up to 150 meters onto flat rocky ossuaries, breaking them into pieces small enough to swallow. The verb in Biblical Hebrew from which this word stems means: 'to break bread.' Modern Hebrew is consistent with this interpretation. A number of translations e.g. NIV, JB and LB simply use the more generic 'vulture'."[9]

4. "The third 'unclean' bird is called עָזְנִיָּה in biblical Hebrew. In modern Hebrew we find *ozniyat hanegev* (*Torgos tracheliotus negevensis*) usually translated as the Lappet-faced Vulture, and *ozniyat shekhora* (*Aegypius monachus*) usually translated as the Black Vulture. The latter should however not be confused with the American Black Vulture (*Coragyps atratus*). Biblical Hebrew dictionaries agree with this interpretation. With all the above in mind, a meaningful translation of Lv 11:13c and Dt 14:12b would be as follows, 'the Eagle, the Bearded Vulture, and the Lappet-faced Vulture'."[10]

5. "In Prv 30:17 the context determines that the Hebrew word נֶשֶׁר should rather be translated with 'vulture.' In Lv 11:18 we find the Hebrew word רָחָם which is referred to by some dictionaries as (*Vultur percnopterus*), which is more probably meant to be the Egyptian Vulture (*Neophron percnopterus*)."[11]

6. Leviticus 11:13c

BHS	אֶת־הַנֶּשֶׁר וְאֶת־הַפֶּרֶס וְאֵת הָעָזְנִיָּה׃
Ltrl	lappet-faced vulture—and the—the bearded vulture—the eagle
NIV	the eagle, the vulture, the black vulture,
KJB	the eagle, and the ossifrage, and the osprey,
ASV	the eagle, and the gier-eagle, and the osprey,
WEB	the eagle, and the vulture, and the black vulture,

---

[7] Hattingh, Tian (2012), p. 106.
[8] Hattingh, Tian (2012), p. 104.
[9] Hattingh, Tian (2012), p. xxii.
[10] Hattingh, Tian (2012), p. xiv.
[11] Hattingh, Tian (2012), p. 95.

4. KITES

1. "Lv 11:14 and Dt 14:13 mentions a bird by the Hebrew name of דָּאָה which is though to be the Red Kite (*Milvus milvus milvus*), a sub-species found in Central Europe and around the Mediterranean. The stem of the Hebrew verb consisting of the same consonants, describes the action of a wolf sneaking up to its prey, or of a hovering raptor pouncing on its prey. Lv 11:14 and Dt 14:13 also mentions a bird by the Hebrew name of אַיָּה which is thought to be the Black Kite (*Milvus migrans*), as the name might be an imitation of its cry. There are seven sub-species of which two are found in the Middle East. *Milvus migrans migrans* migrates to sub-Saharan Africa, and *Milvus migrans aegyptius* is found mainly in Egypt."[12]

2. "In Job 15:23 (Chapter 82.22.3) a word is found that is very close to that of the Black Kite, but it cannot be safely translated as such. The Black Kite is mentioned in Job 28:7 (Chapter 82.22.5), associating it with exceptional eyesight."[13]

3. Job 28:7

BHS	וְלֹא שְׁזָפַתּוּ עֵין אַיָּה׃
Ltrl	black kite—the eye of—he saw it—and not
NIV	no falcon's eye has seen it.
KJB	and which the vulture's eye hath not seen:
ASV	neither hath the falcon's eye seen it:
WEB	neither has the falcon's eye seen it.

5. FALCONS

1. "The Hebrew word נֵץ refers to the desert subspecies of the Peregrine Falcon (*Falco peregrinus pelegrinoides*), which is common in the Middle East and found as far as Iraq and even into Iran. The word occurs only three times in the Hebrew Bible namely in Lv 11:16, Dt 14:15, and Job 39:26 (Chapter 82.22.8). None of these contexts give us any further details, except that Job mentions that the bird is heading south, which might be a reference to a migratory direction."[14]

2. "The Peregrine Falcon (*Falco peregrinus*) is considered by some to be the fastest bird, reaching speeds up to 180 km per hour in a stoop. However, this is debatable, as the Common Swift (*Apus apus*) is said to be capable of speeds up to 216 km per hour for short bursts."[15]

3. Job 39:26

---

[12] Hattingh, Tian (2012), p. 106.
[13] Hattingh, Tian (2012), p. 108.
[14] Hattingh, Tian (2012), p. 108.
[15] Hattingh, Tian (2012), p. 108.

BHS	הֲֽמִבִּינָ֣תְךָ֭ יַֽאֲבֶר־נֵ֑ץ יִפְרֹ֖שׂ כְּנָפָ֣ו לְתֵימָֽן׃
Ltrl	to south—his wings—he will spread—falcon—he will fly—by your wisdom?
NIV	Does the hawk take flight by your wisdom and spread its wings toward the south?
KJB	Doth the hawk fly by thy wisdom, *and* stretch her wings toward the south?
ASV	Is it by thy wisdom that the hawk soareth, (And) stretcheth her wings toward the south?
WEB	Is it by your wisdom that the hawk soars, and stretches her wings toward the south?

83.4 FOWL-LIKE BIRDS

1. INTRODUCTION

1. The Latin word *gallus*, which means, "cock," has led to the name of the order Galliformes. It includes families like chickens (Red Junglefowl), quail, partridges, pheasants, guineafowl, grouse, and turkeys.

2. "All the families in this order have been closely associated with man throughout recorded history. There are at least two reasons:

    a) As opposed to sparrows and even doves and pigeons, they are relatively large birds that provide a protein-rich source of food to their predators and to humans. All of them have light, succulent breast meat with a pleasing flavor. This is mainly because they have well developed breast muscles. (KFC says the drumsticks are not bad either).

    b) Because they lay relatively large and highly nutritious eggs, they all have the characteristics of the domestic chicken."[16]

3. "Various species from this order were amongst the earliest, if not the first, birds taken from the wild and domesticated by man. They are mainly granivorous and herbivorous but are also slightly omnivorous. Because of this diet, they are excluded from the 'unclean' birds mentioned in Lv 11:13–19 and Dt 14:12–18."[17]

2. PARTRIDGES

1. "Although partridges are found in the Mediterranean, e.g. the Barbary Partridge (*Alectoris barbara*), the Red-legged Partridge (*Alectoris rufa*), the Grey Partridge (*Perdix perdix*), and the Rock Partridge (*Alectoris graeca*), it is really only the Chukar (*Alectoris chukar*) that is common in the Middle East. The Arabian Partridge (*Alectoris melanocephala*), and Philby's Partridge (*Alectoris philyi*), are restricted to small areas in Arabia. On the steep, rocky slopes of the desert and semi-desert areas, one finds the Sand Partridge (*Ammoperdix heyi*)."[18]

---

16 Hattingh, Tian (2012), p. 109.
17 Hattingh, Tian (2012), p. 110.
18 Hattingh, Tian (2012), p. 111.

2\. In Jer 17:11 we find a proverb accurately describing a behavioral pattern of this family that, although mainly monogamous, instances of successive bigamy have been reported and subsequently been substantiated by field observations.

3\. Jeremiah 17:11a

BHS	קֹרֵאˣ דָּגַרˣ וְלֹא יָלָד
Ltrl	he bore / begot—but not—he gathers—a partridge
NIV	Like a partridge that hatches eggs it did not lay
KJB	As the partridge sitteth *on eggs*, and hatcheth *them* not;
ASV	As the partridge that sitteth on eggs which she hath not laid,
WEB	As the partridge that sits on [eggs] which she has not laid,

11ᵃ "LXX put before Grk = Heb, translation double."

1. This footnote states that the Greek Septuagint has εφώνησε meaning, "to speak out loud" before the first word of the verse. It equates the Greek word to the Hebrew word קָרָא which means, "he called" or "he proclaimed." This footnote then correctly states that this an erroneous doubling of the same three consonants by the Septuagint translator.

11ᵇ "LXX (Targum) Grk (Heb Aramaic)."

1. This footnote states that the Greek Septuagint has συνήγαγεν which means, "to gather together." This confirms the MT verb that actually means, "to gather together as a brood."

3. QUAIL

1. "Today it is widely accepted that the Hebrew word שְׂלָו refers to the Common Quail (*Coturnix coturnix*), previously known as *Coturnix communis*. In the Bibles they are best known as a food source for the Israelites in the Sinai Peninsula as described in Ex 16 and Nm 11 and referred to in Ex 16:13 and in Nm 11:31."[19]

2. Exodus 16:13

BHS	וַיְהִי בָעֶרֶב וַתַּעַל הַשְּׂלָוˣ
Ltrl	the quail—and she ascended—in the evening—and it was
NIV	That evening quail came
KJB	And it came to pass, that at even the quails came up,
ASV	And it came to pass at even, that the quails came up,
WEB	It happened at evening that quail came up

13ᵃ "SP Heb, LXX Grk, SyP Syriac."

---

19 Hattingh, Tian (2012), p. 115.

1. Three versions are mentioned in this footnote concerning the word. The Samaritan Pentateuch is the only version that dos not agree with the MT. The added yod could be a pronominal suffix, but it would not make sense in this context. The Greek Septuagint has ορτυγομήτρα which means, "mother-quail," and probably is in response to the female form of the preceding verb in the MT. This footnote does not mention it, but the Aleppo Codex has the same consonants as the MT.

2. The Common Quail is generally reluctant to fly, but once they are airborne, they fly swiftly and directly to their destination. This enables them to cover large distances, including flying over lakes, the sea, and making desert crossings. They typically fly only a few meters above the water and/or dunes. However, the weight of the bird makes it vulnerable to the strength and direction of the prevailing wind. It is known that after experiencing adverse wind conditions in flight, they are so exhausted after crossing a large body of water that they are forced to land and rest as soon as they reach the opposite shore. It is then that they are unable to flee away from danger, making harvesting them and/or preying on them, an easy task.

4. RED JUNGLEFOWL

1. "The crow of the domestic or village cock is one of the most familiar natural noises the world over. What may not be such common knowledge is the fact that the Red Junglefowl (*Gallus gallus*), most likely the wild ancestor of the domestic chicken, has an extensive vocal repertoire."[20]

2. In Jb 38:36 there are two problematic words. The first is טֻחוֹת which appears only twice in the Hebrew Bible, namely in Job 38:36, and in Ps 51:8. It most often translated as "inward parts," "heart," and "kidneys." The second word is שֶׂכְוִי which is found only this once in the Hebrew Bible and most often translated with "the mind." However, it is also known to mean, "cock" or "rooster."

3. With all the above in mind, there are two schools of thought on how Job 38:36 should be translated, as can be seen from the following examples (Chapter 82.22.7).

4. Job 38:36

BHS	מִי־שָׁת בַּטֻּחוֹת חָכְמָה אוֹ מִי־נָתַן לַשֶּׂכְוִי בִינָה׃
Ltrl	—he gave—who—or—wisdom—in the ibis—he has placed–who understanding—to the rooster
NLT	Who gives intuition to the heart and instinct to the mind?
CSB	Who put wisdom in the heart or gave the mind understanding?
KJB	Who hath put wisdom in the inward parts? or who hath given understanding to the heart?
NIV	Who gives the ibis wisdom or gives the rooster understanding?
GNT	Who tells the ibis when the Nile will flood, or who tells the rooster that rain will fall?

5. In Prv 30:31 we find the word זַרְזִיר which appears only here. Its meaning is unclear and it has been translated as the adjective "girded," and the nouns "greyhound," "war-horse," "raven," "starling," and "cock."

---

[20] Hattingh, Tian (2012), p. 112.

5. INDIAN PEAFOWL

1 "Twice in the Hebrew Bible, the Hebrew word תֻּכִּיִּים is used, namely in 1 Kings 10:22 and 2 Chr 9:21, listing some of the importations made by Solomon. In both cases the word is preceded by the word קֹפִים translated as 'apes'."[21]

2 1 Kings 10:22

BHS	וְקֹפִים וְתֻכִּיִּים:
Ltrl	and peacocks—and apes
NIV	and apes and baboons.
KJB	and apes, and peacocks.
ASV	and apes, and peacocks.
WEB	and apes, and peacocks.

83.5 NOCTURNAL RAPTORS

1. INTRODUCTION

1 "The order *Strigiformes* consists of the nocturnal (and solitary) birds of prey, collectively known as the Owls. Owls of all kinds have fascinated humans since ancient times. They are either feared (Africa) or venerated (Australia), despised (e.g. as 'unclean' in the Bibles), or admired as wise. Biblical evidence confirms this with no less than 25 references to nine species in the Hebrew Bible, and usually associated with desolation, destruction and ruin. Paintings of owls on cave walls in France date back fifteen to twenty thousand years."[22]

2. BARN-OWL

1 "The Common Barn-owl (*Tyto alba*) is called in this way to clearly distinguish it from other species in the Barn Owl family. The Common Barn-owl has the distinction of being one of the world's most widely distributed land birds, as well as the most intensively studied of all owls, particularly in Europe and North America. However, of the 28 subspecies presently recognized, most are poorly known, and some isolated populations may represent separate species."[23]

2 "The Hebrew word תִּנְשֶׁמֶת from the stem נָשַׁם meaning, 'to pant' or 'to breath,' is found on three occasions in the Hebrew Bible. In the lists of 'unclean' birds, the word is found in Lv 11:18 and Dt 14:16 and it is generally accepted as referring to the Common Barn-owl (*Tyto alba*). The only other occurrence of this word is in Lv 11:30, where a list of 'unclean' animals 'that move about on the ground,' is given, and there it is translated as chameleon' (*Cameleo cameleo*). The hissing of the Common Barn-owl and the chameleon when threatened may have led to this particular Hebrew stem being used. Unfortunately this stem is used in only one other instance namely in Is 42:14 in connection with the panting of a woman in childbirth. In modern Hebrew the Common Barn-owl has retained the Biblical Hebrew name."[24]

---

21 Hattingh, Tian (2012), p. 124.
22 Hattingh, Tian (2012), p. 126.
23 Hattingh, Tian (2012), p. 127.
24 Hattingh, Tian (2012), p. 130.

3. TYPICAL OWLS

1 There are no less than six Typical Owls mentioned in the Hebrew Bible.[25]

No.	Hebrew	English	Scripture examples
1	אֹחַ	Eurasian Eagle-owl	Is 13:21.
2	שָׂעִיר	Eurasian Scops-owl	Is 13:21, 34:14; 2 Kgs 23:8.
3	תַּחְמָס	Pallid Scops-owl	Lv 11:16, Dt 14:15.
4a	כּוֹס	Little Owl	Lv 11:17, Dt 14:16, Ps 102:7.
4b	קָאָת	Little Owl	Lv 11:18, Dt 14:17, Ps 102:7.
5	יַנְשׁוּף	Northern Long-eared Owl	Lv 11:17, Dt 14:16, Is 34:11.
6	קִפֹּד	Short-eared Owl	Is 14:23, Is 34:11, Zep 2:14.

2 Eurasian Eagle-owl (*Bubo bubo*)

1 The Hebrew word אֹחַ in Is 13:21, unfortunately is found nowhere else in the Hebrew Bible. This word seems to be onomatopoetic (a sound imitation) of one of the sounds uttered by this species.

3 Eurasian Scops-owl (*Otus scops*)

1 The Hebrew word שָׂעִיר has three possible meanings namely, the adjective "hairy," the noun "he-goat" or "buck," and the noun "satyr" or "demon." In Lv 17:7 and 2 Chr 11:15 the context dictates it to be translated as "demon." In 2 Kgs 23:8 the MT text reads "the high places of the gates," but footnote 8ᵉ suggest that it should read "the high places of the demon / hairy being / Scops-owl."

2 In Greek mythology, a **satyr** is one of a class of lustful, drunken woodland gods. In Greek art they were represented as a man with a horse's ears and tail, but in Roman representations as a man with a goat's ears, tail, legs, and horns.

8ᵉ "Read probably Heb." In the MT the form is הַשְּׁעָרִים but this footnote suggests הַשְּׂעִירִים in which the diacritical point of the first letter of the word after the hey of the definite article is moved to the left, and the qamets under the 'ayin is changed to a chireq. Unfortunately this footnote does not provide any reason why the alternative spelling should be considered.

4 Pallid Scops-owl (*Otus brucei*)

1 The Hebrew word תַּחְמָס occurs only in the lists of "unclean" birds, namely in Lv 11:16 and Dt 14:15. It is therefore impossible to ascribe the word beyond any reasonable doubt to a specific species.

---

25 Hattingh, Tian (2012), p. 132.

5a Little Owl (*Athene noctua saharae*)

    1 "There are no less than 13 recognized races of Little Owl (*Athene noctua*) spread across Europe and Asia. Here, our interest lies with two of these subspecies. As its English name suggests, it is a small owl, about twenty-five centimeters in length, and a common a semi-desert dweller in the Middle East."[26]

    2 This subspecies is generally associated with the Hebrew word כוֹס found in Lv 11:17, Dt 14:16, and Ps 102:7.

5b Little Owl (*Athene noctua lilith*)

    1 "In Jewish folklore, from the Alphabet of Sirach (c. 700–1000 CE) onwards, Lilith appears as Adam's first wife, who was created at the same time and from the same clay as Adam (Gen 1:27). This contrasts with Eve, who was created from one of Adam's ribs (Gen 2:22). The legend developed extensively during the Middle Ages. For example, in the 13th-century writings of Isaac ben Jacob ha-Cohen, Lilith left Adam after she refused to become subservient to him and then would not return to the Garden of Eden after she had coupled with the archangel Samael (Satan)."[27]

    2 This subspecies is generally associated with the Hebrew word קָאַת found in Lv 11:18, Dt 14:17, and Ps 102:7, Is 34:11, and Zep 2:14.

6 Northern Long-eared Owl (*Asio otus*)

    1 This species is generally associated with the Hebrew word יַנְשׁוּף found in Lv 11:17, Dt 14:16, and Is 34:11.

7 Short-eared Owl (*Asio flammeus*)

    1 "In Is 14:23 and 34:11 the Hebrew word קִפֹּד is also translated as 'hedgehog' or 'porcupine.' The fact that the other three creatures named by the author in Is 34:11 are birds, would seem to suggest that in this case the word should rather be translated as 'Short-eared Owl.' The context in Zep 2:14 confirms this, as a hedgehog or porcupine would not easily be found to 'roost on her columns' (NIV)."[28]

    2 Zephaniah 2:14

BHS	גַּם־קָאַת גַּם־קִפֹּד
Ltrl	short-eared owl—also—little owl—also
NIV	The desert owl and the screech owl
KJB	both the cormorant and the bittern
ASV	both the pelican and the porcupine
WEB	Both the pelican and the porcupine

---

26 Hattingh, Tian (2012), p. 136, 137.
27 Hattingh, Tian (2012), p. 140.
28 Hattingh, Tian (2012), p. 144–150.

83.6 PIGEONS AND DOVES

1. INTRODUCTION

1. "This family could be called the typical Pigeons and Doves, and contain 181 species. Laymen tend to call the smaller members of the family 'doves,' and the larger members pigeons,' but size alone does not always distinguish the two groups. For example, the Rock Dove (*Columba livia*), is often called the 'Rock Pigeon'."[29]

2. "Doves are often associated with fertility, probably because of their high reproductive capabilities. Although not all doves are peaceful, the goddesses of love from Rome (Venus) and ancient Greece (Aphrodite) are both associated with the dove."[30]

2. DOVES

1. "The Rock Dove (*Columba livia*), the Collared Dove (*Streptopelia decaocto*), the Turtle Dove (*Streptopelia turtur*), and the Laughing Dove (*Streptopelia senegalensis*), often known as the Palm Dove, are all common birds in the Middle East. The Common Woodpigeon (*Columba palumbus*) is a rare wintering species, and the Namaqua Dove (*Oena capensis*) may occur accidentally from Arabia."[31]

2. "The Hebrew word יוֹנָה is a generic term usually translated as 'dove.' It is derived from the stem אָנָה (Is 3:26, 19:8), which means, 'to mourn,' probably applied to the dove because of the call of some species like the Laughing Dove, for example. As in neighboring cultures, the Hebrew also has a love connotation, the noun being used as a term of endearment for a beloved girl on three occasions in the Song of Songs namely in 2:14, 5:2 and 6:9. In the sacrificial passages of Lv 5:7, 5:11, 12:6, 12:8, 14:22, 14:30, 15:14, 15:29, and Nm 6:10 it is usually translated into English as a 'young pigeon'."[32]

3. "The Laughing Dove is also common in the Middle East, and would certainly be acceptable as sacrifices. However, the Hebrew word תֹּר plural תֹּרִים is a sound imitating word, based on the call of the Turtle Dove (*Streptopelia turtur*), as is the case with its scientific generic name. It is referred to in all the sacrificial passages of Lv 5:7, 5:11, 12:6, 12:8, 14:22, 14:30, 15:14, 15:29, and Nm 6:10, making the sacrificial prescription unmistakable."[33]

4. "One of the most famous birds in Bibles is found in Gen 8:8–12, where the story about Noah trying to determine to what extent the floodwaters have receded is told. He sent out a raven, which did not return. But because he wanted to confirm that land was actually bare, he sent out the terrestrial dove."[34]

---

29 Hattingh, Tian (2012), p. 147.
30 Main source: Wikipedia contributors. *"Lilith."* Wikipedia, The Free Encyclopedia, 4 October, 2019. Web: 4 October, 2019. Slightly edited.
31 Hattingh, Tian (2012), p. 150.
32 Hattingh, Tian (2012), p. 155.
33 Hattingh, Tian (2012), p. 157.
34 Hattingh, Tian (2012), p. 157.

5   In Gen 8:8 there is a footnote (8ᵃ) suggesting that, as in verses 10 and 12, Noah waited seven days after sending out the raven before he sent out the dove. Neither the Greek Septuagint, nor the Aleppo Codex had added this information in verse 8.

6   In Hos 7:11–12 the dove is described as "a silly, senseless dove" (NIV).

83.7   PERCHING BIRDS / SONGBIRDS

1. INTRODUCTION

1   "The order *Passeriformes* (Latin: *passer* which means 'sparrow') are by far the largest bird order in terms of numbers. There are more than 5,100 species in total or 60 percent of all known living birds. It is the most complex order (114 families), and the most highly developed order of birds. In the animal kingdom, they form one of the most diverse terrestrial vertebrate orders. The order has roughly twice as many species as the largest of the mammal orders, the *Rodentia*."[35]

2. SWALLOWS

1   "The Swallows (and Martins) are a group of birds that are well known and loved by people all over the world. They are almost cosmopolitan (embrace multicultural demographics) in their distribution. In other words, they can be found on all continents except Antarctica. They consist of 79 living species in about 20 genera."[36]

2   In the Hebrew Bible, the word דְּרוֹר is translated with "swallow." In Ps 84:4 it is said that swallows were nesting in the Temple area (item 4.3 below), and in Prv 26:2 the aerial lifestyle of the swallow is implied.

3. RAVENS

1   "Ravens, and more so crows, possess remarkable personalities, which can rightly be described as assertive and full of self-confidence. They are also seen as brash, bold, and aggressive. In addition to this, they are highly active, and particularly noisy. They possess an extensive dietary range, meaning they will eat almost anything that they can swallow, animal or vegetable, dead or alive. This, coupled with their boldness and intelligence, has enabled them to adapt completely to a lifestyle co-existent with man. This is the case even where the habitat has radically been altered by the destructive activities of humans and the use of their machines. Therefore they are distributed almost world-wide. However, they are absent from Antarctica, New Zealand, southern South-America, and certain oceanic islands."[37]

2   "The Hebrew word עֹרֵב is usually translated as 'raven,' probably meaning the Common Raven (*Corvus corax*), but the Hooded Crow (*Corvus corone cornix*), is also a common sighting in cities and other urban areas. The Carrion Crow (*Corvus corone corone*), and to a lesser extent, the Rook (*Corvus frugilegus*), are common in the Middle East, and would probably fit well into any of the biblical references."[38]

---

35   Hattingh, Tian (2012), p. 158.
36   Hattingh, Tian (2012), p. 158.
37   Hattingh, Tian (2012), p. 158.
38   Hattingh, Tian (2012), p. 160.

3 "Because of their extensive dietary range, ravens are included in the lists of 'unclean' birds in Lv 11:15 and Dt 14:14. In 1 Kgs 17:4, and 17:6 ravens are said to supply Elijah with food. Ravens are more shy and vigilant than the crows. They prefer mountainous terrain or solitary wooded areas suitable for nesting, and would fit into the context of the story. In Gen 8:7 we find probably one of the most well known references to birds in the Hebrew Bible, as the raven is the first to leave Noah's ark. Because of the difference in personality, it would seem that it in actual fact was one of the crows that were sent. Both Job 38:41 (Chapter 82.22.7) and Ps 147:9 suggest that parents in this family have their hands full with ravenous chicks. Prv 30:17 refer to the practice by crows to peck at the eyes of a fresh carcass. Sg 5:11 takes note of the raven's plumage, and Is 34:11 of its preference to live in solitary areas."[39]

4. SPARROWS

1 "As its vernacular name indicates, the House Sparrow (*Passer domesticus*) is the most abundant and successful urban dweller of all birds. Step off a plane at any airport, and you will probably be welcomed by the chattering local family. The House Sparrow originated in the Middle Eastern region. Originally, they were native to Europe, western Asia and northern Africa, but they have since followed European civilization all over the world."[40]

2 "In the Middle East region one can readily find the House Sparrow, the Spanish Sparrow (*Passer hispaniolensis*), the Rock Sparrow (*Petronia petronia*), and the Dead Sea Sparrow (*Passer moabiticus*) in their respective distribution ranges. Ps 84:4 and Ps 102:8 refer to a bird sitting alone on the housetop, which hardly suggests a sociable House Sparrow, and could be referring to the Blue Rock Thrush (*Monticola solitarius*) which is a shy, solitary bird, as indicted by its name, that perches on rock summits and even houses."[41]

3 Psalm 84:4

BHS	גַּם־צִפּוֹר מָצְאָה בַיִת וּדְרוֹר קֵן לָהּ
Ltrl	for her—a nest—and a swallow—a house—she found—birds—even
NIV	Even the sparrow has found a home, and the swallow a nest for herself,
KJB	Yea, the sparrow hath found an house, and the swallow a nest for herself
ASV	Yea, the sparrow hath found her a house, And the swallow a nest for herself,
WEB	Yes, the sparrow has found a home, and the swallow a nest for herself,

1 The Hebrew word צִפּוֹר is a feminine generic term referring to birds in general. In the Hebrew Bible it appears 40 times in several forms, like in צִפֹּרָה which is the name of Moses' wife in Ex 2:21, 4:25, and 18:2. The f. sg. noun per se appears 11 times like here in Ps 84:4, and in Gen 7:14; Dt 4:17, 14:11; Ps 8:8, 11:1, 84:4; Prv 7:23; Ez 39:4, Am 3:5.

---

39 Hattingh, Tian (2012), p. 163.
40 Hattingh, Tian (2012), p. 166.
41 Hattingh, Tian (2012), p. 167.

83.8 UNCLEAN BIRDS

1. INTRODUCTION

"The following biblical Birds are mentioned only twice in the Bibles. Because of the lack of any further cross references, we do not have conclusive evidence as to what bird, or possibly animal, is meant.

1	Cormorant (*Phalacrocorax carbo*)	Lv 11:17 and Dt 14:17
2	Pallid Scops-owl (*Otus brucei*)	Lv 11:16 and Dt 14:15
3	Hoopoe (*Upupa epops*)	Lv 11:19 and Dt 14:18
4	Red Kite (*Milvus milvus milvus*)	Lv 11:14 and Dt 14:13
5	Egyptian Vulture (*Neophron percnopterus*)	Lv 11:18 and Dt 14:17
6	Lappet-faced Vulture (*Torgos tracheliotus negevensis*)	Lv 11:13 and Dt 14:12
7	Common Barn-owl (*Tyto alba*)	Lv 11:18 and Dt 14:16
8	Bearded Vulture (*Gypaetus barbatus*)	Lv 11:13, and Dt 14:12
9	Sea-gulls (*Laridae*) No less than eleven species of the family Laridae occur in the Middle East. Two of the more common ones are the Black-headed Gull (*Larus ridibundus*), and the Little Gull (*Larus minutes*).	Lv 11:16 and Dt 14:15
10	Herons (*Ardeidae*) The Hebrew word 'anaphah only occurs in the list of 'unclean' birds in Lv 11:19 and Dt 14:18. Modern Hebrew utilizes this word as a generic term for the Herons found in the Middle East, namely the Grey Heron (*Ardea cinerea*), Purple Heron (*Ardea purpurea*), and the Goliath Heron (*Ardea goliath*). The Biblical Hebrew stem from which this word is derived means 'to be angry.' Maybe the overall impression left by looking at the face of a heron might have led to this deduction."[42]	

83.9 BIRD SPECIES IN THE HEBREW BIBLE

1   Bat (Hebrew: *'atalleph*) (*Chiroptera Spp.*)

Lv 11:19	Dt 14:18	Is 2:20

2   Bulbul, Yellow-vented (Hebrew: *'agur*) (*Pycnonotus xanthopygos*)

Is 38:14	Jer 8:7

3   Cuckoo, Lark-heeled (Hebrew: *barbur*) (*Centropus aegyptius*)
    1 Kgs 5:3

---

[42] Hattingh, Tian (2012), p. 168.

4   Cormorant (Hebrew: *shalah*) (*Phalacrocorax carbo*)

Lv 11:17	Dt 14:17

5   Dove, Rock (Hebrew: *jonah*) (*Columbia livia*)

Gen 8:8	Gen 8:9	Gen 8:10	Gen 8:11	Gen 8:12	Lv 5:7
Lv 5:11	Lv 12:6	Lv 12:8	Lv 14:22	Lv 14:30	Lv 15:14
Lv 15:29	Nm 6:10	Ps 55:7	Ps 56:1	Ps 68:14	So 1:13
So 1:15	So 2:14	So 4:1	So 5:2	So 5:12	So 6:9
Is 38:14	Is 59:11	Is 60:8	Jer 48:28	Hos 7:11	Ho 11:11
Na 2:7	Ez 7:16				

6   Dove, Turtle (Hebrew: *tor*) (*Streptopelia turtur*)

Gen 15:9	Lv 1:14	Lv 5:7	Lv 5:11	Lv 12:6	Lv 12:8
Lv 14:22	Lv 14:30	Lv 15:14	Lv 15:29	Nm 6:10	Ps 74:19
So 2:12	Jer 8:7				

7   Eagle (Hebrew: *nesher*) (*Accipitridae Spp.*)

Ex 19:4	Lv 11:13	Dt 14:12.	Dt 28:49	Dt 32:11	2 Sm 1:23
Jb 9:26	Jb 39:27	Ps 103:5	Prv 23:5	Prv 30:19	Is 40:31
Jer 4:13	Jer 48:40	Jer 49:16	Jer 49:22	Lam 4:19	Ez 1:10
Ez 10:14	Ez 17:3	Ez 17:7	Dn 4:30	Dn 7:4	Od 1:4
Mi 1:16	Hb 1:8				

8   Falcon (Hebrew: *nets*) (*Falco peregrinus*)

Lv 11:16	Dt 14:15	Jb 39:26

9   Heron (Hebrew: *'anaphah*) (*Ardeidae Spp.*)

Lv 11:19	Dt 14:18

10   Hoopoe (Hebrew: *dukhiphath*) (*Upupa epops*)

Lv 11:19	Dt 14:18

11   Junglefowl, Red (Hebrew: *sekwi*) (*Gallus gallus*)
     Jb 38:36

12 Kite, Black (Hebrew: *'ajjah*) (*Milvus migrans migrans*)

| Lv 11:14 | Dt l4:13 | Jb 15:23? | Jb 28:7 |

13 Kite, Red (Hebrew: *da'ah*) (*Milvus milvus milvus*)

| Lv 11:14 | Dt 14:13 |

14.1 Ostrich (Hebrew: *ja'anah*) (*Struthio camelus*)

Lv 11:16	Dt l4:15	Jb 30:29	Is 13:21	Is 34:13	Is 43:20
Jer 50:39	Lam 4:3	Hos 11:11	Mi 1:8		

14.2 Ostrich, female (Hebrew: *renanim*) (*Struthio camelus*)
Jb 39:13

15 Owl, Common Barn (Hebrew: *tinshemet*) (*Tyto alba*)

| Lv 11:18 | Dt 14:16 |

16 Owl, Eagle (Hebrew: *och*) (*Bubo bubo*)
Is 13:21

17 Owl, Little (Hebrew: *kos*) (*Athene noctua saharae*)

| Lv 11:17 | Dt 14:16 | Ps 102:7 |

18 Owl, Little (Hebrew: *qa'ath*) (*Athene noctua lilith*)

| Lv 11:18 | Dt 14:17 | Ps 102:7 | Is 34:11 | Zeph 2:14 |

19 Owl, Long-eared, Northern (Hebrew: *janshoph*) (*Asio otus*)

| Lv 11:17 | Dt 14:16 | Is 34:11 |

20 Owl, Scops, Eurasian (Hebrew: *sair*) (*Otus scops scops*)

| Lv l7:7 | 2 Kgs 23:8 | 2 Chr 11:15 | Is 13:21 | Is 34:14 |

21 Owl, Scops Pallid (Hebrew: *tahmas*) (*Otus brucei*)

| Lv 11:16 | Dt 14:15 |

22 Owl, Short-eared (Hebrew: *qippod*) (*Asio flammeus*)

| Is 14:23 | Is 34:11 | Zeph 2:14 |

23 Owl, Tawny (Hebrew: *qippoz*) (*Strix aluco*)
   Is 34:15

24 Partridge (Hebrew: *qore'*) (*Ammoperdix heyi*)

| 1 Sm 26:20 | Jer 17:11 |

25 Peafowl, Indian (Hebrew: *tukkijjim*) (*Pavo cristatus*)

| 1 Kgs 10:22 | 2 Chr 9:21 |

26 Plover, Egyptian (Hebrew: *stippor*) (*Pluvianus aegyptius*)
   Jb 40:29

27 Quail (Hebrew: *slaw*) (*Coturnix coturnix*)

| Ex 16:13 | Nm 11:31 | Nm 11:32 | Ps 105:40 |

28 Raven (Hebrew: *'orev*) (*Corvus Spp.*)

| Gen 8:7 | Lv 11:15 | Dt 14:14 | 1 Kgs 17:4 | 1 Kgs 17:6 | Jb 38:41 |
| Ps 147:9 | Prv 30:17 | Eccl 5:11 | So 5:11 | Is 34:11 | |

29 Sea-gull (Hebrew: *shahaph*) (*Laridae*)

| Lv 11:16 | Dt 14:15 |

30 Stork (Hebrew: *hasidhah*) (*Ciconidae*)

| Lv 11:19 | Dt 14:18 | Jb 39:13 | Ps 104:17 | Jer 8:7 | Zech 5:9 |

31 Swallow (Hebrew: *dror*) (*Hirundinidae Spp.*)

| Ps 84:4 | Prv 26:2 |

32 Swift (Hebrew: *sis*) (*Apus apus*)

| Is 38:14 | Jer 8:7 |

33 Vulture, Bearded (Hebrew: *peres*) (*Gypaetus barbatus*)

Lv 11:13	Dt 14:12

34 Vulture, Griffon (Hebrew: *dajjah, nesher*) (*Gyps fulvus*)

Dt 14:13	Is 34:15	Mi 1:16	Prv 30:17

35 Vulture, Lapped-faced (Hebrew: *oznijah*) (*Torgos tracheliotus negevensis*)

Lv 11:13	Dt 14:12

36 Vulture, Egyptian (Hebrew: *raham*) (*Neophron percnopterus*)

Lv 11:18	Dt 14:17

XVII
NAMES
OF
GOD

84 Introduction

84.1 INTRODUCTION 1

1. In the vast number of modern English translations that are currently available, an almost universal consensus has been reached on how the different "names" of God should be translated into English. The 188 appellations used to name the one God of the Hebrew people in their Holy Scriptures (called the Tanakh) are investigated in the next three chapters of this volume. For the sake of quick referencing, these "names" have been numbered in the right hand margin of Chapters 85–87 below.

2. Rabbinic Judaism describes seven names which are so holy that, once written should not be erased. They are: YHWH (Chapter 86.1), and six others which can be categorized as titles. El (Chapter 85.1), Eloah (Chapter 85.2.3), Elohim (Chapter 85.2.1), Shaddai (Chapter 85.3.1), Ehyeh (Chapter 87.5), and Tsevaot (Chapter 86.3.7). Other names are considered mere epithets or titles reflecting different aspects of God.[1]

---

[1] Hattingh, Tian (2012), p. 169.

85　EL

| 85.1 | אֵל | 1 |

1. אֵל (traditionally written in English as "El") appears in Ugaritic, Phoenician and other 2nd and 1st millennium BCE texts both as generic "god" and as the head of the divine pantheon. In the Hebrew Bible El appears very occasionally alone (Ex 34:14; Nm 12:13). As it will be shown in this chapter, El usually appears with some epithet or attribute attached. For example: El Shaddai (Chapter 85.3.1), El Elyon (Chapter 85.3.3), etc. In these instances it is usually interpreted and translated as "God," but it is not always clear whether these uses of El refer to the deity in general or to the god El in particular.

2. The word El, is a m. sg. noun occurring 247 times in the Hebrew Bible, and has the basic meaning of "god." However, it has many subordinate applications to express the concept of power and/or might. In prose it is most commonly used with a defining word, usually an adjective or a genitive. Next we will mention a selection of those applications.

3. The most common application in the Hebrew Bible is to identify the one only true God of Israel. Unaltered this application appears 163 times in the Hebrew Bible.

    a) El appearing alone, as in Nm 12:13, is an indication that the only true God needs no article or any other predicate to define Himself. In Gen 33:20 and elsewhere, El is portrayed as a divine name. Mal 2:10 calls God "One."

Examples from the Tanakh		
Mal 2:10	Gen 33:20	Nm 12:13
אֵל אֶחָד	אֵל אֱלֹהֵי יִשְׂרָאֵל	אֵל
one God	El, God of Israel	God

   b) Over and above the basic form, El is also contextually associated with a vast number of qualities, descriptions and positions of God, including many forms of five variations (Chapter 85.2), and seven combinations (Chapter 85.3).

Examples from the Tanakh				
Gen 9:26	Is 5:17	Dt 10:17	Dt 7:9	Gen 31:13
אֱלֹהֵי	וְהָאֵל הַקָּדוֹשׁ	הָאֵל הַגָּדֹל	הָאֵל הַנֶּאֱמָן	הָאֵל
God of	and the holy God	The great God	The faithful God	The God
Ex 15:2	Ex 15:2	Gen 49:25	Gen 35:1, 3	Gen 39:21
אֶל בֵּית-אֵל	אֵלִי	מֵאֵל	לָאֵל	לְאֵל יָדִי
God of Bethel	my God	from God	to God	in the power

4 Another application is employed to indicate men (and a city) of power and rank.

Examples from the Tanakh			
Jon 3:3	Ez 31:11	Ez 32:21	Jb 41:17
לֵאלֹהִים	אֵיל גּוֹיִם	אֵלֵי גִבּוֹרִים	אֵלִים
exceedingly	mighty one of nations	mighty heroes	mighty men

5 To indicate power and strength.

Examples from the Tanakh			
Neh 5:5	Dt 28:32	Prv 3:27	Gen 31:29
וְאֵין לְאֵל יָדֵנוּ	וְאֵין לְאֵל יָדֶךָ	לְאֵל יָדֶיךָ	יֶשׁ־לְאֵל יָדִי
and not in our power	and no power in your hand	in the power of your hand	It is in the power of my hand

6 To characterize mighty things in nature.

	Examples from the Tanakh		
	Ps 36:7	Is 14:13	Ps 80:11
	כְּהַרְרֵי־אֵל	לְכוֹכְבֵי־אֵל	אַרְזֵי־אֵל
Litr.	like the mountains of God	to the stars of God	the cedars of God
Idm.	like the mighty mountains	to the mighty stars	the mighty cedars

7 To indicate the gods of the nations / supreme God.

Examples from the Tanakh			
Dt 32:12	Ps 44:21	Ex 34:14	Dn 11:36
אֵל נֵכָר	לְאֵל זָר	לְאֵל אַחֵר	אֵל אֵלִים
foreign god	to a strange god	to other gods	the God of gods

Refer to Chapter 85.3.8 for other names containing El.

8   Inseparable Prepositions

El takes the Inseparable Prepositions, often combined with the article (Chapter 17.4 in Vol. 1).

Examples from the Tanakh			
Gen 49:25; Ps 104:21	Jb 13:7	Gen 35:1, 3	Dt 33:26
Jb 20:29, 35:2	Jb 21:22, 22:2	Jb 13:8	Jb 40:9
הָלָאֵל	הַלְאֵל	לָאֵל	כָּאֵל
for God?	for God?	to / for (the) God	like God
(4 times)	(3 times)	(10 times)	(twice)

9   Declensional Suffixes

To indicate possession by adding declensional suffixes. El being a m. sg. noun (Chapter 10.11.A.2.2 in Vol. 1) takes the Type I suffixes. (Chapter 10.8 in Volume 1). Other than Elohim, which uses ten declensional suffixes (Chapter 85.2.1.6), El only uses the 1cs suffix, and this form appears twelve times in the Hebrew Bible with ten of these in Psalms.

a)   my God   אֵלִי

† Examples from the Tanakh
Ex 15:2; Is 44:17; Ps 18:3, 22:2, 22:2, 22:11, 63:2, 68:25, 89:27, 102:25, 118:28, 140:7

The two instances of "Eli" in Ps 22:2 is of particular significance to the Christian religion. The Hebrew phrase in Ps 22:2a is quoted in the New Testament in Mt 27:46 and Mrk 15:34 as the fourth of the so-called "Seven Words" of Jesus Christ during his crucifixion. The vernacular spoken by Jesus was Aramaic and not Hebrew. St. Mark uses the Aramaic phrase, which then includes the form "Eloi," whereas St. Matthew choose to use the original Hebrew "Eli."

b)   the mighty / Gods

† Examples from the Tanakh	
Jb 41:17; Ps 29:1, 89:7	Dn 11:36
אֵלִים	אֵלִים
the mighty	gods

	Name	Literal meaning	Example	
1	אֵל אֵלִים	God of gods	Dn 11:36	2

10 Waw

There are seven occurrences where El is found with a waw.

† Examples from the Tanakh			
Gen 28:3, 43:14	Ps 7:11, 78:35	Jb 23:16, 34:5	Is 5:16
וְאֵל	וְאֵל	וְאֵל	וְהָאֵל
and God	and God	and God	and God

11 Article

Of the 20 occurrences where El takes the article, 13 of these form combinations.

	Name	Literal meaning	Examples	
1	הָאֵל	the God	Gen 46:3	3
2	הָאֵל בֵּית־אֵל	the God of Bethel	Gen 31:13	4
3	הָאֵל הַנֶּאֱמָן	the God who keeps	Dt 7:9	5
4	הָאֵל הַגָּדֹל	the great God	Dt 10:17	6
5	הָאֵל מָעוּזִּי	the God my fortress	2 Sm 22:33	7
6	הָאֵל הַנֹּתֵן נְקָמֹת	the God who gives vengeance	2 Sm 22:48	8
7	הָאֵל הַגָּדוֹל וְהַנּוֹרָא	the great and terrible God	Neh 1:5	9
8	הָאֵל הַמְאַזְּרֵנִי	the God who girds me	Ps 18:32	10
9	הָאֵל יְשׁוּעָתֵנוּ	the God who is our salvation	Ps 68:20	11
10	הָאֵל עֹשֵׂה פֶלֶא	the God who works wonders	Ps 77:14	12
11	הָאֵל יְהוָה	the God, Yahweh	Ps 85:9	13
12	הָאֵל ׀ יְהוָה	God, Yahweh	Is 42:5	14
13	הָאֵל הַגָּדוֹל הַגִּבּוֹר	the great and mighty God	Jer 32:18	15
14	הָאֵל הַגָּדוֹל הַגִּבּוֹר וְהַנּוֹרָא	the great, mighty and terrible God	Neh 9:32	16

In Jb 8:3 we find the form הַאֵל and the phrase literally means, "God subverts judgment." Because of this, most English translations opted to take the patach to be chatuph-patach. The prefix then becomes an interrogative hey (Chapter 21.7 in Vol. 1), and in doing so, they changed the phrase (and sentence) into a question.

85.2 VARIATIONS OF EL

1	אֱלֹהִים	17

1 Introduction

The word אֱלֹהִים traditionally written in English as "Elohim," is the first name for God found in the Hebrew Bible (Gen 1:1). In the very first sentence in the Hebrew Bible, God (Elohim) speaks the universe into existence, demonstrating the superlative nature of God's power. Elohim appears 2,602 times throughout the Hebrew Bible, but is not found in the Book of Esther.

	Examples from the Tanakh				
	Nm 22:18	Gen 27:20	Gen 5:22	Gen 9:26	Gen 1:1
	אֱלֹהַי	אֱלֹהֶיךָ	הָאֱלֹהִים	אֱלֹהֵי	אֱלֹהִים
	my God	your God	God	God of	God
occurrences:	101	325	366	398	680

Refer to Chapter 86.2 below for combinations of these forms with Yahweh.

2 Derivation and Meaning:

The derivation of the name Elohim is unclear and therefore debatable. It has the unusual characteristic of being a m. pl. noun that is used to describe the One God of Israel as seen above. However, it may also mean, "gods." This is also the case for the singular form El. Both forms are used with or without the article.

For the purposes of this publication we will assume that Elohim is the plural form of Eloah. Apart from the first meaning mentioned above, Elohim has a number of additional meanings including the following:

a) other god(s).	c) gods of the nations
b) foreign god(s).	d) sons of God = angels

a)

Examples from the Tanakh		
Dt 10:17	Ex 18:11	Ex 20:3, 23:13
הוּא אֱלֹהֵי הָאֱלֹהִים	מִכָּל־הָאֱלֹהִים	אֱלֹהִים אֲחֵרִים
he is the God of the gods	than all the gods	other gods

b)

Examples from the Tanakh		
Dt 31:16	Gen 35:2,(4)	Js 24:20,(23)
אֱלֹהֵי נֵכַר־הָאָרֶץ׃	אֶת־אֱלֹהֵי הַנֵּכָר	אֱלֹהֵי נֵכָר
the foreign gods of the land	the gods of the foreign	gods of foreign

c)

Examples from the Tanakh		
Dt 29:17	2 Chr 32:17,(19)	2 Kgs 18:33, 19:12
אֶת־אֱלֹהֵי הַגּוֹיִם הָהֵם	כֵּאלֹהֵי גּוֹיֵי הָאֲרָצוֹת	אֱלֹהֵי הַגּוֹיִם
the gods of those nations	as the gods of the nations of the lands	gods of the nations

d)

Examples from the Tanakh		
Ps 97:7	Gen 6:2, 4	Jb 1:6, 2:1, 38:7
כָּל־אֱלֹהִים	בְּנֵי־הָאֱלֹהִים	בְּנֵי הָאֱלֹהִים
all gods / angels	sons of God	sons of God

3 Plural absolute

As mentioned above (section 1.1), the plural absolute form "Elohim" appears 680 times in the Hebrew Bible. It is sometimes used in phrase where a construct form would seem to be more appropriate. For example:

	Name	Literal meaning	Examples	
1	אֱלֹהִים אֱמֶת	God of truth	Jer 10:10	**18**
2	אֱלֹהִים קְדֹשִׁים	Holy God	Js 24:19	**19**
3	אֱלֹהִים חָי	Living God	2 Kgs 19:4, 16; Is 37:4, 17	**20**
4	אֱלֹהִים חַיִּים	Living God	Dt 5:26; 1 Sm 17:26	**21**
5	אלהים עֶלְיוֹן	God Most High	Ps 57:2	**22**

4   Plural construct

As mentioned in section 1.1 above, the construct form of Elohim namely אֱלֹהֵי meaning, "God(s) of . . . ," appears 398 times in the Hebrew Bible. The plural is used to indicate the singular God (of Israel). In addition, the construct form is used to indicate a possessive relationship with God. These instances can be placed within three groups namely:

a)   indicating certain attributes of God.

	Name	Literal meaning	Examples	
1	אֱלֹהֵי קֶדֶם	God of aforetime	Dt 33:27	23
2	אֱלֹהֵי מַעַרְכוֹת	God of the armies	1 Sm 17:45	24
3	אֱלֹהֵי הָאֱלֹהִים	God of the gods	Dt 10:17	25
4	אֱלֹהֵי אֲבוֹתֵינוּ	God of our help	1 Chr 12:18	26
5	אֱלֹהֵי צְבָאוֹת	God of hosts	2 Sm 5:10	27
6	אֱלֹהֵי מִשְׁפָּט	God of justice	Is 30:18	28
7	אֱלֹהֵי חַסְדִּי	God of my mercy	Ps 59:17	29
8	אֱלֹהֵי מִקָּרֹב	God of nearness	Jer 23:23	30
9	אֱלֹהֵי תְהִלָּתִי	God of my praise	Ps 109:1	31
10	אֱלֹהֵי צִדְקִי	God of my righteousness	Ps 4:1	32
11	אֱלֹהֵי צוּרִי	God of my rock	2 Sm 22:3	33
12	אֱלֹהֵי צוּר	God of the rock	2 Sm 22:47	34
13	אֱלוֹהֵי יִשְׁעִי	God of my salvation	Ps 27:9	35
14	אֱלוֹהֵי תְּשׁוּעָתִי	God of my salvation	Ps 51:14	36
15	אֱלֹהֵי יִשְׁעֵךְ	God of your salvation	Is 17:10	37
16	אֱלוֹהֵי יִשְׁעֵנוּ	God of our salvation	1 Chr 16:35	38
17	אֱלֹהֵי הָרוּחֹת	God of the spirits	Nm 16:22	39
18	אֱלֹהֵי מָעוּזִּי	God of my strength	Ps 43:2	40
19	אֱלֹהֵי אֱמֶת	God of truth	2 Chr 15:3	41

b) indicating the relationship between God and certain people.

	Name	Literal meaning	Examples	
1	אֱלֹהֵי אַבְרָהָם	God of Abraham	Gen 26:24, 28:13, 31:42	**42**
2	אֱלֹהֵי יִצְחָק	God of Isaac	Ex 3:6, 15, 4:5	**43**
3	אֱלֹהֵי יַעֲקֹב	God of Jacob	2 Sm 23:1; Ps 20:1, 46:7, 11	**44**
4	אֱלֹהֵי יִשְׂרָאֵל	God of Israel	Gen 33:20; Ex 5:1, 32:27	**45**
5	אֱלֹהֵי הָעִבְרִיִּים	God of the Hebrews	Ex 3:18, 5:3, 7:16	**46**
6	אֱלֹהֵי אֵלִיָּהוּ	God of Elijah	2 Kgs 2:14	**47**
7	אֱלֹהֵי אָבִי	God of my father	Gen 31:24, 32:9; Ex 15:2	**48**
8	אֱלֹהֵי אָבִיךָ	God of your father	Gen 46:3, 50:17; Ex 3:6	**49**
9	אֱלֹהֵי אֲבוֹתֵיכֶם	God of your fathers	Ex 3:13, 15, 16; Dt 1:11	**50**
10	אֱלֹהֵי אֲבֹתָיו	God of his fathers	2 Kgs 21:22; 2 Chr 28:25	**51**
11	אֱלֹהֵי אֲבֹתֵינוּ	God of our fathers	Dt 26:7; Ezr 7:27	**52**
12	אֱלֹהֵי אֲבִיהֶם	God of their father	Gen 31:53	**53**
13	אֱלֹהֵי אֲבֹתָם	God of their fathers	Ex 4:5; Dt 29:25; Jgs 2:12	**54**
14	אֱלֹהֵי אֲבֹתֵיהֶם	God of their fathers	1 Chr 29:20; 2 Chr 7:22	**55**
15	אֱלֹהֵי אֲדֹנִי	God of my master	Gen 24:12, 27, 42, 48	**56**
16	אֱלֹהֵי אַבְרָהָם יִצְחָק וְיִשְׂרָאֵל	God of Abraham, Isaac, and Israel	1 Chr 29:18	**57**

c) indicating the relationship between God and certain places.

	Name	Literal meaning	Examples	
1	אֱלֹהֵי יְרוּשָׁלָיִם	God of Jerusalem	2 Chr 32:19	**58**
2	אֱלֹהֵי הַשָּׁמַיִם	God of the heavens	Gen 24:3, 7	**59**
3	אֱלֹהֵי הָאָרֶץ	God of the land / earth	2 Kgs 17:26, 27	**60**
4	אֱלֹהֵי הָרִים	God of the mountains	1 Kgs 20:28	**61**
5	אֱלֹהֵי שֵׁם	God of Shem	Gen 9:26	**62**
6	אֱלֹהֵי עֲמָקִים	God of the valleys	1 Kgs 20:28	**63**

5 Inseparable Prepositions

   Elohim takes four Inseparable Prepositions (Chapter 17.4 in Vol. 1).

a) With the inseparable preposition בּ it appears 36 times.

Examples from the Tanakh			
Is 50:10	1 Sm 17:43	Is 61:10	2 Sm 22:30
בֵּאלֹהָיו	בֵּאלֹהָיו	בֵּאלֹהַי	בֵּאלֹהַי
on his God	by his gods	in my God	by my God
(once)	(once)	(once)	(once)
Js 22:16; 1 Chr 5:25	Hb 3:18	Is 65:16, 16	Hos 12:6
בֵּאלֹהֵי	בֵּאלֹהֵי	בֵּאלֹהֵי	בֵּאלֹהֶיךָ
against the God of	in the God of	by the God of	to your god
(twice)	(once)	(twice)	(once)
Hos 13:16	Nm 21:5	Neh 13:27	Js 24:27
בֵּאלֹהֶיהָ	בֵּאלֹהִים	בֵּאלֹהֵינוּ	בֵּאלֹהֵיכֶם
against her God	against God	against our God	your (pl.) God
(once)	(23 times)	(once)	(once)

	Name	Literal meaning	Examples	
1	בֵּאלֹהֵי אָמֵן	(by) the God of truth	Is 65:16, 16	64
2	בֵּאלֹהִים לַעְזוֹר	(for) God has power to help	2 Chr 25:8	65

b) With the inseparable preposition לְ it appears 124 times, of which 93 times are without any suffix.

Examples from the Tanakh			
Lv 21:7	Ps 69:3	Gen 46:1	Gen 17:7, 8
לֵאלֹהָיו	לֵאלֹהַי	לֵאלֹהֵי	לֵאלֹהִים
to his God	for my God	to the God of	by my God
(5 times)	(3 times)	(15 times)	(78 times)
Ex 5:8	Nm 25:2	Ex 23:24	Ex 8:25
לֵאלֹהֵינוּ	לֵאלֹהֵיהֶן	לֵאלֹהֵיהֶם	לֵאלֹהֵיכֶם
to our God	to their gods	to their gods	to your God
(9 times)	(twice)	(7 times)	(3 times)

	Name	Literal meaning	Examples	
1	לֵאלֹהֵי אָבִיו	(for) the God of his father	2 Chr 34:3	66
2	לֵאלֹהֵי דָוִיד	(for) the God of David	2 Chr 34:3	67
3	לֵאלֹהֵי מָרוֹם	(to) the God of heights	Mi 6:6	68
4	לֵאלֹהִים עוּזֵּנוּ	(to) God our strength	Ps 81:1	69
5	לֵאלֹהִים לְכֹל מִשְׁפְּחוֹת יִשְׂרָאֵל	the God of all the families of Israel	Jer 31:1	70

c) With the inseparable preposition כ it appears 5 times.

† Examples from the Tanakh		
Gen 3:5; Ps 77:13; Zec 12:8	1 Sm 2:2	2 Chr 32:17
כֵּאלֹהִים	כֵּאלֹהֵינוּ	כֵּאלֹהֵי
like God	like our God	as the gods
(3 times)	(once)	(once)

d) With the inseparable reposition מ it appears 20 times, of which four times are without any suffix.

Examples from the Tanakh			
Dt 6:14, 13:7	Jer 51:5	2 Sm 22:22	Lv 19:14
מֵאֱלֹהֵי	מֵאלֹהָיו	מֵאֱלֹהַי	מֵאֱלֹהֶיךָ
from the gods of	by his God	from my God	your god
(4 times)	(once)	(3 times)	(5 times)
1 Chr 5:22; 2 Chr 25:20	2 Chr 35:21	Ezr 8:23	
מֵהָאֱלֹהִים	מֵאֱלֹהִים	מֵאֱלֹהֵינוּ	
of God	from God	our God	
(twice)	(4 times)	(once)	

	Name	Literal meaning	Examples	
1	מֵאֱלֹהֵי יִשְׁעוֹ	(from) the God of his salvation	Ps 24:5	71
2	מֵאֱלֹהִים אֲשֶׁר־עִמִּי	(from) the God who is with me	2 Chr 35:21	72

6   Declensional Suffixes

Declensional Suffixes are used to indicate possession. אֱלֹהִים is a m. pl. noun (Chapter 10.11.A.2.2 in Vol. 1), thus taking the Type II suffixes. (Chapter 10.8 in Vol. 1). Without a prefix and/or a suffix it appears 1,078 times (Chapter 85.2.1.1 below). In addition, it appears 913 times with nine suffixes.

Examples from the Tanakh				
Ex 3:18	Ex 34:16	Ex 32:11	Nm 22:18	Gen 9:26
אֱלֹהֵינוּ	אֱלֹהֵיהֶן	אֱלֹהָיו	אֱלֹהָי	אֱלֹהֵי
our God	their gods	his God	my God	the God of
(174 times)	(3 times)	(58 times)	(101 times)	(398 times)
Ex 10:7	Prv 2:17	Gen 43:23	Gen 27:20	Ps 146:10
אֱלֹהֵיהֶם	אֱלֹהֶיהָ	אֱלֹהֵיכֶם	אֱלֹהֶיךָ	אֱלֹהַיִךְ
their God	her God	your God	your God	your God
(71 times)	(5 Times)	(162 times)	(325 times)	(14 times)

	Name	Literal meaning	Examples	
1	וֵאלֹהֵי אֲבִיכֶם	(but) the God of your father	Gen 31:29	73
2	וֵאלֹהֵי נָחוֹר	(but) the God of Nahor	Gen 31:53	74

7   Waw

a)   With waw there are 32 occurrences. Suffixes are often attached.

Examples from the Tanakh			
Ru 1:16	2 Sm 7:23	Gen 24:3	Ps 5:2, 42:11
וֵאלֹהַיִךְ	וֵאלֹהָיו	וֵאלֹהֵי	וֵאלֹהַי
and your God	and its gods	and the God of	and my God
(3 times)	(once)	(13 times)	(6 times)
Ex 23:32	Jgs 2:3		Gen 22:1
וְלֵאלֹהֵיהֶם	וֵאלֹהֵיהֶם		וְהָאֱלֹהִים
and with their gods	and their gods		and God
(once)	(once)		(7 times)

b) With a waw followed by a prefix there are six occurrences.

† Examples from the Tanakh		
Is 40:27	Is 8:21	2 Chr 22:7
וּמֵאֱלֹהַי	וּבֵאלֹהָיו	וּמֵאֱלֹהִים
and from my God	and their God	and from God
(once)	(once)	(once)
Nm 33:4	Ps 18:29	Is 48:1
וּבֵאלֹהֵיהֶם	וּבֵאלֹהַי	וּבֵאלֹהֵי
and on their gods	and by my God	and the God of
(once)	(once)	(once)

2	אֱלָהּ		75
	אֱלָהָא	(Aramaic spelling)	76

1 Introduction

These words are traditionally written as "Elah(a)," and mean, "God." They occur 95 times in the Hebrew Bible, with 29 of these occurrences utilizing the Aramaic spelling especially in Daniel and Ezra.

† Examples from the Tanakh		
Ezr 4:24; 5:2, 2, 8, 13, 14	Dn 2:18, 23, 28	Ezr 5:1, 11
Ezr 5:15, 16, 17; 6:3, 5, 5	Dn 2:37, 44, 45, 47	Ezr 6:14; 7:12
Ezr 6:7, 7, 8, 12, 16, 17, 18; 7:24	Dn 3:15, 28, 29	Ezr 7:19, 21, 23
Dn 2:20; 3:26; 4:2	Dn 6:7, 12	
Dn 5:3, 18, 21, 26; 6:20, 26		
God אֱלָהָא	God אֱלָהּ	God אֱלָהּ

2   Elah(a) combinations

Elah(a) combines with nouns and adjectives to describe certain attributes of God.

	Name	Literal meaning	Examples	
1	אֱלָהָא רַבָּא	great God	Ezr 5:8	77
2	אֱלָהָא חַיָּא	living God	Dn 6:21	78
3	אֱלָהּ יִשְׂרָאֵל	God of Israel	Ezr 5:1, 6:14	79
4	אֱלָהּ יְרוּשְׁלֶם	God of Jerusalem	Ezr 7:19	80
5	אֱלָהּ שְׁמַיָּא וְאַרְעָא	God of heaven and earth	Ezr 5:11	81
6	אֱלָהּ שְׁמַיָּא	God of heaven	Ezr 6:9, 10	82
7	אֱלָהּ אֲבָהָתִי	God of my fathers	Dn 2:23	83
8	אֱלָהּ רַב	great God	Dn 2:45	84
9	אֱלָהּ אֱלָהִין	God of Gods	Dn 2:47	85

3   Inseparable Prepositions

They take only the inseparable preposition ל and appear ten times with it (Chapter 17.4 in Vol. 1).

Examples from the Tanakh					
Ezr 5:12, 6:9	Dn 3:12	Dn 5:4	Dn 3:28	Dn 3:18	Dn 3:14
לֶאֱלָהּ	לֵאלָהָךְ	לֵאלָהֵי	לֵאלָהֲהוֹן	לֵאלָהָיִךְ	לֵאלָהַי
to the God of	*your gods*	*the gods of*	*their God*	*your gods*	*my gods*
(5 times)	(once)	(once)	(once)	(once)	(once)

4   Declensional Suffixes

Declensional Suffixes are used to indicate possession. Elah(a) is a m. sg. noun (Chapter 10.11.B.3 in Vol. 1), thus taking the Type I suffixes (Chapter 10.8 in Vol. 1). Without a prefix and/or a suffix Elah(a) appears 49 times. In addition to that, it appears 31 times with nine suffixes.

Examples from the Tanakh				
Dn 3:28, 29	Ezr 5:5, 7:16	Dn 2:47	Ezr 7:17, 18	Ezr 7:14
אֱלָהֲהוֹן	אֱלָהֲהֹם	אֱלָהֲכוֹן	אֱלָהֲכֹם	אֱלָהָךְ
the God	*their God*	*your God*	*your God*	*your God*
(twice)	(twice)	(once)	(twice)	(8 times)

Dn 4:8, 6:22	Dn 2:11	Dn 6:5	Dn 3:17
אֱלָהִי	אֱלָהִין	אֱלָהֵהּ	אֱלָהַנָא
my God	*gods*	*his God*	*our God*
(twice)	(9 times)	(4 times)	(once)

	Name	Literal meaning	Examples	
1	אֱלָהֵהּ דִּי־דָנִיֵּאל	the God of Daniel	Dn 6:26	86
2	אֱלָהֲהוֹן דִּי־שַׁדְרַךְ	the God of Shadrach	Dn 3:28, 29	87

5   Waw

With waw there are three occurrences of Elah(a).

Examples from the Tanakh		
Dn 5:23	Dn 5:23	Ezr 6:12
וְלֵאלָהֵי	וְלֵאלָהָא	וֵאלָהָא
and the gods	*and the God*	*and the God*
(once)	(once)	(once)

6   Aramaic

There are four suggested (but disputed) occurrences of Aramaic in the Hebrew Bible. These occurrences consist of three words and a phrase in:

Ps 2:12	"son"
Gen 15:1	"in a vision"
Nm 23:10	"stock" or "fourth part"
Jb 36:2a	the phrase "Suffer me a little, and I will show thee."

However, there are four more occurrences, and these are all undisputed. They are the following:

1   Gen 31:47: a Hebrew place name, Jegar-Sahadutha.

2   Jer 10:11: a single sentence denouncing idolatry occurs in the middle of a Hebrew text.

3   Dn 2:4b—7:28: five stories about Daniel and his colleagues, and including an apocalyptic vision.

4   Ezr 4:8—6:18 and 7:12—26: quotations of documents from the 5th century on the restoration of the Temple in Jerusalem.

| 7 | עִלָּיָא | 88 |

In Dn 4:14, 21, 22, 29, 31, and 7:25 we find this Aramaic adjective meaning, "high," but which always has an emphatic meaning and therefore translated as "highest." This resulted in it being used as a name of God and is then translated as "The Most High."

| 8 | אֱלָהָא עִלָּיָא | 89 |

This Aramaic word appears with the Hebrew word Elah in the following places: Dn 3:26, 32, and 5:18, 21. It is translated as "The Most High God."

Examples from the Tanakh	
Dn 3:26	Dn 4:14
אֱלָהָא עִלָּיָא	עִלָּיָא
The Most High God (4 times)	*The Most High (6 times)*

3	אֱלוֹהַּ	90
	אֱלוֹהַּ	91

1 Introduction

This word is traditionally written as "Eloah," meaning, "God," and occurs 60 times in the Hebrew Bible. It has a Mappiq in the final hey most of the times. It is a m. sg. noun probably formed by inference (an educated guess) from the plural אֱלֹהִים

2 Derivation and Meaning

The word closely resembles those used in both Arabic and Aramaic to express the meaning of "god." In Hebrew it is used to indicate the following:

a) Heathen deities in the four passages below.

b) The God of Israel in the remaining passages. Examples below.

The word Eloah ends with a furtive patach and a hey containing a Mappiq (Chapters 8.1 and 8.2 in Vol. 1).

a)

† Examples from the Tanakh			
2 Kgs 17:31	Hb 1:11	Dn 11:37	2 Chr 32:15
אֱלָהּ	לֵאלֹהוֹ	אֱלוֹהַּ	אֱלוֹהַּ
god (Qere)	*to his god*	*God*	*god*

b)

Examples from the Tanakh			
Ps 18:31, 50:22	Jb 9:13, 10:2	Jb 3:4, 23, 4:9, 17	Dt 32:15, 17
Ps 114:7, 139:19	Jb 11:5, 6, 7	Jb 5:17, 6:4, 8, 9	Neh 9:17
אֱלוֹהַ	אֱלוֹהַ	אֱלוֹהַ	אֱלוֹהַ
God	God	God	God

3

	Name	Literal meaning	Examples	
1	אֱלָהֵהּ דִּי־דָנִיֵּאל	the God of Daniel	Dn 6:27	**92**
2	אֱלָהָא חַיָּא	the living God	Dn 6:26	**93**
3	אֱלוֹהַ סְלִיחוֹת	the God of forgiveness	Neh 9:17	**94**
4	אֱלוֹהַ עֹשִׂי	God my maker	Jb 35:10	**95**
5	אֱלוֹהַ עֹשִׂי	God is awesome majesty	Jb 37:22	**96**
6	אֱלוֹהַ יַעֲקֹב	God of Jacob	Ps 114:7	**97**
7	אֱלוֹהַ גֹּבַהּ שָׁמַיִם	God in the high heaven	Jb 22:12	**98**
8	אֱלוֹהַ יִשְׁמְרֵנִי	God watches over me	Jb 29:2	**99**
9	אֱלוֹהֵי יִשְׁעִי	God of my salvation	Ps 18:46	**100**
10	אֱלוֹהַי הַמֶּלֶךְ	my God, the King	Ps 145:1	**101**

In Ps 146:5 we also find "God of Jacob," but in a peculiar combination where the relative particle שׁ is prefixed to El. For example,

| שֶׁאֵל יַעֲקֹב | he who (has) the God of Jacob | Ps 146:5 |

4 Inseparable Prepositions

אֱלוֹהַ with the inseparable preposition ל occurs twice, and with כְּ it occurs once (Chapter 17.4 in Vol. 1).

† Examples from the Tanakh	
Jb 4:17	Jb 12:4, 36:2
מֵאֱלוֹהַ	לֶאֱלוֹהַּ
than God	*on God*
(once)	(twice)

5 Declensional Suffixes, Waw

Eloah uses only one declensional suffix (1cp), and has three occurrences with a waw.

† Examples from the Tanakh		
Dn 11:38, 38	Jb 24:12	Ps 143:10, 145:1
וְלֶאֱלֹהַּ	וֶאֱלוֹהַּ	אֱלֹהַי
and a god	*yet God*	*my God*
(twice)	(once)	(twice)

4	עֶלְיוֹן	102

1 Introduction

The word "Elyon" appears 58 times in the Hebrew Bible, of which 42 refer to God. It appears in many poetic passages, especially in Psalms (19 times). It is firmly identified with Yahweh, as is seen in 2 Sm 22:14 and Ps 97:9:

Examples from the Tanakh		
2 Sm 22:14	Ps 50:14	Nm 24:16; Dt 32:8
וְעֶלְיוֹן	לְעֶלְיוֹן	עֶלְיוֹן
and the Most High	*to the Most High*	*the Most High*

5	אֱלָהָא חַיָּא	103

1 Introduction

These words, traditionally written as "Elaha-hayya," means, "living God." The phrase is remarkable, uttered as it is by a heathen king.

Examples from the Tanakh
Dn 6:21, 27
אֱלָהָא חַיָּא
the living God

85.3 EL CONSTRUCTIONS

אֵל is used in conjunction with other words to form constructions that designate various aspects of God's character.

1	אֵל שַׁדַּי	104

1 Introduction

Ltrl:	God of my breasts	NIV:	Almighty God
KJB:	the Almighty God	NLT:	Almighty God

El Shaddai occurs eight times in the Hebrew Bible. It is used almost exclusively in Genesis. According to Ex 6:2, 3 this was the primary name by which God was known to the Patriarchs. The word "shaddai" was used later (by itself) in the Hebrew Bible (Nm 24:4, Is 13:6, Ez 1:24).

2   Derivation and Meaning

There are at least three possible ways in which this term can be explained.

a) The word "shaddai" is a feminine noun meaning, "breast" with a Type II 1cs suffix. Type II suffixes indicate a plural noun (Chapter 10.8 in Vol. 1). The literal translation of the term would then be, "God of my breasts," and the idiomatic translation: "God of nourishment." This would then indicate a God who is satisfying the needs of His people as a mother would her child. He would then be, "God our Sustainer," or "The All Sufficient God." On its own "shaddai" occurs 48 times in the Hebrew Bible. It is used as the name of God by Balaam (Nm 24:4, 16); by Naomi (Ruth 1:20); and 31 times in the Book of Job.

b) Some scholars believe that the name is derived from an Akkadian word "tsadu," meaning, "mountain." This would suggest strength and power. The idiomatic translation would then be "Mighty God" or "Omnipotent God." This translation is commonly found in the Latin Vulgate and Greek Septuagint.

c) Some other scholars believe that the word "shaddai" originated from the verb "shadad" meaning, "to deal violently with," or "strong to overpower."

Examples from the Tanakh			
Gen 35:11	Gen 28:3	Gen 17:1	Gen 49:25
אֵל שַׁדַּי	וְאֵל שַׁדַּי	אֵל שַׁדַּי	שַׁדַּי
God Almighty	*and God Almighty*	*God Almighty*	*Almighty*
Ez 10:5	Gen 43:14	Ex 6:3	Gen 48:3
אֵל שַׁדַּי	וְאֵל שַׁדַּי	בְּאֵל שַׁדַּי	אֵל שַׁדַּי
God Almighty	*and God Almighty*	*as God Almighty*	*God Almighty*

| 2 | אֵל גִּבּוֹר | 105 |

1 Introduction

Ltrl:	God mighty / Messiah	NIV:	Mighty God
KJB:	The mighty God	NLT:	Mighty God

The word "gibbor" meaning, "strong, mighty" appears 159 times in the Hebrew Bible. The combination of "El gibbor" appears twice in Isaiah. In addition, there are seven other occurrences of "gibbor" that refer to God as fighting.

2 Derivation and Meaning

Of the last eight words ("'avi ad" is actually two words) in Is 9:5, the last six words obviously fall into three couplets. Scholars are of the opinion that the first two words should also be taken together, and that we then have four elements of one compound name namely: (a) Wonderful-Counselor, (b) God-the-Mighty-One, (c) Father of Eternity, (d) Prince of Peace.

At that time, the kings of Egypt and Assyria delighted in long lists of epithetic names when describing the greatness and glory of their kings. It is therefore quite understandable that Isaiah would want to do the same when naming the King that he was writing about.

Examples from the Tanakh		
Is 9:5, 10:2	Dt 10:17; Neh 9:32	Jgs 6:12; Zep 3:17
אֵל גִּבּוֹר	הַגִּבֹּר	גִּבּוֹר
Mighty God / Messiah	*the Mighty*	*mighty*
Jer 32:18	Ps 24:8	Ps 24:8
הַגִּבּוֹר יְהוָה	יְהוָה גִּבּוֹר	עִזּוּז וְגִבּוֹר
the mighty God Yahweh	*mighty Yahweh*	*strong and mighty*

3 Messiah

In the ancient world olive oil was a very versatile commodity. It was often used in cooking and as a medicine. Shepherds for example used it as a disinfectant whenever they themselves or one of their livestock were injured. The word Messiah is an English transliteration of the Hebrew m. sg. noun מָשִׁיחַ meaning, "anointed one," from the verb מָשַׁח meaning, "to smear, anoint" (Jer 22:14). It occurs 38 times in the Hebrew Bible. However, in Ex 29:7 for example it means, "to anoint," in other words "to smear / pour olive oil on the head of somebody." This ceremony was performed on anyone becoming a king, priest or prophet in the service of Yahweh.

Is 9:1 is quoted in Mt 4:16. In Luke 1:32–33 there is an allusive reference to Isaiah 9:7, but Is 9:5 in never mentioned in the New Testament.

Examples from the Tanakh		
Dn 9:25, (26)	Ex 29:7	Jer 22:14
מָשִׁיחַ נָגִיד	שֶׁמֶן הַמִּשְׁחָה	וּמָשׁוֹחַ
anointed prince	anointing oil	and painted

4　Scriptural requirements

In Judaism, the Messiah is not considered to be God or a pre-existent divine Son of God. He is considered to be a great political leader that has descended from King David. That is why he is referred to as "Messiah ben David," which means, "Messiah, son of David." The Messiah, in Judaism, is considered to be a great charismatic leader that is well oriented with the laws that are followed in Judaism. Many of the scriptural requirements concerning the Messiah, what he will do, and what will be done during his reign are located in Isaiah. For example, He will be descended from King David (Is 11:1).

All Israelites will be returned to their homeland (Is 11:12).

All of the dead will rise again (Is 26:19).

The whole world will worship the One God of Israel (Is 2:11–17).

Some Jews interpret Is. 1:26 to mean that the Sanhedrin will be re-established. The "spirit of the Lord" will be on him and he will have a "fear of God" (Is 11:2).

Evil and tyranny will not be able to stand before his leadership (Is 11:4).

Knowledge of God will fill the world (Is 11:9).

Nations will recognize the wrongs they did to Israel (Is 52:13–53:5).

He will include and attract people from all cultures and nations (Is 11:10).

The Jewish people will experience eternal joy and gladness (Is 51:11).

Once he is King, leaders of other nations will look to him for guidance (Is 2:4).

Death will be swallowed up forever (Is 25:8).

There will be no more hunger or illness, and death will cease (Is 25:8).

He will give you all the worthy desires of your heart (Psalms 37:4).

He will take the barren land and make it abundant and fruitful (Is 51:3).

The ruined cities of Israel will be restored (Ez 16:55).

Weapons of war will be destroyed (Ez 39:9).

The peoples of the world will turn to the Jews for spiritual guidance (Zec 8:23).[1]

1　Hattingh, Tian (2012), p. 170.

| 3 | אֵל עֶלְיוֹן | 106 |

1 Introduction

Ltrl:	God Most High	NIV:	God Most High
KJB:	the most high God	NLT:	God Most High

The single word "elyon" is used 20 times as a name of God.
The construction "El Elyon" occurs five times in the Hebrew Bible.
The word "elyon" appears eight times with other divine names.

2 Derivation and Meaning

It seems that the word "elyon" is derived from the Hebrew root "'alah" meaning, "to go up or ascend or climb." The implication is that it indicates that which is the very highest. Alone and/or in combinations, "elyon" then expresses an exaltation to the extreme sovereignty and majesty of God and His highest preeminence. All of these different terms are therefore commonly translated as "The Most High God" or "Exalted God."

a)

† Examples from the Tanakh			
Ps 73:11	Ps 50:14 Is 14:14	Nm 24:16 Dt 32:8 Lam 3:35, 38	Ps 9:2, 21:7, 46:4 Ps 77:10, 78:17, 82:6 Ps 83:18, 87:5, 89:27 Ps 91:1, 9, 92:1, 107:11
בְּעֶלְיוֹן	לְעֶלְיוֹן	עֶלְיוֹן	עֶלְיוֹן
with the Most High	to the Most High	The Most High	The Most High

b)

† Examples from the Tanakh		
Ps 78:35	Gen 14:18, 19	Gen 14:20, 22
וְאֵל עֶלְיוֹן	לְאֵל עֶלְיוֹן	אֵל עֶלְיוֹן
and The Most High God	to The Most High God	The Most High God

c)

† Examples from the Tanakh			
Ps 57:3	Ps 78:56	Ps 7:17, 47:2 Ps 97:9	2 Sm 22:14 1 Kgs 9:8; Ps 18:13
לֵאלֹהִים עֶלְיוֹן	אֱלֹהִים עֶלְיוֹן	יְהוָה עֶלְיוֹן	יְהוָה וְעֶלְיוֹן
to God The Most High	God Most High	Yahweh Most High	Yahweh and Most High

	Name	Literal meaning	Examples	
1	יְהוָה עֶלְיוֹן	Yahweh, Most High	Ps 7:17	**107**
2	אֱלֹהִים עֶלְיוֹן	God, Most High	Ps 78:56	**108**

4	אֵל עוֹלָם	**109**

1 Introduction

Ltrl:	God Eternity	NIV:	The Eternal God
KJB:	the Everlasting God	NLT:	The Eternal God

The word "'olam" meaning, "eternity" appears 439 times in the Hebrew Bible.

a) The exact construction "El 'olam" occurs only once in the Hebrew Bible. A variation "elohey 'olam" occurs as well.

b) In addition, there are several occasions where God is mentioned in connection with the concept of eternity.

2 Derivation and Meaning

God by nature is without beginning or end. Unimaginable to us humans, he is completely free from all the constraints of time. This phenomenon has led to an array of translations like, "The Everlasting God," "The God of Eternity," "The God of the Universe," "The God of Ancient Days," and more.

a)

† Examples from the Tanakh	
Is 40:28	Gen 21:33
אֱלֹהֵי עוֹלָם	אֵל עוֹלָם
Everlasting God	Everlasting God

b)

Examples from the Tanakh		
Ex 3:15	Dt 33:27	Dt 32:40
זֶה־שְּׁמִי לְעֹלָם	זְרֹעֹת עוֹלָם	חַי אָנֹכִי לְעֹלָם
this is my name forever	Idm: everlasting arms	I live for ever

Neh 9:5

אֶת־יְהוָה אֱלֹהֵיכֶם מִן־הָעוֹלָם עַד־הָעוֹלָם

Yahweh your God from eternity to eternity

Ps 90:2

אֶת־יְהוָה אֱלֹהֵיכֶם מִן־הָעוֹלָם עַד־הָעוֹלָם

Yahweh, your God from eternity to eternity

1 Chr 16:36

בָּרוּךְ יְהוָה אֱלֹהֵי יִשְׂרָאֵל מִן־הָעוֹלָם וְעַד הָעֹלָם

Blessed be Yahweh, the God of Israel, From everlasting even to everlasting

	Name	Literal meaning	Examples	
1	אֱלֹהֵי עוֹלָם	Everlasting God	Is 40:28	**110**

5	אֵל רֳאִי			**111**

1 Introduction

Ltrl:	God seeing / sight	NIV:	the God who sees
KJB:	God sees	NLT:	the God who sees

The word "ro'iy" meaning, "seeing" appears 5 times in the Hebrew Bible, but is used as a name of God only once namely in Gen 16:13 by Hagar.

2 Derivation and Meaning

When Hagar met the Angel of the Lord, she realized she had seen God Himself in a theophany (a visible manifestation to humankind of God or a god).

† Examples from the Tanakh		
Gen 16:13	*the God that sees*	אֵל רֳאִי

| 6 | אֵל קַנָּא | 112 |

1 Introduction

Ltrl:	God jealous	NIV:	jealous God
KJB:	jealous God	NLT:	jealous God

The adjective קַנָּא appears six times in the Hebrew Bible. Five times in combination with El, and once with YHWH. It means, "jealous" in the sense of "jealous of His own honor," or "demanding exclusive service."

Examples from the Tanakh		
Na 1:2	Dt 4:24, 5:9, 6:15	Ex 20:5, 34:14
אֵל קַנּוֹא	אֵל קַנָּא	אֵל קַנָּא
jealous God	*jealous God*	*jealous God*

| 7 | אֵל חָי | 113 |

1 Introduction

Ltrl:	God living	NIV:	the living God
KJB:	the living God	NLT:	the living God

From this metaphor it is evident that God is regarded here as the source of life.

Examples from the Tanakh	
Ps 42:2	Ps 84:3; Js 3:10; Hos 2:1
לְאֵל חָי	אֵל חָי
for the living God	*living God*

8   Other Names

	Name	Literal meaning	Examples	
1	אֵל אֱמֶת	God of truth	Ps 31:6	**114**
2	אֵל דֵּעוֹת	God of knowledge	1 Sm 2:3	**115**
3	אֵל יְשׁוּעָתִי	God of my salvation	Is 12:2	**116**
4	אֵל הַקָּדוֹשׁ	God the Holy One	Is 5:16	**117**
5	אֵל הַשָּׁמָיִם	God of the heavens	Ps 136:26	**118**
6	אֵל הַנֶּאֱמָן	God the Faithful	Dt 7:9	**119**
7	אֵל הַגָּדֹל	The Great God	Dt 10:17	**120**
8	אֵל אֶחָד	One God	Mal 2:10	**121**
9	אֵל־חַנּוּן	Gracious God	Jon 4:2	**122**
10	אֵל סַלְעִי	God of my rock / crag	Ps 42:10	**123**
11	אֵל־הַכָּבוֹד	God of glory	Ps 29:3	**124**
12	אֵל נְקָמוֹת	God of vengeance	Ps 18:48	**125**
13	וְאֵל זֹעֵם	and God that has indignation	Ps 7:12	**126**
14	אֵל שִׂמְחַת גִּילִי	God exceeding my joy	Ps 43:4	**127**
15	אֵל לְמוֹשָׁעוֹת	God of deliverances	Ps 68:21	**128**
16	אֵל קַנּוֹא	Jealous God	Na 1:2	**129**
17	עִמָּנוּ אֵל	Immanuel (with us *is* God)	Is 7:14	**130**
18	אֵל אָבִיךָ	God of your father	Gen 49:25	**131**

85.4 PROPER NAMES CONTAINING EL

A theophoric name (from the Greek, literally meaning, "bearing / carrying a god"), embeds the name of a god, both invoking and displaying the protection of that deity. There are at least 114 theophoric proper names of people and places in the Hebrew Bible that contain El. In these cases El is usually interpreted and translated as "God," but it is not clear whether these refer to the deity in general or to the god El in particular. There are also at least 74 names containing Yah(weh).[2] A selection of examples containing El are shown below.

				Examples
1	יִשְׂרָאֵל	Ltrl: Struggled with God	KJB: Israel	Gen 32:28
2	שְׁמוּאֵל	Ltrl: God has heard Literally it would mean, "his name is El" or "name of El."	KJB: Samuel	1 Sm 1:20
3	אֵלִיָּה	Ltrl: Yahu is God	KJB: Elijah	1 Kgs 17:1, 2 Kgs 1:3
4	אֱלִישָׁע	Ltrl: God is salvation	KJB: Elisha	1 Kgs 19:16
5	גַּבְרִיאֵל	Ltrl: Strength of God	KJB: Gabriel	Dn 8:16, 9:21
6	מִיכָאֵל	Ltrl: Who is like God	KJB: Michael	1 Chr 5:13, 14
7	יִזְרְעֵאל	Ltrl: God sows	KJB: Jezreel	Js 15:56, 17:16
8	יִשְׁמָעֵאל	Ltrl: God hears	KJB: Ishmael	Gen 25:13
9	אֲרִיאֵל	Ltrl: Lioness of God	KJB: Ariel	Is 29:1, 1, 2
10	עִמָּנוּאֵל	Ltrl: with us is God	KJB: Immanuel	Is 7:14, 8:6
11	אֱלִיאֵל	Ltrl: my God is God	KJB: Eliel	1 Chr 5:24, 34; 8:20, 22
12	דָּנִיֵּאל	Ltrl: God is my judge	KJB: Daniel	Dn 2:13, 14, 15, 16, 17, 18
13	אֱלִיעֶזֶר	Ltrl: my God is help	KJB: Eliezer	Gen 15:2; Ex 18:4
14	אֶלְקָנָה	Ltrl: God has created	KJB: Elkanah	Ex 6:24; 1 Sm 1:1
15	אִיתִיאֵל	Ltrl: with me is God	KJB: Ithiel	Neh 11:7; Prv 30:1

---

2 Hattingh, Tian (2012), p. 179.

16	בֵּית־אֵל	Ltrl: house of God	KJB: Bethel	Gen 12:8, 8, 13, 3, 3
17	אֱלִיהוּא	Ltrl: He is my God	KJB: Elihu	Jb 32:2, 4, 5, 6
18	אֱלִיפֶלֶט	Ltrl: God is deliverance	KJB: Eliphelet.	2 Sm 5:16
20	אֶלְיָדָע	Ltrl: God knows	KJB: Eliada	2 Sm 5:16
21	יְחֶזְקֵאל	Ltrl: God will strengthen	KJB: Ezekiel	Ez 1:3
22	פְּנִיאֵל	Ltrl: Face of God	KJB: Peniel	Gen 32:30
23	אֵל אֱלֹהֵי יִשְׂרָאֵל	Ltrl: God, the God of Israel	KJB: EleloheIsrael	Gen 33:20

86 YHWH

86.1	יְהוָה	132

1 Introduction

יְהוָה is the so-called *Tetragrammaton*, from the Greek Τετραγράμματον, meaning, "(consisting of) four letters." It is the Hebrew name of God that in English is transliterated into four letters namely YHWH and frequently Anglicized as Yahweh or Jehovah. Because of the traditional Greek form, and based on other grammatical indications it is pronounced as "Yahweh" (Refer to "Jehovah" in Chapter 87.2.3 below).

It is the most frequently used name of God in the Hebrew Bible, and occurs 6,823 times in the Hebrew Bible of which 1,419 are found in the Torah. It is found 31 times in Job, in Daniel seven times (only in Chapter 9), and 39 times in the elohistic Psalms (Ps 42—83). YHWH does not appear in the books of Esther and Song of Songs, prompting some scholars to doubt their status in the Hebrew canon.

The original Hebrew Bible text was an abjad (text consisting of consonants only). To indicate (mostly long) vowels, consonant letters were inserted into the original text during the classical biblical Hebrew phase. The consonant letters yod, waw, hey, and aleph were used. These letters are collectively called matres lectionis (mothers of reading). These letters are also called "vocalic place holders," as they hold the place for a vowel. The three letters used in YHWH namely yod, hey and waw, are all three *matres lectionis*. This prompted Josephus to state that YHWH consists of "four vowels."

2 YHWH Spelling

Six different spellings of YHWH are found in the Leningrad Codex (1008–1010), the codex on which, among others, *BHS* is based:

יְהוָה	Gen 2:4	יֱהוִה	Jgs 16:28	יְהוִה	1 Kgs 2:26
יְהֹוָה	Gen 3:14	יֶהוִה	Gen 15:2	יְהֹוִה	Ez 24:24

With the waw conjunctive the form is וַיהוָה and with "le-" the form is לַיהוָה.

3 Derivation and Meaning

There is no agreement among scholars on the origins and meaning of YHWH. It does not seem to have any reasonable etymology and therefore no real meaning per se. Recently many scholars explain it as being the hiph'il impf. 3ms of the word "to be." It would then literally mean, "the one bringing into being," or "life giver," or "creator / giver of existence." But most scholars take it as the qal binyan, meaning, "the one who is," or "the existing, ever living."

Because of the similarities, it is often connected to and explained in terms of the word meaning, "I Am" in God's revelation to Moses on Mt. Horeb in Ex 3:14. By using that word, God is portraying himself as the self-existent One, the "I am," who is worthy of all worship and honor. However, this appears to be an attractive albeit superficial theological invented to explain the meaning of YHWH.

The exact origins of YHWH is highly disputed. It may have begun as an epithet (nickname) of El. El is a Northwest Semitic word meaning, "god" or "deity" in general. As a proper name it refers to any one of multiple major ancient Near Eastern deities. The earliest plausible mentions of YHWH are in Egyptian texts that refer to a similar-sounding place name associated with the Shasu nomads of the southern Transjordan area.

Examples from the Tanakh	
Ex 30:20	Ps 130:1, 5, 7
לַיהוָה	יְהוָה
to the LORD	LORD

YHWH is traditionally written in English Bibles as "LORD" to distinguish it from Adonai which is traditionally written as "Lord."

It should be kept in mind that, like words, names have meaning, but names are primarily used to identity a particular person. Wide scholarly consensus on this point has led to it recently becoming more popular to translate YHWH into English with "Jahweh" or "Yahweh" instead of "God" or "Lord." This is especially applicable to the following contexts:

a) Where the name is in focus.

b) Where YHWH is joined to Elohim or Adonai.

c) Where YHWH is in a descriptive phrase (e.g., "YHWH, the God of Israel").

86.2 COMBINATIONS WITH ELOHIM

YHWH is used with Elohim and suffixes, especially in Deuteronomy. The specific number of occurrences refer to those of Elohim as mentioned in Chapter 85.2.3 above.

		Examples		
1	יְהוָה אֱלֹהִים Ltrl:Yahweh God KJB:LORD God	(34 times)		133
		Gen 2:4—3:23; Ex 9:30; 2 Sm 7:25 1 Chr 17:16, 17, 28:30, 29:1; Jon 4:6 2 Chr 1:9, 6:41, 42, 26:18; Ps 72:18, 84:12		
2	יְהוָה אֱלֹהֶיךָ Ltrl:Yahweh your God KJB:the Lord your God	(234 times in Dt)	(325 times in total)	134
		Gen 27:20, Ex 15:26, 20:2, 5, 7, 10, 12, 19 Dt 1:21, 31, 2:7, 30, 4:3, 10, 19, 5:6, 9, 11, 12		
3	יְהוָה אֱלֹהֵיכֶם Ltrl:Yahweh your God KJB:the Lord your God	(46 times in Dt)	(162 times in total)	135
		Ex 6:7, 8:28, 10:8, 16, 17, 16:12, 23:25 Lv 11:44, 18:2, 4, 30, 19:2, 3, 4, 10, 25, 31, 34 Dt 1:10, 26, 30, 32, 3:18, 20, 21, 22, 4:2, 4, 23 Dt 5:32, 33, 6:1, 16, 17, 8:20, 9:16, 23, 10:17		

4	יְהוָה אֱלֹהֵינוּ	(23 times in Dt)	(174 times in total)	136
	Ltrl: Yahweh our God KJB: the Lord our God	Ex 3:18, 5:3, 8:10, 26, 27, 10:25, 26 Dt 1:6, 19, 20, 25, 41, 2:29, 33, 36, 37		
5	יְהוָה אֱלֹהֵיהֶם	(5 times in Dt)	(71 times in total)	137
	Ltrl: Yahweh their God KJB: the Lord their God	Ex 10:7, 29:46; Lv 26:44; Jgs 3:7, 8:34 1 Sm 12:9; 1Kgs 9:9; 2 Kgs 17:7, 9, 14, 16		
6	יְהוָה אֱלֹהָי	(3 times in Dt)	(101 times in total)	138
	Ltrl: Yahweh my God KJB: the Lord my God	Nm 22:18; Dt 4:5, 18:16, 26:14 Js 14:8; 2 Sm 24:24; 1Kgs 3:7, 5:5		
7	יְהוָה אֱלֹהַי	(included in 6 above)		139
	Ltrl: Yahweh my God KJB: the Lord my God	2 Sm 24:24; 1 Kgs 5:4 Ezr 7:28; Ps 7:1, 3		
8	יְהוָה אֱלֹהָיו	(58 times)		140
	Ltrl: Yahweh his God KJB: the Lord his God	Ex 32:11; Lv 4:22; Nm 23:21 Dt 17:19, 18:7; 1 Kgs 5:3, 11:4, 15:3		
9	יְהוָה אֱלֹהֶיךָ	(14 times in total)		141
	Ltrl: Yahweh your God KJB: the Lord your God	Is 60:9; Jer 2:17, 19, 3:13 Mi 7:10; Zep 3:17		

86.3 OTHER COMBINATIONS WITH YHWH

1	יְהוָה יִרְאֶה	142
1	Ltrl: Yahweh he will appear KJB: Jehovahjireh Eng: Yahweh-yireh	† **Examples** Gen 22:14

2   Yahweh-yireh is the place name memorialized by Abraham when God provided the ram to be sacrificed in place of Isaac. In *BHS* there is a footnote stating that the second word of this combination should probably not be the qal impf. 3ms as it is now, but rather be the niph'al impf. 3ms meaning, "he will appear." The translation in KJB therefore correctly translates the last two words of the verse as "Yahweh, he will be seen," and "The Lord Will Provide."

2	יְהוָה מְקַדֵּשׁ	143
1	Ltrl: Yahweh who sanctifies KJB: Yahweh do sanctify Eng: Yahweh-mkaddeish	**† Examples** Ez 37:28 Ex 31:13; Lv 20:8, 21:8, 15, 23 Lv 22:9, 16, 32

2. The name Yahweh-Mkaddeish indicates that Yahweh had both the power and the will to sanctify his people by making them inwardly as well as outwardly holy. Mkaddeis is the pi'el part. m. sg. of the Hebrew verb meaning, "to set apart, to consecrate." From the same root the noun means, "apartness, sacredness, holiness." Sanctification is the separation of an object or person to the dedication of the Holy. When the two words are combined, it can then be literally translated as "The Lord who sets you apart."

3	יְהוָה נִסִּי	144
1	Ltrl: Yahweh my banner KJB: Jehovahnissi Eng: Yahweh-nissi	**† Examples** Ex 17:15

2. The m. sg. noun נֵס means, "standard, ensign, signal, sign, miracle." In this instance it has the meaning of a rallying-point. This name appears only this once in the Hebrew Bible, to commemorate Israel's victory over the Amalekites. By using this name, Moses recognizing that the Lord was Israel's banner under which they defeated the Amalekites. "Nes" is sometimes translated as a pole with an insignia attached to it. For example in Nm 21:8, 9. In battle, opposing nations would fly their insignia on a pole at each of their respective front lines to give their soldiers a feeling of hope and a focal point. This is what God is to us: a banner of encouragement to give us hope and a focal point.

3. See Chapter 82.4 for notes on the so-called *hapax legomenon*. These are words that appear only once in a body of work such as here in the Hebrew Bible. It has no connection to any other verb root, making it impossible to ascertain with certainty what the original author meant.

4	יְהוָה עֹשֵׂנוּ	145
1	Ltrl: Yahweh our maker KJB: Yahweh our maker Eng: Yahweh-osenu	**† Examples** Ps 95:6

2. The word עֹשֵׂנוּ is the qal part. active m. sg. of the verb עָשָׂה which means, "to do, make." Acknowledging God as the Creator of his people is common in the Hebrew Bible (Dt 32:6; Ps 100:3, 149:2; Is 43:21; 44:2).

5	יְהוָה רֹעִי	146
1	Ltrl: Yahweh my shepherd KJB: The LORD *is* my shepherd Eng: Yahweh-ro'iy	**Examples** Ps 23:1; Gen 48:15

2   The word רֹעִי is the qal part. m. sg. of the verb רָעָה meaning, "to pasture, tend, graze," with the 1sc personal pronoun added. Here it is used as an epithet (expressing a quality characteristic of the person / thing mentioned) of God. This metaphor is frequently used later in the Hebrew Bible (Is 40:11, 49:9, 10; Jer 31:10; Ez 34:6–19). It is perhaps implied in Gen 48:15 as "the God who fed me," but first appears, plainly and openly as "shepherd" in the Davidic psalms (Ps 23:1, 74:1, 77:20; 78:53; 79:14; 80:1). In Jb 31:9 and Sg 5:16 we find "my friend" from the same root.

3   Refer to Chapter 87.11

6	יְהוָה רֹפְאֶךָ	147
1	Ltrl: Yahweh, your Healer KJB: Yahweh that healeth thee Eng: Yahweh-roph'eka	**Examples** Ex 15:26

2   The word רֹפְאֶךָ is the qal part. m. sg. of the Hebrew verb רָפָא meaning, "to heal," with the 2ms pronominal suffix. Literally it then means, "your healer." Yahweh-roph'eka then means, "Yahweh, your healer." Refer to: Gen 20:7; Nm 12:13; 2 Kgs 20:5, 8; Jer 3:22, 30:17; Is 30:26, 61:1; Ps 103:3, 107:20.

7	יְהוָה צְבָאוֹת	148
1	Ltrl: Yahweh of armies KJB: the LORD of hosts Eng: Yahweh-tseva'ot	**Examples** 1 Sm 1:3, 11, 4:4, 15:2, 17:45 Ps 24:10, 48:8, 80:4, 19, 84:3 Is 1:24, 3:15, 5:16, 6:5, 9:19, 10:26, 14:22

2   צְבָאוֹת Noun, f. pl. form of צָבָא meaning, "army, war, warfare." It occurs 283 times in the Hebrew Bible, and in almost all of these cases, in combination with Yahweh. It is first used in 1 Sm 1:3, and most frequently used in Isaiah (62 times) and Jeremiah (82 times). The most common translation into English is, "LORD of Hosts" (KJB, ESV, ERV), but other alternatives are, "Lord Almighty" (NIV, GNT), "LORD of Heaven's Armies" (NLT, ISV), "LORD All-Powerful" (CEV), "Yahweh of Armies" (WEB), "Jehovah of hosts" (ASV).

8	יְהוָה שָׁלוֹם	149
1	Ltrl: Yahweh of peace KJB: Jehovahshalom Eng: Yahweh-shalom	**Examples** Jgs 6:24

2   The name given by Gideon to the altar he built after the Angel of the Lord assured him he would not die as he thought he would after seeing Him.

9	יְהוָה שָׁמָּה	150
1	Ltrl: Yahweh there KJB: The LORD Is There Eng: Yahweh-shammah	† **Examples** Ez 48:35

2   The adverb שָׁם meaning, "there," often takes the hey locale (Chapter 19.1 in Vol. 1) as a suffix, resulting in the form שָׁמָּה. This combination occurs only once, namely in Ez 48:35, as the name given to Jerusalem.

10	יְהוָה צִדְקֵנוּ	151
1	Ltrl: Yahweh our righteousness KJB: THE LORD OUR RIGHTEOUSNESS Eng: Yahweh-tsidqenu	**Examples** Jer 23:6, 33:16

2   The m. sg. noun צֶדֶק means, "righteousness," and here has the 1cp pronominal suffix attached which is then translated, "our righteousness" (Chapter 82.28.3).

11	יְהוָה בּוֹרֵא	152
1	Ltrl: Yahweh, the Creator KJB: the LORD, the Creator Eng: Yahweh-borei	**Examples** Is 40:28, 42:5, 45:18

2   The word בּוֹרֵא is the qal part. m. sg. of the verb בָּרָא which in the qal binyan means, "to create" or "shape."

12	יְהוָה קְדוֹשְׁכֶם	153
1	Ltrl: Yahweh, your Holy One KJB: LORD, your Holy One Eng: Yahweh-qedoshchem	† Examples Is 43:15

2 This is the only instance in the Hebrew Bible where the adjective has the 2mp suffix.

13	יְהוָה עֶלְיוֹן	154
1	Ltrl: Yahweh, the Most High KJB: LORD, most high Eng: Yahweh-Eljon	† Examples Ps 7:17

86.4 PROPER NAMES CONTAINING YAH(WEH)

1 A theophoric name (from the Greek, literally meaning, "bearing / carrying a god"), embeds the name of a god, both invoking and displaying the protection of that deity. There are at least 74 names containing Yah(weh) in the Hebrew Bible.[1] A selection of examples are shown below.

		Examples
1	יִרְמְיָהוּ Ltrl: Yahweh exalts KJB: Jeremiah	(121 occurrences) Jer 1:1, 11
2	מוֹרִיָּה Ltrl: Moriy-yah KJB: Moriah	(2 occurrences) Gen 22:2 2 Chr 3:1
3	יוֹתָם Ltrl: Yahweh is perfect KJB: Jotham	(24 occurrences) Jgs 9:5, 7, 21, 57; 2 Kgs 15:5, 7 1 Chr 2:47, 3:12, 5:17
4	יְהוֹיָקִים Ltrl: Yahweh raises up KJB: Jehoiakim	(37 occurrences) 2 Kgs 23:34, 35, 36, 24:1, 5, 6, 19 1 Chr 3:15, 16; 2 Chr 36:4, 5, 8

---

[1] Main source: Wikipedia contributors. "*Names of God in Judaism.*" Wikipedia, The Free Encyclopedia, 14 December, 2018. Web: 17 December, 2018. Slightly edited.

5	יֵהוּא		(58 occurrences)
	Ltrl: Yahweh is He KJB: Jehu		1 Kgs 16:1, 7, 12, 19:16, 17, 17 2 Kgs 9:2, 5, 11, 13, 14, 15, 16, 17, 18
6	מִיכָיָה		(4 occurrences)
	Ltrl: Who (is) like Yahweh? KJB: Micaiah		Jer 26:18, 2 Kgs 22:12 Neh 12:35, 41
7	מִיכָה		(33 occurrences)
	Ltrl: Who (is) like Yahweh? KJB: Micah (a contraction of 6 above)		Mi 1:1; Jgs 17:5, 8, 9, 10, 12, 13 Jgs 18:2, 3, 4, 13, 15, 18, 22
8	צְפַנְיָה		(10 occurrences)
	Ltrl: Yahweh has hidden. KJB: Zephaniah		Zep 1:1; 2 Kgs 25:18; 1 Chr 6:36 Jer 21:1, 29:25, 29, 37:3
9	זְכַרְיָה		(43 occurrences)
	Ltrl: Yahweh remembers. KJB: Zechariah		2 Kgs 14:29, 15:8, 11, 18:2 1 Chr 5:7, 9:21, 37, 15:18, 20, 24

87 Other Names

87.1	אָדוֹן	155

1. Introduction

Ltrl:	lord	NIV:	LORD
KJB:	LORD	NLT:	LORD

2. Derivation and Meaning

Adon, meaning, "lord" appears 325 times in total in the Hebrew Bible. It appears in a number of forms, but the most prevalent forms are:

a) i) Singular, אָדוֹן meaning, "lord, LORD."

   ii) Plural cstr., אֲדֹנֵי meaning, "lord of, lords of." It appears 164 times, and will be dealt with in this section.

b) אֲדֹנִי meaning, "my Lord." It appears 161 times in the Hebrew Bible, and will be dealt within this section.

c) אֲדֹנָי appears a total of 448 times in the Hebrew Bible, and it will be dealt with in Chapter 87.2 below.

אָדוֹן is a common m. sg. noun, appearing in the singular and plural. It is derived from an Ugaritic word meaning, "lord" or "father."

   i) The singular form refers to men and God.

Examples from the Tanakh				
Hebrew	Title	Person	Text	
אָדוֹן לְבֵיתוֹ	lord of his house	Joseph	Ps 105:21	
אָדוֹן לָנוּ	lord over us	a ruler	Ps 12:5	
אָדוֹן	lord	Jehoiakim	Jer 22:18	
הָאָדֹן יְהוָה	the Lord Yahweh	God	Ex 23:17	156
אֲדוֹן כָּל־הָאָרֶץ	Lord of all the earth	God	Js 3:11, 13	157

ii) The plural form also refers to men and God.

Examples from the Tanakh				
Hebrew	**Title**	**Person**	**Text**	
אֲדֹנֵי הָהָר	owner of the hill	Omri	1 Kgs 16:24	
אֲדֹנָיו	his master	Hebrew servant	Ex 21:4	
אֲדוֹנֶיהָ	her lord	husband	Jgs 19:26, 27	
אֲדֹנֶיךָ	your master	Elijah	2 Kgs 2:3, 5, 16	
אֲדֹנֵיהֶם	their lord	Nobles	Neh 3:5	
אֲדֹנֶיךָ	your lord	David's king	1 Sm 29:10	
אֲדֹנֵיהֶם	their lord	servants	Jgs 3:25	
לַאֲדֹנֵי הָאֲדֹנִים	Lord of Lords	God	Ps 136:3	**158**
יְהוָה אֲדֹנֵינוּ	Yahweh our Lord	God	Ps 8:2, 10	**159**

In this form, the 1sc declensional suffix is added to the singular form of the noun. Occasionally speakers will use Adon(i) to refer to God, and more often than not it will be in the Psalms. Adonay is most commonly and in a number of ways used to refer to God as will be seen in the next section. Adon(i) is used 215 times to refer to a wide variety of people including the following:

Examples from the Tanakh			
Hebrew	**Title**	**Person**	**Text**
אֲדֹנִי	my master	Abraham's servant	Gen 24:12
אֲדֹנִי	my lord	Joseph	Gen 42:10
אֲדֹנִי	my lord	Saul	1 Sm 22:12
אֲדֹנִי	my lord	Elijah	1 Kgs 18:7
אֲדֹנִי	my lord	an angel	Js 5:14
אֲדֹנִי	my lord	husband Abraham	Gen 18:12
אֲדֹנִי	my lord	father, Laban	Gen 31:35
אֲדֹנִי	my lord	Eli	1 Sm 1:15
אֲדֹנִי	my lord	Joab	2 Sm 11:11

3 Proper names

There are five proper names of people in the Hebrew Bible that contain Adon(i). A selection of examples are shown below.

		Examples
1	אֲדֹנִי־צֶדֶק Ltrl: Lord of righteousness KJB: Adoni-zedek	(2 occurrences) Js 10:1, 3
2	אֲדֹנִיָּה Ltrl: my Lord is Yahweh KJB: Adonijah	(26 occurrences) 1 Kgs 1:5, 7, 8, 9, 11, 13, 18, 24 1 Kgs 1:25, 41, 42, 43, 49, 50, 51
3	אֲדֹנִירָם Ltrl: my Lord is exalted KJB: Adoniram	(2 occurrences) 1 Kgs 4:6, 5:14
4	אֲדֹנִיקָם Ltrl: my Lord has arisen KJB: Adoniqam	(3 occurrences) Ezr 2:13, 8:13; Neh 7:18
5	אֲדֹנִי־בֶזֶק Ltrl: Lord of Bezek KJB: Adoni-Bezek	(3 occurrences) Jgs 1:5, 6, 7

87.2	אֲדֹנָי	160

1 Introduction

Ltrl:	"my lords'" (both plural and possessive).	NIV:	Lord
KJB:	Lord	NLT:	Lord

אֲדֹנָי traditionally written as "Adonai" or "Adonay," is a masculine noun used as a proper name of God only and often as a substitute for Yahweh. Adonai appears 448 times in total in the Hebrew Bible, using the above spelling 419 times. In Isaiah it is heavily used, and occurs 200 times in Ezekiel alone. It appears eleven times in Daniel Chapter 9. It is first used as early as Gen 15:2 in the Hebrew Bible.

2   Derivation and Meaning

Adonai is an older and more emphatic form of the plural form of Adonim, known as a *pluralis excellentive.* The termination is regarded as a suffix by some. It is a term describing the Divine sovereignty, originally from adan, meaning, "to rule" or "to judge." In combination with YHWH it is thus often translated as "Sovereign Lord" to express this nuance (NIV, Jer 32:17; Am 7:5). It is often connected with the Phoenician "aden," an honorary epithet (nickname) of deity, and recognized as such in Dt 10:17.

In the Hebrew Bible Yahweh is more often used when describing God's dealings with His people, while Adonai is used more when He deals with the Gentiles.

Examples from the Tanakh			
1 Kgs 3:10	Ex 4:10, 13	Gen 20:4	Gen 18:27, 31
בְּעֵינֵי אֲדֹנָי	בִּי אֲדֹנָי	אֲדֹנָי	אֶל־אֲדֹנָי
in the eyes of the Lord	please Lord	Lord	to the Lord

3   Jehovah

On the basis of Gen 20:4 and Lv 24:11, YHWH was regarded as a *nomen ineffable* (a name so great or extreme that it cannot be described in words / a name not to be spoken because of its sacredness / an unutterable name).

Even as early as the time of Ezra, and certainly during the third century AD, the Jewish people stopped pronouncing YHWH in fear of contravening the third commandment (Ex 20:7). We therefore no longer know for certain the exact pronunciation. YHWH is often read as אֲדֹנָי (Adonai / Adonay) which literally means, "my Lord," or "my lords." However, the Masoretes applied the vowels (slightly modified) that are found in Adonai to YHWH, resulting in יְהֹוָה and then the pronunciation of this combination became "Jehovah." The pronunciation "Jehovah" was not know until 1520, when it was introduced by Petrus Galatinus, an Italian Friar Minor, philosopher, theologian and Orientalist.

Other common substitutions are "hashem" (The Name), and "hakadosh baruch hu" (The Holy One, blessed be He). When the name YHWH occurs in conjunction with Adonai, the former is read as Elohim and pointed (given vowels) as יְהֹוִה to avoid having to read Adonai twice.

4

	Name	Literal meaning	Examples	
1	אֲדֹנָי יְהֹוִה	Lord YHWH	Gen 15:2	**161**
2	אֲדֹנָי יְהֹוִה	Lord YHWH	Ez 39:1	**162**
3	יְהֹוָה אֲדֹנָי	YHWH, the Lord	Ps 141:8	**163**
4	אֲדֹנָי הָאֱלֹהִים	Lord God	Dn 9:3	**164**
5	אֲדֹנָי הַגָּדוֹל וְהַנּוֹרָא	The Lord who is great and terrible	Neh 4:8	**165**

6	אֲדֹנָי אֱלֹהַי	Lord, my God	Ps 38:15	**166**
7	אֲדֹנָי תְּשׁוּעָתִי	Lord, my salvation	Ps 38:22	**167**
8	מָגִנֵּנוּ אֲדֹנָי	Lord, our shield	Ps 59:12	**168**
9	אֲדֹנָי אֱלֹהַי	Lord, my God	Ps 86:12	**169**
10	אֲדֹנָי אֱלֹהֵינוּ	Lord, our God	Ps 90:17	**170**
11	אֲדֹנָי יְהוִה צְבָאוֹת	Lord, God of hosts	Is 22:12	**171**
12	אֲדֹנָי יְהוִה קָדוֹשׁ	Lord, God the Holy One	Is 30:15	**172**

87.3		יָהּ		**173**
1		Introduction Ltrl: lord KJB: Lord		(48 occurrences)

"Yah" is a m. sg. noun meaning, "Lord." It is commonly regarded as an abbreviated form of Yahweh.

2	The 48 occurrences are as follows:			Total
	Exodus		15:2, 17:6	2
	Isaiah		12:2, 26:4, 38:11, 38:11	4
	Psalms:	Yah	68:4, 68:18, 77:11, 89:8, 94:7, 94:12, 115:18, 118:5, 118:5, 118:14, 118:17, 118:18, 118:19, 122:4, 130:3, 135:4, 150:6.	17
		Hallelujah	102:18, 104:35, 105:45, 106:48, 111:1, 112:1, 113:1, 113:9, 115:17, 115:18, 116:19, 117:2, 135:1, 135:3, 135:21, 146:1, 146:10, 147:1, 147:20, 148:1, 148:14, 149:1, 149:9 150:1, 150:6.	25

In Ps 68:4 and Is 26:4, Yah has an inseparable preposition.

3   Yah is the form generally used in the termination of a number of proper names:

English	Hebrew	Meaning	Examples
Isaiah	יְשַׁעְיָה	Salvation of Yah	2 Kgs 19:2
Jeremiah	יִרְמְיָה	Yah exalts	2 Kgs 23:31
Zechariah	זְכַרְיָה	Yah remembered	2 Kgs 14:29
Elijah	אֵלִיָּה	Yah is God	1 Kgs 17:1
Nehemiah	נְחֶמְיָה	Yah comforts	Neh 1:1
Joshua	יְהוֹשׁוּעַ	Yahweh is salvation	Ex 17:9
Hezekiah	חִזְקִיָּה	Yah has strengthened	2 Kgs 16:20
Irijah	יִרְאָיָּה	Yah sees	Jer 37:13
Obadiah	עֹבַדְיָה	Servant of Yah.	1 Kgs 18:3
Mount Moriah	מוֹרִיָּה		Gen 22:2

4	הַלְלוּ־יָהּ	(24 occurrences)
	Ltrl: praise (2mp) the Lord! KJB: Praise ye the LORD!	Ps 104:35; 106:1, 48; 111:1; 112:1; 113:1, 9; 115:8; 116:19; 117:2; 135:1, 25; 146:1,10; 147:1, 20; 148:1,14; 149:1, 9; 150;1, 6.

5   יָהּ first appears in early poems (Ex 15:2), and in the later Psalms especially the Hallels (Ps 113—118). In the Psalms it is part of the construction הַלְלוּ־יָהּ traditionally written as "Hallelujah." The verb הָלַל in the pi'el binyan means, "praise." The pi'el imp. 2mp הַלְלוּ then means, "praise ye (m.pl.)!," and occurs thirty-three times in the Hebrew Bible. In 24 of these occurrences הַלְלוּ is followed directly by יָהּ and the combination is הַלְלוּ־יָהּ which then literally means, "Praise ye (m.pl.)!, the Lord." (Chapter 46.4 in Vol. 2)

87.4	עַתִּיק יוֹמִין	174
1	Introduction Ltrl: ancient days KJB: Ancient of days	† Examples Dn 7:9, 13, 22

2	This name of God has two forms, and appears only in the Book of Daniel. The word עַתִּיק is an Aramaic adjective, related to the same word in Hebrew that means, "old, ancient." It is used in the sense of God being eternal.

87.5	אֶהְיֶה אֲשֶׁר אֶהְיֶה	175
1	Introduction Ltrl: I will be what I will be KJB: I Am that I Am	† Examples Ex 3:14

2	Ehyeh asher ehyeh is the first of three responses given to Moses when he asks for God's name. The King James Version uses it as a proper name for God. The Aramaic Targum Onkelos leaves the phrase untranslated.
3	The word "ehyeh" is the first person sg. Impf. form of the verb "hayah," meaning, "to be," and is usually translated into English as "I will be." Because Classical Hebrew had an aspectual system rather than grammatical tense, in which the impf. denotes any actions that are not yet completed, the verb form "ehyeh" can be translated as, "I am / I am being / I will be," for example in Ex 3:12.
4	Although "Ehyeh asher ehyeh" is generally rendered in English as "I am that I am," better renderings might be, "I will be what I will be" or "I will be who I will be," or "I shall prove to be whatsoever I shall prove to be" or even "I will be because I will be." The word asher is a relative pronoun whose meaning depends on the immediate context, so that "that," "who," "which," or "where" are all possible translations.

87.6	מֶלֶךְ גָּדוֹל	176
1	Ltrl: a king great KJB: a great King NIV a great king	† Examples Ps 47:2, 48:2, 95:3; Mal 1:14b

2	In Malachi it is the LORD Almighty that calls himself a great King. In the Psalms, the authors are describing God as a great King. As the above examples show, English translations are not consistent in using "king" as a name of God.

87.7	פַּחַד יִצְחָק	177
1	Ltrl: the fear of Isaac KJB: the fear of Isaac NIV the Fear of Isaac	† Examples Gen 31:42, 31:53

| 2 | This phrase has been the subject of much debate, with a variety of suggestions about the precise meaning of the verb pachad itself ("thigh"? "kinsman"?). The question remains: is this a reference to Isaac's deity ("Fear of . . ."), or to Isaac's experience of or posture before his deity ("fear of . . ."). |

87.8	אֲבִיר יַעֲקֹב	178
1	Ltrl: the mighty one of Jacob KJB: the mighty God of Jacob NIV the Mighty One of Jacob	† Examples Gen 49:24; Ps 132:2, 5 Is 1:24, 49:26, 60:16

| 2 | אָבִיר The sg. cstr. form of the adjective אַבִּיר meaning, "mighty, valiant." |
| 3 | In Ps 132:2, 5 the form is actually לַאֲבִיר meaning, "to the Mighty One of Jacob." |

87.9	אֲבִיר יִשְׂרָאֵל	179
1	Ltrl: the mighty one of Israel KJB: the Mighty One of Israel NIV the Mighty One of Israel	† Examples Is 1:24

| 2 | This phrase appears only this once in the Hebrew Bible. |

87.10	אֶבֶן יִשְׂרָאֵל	180
1	Ltrl: the rock of Israel KJB: the stone of Israel NIV the Rock of Israel	† Examples Gen 49:24

| 2 | This phrase appears only this once in the Hebrew Bible. |

87.11	רֹעֶה	181
1	Ltrl: Shepherd NASB Shepherd	† Examples Gen 49:24, Eccl 12:11

| 2 | This noun appears 164 times in the Hebrew Bible, but in these two instances it serves as a Divine Name of God. |

87.12	רֹעֵה יִשְׂרָאֵל	182
1	Ltrl: the Shepherd of Israel KJB: O Shepherd of Israel	† Examples Ps 80:2

2   This phrase appears only this once in the Hebrew Bible.

87.13	קָדוֹשׁ	183
1	Ltrl: Holy One KJB: the Holy One NIV the Holy One	**Examples** Jb 6:10 Prv 9:10, 30:10

2   This appellation appears 12 times in the Hebrew Bible. In Proverbs and Hos 11:12 it has the plural form, and in some instances like Is 10:17, 43:15, 49:7, and Hab 1:12 it has a suffix.

3   This term is an adjective meaning, "sacred, holy," that is used to describe God as separate and apart from human infirmity, impurity, and sin. It has become the divine name of God originating from the trisagion ("Thrice Holy") in Is 6:3.

87.14	קְדוֹשׁ יִשְׂרָאֵל	184
1	Ltrl: the Holy One of Israel KJB: the Holy One of Israel NIV the Holy One of Israel	**Examples** 2 Kgs 19:22; Ez 39:7 Ps 71:22, 78:41, 89:18

2   This appellation appears 32 times in the Hebrew Bible. In addition to the examples above, it appears 25 times in Isaiah (Is 1:4; 5:19, 24; 10:17, 20, etc.), and twice in Jeremiah (Jer 50:29, 51:5).

87.15	קְדוֹשׁ יַעֲקֹב	185
1	Ltrl: the Holy One of Jacob KJB: the Holy One of Jacob NIV the Holy One of Jacob	† **Examples** Is 29:23

2   This appellation appears only here in the Hebrew Bible.

87.16	מוֹשִׁיעַ	186
1	Ltrl: Savior NASB Savior	**Examples** Is 19:20, 45:15, 21, 63:8

2   מוֹשִׁיעַ Hiph'il part. m. sg. active of the root ישע meaning, "to save, deliver." The participle then means the noun, "savior."

3   This particiciple appears 208 times in the Hebrew Bible, but in nine instances it serve s as a Divine Name of God. Apart from the four part. m. sg. instances mentioned above, it appears five times in four forms with suffixes attached:

a)   With a 2ms pronominal suffix ("your Savior") in Is 43:3

b)   With a 2fs pronominal suffix ("your Savior") in Is 49:26, 60:16

c)   With a 3ms pronominal suffix ("it's Savior") in Jer 14:8

d)   With a 3mp pronominal suffix ("their Savior") in Ps 106:21

87.17	גֹּאֵל	187
1	Ltrl: Redeemer NASB Redeemer	† Examples Is 49:7, 59:20

2   גֹּאֵל Qal part. m. sg. active of the verb גָּאַל meaning, "to redeem (compensate for the faults, sins, or bad aspects of someone or something); to act as kinsman." The participle then means the noun, "redeemer." This is Isaiah quoting YHWH and therefore it becomes a Divine Name spelt with a capital, "Redeemer."

3   This participle appears 105 times in the Hebrew Bible, but only in 18 instances does it serve as a Divine Name of God. Apart from the part. m. sg. mentioned above, it appears in six forms with suffixes attached:

a)   With a 1cs pronominal suffix ("my Redeemer") in Job 19:25, Ps 19:14

b)   With a 1cp pronominal suffix ("our Redeemer") in Is 47:4, 63:16

c)   With a 2ms pronominal suffix ("your Redeemer") in Is 44:24, 48:17

d)   With a 2fs pronominal suffix ("your Redeemer") in Is 41:14, 43:14, 49:26, 54:5, 8, 60:16

e)   With a 3ms pronominal suffix ("his Redeemer") in Is 44:6

f)   With a 3mp pronominal suffix ("their Redeemer") in Ps 78:35, Prv 23:11, Jer 50:34.

87.18	נֵצַח יִשְׂרָאֵל	188
1	Ltrl: the Eminence of Israel NASB the Glory of Israel	† Examples 1 Sm 15:29

2   נֵצַח Noun, m. sg. meaning, "eminence, enduring, everlastingness, perpetuity." This noun appears 44 times in the Hebrew Bible, but only in this instance is it used as an appelation of God. In 1 Chr 29:11 it is used to describe an attribute of YHWH. In the other 42 cases it is used to express endurance in time ("unto the end") and everlastingness ("for ever").

Index

1 Chronicles, 82.17
1 Corinthians, 82.27.8
1 Kings, 82.15
1 Samuel, 82.13
2 Chronicles, 82.18
2 Kings, 82.16
2 Samuel, 82.14

Abel, 82.5.4
abjad, 80.2, 82.5.5, 86.1.1
ABP, 82.10.1, 82.20.3, 82.23.5, 82.28.3
Abraham, 82.2.6.1, 82.5.8, 82.5.10, 82.5.11, 82.5.12, 82.5.14, 82.34.4, 85.2.1.4, 86.3.1
Abram, 82.5.7, 82.5.8, 82.5.10
Acts, 82.5.7
Adam, 82.5.3, 82.9.4, 82.27.9
Adar, 82.19.1
Adonai, 86.1.3
Adoni-Bezek, 87.1.1.3
Adonijah, 87.1.1.3
Adoniqam, 87.1.1.3
Adoniram, 87.1.1.3
Adoni-zedek, 87.1.1.3
Africa, 82.23.5, 83.5.1.1, 83.7.4.1
Africa, sub-Saharan, 83.3.1.2, 83.3.4.1
African, 82.38.2
Afrikaans, 82.5.18, 82.20.2, 82.23.5
Akkadian, 80.1.7.4, 82.14.1
Algeria, 82.38.2
All-Powerful, 82.41.1
Almighty, 82.41.1, 82.42.2, 82.43.1
America, North, 83.3.1.2, 83.5.2.1

America, South, 83.3.1.2, 83.7.3.1
American(s), 82.8.2
Amminadib, 82.26.3
Amos, 82.34
Amoz, 82.27.1
Anglicized, 86.1.1
Antarctica, 83.7.2.1, 83.7.3.1
Anthrax, 83.3.3.1
anthropomorphism, 82.2.6.5
antonym, 82.1.3
apes, 83.4.5.1, 83.4.5.2
Aphrodite, 83.6.1.2
apocopate, 82.5.1
apostasy, 82.2.6.6, 82.2.6.7, 82.2.6.8
Aquila, 82.15.2, 82.23.7
Arabah, 82.27.10
Arabia, 83.4.2.1, 83.6.2.1
Arabian peninsula, 83.2.1.1
Arabic, 80.1.7.4, 82.2.7.14, 82.2.7.18, 82.10.1, 82.16.1, 82.27.1, 82.27.10
Aram, 80.4, 80.5
Aramaic, 80.1.5, 80.1.7.4, 82.10.1, 82.19.1, 82.28.5, 82.31.2, 82.31.3, 82.31.3, 83.4.2.3, 85.1.9, 85.2.2.1, 85.2.2.6
Aran, 80.4, 80.5
Arava(h), 82.27.10
Arial font, 80.1.7.4
Ariel, 85.4
Aristotle, 82.9.4, 82.27.9, 83.1.1
Armies, Heaven's, 82.41.1, 82.43.2
article, definite, 82.5.1, 82.5.2, 82.5.17, 82.6.5, 82.7.2, 82.14.4, 82.23.6, 82.26.2, 82.27.3, 82.27.4, 82.30.6, 85.1.11, 85.2.1.2

Ascents, Song of, 82.23.18
Asher, 82.32.3
Asia, 83.5.3.5, 83.7.4.1
Assyria(n), 82.28.2, 82.32.4
atnach, 82.23.20
Atonement, Day of, 82.30.5
Australia, 83.5.1.1
Azazel, 82.7.3

Baboon, 83.4.5.2
Babylon, 82.19.2
Babylonian, 80.4, 82.8.2, 82.28.5
back-translations, 80.1.3, 80.1.6
Barn-owl, Common, 83.5.2, 83.5.2.1, 83.5.2.2, 83.8.1, 83.9.15
Bartgeier, 83.3.3.3
Bedouin, 82.23.5
Benjamin, 82.32.3
Bethel, 85.1.11, 85.4
Bethlehem, 80.2, 82.37.2
Bezek, 87.1.1.3
BHS, 80.1.1, 80.1.2, 80.1.3, 80.1.6, 80.2, 80.4, 80.5, 82.1.5, 82.1.7, 82.2.6, 82.2.6.5, 82.2.6.6, 82.2.6.7, 82.2.6.8, 82.3.1.5, 82.20.3, 85.1.7, 86.1.2, 86.3.1
Bible, Bishops, 82.5.5, 82.42.4
Bible, Douay-Rheims, 82.6.6, 82.8.2
Bible, Geneva, 82.5.5, 82.42.4
Bible, King James, 80.1.7.4
Bible, Matthew's, 82.5.5
Bibles, English, 82.1.4
Bilha, 82.32.3
binominal, 83.1.4

bird(s), 82.5.2, 82.5.6, 82.7.2, 82.9.2, 82.9.4, 82.22.11, 82.23.12, 82.27.9, 82.32.3, 82.32.4, 83.1.2, 83.1.3, 83.1.4, 83.2.1.3, 83.3.3.1, 83.3.3.2, 83.3.4.1, 83.3.5.1, 83.4.1.2, 83.4.1.3, 83.4.3.2, 83.5.1.1, 83.5.2.1, 83.5.2.2, 83.5.3.7, 83.6.2.1, 83.6.2.4, 83.7.1.1, 83.7.2.1, 83.7.4.1, 83.7.4.2, 83.7.4.3
bird(s), fowl-like, 83.4
birds of prey, 82.22.8
birds of prey, diurnal, 83.3
birds of prey, nocturnal, 83.5.1.1
birds, clean, 83.3.2.1
birds, flightless, 83.2
birds, perching, 83.7
birds, song, 83.7
birds, unclean, 82.7.2, 82.9.2, 83.3.2.1, 83.3.3.4, 83.5.3.4, 83.7.3.3, 83.8
Bittern, 82.27.9
Boaz, 80.3, 80.4, 80.5, 82.12.2, 82.27.11
Bochart, Samuel, 83.2.1.3
Bomberg, 82.24.1
Booths, Feast of the, 82.23.4
Brotzman, Tully, 80.1.2, 80.1.3, 80.4
Bulbul, Yellow-vented, 83.9.2
Buzzard, 82.9.2, 82.27.9

Cain, 82.5.4
Cairo, 82.6.4
Calvin, John, 82.5.1, 82.42.4
Canaan, 82.6.4, 82.6.5
Canal, Suez, 82.6.4
Canon, Hebrew, 82.9.4, 82.27.9, 83.1.1
Cathedral, Chartres, 82.6.6
Catholic, 82.5.3
Celebration, Year of, 82.7.7

Chaldean, 82.19.1, 82.23.1, 82.31.3
chamberlain, 82.5.16
chameleon, 83.5.2.2
cherub, 82.30.5
Chinese, Mandarin, 82.5.18, 82.9.3
Christ, Jesus, 82.7.3, 82.23.7, 85.1.9
Christian, 82.1.2, 80.1.7.4, 82.5.11, 82.5.17, 82.8.2, 82.20.2
Christian, 82.27.3, 85.1.9
Christianize, 82.23.1, 82.28.4
Chukar, 83.4.2.1
Coccus, 82.27.1
cock, 83.4.1.1, 83.4.4.1, 83.4.4.2, 83.4.4.5
Codex, Aleppo, 82.5.6, 82.6.5, 82.23.1, 83.4.3.2, 83.6.2.5
Codex, Leningradensis, 80.4, 80.5, 82.1.4, 82.6.5, 82.17.1, 82.20.2, 82.23.1, 86.1.2
Commandments, Ten, 82.6.5
Condor, Andean, 83.3.1.2
Condor, California, 83.3.1.2
Coptic, 80.1.7.4
Cormorant, 82.27.9, 83.8.1, 83.9.4
Crow, Carrion, 83.4.4.1, 83.7.3.1, 83.7.3.2, 83.7.3.3
Crow, Hooded, 83.7.3.2
Cuckoo, Lark-heeled, 83.9.3

Dan, 82.32.3
Daniel, 82.2.4, 82.31, 82.31.1, 82.31.2, 82.31.5, 85.2.2.1, 85.2.2.4, 85.2.2.6, 85.4, 86.1.1
Darius, King, 82.19.1
David, 82.2.7.8, 82.12.2, 82.14.4, 82.23.4, 82.23.8, 82.23.17
David, 82.25.1, 82.26.2, 82.32.1, 82.32.3, 85.2.1.4
Day Star, 82.27.5

Dead Sea, 82.27.10
Death, 82.27.2, 82.32.6, 82.33.4
Deborah, 82.9.3, 82.11.1
Decalogue, 82.6.5
Deer, European Red, 82.26.2
Deer, Red, 82.23.10
demythologize, 82.27.9
denominative, 82.6.6, 82.7.2, 82.24.2
Desert, Judean, 82.23.5
Deuteronomy, 82.9, 86.2
Dina, 82.32.3
dirge, 82.5.4
dittography, 80.2, 80.4, 82.23.8, 82.39.2
diurnal, 83.3.1.1
Divine Name, 87.11.2, 87.16.3, 87.17.2, 87.17.3
dove(s), 82.5.6, 82.26.2, 82.27.10, 82.32.3, 82.32.4, 82.36.1, 83.4.1.2, 83.6.1.1, 83.6.1.2, 83.6.2, 83.6.2.4, 83.6.2.5, 83.6.2.6
Dove, Collared, 83.6.2.1
Dove, Laughing, 82.26.2, 82.36.1, 83.6.2.1, 83.6.2.2, 83.6.2.3
Dove, Namaqua, 83.6.2.1
Dove, Palm, 83.6.2.1
Dove, Rock, 83.6.1.1, 83.6.2.1, 83.9.5
Dove, Turtle, 83.6.2.1, 83.6.2.3, 83.9.6
DSS, 82.27.13
Dutch, 82.5.18, 82.23.10
Dutch, Old, 82.20.2.2

eagle, 82.9.2, 82.9.4, 82.20.2, 82.22.2, 82.22.11, 82.24.2, 82.27.10, 82.35.1, 82.37.1, 83.3.2.2, 83.3.2.4, 83.3.3.4, 83.3.3.6, 83.9.7
Eagle-owl, Eurasian, 83.5.3.1, 83.5.3.2

Eagles, True / Booted, 83.3.1.3
Ecclesiastes, 82.25, 82.25.1
Eden, Garden of, 83.5.3.5
Editions, 80.1.7.4, 80.4, 82.2.7.2, 82.6.5, 82.17.1, 82.23.7
Edom, 82.16.1
Egypt, 82.6.3, 82.6.4, 82.6.5, 82.14.2, 82.23.5, 82.27.15, 82.32.3, 82.32.4, 82.32.5, 82.38.2, 82.42.4, 83.3.4.1
Egyptian(s), 80.1.7.4, 82.6.1, 82.6.3, 82.22.10, 86.1.3
Ehyeh, 84.1.2
Eilat, Gulf of, 82.6.4, 82.25.1, 82.33.1, 84.1.2, 85.1.1, 85.1.2
El, 85.1.3, 85.1.7, 85.1.8, 85.1.9, 85.1.10, 85.1.11, 85.2.1.2, 85.4, 86.1.3
El Elyon, 85.1.1
El Shaddai, 85.1.1
Elah(a), 85.2.2.1, 85.2.2.2, 85.2.2.4, 85.2.2.8
ElelohelIsrael, 85.4
Eli, 85.1.9
Eliada, 85.4
Eliel, 85.4
Eliezer, 85.4
Elihu, 85.4
Elijah, 82.15.1, 83.7.3.3, 85.2.1.4, 85.4
Elimelech, 80.4, 80.5
Eliphelet, 85.4
Elisha, 82.15.1, 85.4
Elkanah, 85.4
Eloah, 84.1.2, 85.2.3.1
Elohim, 82.34.2, 84.1.2, 85.1.9, 85.2.1.1, 85.2.1.2, 85.2.1.3, 85.2.1.4, 85.2.1.5, 86.1.3, 86.2
Eloi, 85.1.9
English, archaic, 82.5.18
English, modern, 82.1.3, 82.1.4, 82.5.18, 82.5.3, 82.5.4, 82.6.3, 82.15.1, 82.27.10
English, Old, 82.23.10

epexegtic, 82.5.2
Ephraim, 82.32.3
Ephraimite(s), 82.11.3, 82.32.1
Ephratah, 82.37.2
Esther, 82.2.4, 82.9.3, 82.21, 86.1.1
Etham, 82.6.4
Ethiopian, 82.28.2
Ethiopic, 80.1.7.4
eunuch, 82.5.16
euphemism, 82.2.7, 82.2.7.13
Europe, 82.8.2, 83.3.4.1, 83.5.2.1, 83.5.3.5, 83.7.4.1
Eve, 82.27.9, 83.5.3.5
Exodus, 82.6, 82.6.4, 82.7.1, 83.4.3.2
Ezekiel, 82.2.4, 82.6.6, 82.30, 82.30.1, 82.30.5, 82.31.1, 85.4
Ezra, 82.7.1, 82.19, 82.19.2, 85.2.2.1

falcon, 82.22.4, 82.22.8, 82.27.9, 83.3.1.3, 83.3.4.3, 83.3.5, 83.3.5.3, 83.9.8
Falcon, Peregrine, 83.3.5.1, 83.3.5.2
Father, Eternal, 82.27.4
Father, Everlasting, 82.27.4
Flood, Great, 82.5.6
fowl, 82.7.2, 82.22.8, 82.32.3
Fraktur, 80.1.7.4
France, 83.5.1.1
French, 82.23.10

Gabriel, 85.4
Gad, 82.32.3
Galilee, Sea of, 82.16.1
gazelle, 82.26.2
Genesis, 82.5
Geniza, Cairo, 82.2.7.4, 82.5.4, 82.6.5, 82.6.6, 82.23.4, 82.23.5, 82.23.6, 82.25.2, 82.26.2, 82.31.1

Gentiles, 82.34.4
German, 80.1.5, 82.5.18, 82.8.2, 82.23.10
Gideon, 82.11.2
Gilead, Mount, 82.26.2
Gileadites, 82.11.3
Gilgal, 82.10.2
Gittite, 82.23.4
gloss, 82.23.1
God, Holy, 85.2.1.3
God, Living, 85.2.1.3
God, Mighty, 82.27.4
God, Most High, 85.2.1.3
God, The Most High, 85.2.2.8
Gomorrah, 82.5.11, 82.34.2
gopher, 82.5.5
Goshen, 82.6.4
granivorous, 83.4.1.3
Great Assembly, 82.2.2, 82.2.3, 82.2.4
Great Synagogue, 82.2.2
Great Synod, 82.2.2
Greece, 83.6.1.2
Greyhound, 83.4.4.5
Grizim, 82.6.5
grouse, 83.4.1.1
guineafowl, 83.4.1.1
Gull, Black-headed, 83.8.1
Gull, Little, 83.8.1
Gull, Sea, 83.8.1, 83.9.29

Habakkuk, 82.39
Hacaliah, 82.20.1
Hadassah, 82.21.1
Hagar, 82.9.3
Haggai, 82.41
hapax legomenon, 82.1.6, 82.4.1, 82.4.2, 82.4.3, 82.5.5, 82.22.3, 82.23.15, 82.23.20, 82.26.2, 82.27.5, 82.27.9, 82.30.7, 82.39.2
haplography, 82.2.7.14, 82.17.1, 82.23.10
Haran, 82.5.7

Index

hawk, 82.22.4, 82.27.9, 82.22.11, 83.3.5.3
Heathens, 82.34.4
Hebrew, 82.1.5
Hebrew, biblical, 82.1.3, 82.5.18, 82.23.1, 83.1.2, 83.3.3.3, 83.3.3.4, 83.5.2.2, 83.8.1
Hebrew, modern, 82.22.8, 83.3.3.3, 83.3.3.4, 83.8.1
Hebrews, 82.5.17, 82.7.3, 82.23.6, 82.28.5
hedgehog, 82.27.9, 83.5.3.7
Hellenistic, 82.2.2
hemistich, 82.39.2
herbivorous, 83.4.1.3
Heron, 83.8.1, 83.9.9
Heron, Goliath, 83.8.1
Heron, Grey, 83.8.1
Heron, Purple, 83.8.1
Hexapla, 80.4
Hieronymus, 82.23.4, 82.23.5, 82.31.3
Hilkiah, 82.28.1
Holocaust, 82.8.2
Holy One, 87.13.1, 87.14.1, 87.15.1
homoioarcton, 80.5
homoioteleuton, 80.2, 82.28.6
hoopoe, 83.8.1, 83.9.10
Horeb, Mt., 86.1.3
Hosea, 82.32, 82.32.1
howler, 82.27.9
hyenas, 82.27.9

Ibex, Nubian, 82.23.5
ibis, 82.22.10, 82.23.12, 83.4.4.4
Immaculate One, Army of the, 82.5.3
Immanuel, 82.27.3, 85.4
Iran, 83.3.5.1
Iraq, 83.3.5.1
Iron age, 82.9.3
Isaac, 82.34.4, 82.5.10, 85.2.1.4, 86.3.1

Isaiah, 82.27, 82.27.1, 87.14.2, 87.17.2
Ishmael, 85.4
Ishtar, 82.21.1
Israel, ancient, 82.9.3
Israel, Rock of, 82.5.19
Israelites, 82.6.4, 82.30.4, 83.4.3.1
Issachar, 82.32.3
Ithiel, 85.4
ittur sopherim, 82.1.6, 82.3.1, 82.3.1.5

Jabez, 82.17.1
jackals, 82.22.9, 82.27.9, 82.29.2, 82.37.1
Jacob, 82.5.13, 82.5.15, 82.5.17, 82.5.19, 82.14.4, 82.32.3
Jacob, 82.34.4, 85.2.1.4, 87.15.1, 87.8.1, 87.8.2
jaguar, 82.38.2
Jahweh, 86.1.3
Jegar-Sahadutha, 85.2.2.6
Jehoiachin, 82.18.2
Jehoiakim, 86.4
Jehovah, 82.41.1, 82.5.11, 82.5.4, 86.1.1
Jehovahjireh, 86.3.1
Jehu, 86.4
Jeremiah, 82.28, 82.28.1, 82.30.5, 83.4.2.3, 86.4, 87.14.2
Jerome, 82.6.6, 82.29.1, 82.33.4
Jerusalem, 82.7.3, 82.8.2, 82.23.18, 82.25.1, 82.32.3, 85.2.2.2, 85.2.2.6
Jesse, 82.12.2, 82.14.4
Jesus, 82.10.1, 82.23.4, 82.43.3
Jewish, 82.1.2, 82.2.2, 82.2.4, 82.7.1, 82.7.3, 83.5.3.5
Jews, 82.8.2
Jezreel, 85.4
Job, 82.22, 82.22.1, 82.23.12, 83.2.1.2, 83.2.1.3, 83.3.4.3, 83.3.5.1, 83.3.5.3, 83.4.4.3, 83.4.4.4, 83.7.3.3, 86.1.1

Joel, 82.33, 82.33.1, 82.33.4
Jonadab, 82.14.2
Jonah, 81.1, 82.36, 82.36.2
Jonathan, Targum of, 82.9.4
Jordan, 82.6.5, 82.10.2, 82.16.1, 82.23.5, 82.27.10, 83.2.1.1
Joseph, 82.10.1, 82.32.3, 82.5.16
Joseph, House of, 82.32.3
Josephus, 82.31.3, 86.1.1
Joshua, 82.10, 82.10.1, 82.10.2, 82.32.1
Jotham, 86.4
Jubilee Year, 82.7.7
Judah, 82.5.16, 82.31.1, 82.32.3, 82.32.3, 82.37.2
Judaism, 84.1.2
Judaism, Rabbinic, 82.9.1
Judea, 82.16.1
Judges, 82.11, 82.11.1, 82.11.2
Junglefowl, Red, 83.4.1.1, 83.4.4, 83.4.4.1, 83.9.11

Kermes, 82.27.1
Ketiv, 80.2, 80.3, 80.4, 82.24.2, 82.26.2, 82.29.2, 82.30.2, 82.31.5, 82.37.1
KFC, 83.4.1.2
King, great, 82.43.1
Kings, 83.4.5.2, 82.6.4
kite, 82.22.4, 83.3.1.3, 83.3.4
Kite, Black, 83.3.4.1, 83.3.4.2, 83.3.4.3, 83.9.12
Kite, Red, 83.3.4.1, 83.8.1, 83.9.13
klipspringer, 82.23.5
Kolbe, St. Maximillian, 82.5.3
Kremlin, 80.5

Lakes, Bitter, 82.6.4
Lamentations, 82.29
Lammerbeier, 83.3.3.2
Latin, 80.1.7.4, 80.4, 82.2.7.15, 82.28.2, 82.28.5, 82.6.6, 83.4.1.1, 82.14.4

Latin, Old, 80.1.7.4, 80.3, 80.4, 82.2.7.8, 82.2.7.10, 82.2.7.14, 82.9.4, 82.13.4, 82.14.4
Law, Mosaic, 82.9.4, 82.27.9, 83.1.1
Leah, 82.32.3
Lebanon, 82.23.5
Lechem, 82.37.2
leopard, 82.28.2, 82.38.2
Levi(te), 82.6.1, 82.32.3
Leviticus, 82.7
lex difficilior, 82.23.7
Lilith, 82.27.9, 83.5.3.5
Lion, African, 82.38.2
Lion, Atlas, 82.38.2
Lion, Berber, 82.38.2
Lion, Egypt, 82.38.2
Lion, North African, 82.38.2
Lion. Barbary, 82.38.2
Lucianic, 80.4
Lucifer, 82.27.5
Luther, 82.5.1

Malachi, 82.43, 82.43.1
mammal, 83.7.1.1
Manasseh, 82.2.7.2, 82.32.3
Mappiq, 85.2.3.1
Mariology, 82.5.3
Mark, St., 85.1.9
martin, 83.7.2.1
Mary, 82.5.3, 82.10.1
Masorah Magna, 80.4
Masorah Parva, 80.4
Masoretes, 80.2, 82.5.1, 82.5.17, 82.27.6, 82.31.1
matres lectionis, 86.1.1
Matthew, St., 85.1.9
Medieval, 82.23.7
Mediterranean, 83.3.4.1, 83.4.2.1
Melchizedek, 82.5.8
Mesopotamia, 82.5.7
Messiah, 82.27.4
Metonymy, 80.4, 80.5
mezuzah, 82.13.1

Micah, 82.37, 86.4
Micaiah, 86.4
Michael, 85.4
Middle Ages, 83.5.3.5
Middle East, 82.23.5, 82.27.9, 82.39.2, 83.3.4.1, 83.3.5.1, 83.4.2.1, 83.5.3.5, 83.6.2.1, 83.7.3.2, 83.7.4.1, 83.7.4.2, 83.8.1
Mighty One, 87.8.1, 87.8.2, 87.9.1
Militia Immaculatae, 82.5.3
Miriam, 82.9.3
misogyny, 82.38.3
Moab, 80.2, 80.4, 80.5, 82.16.1
Moabite, 82.12.2
Moabitess, 80.3, 80.4, 80.5
Monastery, St. Mark's, 82.27.1, 82.27.13
Mordecai, 82.21.1
Moriah, 86.4
Morocco, 82.38.2
Moses, 82.2.6.3, 82.6.1, 82.6.2, 82.6.6, 82.10.1, 82.27.15, 82.32.4, 83.7.4.3, 86.1.3
Most High, The, 85.2.2.7, 85.2.2.8
Mountains, Atlas, 82.38.2
Muslim(s), 82.8.2

Nahor, 82.5.14, 85.2.1.6
Nahum, 82.38, 82.38.1
Naomi, 80.2, 80.3, 80.4, 80.5
Naphtali, 82.32.3
necromancer, 82.27.7
Negev, the, 82.23.5
Nehemiah, 82.20, 82.20.1, 82.32.1
Neo-Aramaic, 82.23.1
Nephilim, 82.5.5
New York Times, 82.8.2
New Zealand, 83.7.3.1
Nile, 82.22.10, 82.23.12
Nineveh, 82.38.1
Nisan, 82.7.1
Noah, 82.5.2, 82.5.6, 82.6.1, 82.6.5, 83.6.2.4, 83.6.2.5, 83.7.3.3

Non-Hebrews, 82.34.4
Notre Dame, 82.6.6
Numbers, 82.8

Oak, Palestine, 82.14.3
Obadiah, 82.35, 82.35.1
Onkelos, 82.14.1
Origen, 80.4, 82.26.2
ornithologist, 82.5.6, 82.9.4, 82.27.9, 82.38.2
Ornithology, 82.9.4, 82.27.9, 83.1.1
Orpa, 80.2
osprey, 82.9.2, 83.3.1.2, 83.3.3.6
ossifrage, 82.9.2, 83.3.3.6
ostrich, 82.22.11, 82.29.2, 82.37.1, 83.2.1.3, 83.9.14, 82.22.9
Ostrich, Arabian, 83.2.1.1
Ostrich, daughter of, 83.2.1.2
Ostrich, female, 83.9.14
Ostrich, Middle Eastern, 83.2.1.1
Ostrich, Southern, 83.2.1.1
Ostrich, Syrian, 83.2.1.1
Ottoman, 82.8.2
owl(s), 82.22.9, 82.27.9, 82.37.1, 83.3.1.1, 83.5.1.1
Owl, Desert, 82.27.9
Owl, Eagle, 83.9.16
Owl, Great, 82.27.9
Owl, Little, 82.27.9, 83.5.3.1, 83.5.3.5, 83.9.17, 83.9.18
Owl, Northern Long-eared, 82.27.9, 83.5.3.1, 83.5.3.6, 83.9.19
Owl, Screech, 82.27.9
Owl, Short-eared, 82.27.9, 83.5.3.1, 83.5.3.7, 83.9.22
Owl, Tawny, 82.27.9, 83.9.23
owls, typical, 83.5.3, 83.5.3.1

Palestine, 82.10.1, 82.14.3
Palestinian, 80.4
Papyrus, Nash, 82.6.5

paragogic, 82.39.2, 82.42.4
partridge, 83.4.1.1, 83.4.2, 83.4.2.1, 83.4.2.3, 83.9.24
Partridge, Arabian, 83.4.2.1
Partridge, Barbary, 83.4.2.1
Partridge, Grey, 83.4.2.1
Partridge, Philby's, 83.4.2.1
Partridge, Red-legged, 83.4.2.1
Partridge, Rock, 83.4.2.1
Partridge, Sand, 83.4.2.1
Passover, 82.6.3, 82.7.1
peacock, 83.2.1.3, 83.4.5.2
Peafowl, Indian, 83.4.5, 83.9.25
pelican, 82.27.9
Peniel, 85.4
Peninsula, Sinai, 83.4.3.1
Pentateuch, 82.6.6, 82.27.11
Pentateuch, Samaritan, 80.1.7.4, 82.5.1, 82.5.10, 82.5.13, 82.5.14, 82.5.2, 82.5.7, 82.6.4, 82.6.5, 82.7.2, 82.8.1, 82.9.4, 83.3.2.3, 83.4.3.2
Peres, 82.31.3
Persia, 82.21.1
Peshitta, Syriac, 80.1.7.4, 80.2, 80.3, 80.4, 80.5, 82.5.2, 82.5.7, 82.6.5, 82.9.4, 82.13.4, 82.14.1, 82.14.4, 82.2.6.15, 82.23.4, 82.27.15
Pharaoh, 82.5.16
pheasant, 83.4.1.1
Phoenician, 82.5.1, 85.1.1
pigeon(s), 82.5.6, 82.9.4, 83.6, 83.6.1.1
Pigeon, Rock, 83.6.1.1
pigeonbird, 83.4.1.2
Plover, Egyptian, 83.9.26
plumb line, 82.34.3
polygenesis, 80.4
polytheistic, 82.34.2
pomegranate, 82.26.2
porcupine, 82.27.9, 83.5.3.7
Potiphar, 82.5.16
Preacher, 82.25.1
Priest, High, 82.27.10

Prince of Peace, 82.27.4
Prophets, 83.1.1
Prophets, Minor, 82.2.4
Prophets, the, 82.9.4, 82.27.9
Protestant, 82.42.4
Proverbs, 82.24, 82.24.3, 87.13.2
Psalm(s), 82.23, 82.23.4, 82.23.18, 83.7.4.3, 85.1.9, 86.1.1
Psalm, Gradual, 82.23.18
Psalm, of Ascents, 82.23.18
Psalm, Pilgrim, 82.23.18
Psalmists, 82.43.1
Purim, 82.2.4

Qal, 87.17.2
Qere, 80.2, 80.3, 80.4, 82.2.6.5, 82.23.20, 82.24.2, 82.26.2, 82.29.2, 82.29.2, 82.30.2, 82.31.5, 82.37.1, 82.37.2, 82.42.4
quail, 83.4.1.1, 83.4.3, 83.4.3.2, 83.9.27
Quail, Common, 83.4.3.1, 83.4.3.2
Quail, Common
Qumran, 80.3, 82.2.7.3, 82.2.7.18, 82.9.4, 82.13.2, 82.23.17, 82.27.13

rabbinic, 82.2.3, 82.2.7, 84.1.2
Rachel, 82.32.3
Rahab, 82.9.3
Rameses, 82.6.4
raptor, 82.35.1, 82.37.1
Raptors, Nocturnal, 83.5
raven(s), 82.5.6, 82.22.10, 82.27.9, 83.4.4.5, 83.6.2.4, 83.6.2.5, 83.7.3, 83.7.3.1, 83.7.3.2, 83.7.3.3, 83.9.28
Redeemer, 87.17.1, 87.17.2, 87.17.3
Reeds, Sea of, 82.6.4
relic, 82.5.2

retroversions, 80.1.3
Reuben, 82.32.3
Righteousness, 82.28.4, 82.43.3
Rock Thrush, Blue, 83.7.4.2
Roman(s), 82.8.2
Rome, 83.6.1.2
rook, 83.7.3.2
rooster, 82.22.10, 83.4.4.2, 83.4.4.4
Ruben, 82.5.16
Russia, 80.5, 82.8.2
Ruth, 80.2, 80.3, 80.4, 80.5, 80.5, 82.12, 82.12.1, 82.27.11
Ruth, Book of, 80.1.1, 80.1.2, 80.4, 82.12.2

Sabbath, 82.5.1, 82.5.2, 82.6.5, 82.29.1
Sainte-Chapelle, 82.6.6
Salmah, 80.4
Salman, 80.5
Salmon, 80.4, 80.5
Samaria, 82.16.1
Samaritan, 82.5.1
Samuel, 82.13.1, 85.4
Sarah, 82.5.10
Satan, 82.7.3
Saul, 82.32.3
Savior, 82.28.4, 87.16.1, 87.16.2, 87.16.3
scapegoat, 82.7.3
Scops owl, Eurasian, 83.5.3.1, 83.5.3.3, 83.9.20
Scops owl, Pallid, 83.5.3.1, 83.5.3.4, 83.8.1, 83.9.21
script, square, 80.1.7.4
Scriptures, 82.2.6.4
Scriptures, Holy, 84.1.1
Scroll, Isaiah, 82.27.13
Scrolls, 80.1.7.4, 82.27.1
Scrolls, Dead Sea, 82.23.7, 82.27.6, 82.27.13
Scrolls, Qumran, 82.14.4
Sea, Dead, 82.16.1

Sea, Red, 82.6.4, 82.27.9
Sebir, 82.31.1
Sechem, 82.6.5
secretary bird, 83.3.1.2
Segholate, 82.23.1
Sela, 82.27.6
Semitic, Northwest, 86.1.3
Senath, 82.32.3
Septuagint, Ori, 82.28.6
Septuagint, original, 80.2, 82.6.5, 82.10.1, 82.16.2, 82.23.8, 82.28.3, 82.28.6, 82.30.5, 83.3.2.4
Shaddai, 82.22.7, 84.1.2
Shadrach, 85.2.2.4
Shasu, 86.1.3
Shema, the, 82.9.1
Shemoneh 'Esreh, 82.2.4
Sheol, 82.14.1, 82.27.2
Shepherd(s), 87.11.1, 87.12.1, 82.23.8
shibboleth, 82.11.3
Shiloh, 82.13.1
Shusan, 82.21.1
siblicide, 82.9.4
sigla, 80.1.4
silluq, 82.23.20
Simeon, 82.32.3
simile, 82.26.2
Sodom, 82.5.11, 82.34.2
Solomon, 82.18.1, 82.26.1, 82.32.3, 83.4.5.1
Solomon, Song of, 82.26
Son of Man, 82.30.6
Songs, Song of, 82.9.3, 83.6.2.2, 86.1.1
sorcerer, 82.27.7
Spanish, informal, 82.5.18
sparrow(s), 83.4.1.2, 83.7.1.1, 83.7.4
Sparrow, Dead Sea, 83.7.4.2
Sparrow, House, 83.7.4.1, 83.7.4.2
Sparrow, Rock, 83.7.4.2
Sparrow, Spanish, 83.7.4.2

Spirit, 82.42.2
starling, 83.4.4.5
Statenvertaling, 82.20.2
Stephen, 82.5.7
stork, 83.2.1.3, 83.9.30
Succoth, 82.6.4
Sun, 82.43.3
swallow(s), 83.7.2, 83.7.2.1, 83.7.2.2, 83.9.31
swift, 83.9.32
Swift, Common, 83.3.5.2
Symmachus, 82.2.7.18, 82.9.4, 82.15.2, 82.23.4, 82.23.6, 82.23.7, 82.23.8, 82.26.2, 82.42.4
Syriac, 83.4.3.2
Syrohexapla, 82.27.15
Syrohexaplaris, 82.2.7.2

Tabernacle, the, 82.13.1
Tabernacles, Feast of the, 82.23.4
Talmudic, 82.5.11
Tamar, 82.9.3
Tanakh, 83, 82.2.1, 82.5.1, 84.1.1
Tanis, Lake of, 82.6.4
Targum, Jonathan, 82.3.1.1, 82.3.1.3
Targum, Jonathan
Tekoa, 82.34.1
Tell ed-Daba, 82.6.4
Temple area, 83.7.2.2
Temple, First, 82.8.2
Temple, Second, 82.2.2, 82.8.2
Temple, the, 82.19.1, 82.23.18, 82.31.4
terebinth, 82.14.3
term, generic, 82.5.1, 82.6.1, 82.9.4, 82.22.8, 82.24.3, 82.26.2, 82.27.9, 82.35.1, 82.36.1, 82.37.1, 82.38.2, 83.3.3.3, 83.6.2.2, 83.6.2.3, 83.7.4.3, 85.1.2
terrestrial, 83.7.1.1

Tertullianus, 82.2.6.17
Testament, New, 82.1.2, 82.5.17, 82.27.3, 85.1.9
Testament, Old, 80.1.7.4, 82.1.5
Tetragrammaton, 82.9.1, 82.23.17, 86.1.1
Text, Masoretic, 80.1.3, 80.1.6, 80.1.7.4, 82.27.13
Theodotion, 82.2.7.9
theophoric, 85.4
Thrice Holy, 87.13.3
Tiberian, 80.4
tiqqun sopherim, 82.2.1, 82.2.3, 82.2.5, 82.2.6.1–18
tiqquney sopherim, 82.1.6, 82.2.6, 82.2.7
Torah, 86.1.1
Transjordan, 86.1.3
Tsevaot, 84.1.2
turkey, 83.4.1.1
Tyndale, William, 82.5.5

Ugaritic, 80.1.7.4, 82.14.1, 85.1.1
University, Hebrew, 82.27.13
USA, 82.8.2
USSR, 80.5
Uz, 82.22.1

Venus, 83.6.1.2
vertebrate, 83.7.1.1
vorlage, 80.1.3, 80.1.5, 80.1.6, 80.2
vulture, 82.9.2, 82.22.4, 82.22.8, 82.27.9, 82.37.1, 83.3.1.3, 83.3.3, 83.3.3.3, 83.3.3.5, 83.3.4.3
Vulture, American Black, 83.3.3.4
Vulture, Bearded, 82.9.2, 83.3.3.3, 83.3.3.6, 83.8.1, 83.9.33
Vulture, Black, 82.9.2, 83.3.3.4
Vulture, Egyptian, 83.3.3.5, 83.8.1, 83.9.36
Vulture, Griffon, 82.9.2, 82.27.9, 83.9.34

Vulture, Lamb, 83.3.3.2
Vulture, Lapped-faced, 82.9.2, 83.3.3.4, 83.3.3.6, 83.8.1, 83.9.35
Vulture, New World, 83.3.1.2
Waltke and O'Connor, 80.4

War, World, 82.23.5, 83.2.1.1
warhorse, 83.4.4.5
waw, 85.1.10, 85.2.1.7, 85.2.2.5

wolf, 82.27.9
Woodpigeon, 83.6.2.1
Writings, the, 82.9.4, 82.27.9, 83.1.1
Wycliffe, John, 82.5.5

Yael, 82.9.3, 82.23.5
Yah, 82.28.1, 86.4
Yah, Servant of, 82.35.1
Yahu, 85.4

Yahweh-yireh, 86.3.1
Yiddish, 82.8.2

Zebulun, 82.32.3
Zechariah, 82.42, 86.4
Zephaniah, 82.40, 82.40.1, 83.5.3.7, 86.4
Zilpa, 82.32.3
Zion, 82.27.6
Zion, Mount, 82.23.18

References

PUBLICATIONS

Barrett, David B., Kurian, George T., Johnson, Todd M., (2001). *World Christian Encyclopedia: a comparative survey of churches and religions in the modern world.* 2nd ed. Oxford; New York: Oxford University Press.

Brotzman, Ellis R., Tully, Eric J., (2016). *Old Testament Textual Criticism: A Practical Introduction.* Grand Rapids, Michigan: Baker Academic.

Brown, F., et al. (1906). *The Brown-Driver-Briggs Hebrew and English Lexicon.* Massachusetts: Hendrickson Publishers, Inc.

Davidson, B. (1850). *The Analytical Hebrew and Chaldee Lexicon.* Second Edition. Hendrickson Publishers. Peabody, MA.

Elliger, K (Ed.), Rudolph, W (Ed.). (1998). *Biblia Hebraica Stuttgartensia.* Stuttgart. Deutsche Bibelgesellschaft.

Hattingh, Tian. (2012). *Birds and Bibles in History.* London. The London Press.

Kelly, Page H., Crawfor, Timothy G., Mynatt, Daniel S., (1998). *The Masorah of Biblia Hebraica Stuttgartensia: Introduction and Annotated Glossary.* Grand Rapids, Michigan. Wm. B. Eerdmans Publishing.

McCarthy, Carmel (1981). *The Tiqqune Sopherim and Other Theological Corrections in the Masoretic Text of the Old Testament.* Freiburg, Switzerland / Göttingen, Germany: Universitätsverlag / Vandenhoeck Ruprecht.

Ross, Allen P. (2001). *Introducing Biblical Hebrew.* Ada, Michigan: Baker Academic.

Scott, William R. (1987). *A Simplified Guide to BHS: Critical Apparatus, Masora, Accents, Unusual Letters & Other Markings.* N. Richland Hills. BIBAL Press.

Waltke, Bruce K. and O'Connor, Michael Patrick. (1990). *An introduction to Biblical Hebrew Syntax.* Winona Lake, Indiana. Eisenbrauns.

AUDIO BOOK

Kushner, Aviya (2015). *The Grammar of God.* Holland, Ohio. Dreamscapes Media, LLC.

WEBSITES

www.animatedhebrew.com

This site was started in 2004 by Charles Grebe, M.A. in Theological Studies (OT). The site contains a number of interesting items. The most important and useful of these is a link to 35 hours of audio-visual lectures based on the textbook Introducing Biblical Hebrew by Allen B. Ross. The lectures are also available on YouTube at the link https://www.youtube.com/user/animatedhebrew

www.biblehub.com

This site is of use to Bible students in general, including the OT and NT. Also included are parallel translations, an interlinear Hebrew Bible, and a useful search facility.

BIBLE VERSIONS ONLINE

Aleppo Codex

Biblehub.com. (2019). *Aleppo Codex.* Available at: https://biblehub.com/ale/genesis/1.htm

Leningrad Codex

Scripture4all.org. (2019). *Westminster Leningrad Codex with vowels.* Available at: https://www.scripture4all.org/OnlineInterlinear/Hebrew_Index.htm

Masoretic Text

Sarshalom.us. (2019). *The Sar Shalom Hebrew-English Bible.* Available at: http://www.sarshalom.us/resources/scripture/asv/bible.html

Samaritan Pentateuch

Stepbible.org. (2019). *Samaritan Pentateuch in English.* Available at: https://www.stepbible.org/?q=version=SPE|reference=Gen.1&options=VNHUG Accessed 14 Oct. 2019.

Greek Septuagint

Biblehub.com. (2019). *Apostolic Bible Polyglot.* Available at: https://biblehub.com/interlinear/apostolic/genesis/1.htm

Latin Vulgate

Vulgate.org. (2019). *Douay-Rheims, Latin Vulgate, King James.* Available at: http://www.latinvulgate.com

Biography

Christiaan (Tian) Hattingh was born and bred in South Africa. In 1974 he completed a four year training course as a Forest Manager from the Saasveld Forestry College, now part of the Nelson Mandela Metropolitan University. In 1987 he completed a B.A. degree in Psychology and Philosophy at the University of South Africa. Starting in 1974, he studied biblical Hebrew for three years at the same university, and although he never achieved a formal academic qualification in the subject, he soon felt obliged to share his knowledge with others that were equally interested in learning more from the HB Bible. As a result of this yearning, he later conducted part-time classes for Beginners at the local Technicon in Rustenburg, South Africa where he was living at the time.

He has been an avid birder for the past 42 years, and is a founding member of the Rustenburg branch of BirdLife South Africa. He has been birding in Botswana, Zimbabwe, Namibia, Malawi, China, Thailand, and lately in Vietnam. He visited Israel several times, first as a Christian pilgrim, and later to study the birds of the region more closely. Returning to South Africa in 2001, he presented talks on "Birding in Israel" at several BirdLife South Africa branches.

In 2002 he moved to mainland China, where he became an ESL / IELTS teacher. In February of 2012 he published *Birds and Bibles in History*, ISBN 978-1-907313-70-7 covering the history of the Tanakh, the history of Ornithology, and all 409 references to birds in the HB Bible and Christian New Testament. From September 2014 he conducted classes for Beginners in biblical HB in the city of Shenzhen in China until March 2016 when he relocated to Vietnam. He has been an ESL Teacher, an IELTS Instructor, and on-line biblical HB teacher there since then.

Personal website: www.tianhattingh.com

www.ingramcontent.com/pod-product-compliance
Lightning Source LLC
Chambersburg PA
CBHW081333080526
44588CB00017B/2605